Healthy Development in Young Children

Healthy Development in Young Children

Evidence-Based Interventions for Early Education

Edited by
Vincent C. Alfonso and George J. DuPaul

AMERICAN PSYCHOLOGICAL ASSOCIATION
PUBLISHING

Published by
American Psychological Association
750 First Street, NE
Washington, DC 20002
https://www.apa.org

Order Department
https://www.apa.org/pubs/books
order@apa.org

In the U.K., Europe, Africa, and the Middle East, copies may be ordered from Eurospan
https://www.eurospanbookstore.com/apa
info@eurospangroup.com

Typeset in Meridien and Ortodoxa by Circle Graphics, Inc., Reisterstown, MD

Printer: Sheridan Books, Chelsea, MI
Cover Designer: Anne C. Kerns, Anne Likes Red, Silver Spring, MD

Library of Congress Cataloging-in-Publication Data

Names: Alfonso, Vincent C., editor. | DuPaul, George J., editor.
Title: Healthy development in young children : evidence-based interventions
  for early education / edited by Vincent C. Alfonso and George J. DuPaul.
Description: Washington : American Psychological Association, 2020. |
  Includes bibliographical references and index.
Identifiers: LCCN 2020003676 (print) | LCCN 2020003677 (ebook) |
  ISBN 9781433832314 (paperback) | ISBN 9781433833700 (ebook)
Subjects: LCSH: Child psychology. | Educational psychology. | Learning,
  Psychology of. | Effective teaching.
Classification: LCC BF721 .H343 2020 (print) | LCC BF721 (ebook) |
  DDC 155.4—dc23
LC record available at https://lccn.loc.gov/2020003676
LC ebook record available at https://lccn.loc.gov/2020003677

http://dx.doi.org/10.1037/0000197-000

Printed in the United States of America

10 9 8 7 6 5 4 3 2 1

*We dedicate this volume to past, present, and future members of the
Coalition for Psychology in Schools and Education, whose work continues
to influence research, policy, and practice for children and adolescents.
In addition, we dedicate this volume to all young children in the world
who challenge, inspire, and motivate us each and every day.*

CONTENTS

CONTRIBUTORS

Vincent C. Alfonso, PhD, Gonzaga University, Spokane, WA
Jhonelle Bailey, BA, University of Miami, Coral Gables, FL
Baptiste Barbot, PhD, Pace University, New York, NY
L. Morgan Beidleman, MEd, University of Denver, Denver, CO
Karen L. Bierman, PhD, The Pennsylvania State University, State College
Noelita Bowman, PhD, Baltimore County Public Schools, Towson, MD
Jennifer Bugos, PhD, University of South Florida, Tampa
Rebecca Bulotsky-Shearer, PhD, University of Miami, Coral Gables, FL
Courtney L. Cleminshaw, MEd, Lehigh University, Bethlehem, PA
Amanda B. Clinton, PhD, American Psychological Association,
  Washington, DC
Timothy W. Curby, PhD, George Mason University, Fairfax, VA
Darlene DeMarie, PhD, University of South Florida, Tampa
Amanda M. Dettmer, PhD, Yale Child Study Center, New Haven, CT
George J. DuPaul, PhD, Lehigh University, Bethlehem, PA
Joseph R. Engler, PhD, Gonzaga University, Spokane, WA
Jenna Futterer, BS, University of Miami, Coral Gables, FL
Leslie C. Ho, MS, The Pennsylvania State University, State College
Robin L. Hojnoski, PhD, Lehigh University, Bethlehem, PA
Tammy L. Hughes, PhD, Duquesne University, Pittsburgh, PA
Jennifer Katz-Buonincontro, PhD, Drexel University, Philadelphia, PA
Lisa Lenhart, PhD, University of Akron, Akron, OH
Janice C. C. Lepore, PsyD, Independent Practice, Lutherville, MD
Celeste M. Malone, PhD, Howard University, Washington, DC
Michèle M. M. Mazzocco, PhD, University of Minnesota, Minneapolis
Heather A. Mildon, MEd, Anchorage School District, Anchorage, AK

Kristen N. Missall, PhD, The University of Washington, Seattle
Chelsea Morris, PhD, University of West Georgia, Carrollton
Gena Nelson, PhD, Boise State University, Boise, ID
Marissa Park, MSEd, Duquesne University, Pittsburgh, PA
Cydney V. Quinn, MSEd, Duquesne University, Pittsburgh, PA
Amber Radzicki, MSEd, Duquesne University, Pittsburgh, PA
Tara C. Raines, PhD, University of Denver, Denver, CO
Kathleen Roskos, PhD, John Carroll University, University Heights, OH
Yadira Sánchez, PsyD, Duquesne University, Pittsburgh, PA
Michael Sanders, MS, The Pennsylvania State University, State College
Eric L. Schmidt, CPSI, Playground Equipment Services, Cincinnati, OH
Ashley Schoenenberger, MSEd, Duquesne University, Pittsburgh, PA
Tina L. Stanton-Chapman, PhD, University of Cincinnati, Cincinnati, OH
Pablo P. L. Tinio, PhD, Montclair State University, Montclair, NJ

PREFACE AND ACKNOWLEDGMENTS

What topics could generate more positive affect and support than early childhood development and education? Most individuals, whether they are parents or not, enjoy children especially when they are young, innocent, and curious. The evidence for the effectiveness of early learning and early intervention, bipartisan support for not only the continuation but also the expansion of early childhood programs, and decades of federal legislation addressing early childhood education have catapulted early childhood development and education to the forefront of many people's minds.[1] Early education and intervention are critically important because they set the stage for children's long-term educational success, healthy social–emotional functioning, and independent and autonomous contributions to society. As such, the main purpose of this volume is to contribute to the early childhood literature and research by narrowing the science–practice gap via state-of-the art information on assessment, methods to ensure early academic success, strategies to promote high-quality learning environments, and important issues for special populations (e.g., working with individuals from diverse backgrounds).

We are affiliated with the Coalition for Psychology in Schools and Education (CPSE), an organization sponsored by the Education Directorate of the American Psychological Association (APA) with a mission to promote applications of psychological research to improve the quality of public and private pre-K to 12 education. Effectively, the CPSE attempts to improve the delivery

---

[1] Alfonso, V. C., Ruby, S., Wissel, A. M., & Davari, J. (2020). School psychologists in early childhood settings. In F. C. Worrell, T. L. Hughes, & D. D. Dixson (Eds.), *The Cambridge handbook of applied school psychology* (pp. 579–597). Cambridge, England: Cambridge University Press.

of psychological principles and content offered to educational professionals as well as to build interdisciplinary collaboration to address the needs of children in schools.[2]

The CPSE meets in person two times per year and is typically composed of at least 23 professionals from APA divisions and affiliate groups. At each meeting agenda items include but are not limited to CPSE updates, guest speakers, project updates, working group breakout sessions, and discussions of future coalition projects. A theme for several CPSE projects in 2017 and 2018 was early childhood education. Indeed, at least three projects were already under way at that time, including a kindergarten survey, *Top 20 Principles From Psychology for Early Childhood Teaching and Learning*,[3] and the *High 5* brochure.[4]

Concomitantly, Vincent C. Alfonso had been in contact with Linda Malnasi McCarter, senior acquisitions editor, regarding a publication with APA Books. Prior to the December 2017 CPSE meeting at APA headquarters in Washington, DC, we (along with several other CPSE members) met with Malnasi McCarter; Ed Meidenbauer, director of video media in APA's Publications and Databases; Dr. Rena Subotnik, director of the CPSE; and Maha Khalid, assistant director of the CPSE, to discuss possible early childhood publications and media (e.g., books, videos). After some discussions and deliberation at the December 2017 CPSE meeting, the genesis of *Healthy Development in Young Children: Evidence-Based Interventions for Early Education* took place.

Preparing this volume has been nothing short of pleasurable, motivating, and rewarding! The invited authors of the 15 chapters expended much time and energy writing, revising, and finalizing them so that they would be professional, readable, and practical. We believe they accomplished the task and are grateful to all authors, especially the following CPSE members: Amanda Clinton, Tim Curby, Darlene DeMarie, Amanda Dettmer, Tammy Hughes, Janice Lepore, Celeste Malone, Tara Raines, Yadira Sánchez, and Pablo Tinio. We would be very remiss not to acknowledge Rena Subotnik, who supported this volume from the outset, allowed us to create it the way we saw fit, and celebrated its publication with us. Thank you, Rena, for all that you have done and continue to do for the CPSE! A quiet, but always staunch, supporter has been Maha Khalid. We are appreciative for all her behind-the-scenes work, consistent guidance, and pleasant demeanor. Linda Malnasi McCarter has been a joy to work with, and her editor-friendly oversight of the project

[2]American Psychological Association. (n.d.-a). *Coalition for Psychology in Schools and Education*. Retrieved from https://www.apa.org/ed/schools/coalition
[3]American Psychological Association, Coalition for Psychology in Schools and Education. (2019). *Top 20 principles from psychology for early childhood teaching and learning*. Retrieved from https://www.apa.org/ed/schools/teaching-learning/top-twenty/early-childhood
[4]American Psychological Association. (n.d.-b). *High 5: Must-ask questions for parents in search of the best early childhood program*. Retrieved from https://www.apa.org/education/k12/high-five

is largely responsible for its completion. Finally, we greatly appreciate the careful review and constructive feedback provided by Ida Audeh, development editor; Elizabeth Brace, production editor; and Catherine Malo, copyeditor. If it were not for these individuals, the quality of the text, tables and figures, and indexes would not be so high. Thank you all for making this project such a success and a major contribution to the field.

Healthy Development
in Young Children

Introduction

The Importance of Early Childhood Development, Education, and Intervention

Vincent C. Alfonso and George J. DuPaul

In recent decades, especially the past 2, early childhood development, education, and intervention have been major topics in professional print outlets such as articles, books, and presentations; social media outlets, including blog posts, YouTube videos, and TED Talks; the Internet in general; and local, state, and national debates and legislation. For example, social–emotional learning, early literacy, numeracy, play, diversity, and creativity have become an increasing focus among early childhood educators, parents, and legislators. Although not designed as a best-practices text, this volume has that flavor, as each chapter addresses what can be done now to assist young children to develop and maintain a healthy trajectory in life to become valuable contributors to society.

We assembled committed scholar–practitioners and expert researchers from around the country to translate accumulated empirical evidence into everyday practice to improve the lives of young children, educate parents and other caregivers, and influence government officials to support early childhood development, education, and intervention. In the pages that follow, we offer our rationale for proposing and producing this volume, an overview of the contents that are divided into five parts, and concluding thoughts on the topic and the future of early childhood education and intervention.

http://dx.doi.org/10.1037/0000197-001
Healthy Development in Young Children: Evidence-Based Interventions for Early Education,
V. C. Alfonso and G. J. DuPaul (Editors)

RATIONALE

It may seem that early childhood education has been in existence for a long time and that we know much about the development of early academic skills, social–emotional functioning, self-regulation, and other important aspects of life (e.g., Weikart, 1989). However, it is really in the past 50 to 60 years that we have studied early childhood development, education, and intervention in earnest (e.g., Spodek & Saracho, 2003). A critical moment or time period for implementing and studying early childhood education occurred in the mid-1960s, when arguably one of the most significant programs in American education—namely, Head Start—was born (S. L. Ramey, 1999; U.S. Department of Health and Human Services, Administration for Children and Families, Office of Head Start, National Center on Parent, Family, and Community Engagement, 2018; Vinovskis, 2005; Zigler, 1994; Zigler & Bishop-Josef, 2006). Although primarily an early education program for young children in low-resource environments, Head Start and its younger sibling, Early Head Start, have had an impact on our thinking about young children for decades (e.g., Love et al., 2005).

Another important moment or time period was the mid-1980s, when services for young children (i.e., birth–5 years) with disabilities or at risk for disabilities became available (Cortiella & Horowitz, 2014; Education of the Handicapped Amendments of 1986; Rounds, 1991; Shonkoff & Meisels, 1991). Legislation regarding young children with disabilities has continued to the present time (i.e., Individuals With Disabilities Education Improvement Act, 2004) and will likely be an enduring part of American education given the plethora of evidence for the effectiveness of early intervention (Campbell & Ramey, 1994; Clarke & Clarke, 1989; Guralnick, 1991; C. T. Ramey & Ramey, 1998; C. T. Ramey, Sparling, & Ramey, 2014; Rose & Calhoun, 1990).

In addition, we have learned that myriad short- and long-term benefits are associated with early childhood education, including improved literacy (e.g., Dickenson & Neuman, 2006; Good, Simmons, & Smith, 1998; Kilpatrick, 2015), acquisition of number knowledge and skills (Jordan, Kaplan, Ramineni, & Locuniak, 2009; Mazzocco, Feigenson, & Halberda, 2011; Salillas & Wicha, 2012; Vo, Li, Kornell, Pouget, & Cantlon, 2014), higher graduation rates from high school and reductions in special education placement (e.g., McCoy et al., 2017), higher income, greater life satisfaction and quality of life, and a healthier society overall (Barnett, 1995; Gorey, 2001; Heckman, 2011; Masten & Coatsworth, 1998; C. T. Ramey et al., 2014; Weissberg, 2000; Yoshikawa et al., 2013). Thus, given the benefits of early childhood education and intervention for typically developing children, those at risk for disabilities, and those who have a disability, we believed an up-to-date volume that bridges the science–practice gap in educational settings was long overdue, especially when we reviewed what texts were available in the science and practice worlds.

This edited volume is intended primarily for experienced education and mental health practitioners who work in early childhood settings such as day care centers, preschools, special education preschools, and kindergarten.

Practitioners who regularly work with young children (e.g., 2–5 years of age)—whether psychologists, speech–language pathologists, social workers, teachers, special education teachers, or related services professionals—make up the target audience for this volume. However, parents, caregivers, and other adults who work with or care for young children may also benefit from its contents.

OVERVIEW OF PARTS AND CHAPTERS

The 15 chapters in this volume are divided into five parts: Assessment; Preparing for School: Ensuring Academic Success; High-Quality Learning Environments; Special Populations; and Advocacy for Early Education. The first four parts consist of two to six chapters, focuses on young children (typically between 2 and 5 years of age), and offers practical guidelines for working with these young members of society. Chapter 15 is a stand-alone chapter that addresses national policies and laws affecting children's health and education, respectively.

Assessment is addressed in Part I because we believe that for any intervention to be effective, it must be based on reliable and valid data garnered from a variety of assessment methods such as norm-referenced tools (e.g., cognitive and early academic tests, rating scales), observations, and interviews. When multisource, multimethod, and multisetting assessment take place, we have more confidence that our interventions, when delivered with fidelity, will be effective. As such, the first chapter on assessment by Alfonso, Engler, and Lepore focuses on five areas of development (i.e., cognitive, motor skills, language, behavioral and social–emotional functioning, adaptive behavior) that are typically measured and that are most critical for screening for developmental delay and making diagnostic and educational placement decisions. In addition, they offer guidelines in choosing assessment methods and tools stressing psychometric rigor, with a focus on standardization, reliability, validity, and score interpretation.

In Chapter 2, Hojnoski and Missall discuss the importance of assessment and describe various methods for assessing young children's early learning and social–emotional development. The chapter begins with a review of empirical literature to provide a strong rationale supporting effective assessment practices with young children, including early emerging differences in growth trajectories, longitudinal patterns of performance, and the malleability of key constructs, such as early learning and social–emotional competence. Then Hojnoski and Missall discuss key considerations to maximize the benefit of assessment efforts, including defining constructs of interest with an emphasis on practical implications and the critical role that context plays in supporting children's development. After a review of broad approaches to assessment, they conclude with a discussion addressing linking assessment to action to support healthy growth and development.

Part II addresses preparing for school and ensuring academic success. In this part, the authors of six chapters summarize the literature and research on how to prepare young children to be successful in educational settings, what this success looks like, and how to ensure continued success in the school-age years. We know from the more than 50 years of Head Start that early intervention is effective only when it is delivered consistently into about the third grade; otherwise, developmental gains may be short-lived, and regression to earlier stages of development can occur. Bierman, Sanders, and Ho begin this part of the book with a chapter on school readiness. These authors report that two thirds of American children now attend preschool, and 43 of the 50 states offer state-funded prekindergarten. Accordingly, academic expectations for kindergarten have risen, amplifying pressures on early education programs to promote the preacademic and social–emotional skills children need to sit, listen, and learn at school entry. This chapter also provides reviews of the empirical evidence linking various approaches to early education with the effective promotion of school readiness in children growing up in economically disadvantaged circumstances and the narrowing of that socioeconomic gap. The next chapter, written by Roskos and Lenhart, describes the scientific research base, highlighting how far we have come in our understanding of early literacy development and learning (ages 2–5 years). Roskos and Lenhart discuss the early literacy pedagogy grounded in this research base, including key principles and guidance for instruction by parents and teachers. They close with a look into the future of early literacy teaching and learning with a special focus on the growing influence of multimedia in early childhood.

Early number knowledge and skills are the topics covered in Chapter 5 by Nelson and Mazzocco. These authors focus on developmental and individual differences in early numerical abilities and skills to help readers understand how to support the development of numerical thinking in young children and the roles that numerical thinking plays in mathematics achievement. Nelson and Mazzocco also provide readers with resources to support planning and implementation of learning environments and instruction to promote an understanding of early number knowledge and skills sense for all learners.

Next is a chapter on self-regulation in young children by Dettmer, Clinton, and Mildon. The authors describe the biological and behavioral indicators of self-regulation, with insights from comparative psychology, and the long-term benefits that emerge from the early development of this skill. They also discuss the complex relationships between biological bases of behavior and environmental influences, review prevention and intervention programs and methods related to education and schools, and present practical applications of the science of self-regulation to classroom settings.

In Chapter 7, DeMarie and Bugos state that opportunities for play in early childhood are important for children's later academic development. They describe different types of play activities along with the role of these activities in advancing the development of language, literacy, and science, technology, engineering, and mathematics among a diverse group of children. In addition, they note how children's engagement with play materials, their opportunities for expressing language, and adult scaffolds benefit later academic achievement.

The final chapter in this part, Chapter 8, by Bulotsky-Shearer, Futterer, Bailey, and Morris, highlights research on within-child (i.e., internal developmental capacities) and external (e.g., contextual factors within the home) strengths that affect the development of young children's skills (e.g., socioemotional competence). They provide an overview of these factors within a bioecological framework along with a summary of their research conducted within Head Start programs; illustrate the importance of family–school, teacher–child, and child-initiated peer play interactions as critical contexts for supporting engagement in learning, particularly for children from ethnic, racial, and linguistically diverse low-income backgrounds; and present evidence-based, practical suggestions to support these relational contexts as key contributors to early school success, particularly related to the transition to kindergarten.

High-quality learning environments are the topic of Part III, which comprises three chapters. We know that quality of the learning environment is critical in early childhood education and intervention. What makes a quality learning environment, how we can ensure the existence of these environments, and what steps we need to take to improve them are questions addressed in the chapters of this part. For example, Chapter 9, written by DuPaul and Cleminshaw, discusses principles and practices that promote positive guidance in early childhood. These authors see a critical need for early childhood educators to address children's challenging behaviors given the relatively high rates of behavior control difficulties among preschoolers and the importance of self-regulation skills for early school success. They maintain that teachers and parents typically use reactive, punitive strategies to address children's behavior, techniques that often are ineffective in promoting durable behavior change. Thus, DuPaul and Cleminshaw describe methods for teachers and parents to prevent children's challenging behaviors and promote growth in self-regulation skills in the context of a multitiered system of support.

The next chapter in Part III focuses on creating successful early learning environments. According to Curby, a primary task of early childhood is for children to become socially and emotionally competent. The chapter begins with a discussion of the importance of teacher–child interactions as a mechanism for promoting social and emotional competencies in young children. Curby then describes the skills associated with children being socially and emotionally competent, such as being able to identify the antecedents and consequences of emotions. Finally, he describes noncurricular ways in which teachers can promote these competencies in the preschool classroom, such as through validating the emotions that underlie behaviors. The final chapter in this part, Chapter 11, written by Tinio, Katz-Buonincontro, and Barbot, emphasizes creativity and creative potential in early childhood education. Tinio and colleagues stress that early childhood is an optimal time for promoting creativity and imagination in children. They discuss the key cognitive, socioemotional, and environmental factors that support and impede the development and expression of creative and imaginative behaviors. These authors conclude with a discussion of the implications of these interventions on children's cognitive and socioemotional development as well their engagement with and appreciation of the world around them.

The fourth part of this volume consists of three chapters, each of which addresses a special population. When we were conceptualizing this project, we knew we had to include chapters on special populations given the changing demographics in the United States. It is not uncommon to see children from all walks of life in early childhood education settings, as well as young children with disabilities or specific learning and developmental challenges. In Chapter 12, Stanton-Chapman and Schmidt discuss a definition of social competence, how professionals can facilitate the development of social competence in preschoolers with disabilities, and why promoting social competence in children who lack the needed skills is critical in the early childhood years. In Chapter 13, Radzicki, Hughes, Schoenenberger, Park, and Sánchez focus on working with young children who are culturally and linguistically diverse. These authors posit that as the United States becomes more linguistically and culturally diverse, educators need to prepare even more for working with young children and their families. They provide an outline of what culturally sensitive practices should look like, discuss disparities often faced by children from culturally and linguistically diverse backgrounds, and provide recommendations for early childhood professionals to implement culturally competent practices. In the final chapter in this part, Hughes and Quinn report that a substantial research base shows that early negative experiences (i.e., adverse childhood experiences) can lead to lifelong problems and, often, psychopathology that impairs a young child's current and ultimately later life, including adult functioning. According to these authors, early intervention can prevent the consequences of early adversity. They also address how to work with young children living in stressful environments.

Part V, the last chapter of this volume, prepared by Raines, Malone, Beidleman, and Bowman, describes national policies and laws affecting children's health and education. According to Raines and colleagues, policies and laws play a vital part in the growth and development of young children, who can be supported or harmed by the climate created through policy. Understanding the roles legislation and policy play in children's well-being is a key component of providing well-rounded and responsive services. Their chapter reviews policies and laws that have left a lasting impact on resources for children along the developmental spectrum.

CONCLUDING THOUGHTS

This volume addresses many topics in early childhood education, but no individual volume can cover all topics of interest or importance in this area. As such, we welcome feedback, thoughts, and suggestions regarding the current chapters and other topics as well via email at the following addresses: alfonso@gonzaga.edu for Vincent C. Alfonso and gjd3@lehigh.edu for George J. DuPaul. There is no reason to believe that early childhood education research, practice, and policy are going to slow down anytime soon, and we look forward to future publications and presentations that carry on the good work assembled here. Effective translation of evidence-based practices to implementation in real-world, early education settings is critical for promoting the success of all young children, regardless of ability and background.

REFERENCES

Barnett, W. S. (1995). Long-term effects of early childhood programs on cognitive and school outcomes. *The Future of Children, 5*, 25–50. http://dx.doi.org/10.2307/1602366

Campbell, F. A., & Ramey, C. T. (1994). Effects of early intervention on intellectual and academic achievement: A follow-up study of children from low-income families. *Child Development, 65*, 684–698. http://dx.doi.org/10.2307/1131410

Clarke, A. M., & Clarke, A. D. B. (1989). The later cognitive effects of early intervention. *Intelligence, 13*, 289–297. http://dx.doi.org/10.1016/S0160-2896(89)80001-7

Cortiella, C., & Horowitz, S. H. (2014). *The state of learning disabilities: Facts, trends and emerging issues.* New York, NY: National Center for Learning Disabilities.

Dickenson, D., & Neuman, S. (Eds.). (2006). *Handbook of early literacy research* (Vol. 2). New York, NY: Guilford Press.

Education of the Handicapped Amendments of 1986, Pub.L. No. 99-457, § 2294 (1986).

Good, R. H., Simmons, D. C., & Smith, S. B. (1998). Effective academic interventions in the United States: Evaluating and enhancing the acquisition of early reading skills. *School Psychology Review, 27*, 45–56.

Gorey, K. M. (2001). Early childhood education: A meta-analytic affirmation of the short and long-term benefits of educational opportunity. *School Psychology Quarterly, 16*, 9–30. http://dx.doi.org/10.1521/scpq.16.1.9.19163

Guralnick, M. J. (1991). The next decade of research on the effectiveness of early intervention. *Exceptional Children, 58*, 174–183. http://dx.doi.org/10.1177/001440299105800209

Heckman, J. J. (2011). The economics of inequality: The value of early childhood education. *American Educator, 35*(1), 31–35.

Individuals With Disabilities Education Improvement Act, 20 U.S.C. § 1400 (2004).

Jordan, N. C., Kaplan, D., Ramineni, C., & Locuniak, M. N. (2009). Early math matters: Kindergarten number competence and later mathematics outcomes. *Developmental Psychology, 45*, 850–867. http://dx.doi.org/10.1037/a0014939

Kilpatrick, D. A. (2015). *Essentials of assessing, preventing, and overcoming reading difficulties.* Hoboken, NJ: John Wiley & Sons.

Love, J. M., Kisker, E. E., Ross, C., Raikes, H., Constantine, J., Boller, K., . . . Vogel, C. (2005). The effectiveness of early Head Start for 3-year-old children and their parents: Lessons for policy and programs. *Developmental Psychology, 41*, 885–901. http://dx.doi.org/10.1037/0012-1649.41.6.885

Masten, A. S., & Coatsworth, J. D. (1998). The development of competence in favorable and unfavorable environments. Lessons from research on successful children. *American Psychologist, 53*, 205–220. http://dx.doi.org/10.1037/0003-066X.53.2.205

Mazzocco, M. M., Feigenson, L., & Halberda, J. (2011). Preschoolers' precision of the approximate number system predicts later school mathematics performance. *PLoS ONE, 6*(9), e23749. http://dx.doi.org/10.1371/journal.pone.0023749

McCoy, D. C., Yoshikawa, H., Ziol-Guest, K. M., Duncan, G. J., Schindler, H. S., Magnuson, K., . . . Shonkoff, J. P. (2017). Impacts of early childhood education on medium- and long-term educational outcomes. *Educational Researcher, 46,* 474–487. http://dx.doi.org/10.3102/0013189X17737739

Ramey, C. T., & Ramey, S. L. (1998). Early intervention and early experience. *American Psychologist, 53,* 109–120. http://dx.doi.org/10.1037/0003-066X.53.2.109

Ramey, C. T., Sparling, J. J., & Ramey, S. L. (2014). Interventions for students from low resource environments: The Abecedarian approach. In J. T. Mascolo, V. C. Alfonso, & D. P. Flanagan (Eds.), *Essentials of planning, selecting, and tailoring interventions for unique learners* (pp. 439–473). Hoboken, NJ: John Wiley & Sons.

Ramey, S. L. (1999). Head Start and preschool education: Toward continued improvement. *American Psychologist, 54,* 344–346. http://dx.doi.org/10.1037/0003-066X.54.5.344

Rose, T. L., & Calhoun, M. L. (1990). The Charlotte Circle Project: A program for infants and toddlers with severe/profound disabilities. *Journal of Early Intervention, 14,* 175–185. http://dx.doi.org/10.1177/105381519001400206

Rounds, K. A. (1991). Early intervention services for very young children and their families under P.L. 99-457. *Child and Adolescent Social Work Journal, 8,* 489–499. http://dx.doi.org/10.1007/BF00755236

Salillas, E., & Wicha, N. Y. Y. (2012). Early learning shapes the memory networks for arithmetic: Evidence from brain potentials in bilinguals. *Psychological Science, 23,* 745–755. http://dx.doi.org/10.1177/0956797612446347

Shonkoff, J. P., & Meisels, S. J. (1991). Defining eligibility for services under PL 99-457. *Journal of Early Intervention, 15,* 21–25. http://dx.doi.org/10.1177/105381519101500104

Spodek, B., & Saracho, O. N. (2003). On the shoulders of giants: Exploring the traditions of early childhood education. *Early Childhood Education Journal, 31,* 3–10. http://dx.doi.org/10.1023/A:1025176516780

U.S. Department of Health and Human Services, Administration for Children and Families, Office of Head Start, National Center on Parent, Family, and Community Engagement. (2018). *Head Start Parent, Family, and Community Engagement Framework.* Retrieved from https://eclkc.ohs.acf.hhs.gov/sites/default/files/pdf/pfce-framework.pdf

Vinovskis, M. A. (2005). *The birth of Head Start: Preschool education policies in the Kennedy and Johnson administrations.* Chicago, IL: University of Chicago Press. http://dx.doi.org/10.7208/chicago/9780226856735.001.0001

Vo, V. A., Li, R., Kornell, N., Pouget, A., & Cantlon, J. F. (2014). Young children bet on their numerical skills: Metacognition in the numerical domain. *Psychological Science, 25,* 1712–1721. http://dx.doi.org/10.1177/0956797614538458

Weikart, D. (1989). Early childhood education and primary prevention. In R. E. Hess & J. Delong (Eds.), *The NMHA: Eighty years of involvement in the field of prevention* (pp. 285–306). New York, NY: Routledge.

Weissberg, R. P. (2000). Improving the lives of millions of school children. *American Psychologist, 55,* 1360–1373. http://dx.doi.org/10.1037/0003-066X.55.11.1360

Yoshikawa, H., Weiland, C., Brooks-Gunn, J., Burchinal, M., Espinosa, L., Gormley, W., & Zaslow, M. J. (2013, October). *Investing in our future: The evidence base for preschool education* [Policy brief]. Washington, DC: Society for Research in Child Development. Retrieved from https://www.fcd-us.org/the-evidence-base-on-preschool

Zigler, E. (1994). Reshaping early childhood intervention to be a more effective weapon against poverty. *American Journal of Community Psychology, 22,* 37–47. http://dx.doi.org/10.1007/BF02506816

Zigler, E. F., & Bishop-Josef, S. J. (2006). The cognitive child vs. the whole child: Lessons from 40 years of Head Start. In D. G. Singer, R. M. Golinkoff, & K. Hirsh-Pasek (Eds.), *Play = learning: How play motivates and enhances children's cognitive and social emotional growth* (pp. 15–35). New York, NY: Oxford University Press.

ASSESSMENT

1

Assessing and Evaluating Young Children

Developmental Domains and Methods

Vincent C. Alfonso, Joseph R. Engler, and Janice C. C. Lepore

A necessary step in promoting healthy growth and development in young children is ensuring appropriate, accurate, and purposeful assessment and evaluation of developing skills because reliable and valid assessment data are evaluated or interpreted to guide the planning, selecting, and tailoring of interventions (Mascolo, Alfonso, & Flanagan, 2014). On a daily basis, parents, teachers, and other caretakers make decisions about how to meet the short- and long-term needs of the children in their care. These decisions can best be made with a reliable and valid foundation of information about the individual child, including how she or he understands and interacts with the environment and whether she or he is developing the necessary core skills to continue to learn and progress. As Snow and Van Hemel (2008) observed, assessment conducted well can support better program development and more positive outcomes for young children, but assessment conducted poorly can have negative outcomes because evaluation of the data is compromised. The primary goal of this chapter is to offer guidance to teachers, health care providers, and other professionals working with young children to support them in planning, developing, and implementing assessment processes and methods that promote short- and long-term healthy development of the children in their care.

http://dx.doi.org/10.1037/0000197-002
Healthy Development in Young Children: Evidence-Based Interventions for Early Education,
V. C. Alfonso and G. J. DuPaul (Editors)

RATIONALE FOR ASSESSMENT AND EVALUATION
OF YOUNG CHILDREN

Recent years have seen increased emphasis on assessment during early child-hood, including the early elementary and preschool years. This shift has been driven by several factors, including the ever-increasing research highlighting the relationships between early developmental skills and outcome measures such as school readiness (Cristofaro & Tamis-LeMonda, 2012; Friend, Smolak, Liu, Poulin-Dubois, & Zesiger, 2018; see also Chapter 3, this volume), early literacy and reading skills (Duff, Reen, Plunkett, & Nation, 2015; Kim, Im, & Kwon, 2015; O'Neill, Thornton, Marks, Rajendran, & Halperin, 2016; see also Chapter 4, this volume), and social–emotional and behavior development (Eklund, Kilgus, von der Embse, Beardmore, & Tanner, 2017; Shonkoff & Phillips, 2000; Whitcomb, 2018; see also Chapter 2, this volume). Research findings have consistently supported early identification and intervention as valuable tools to promote positive outcomes in young children, including preschoolers (Alfonso, Ruby, Wissel, & Davari, 2020; Ramey & Ramey, 2004; Ramey, Yeates, & Short, 1984).

In addition to the scientific literature, there has been steady movement at the federal and state legislative levels toward screening, assessment, evalua-tion, and intervention during early childhood. At the federal level, statutes include the Individuals With Disabilities Education Improvement Act (2004), the Research Excellence and Advancements for Dyslexia Act (2016), and the Every Student Succeeds Act (2015). At the state level, legislatures are respond-ing with updates to regulations and codes to implement early screening for a range of concerns, including developmental delays, language skills, and early academic development. In many cases, these acts are recognition of the science regarding the efficacy of early intervention and are an attempt to ensure that all children have access to the services and supports that will foster their growth and development. However, implementation of these acts has often been hampered by questions surrounding the assessment processes itself. For example, there appears to be a lack of clarity about specifically what to assess, how to ensure accurate assessments, how to evaluate assessment data, and finally how to apply the information gained in the most effective manner.

Therefore, this chapter first describes the rationale for including five domains of early childhood development whether screening or conducting a compre-hensive assessment.[1] Next, a discussion of what types of assessment methods

---

[1]A brief note regarding the similarities and differences between screening assessment and comprehensive assessment is in order. Each of these assessments tends to include multiple domains or areas of development (e.g., cognitive abilities and processes, adaptive behavior), and their evaluation or interpretive power depends on the psychometric characteristics (e.g., standardization, reliability) of the assessment tools. Screening, however, typically refers to brief, general, low-cost methods that yield initial information about multiple behaviors for individuals or large groups of children (Gridley, Mucha, & Hatfield, 1995). In addition, screening "can be used to

to use follows. Then, we provide a brief discussion of psychometric properties of norm-referenced, standardized instruments necessary to ensure that examiners, assessment experts, practitioners, and clinicians can have confidence that their assessment yielded reliable and valid results (Alfonso & Flanagan, 2009). We conclude the chapter with an example of a psychometrically sound language test for preschoolers to demonstrate how to evaluate the psychometric rigor of these types of measures (Alfonso, Shanock, Muldoon, Benway, & Oades-Sese, 2018; Muldoon, Benway, Shanock, & Alfonso, 2018).

DOMAINS OF ASSESSMENT AND EVALUATION OF YOUNG CHILDREN'S PERFORMANCE

A well-developed assessment plan includes a clear statement about the domains and skills to be measured. Within early childhood, including the preschool years, five domains are most frequently the focus of assessment. These domains are cognitive abilities and processes, motor skills, speech and language skills, social–emotional behavior, and adaptive behavior (Bracken & Nagle, 2007; Snow & Van Hemel, 2008). Together, these domains and associated skills form the foundation for the development of interpersonal relationships, academic learning, emotional health, and interpersonal–social functioning during childhood. As such, a deficit within any of the domains of functioning or associated skills at the foundational level may have a negative effect on future functioning. It is important as a first step in the assessment planning process to develop a clear and agreed-upon definition of the developmental domain(s) as well as identify the set of skills to be assessed and evaluated within that domain, relevant to the referral question(s) at hand.

Cognitive Abilities and Processes

Cognition, as a broad construct, refers to "the mental processes that are involved in perception, attention, memory, problem solving, reasoning and making decisions" (Goldstein, 2008, p. 2). Professionals have access to a variety of theoretically and psychometrically sound measures of cognitive abilities and processes that can provide valuable information about a young child's development. Skills assessed by these measures may include vocabulary knowledge, verbal and nonverbal problem solving, analysis of visual sequences and

---

identify potential learning problems, guide future interventions, or serve as a pre-referral tool" (Emmons & Alfonso, 2005, p. 112). Psychometric characteristics that are particular to screening assessment as opposed to comprehensive assessment are sensitivity and specificity. These terms refer to true positives and true negatives, respectively, as high-quality screening assessments distinguish between children who are at risk for developmental delays and those who are not. Emmons and Alfonso (2005) discussed screening assessment in their critical review of several screening batteries, and the remainder of this chapter discusses comprehensive assessment.

shapes, attention and inhibition, various aspects of memory, and the degree to which a child can process information efficiently (Alfonso & Flanagan, 1999, 2007). In some cases, measures may also assess skills more specifically associated with preacademic and academic skill development, such as phonological awareness–processing and working memory (Brock, Rimm-Kaufman, Nathanson, & Grimm, 2009; Costa, Green, Sideris, & Hooper, 2018; Potocki, Ecalle, & Magnan, 2017).

Engler and Alfonso (2020) reviewed the theoretical, quantitative, and qualitative characteristics of several cognitive tests typically administered to pre-school children. As part of their review, Engler and Alfonso examined the broad and narrow Cattell–Horn–Carroll abilities measured by commonly adminis-tered preschool cognitive tests. They found that all tests reviewed measured comprehension–knowledge, fluid reasoning, visual processing, and working memory capacity. The Woodcock–Johnson IV Tests of Cognitive Abilities (Schrank, McGrew, & Mather, 2014) and the Differential Ability Scales, Second Edition (Elliott, 2007) also measured auditory processing, processing speed, and learning efficiency.

Information about a young child's cognitive profile, including areas of strength and weakness, can be applied to promote healthy growth and develop-ment in a variety of ways, such as providing an enriched learning environment, introducing additional structure or practice for specific skills, and identifying children who would benefit from early intervention services or additional monitoring as they enter academic settings. For example, if a young child is identified as having deficits in the area of working memory, one may rec-ommend intervening to teach the child chunking strategies, use mnemonic devices, or modify the learning environment to break down multistep pro-cedures into individual steps.

Motor Skills

Motor skills are generally considered to be divided into two broad categories: namely, gross motor skills, which involve movements of the large muscles of the body, and fine motor skills, which involve smaller muscle systems such as the hands, fingers, feet, and facial muscles. Motor skills are among the earliest skills to be monitored and assessed. As early as 3 to 6 months of age, parents of infants are asked to monitor their child's ability to raise her or his head, grasp small objects, and roll over independently before moving on to crawling and taking her or his first steps. Healthy developing motor skills allow children to explore their environment, participate in social and play activities, and facil-itate cognitive development and learning (Grissmer, Grimm, Aiyer, Murrah, & Steele, 2010).

Assessment of gross motor skills typically involves observation of a child's ability to walk, run, jump, maintain body posture, and move through the envi-ronment (H. G. Williams & Monsma, 2007). A review of several gross motor assessments was recently completed by Monsma, Miedema, Brian, and Williams (2020). Assessment of fine motor skills typically includes activities such as holding tools for writing or drawing, picking up small objects, transferring objects between hands, smoothly tracking objects with the eyes, and transferring and chewing food. Difficulties in motor development can impact a child's ability to engage in a variety of important tasks including active play with peers, manipulating writing or drawing tools, remaining comfortably seated or positioned within a group, and developing age-appropriate independence in self-care (e.g., fastening clothing, eating). Concerns in these areas are typically evaluated further by a physical or occupational therapist to determine age-appropriate expectations and develop intervention or support plans if needed.

Speech and Language Skills

A child's developing speech and language skills can facilitate or impede a child in establishing relationships, communicating ideas and questions, and seeking comfort or assistance for her or his needs (Nelson & Warner, 2007). Early oral language skills have also been shown to correlate with the development of pre- and early literacy skills (Friend et al., 2018; Neuman & Dickinson, 2011). Assessment of speech and language skills often includes an evaluation of oral language (e.g., receptive and expressive skills) as well as pragmatic communication skills and, in some cases, early literacy skills. Expressive language tasks typically require a child to provide oral definitions of specific words; to reproduce words, phrases, or sentences accurately; and to generate language independently to meet a specific demand (e.g., words within a given category, completing a given sentence).

Receptive language tasks may assess skills such as the ability to identify objects or pictures associated with words or brief definitions, the ability to respond accurately to questions after listening to information, and the ability to track and follow oral instructions. Measures of pragmatic language offer rich information about a child's understanding of the use of language and communication patterns and may focus on skills such as understanding turn-taking in conversation and the ability to recognize, monitor, and modulate tone and volume. Measures of early literacy skills often include tasks to assess the development of phonological awareness and processing skills (e.g., rhyming, sound recognition and isolation, blending) as well as skills such as letter and object naming, alphabetic knowledge, and comprehension skills (McConnell, Bradfield, & Wackerle-Hollman, 2014). Caesar and Ottley (2020) offered an excellent treatise on assessing communication, language, and speech in preschool children. They provided a conceptual framework for understanding language development in young children, reviewed several measures of speech and language development and functioning, and discussed assessment of young children from special populations.

Social-Emotional Behavior

Social–emotional behavior pertains to internal experiences, such as a child's feelings of anxiety, sadness, excitement, or worry, as well as external behaviors, such as how a child interacts with adults and peers, responds to specific task expectations, or copes with unexpected changes in the environment (Whitcomb, 2018; see also Chapter 2, this volume). Often, these behaviors are assessed through direct observation, reports from specific informants (e.g., parents, teachers), or a combination of these methods. A child's ability to share and take turns; her or his typical responses to new teachers or situations; the degree to which she or he is friendly, welcoming, or shy with new peers; and the ability to follow instructions may all be areas of focus of social–emotional assessment. This information is vital to ensuring a child's health and wellness, as early impairments in social–emotional functioning may develop into more significant concerns such as anxiety, depression, or behavioral disorders or may be indicators of other common behavior problems such as attention-deficit/hyperactivity disorder (DuPaul, McGoey, Eckert, & VanBrakle, 2001).

Additionally, the aforementioned social–emotional concerns have been shown to be related to future academic difficulties (Eklund et al., 2017). Impairments in social–emotional functioning during early childhood have also been associated with increased risk for difficulties during later adolescence and adulthood, including lower rates of high school graduation and employment and higher rates of involvement with juvenile justice (Jones, Greenberg, & Crowley, 2015). Moreover, early intervention has been found to strengthen social–emotional skills and to promote improved behaviors and positive outcomes (Bauminger, 2002; Schonert-Reichl et al., 2015).

Adaptive Behavior

Adaptive behavior refers broadly to the set of skills that involve a child's interactions and response, or adaptations, to expectations and changes in the environment. Current operational definitions of adaptive behavior refer to three broad components: conceptual skills, social skills, and practical skills (American Association on Intellectual and Developmental Disabilities, 2010; Arias, Verdugo, Navas, & Gómez, 2013). These broad components are then further broken down into specific skill areas. Conceptual skills may include communication of personal needs and following safety rules; social skills include interacting with others and playing appropriately with toys; and practical skills include dressing oneself, preparing and consuming appropriate food, and maintaining personal hygiene (Harrison & Raineri, 2007).

In the assessment of adaptive behavior skills, it is important to recognize the impact of contextual, situational, cultural, and developmental factors. A toddler may be expected to demonstrate a different level of personal hygiene management compared with an older child. In addition, opportunities to practice and develop skills, as well as family and cultural expectations related to adaptive skills, influence development and performance of different skills across different situations. With that in mind, assessment of adaptive behavior needs to be conducted with an understanding of a child's background and family and cultural context, and oftentimes measures of adaptive behavior include input from adult observers, such as parents and teachers (Harrison & Oakland, 2015; Sparrow, Cicchetti, & Saulnier, 2016).

Adaptive behavior assessment and evaluation are critical to diagnosing intellectual disabilities as well as other developmental disabilities, yet they are often underutilized or misunderstood. Harrison (2020) discussed procedures for assessing adaptive behavior within multidimensional preschool services; described, reviewed, and evaluated typically administered standardized adaptive behavior rating scales and supplemental assessment techniques; and explained how to use the results of adaptive behavior assessment to diagnose developmental disabilities and plan effective intervention programs.

DEVELOPING THE ASSESSMENT PLAN

In deciding the domains of development to assess, one must first consider the intended purpose of the assessment. For example, practitioners should establish the specific question(s) to be answered, specific concerns emerging, and specific environments where the findings will be applied. In light of the plethora of possibilities, assessing development is clearly not a one-size-fits-all process. Rather, those assessing early childhood development must be skilled in the tools and techniques needed to respond appropriately. For example, a screening assessment, which may be intended to distinguish children quickly who are at risk for a given concern from children who are not at risk, is a significantly different assessment than a diagnostic assessment intended to identify a given child's skills and needs and identify target areas for intervention. Similarly, a process that will be used to develop or evaluate a school- or communitywide program will be different from an assessment process intended to inform intervention planning for a small group or an individual. It is also important to keep in mind the level of resources required for a given assessment process—including the resources required from the family and the child. As such, participating in an assessment process requires an investment of time, energy, and trust that the process will result in a positive and desirable outcome. When designing assessment processes, practitioners need to keep each of these factors in mind, carefully balancing the needs, goals, risks, and benefits of the process.

ASSESSMENT OF YOUNG CHILDREN

When young children are assessed, particularly within the domains of functioning previously discussed, the assessment should be comprehensive in nature. Although the term *comprehensive* is used vaguely, there is consensus within the professional community that an assessment should meet three criteria: (a) include data from multiple methods, (b) include data from multiple sources, and (c) include data from multiple settings. Briefly, a comprehensive assessment should be multimethod, multisource, and multisetting. We believe that a comprehensive assessment should utilize multiple methods for gathering assessment data because no one method is sufficient for evaluating and thus understanding a young child's functioning. Different methods for gathering data that a practitioner may want to consider include, but are not limited to, systematic direct observations, interviews, and norm-referenced tests (Salvia, Ysseldyke, & Witmer, 2017; Sattler, 2008; see also Chapter 2, this volume).

Systematic Direct Observations

Systematic direct observations (e.g., frequency, duration, and/or latency recordings) are often considered a necessary component of any early childhood assessment because they allow the practitioner to observe the behavior directly in question. Additionally, behavioral observations can be completed in a setting in which the behavior is considered problematic (Whitcomb, 2018). For example, depending on the source of referral, young children may be observed in settings such as a preschool, daycare, or home (i.e., multisetting). Even within a preschool or daycare setting it is important to observe children in multiple locations because young children may behave differently in the classroom versus the outside play area, for instance.

Each of the settings offers a different perspective for understanding the behavior and, as such, contributes data necessary to address the behavior in question. In addition, behavioral observations allow the practitioner to understand the contextual variables that are co-occurring and may contribute to the behavior difficulty. We recommend that practitioners observe young children in situations where the behavior occurs as well as situations where the behavior does not occur. This gives practitioners a better understanding of the antecedents and consequences of the behavior, both of which may contribute to its maintenance. By following this process, practitioners are able to gather data in a way that meaningfully informs recommendations for remediation, should they be needed.

Interviews

Interviews are also a valuable method of gathering data when assessing young children that can add significantly to the assessment process. Unfortunately, in light of their cognitive and linguistic development, interviewing young children poses several inherent challenges. For example, young children may not have the ability to identify their thoughts and emotions or articulate those to the interviewer. Therefore, it is recommended that interviews be conducted with adult caregivers (i.e., multisource) who are familiar with the young child and can provide a reliable description of the child's developmental abilities. As a rule of thumb, it is recommended that practitioners interview adult caregivers/providers who are most familiar with the child. For example, it would be inappropriate to interview a day care provider who has worked with a child for a short time (i.e., days or couple of weeks) because it is unlikely that the provider can accurately describe the child's development. If, however, the provider has worked with the child for a couple of months, it is more likely that she or he will give an accurate account regarding the child's development. Other adult caregivers to interview may include nannies, external family members, community members, religious affiliation members, and the like.

Interviews have several advantages over behavioral observations. As such, we recommend that interviews be used in conjunction with behavioral observations. First, interviews provide an opportunity to develop rapport with adult caregivers. Rapport is necessary and a cornerstone of the assessment process that allows practitioners to develop relationships with the caregivers/providers. Second, whereas behavioral observations are focused on the present, a well-constructed interview can gather data from the past (e.g., developmental history) and can also identify the desired outcome for the assessment process. Third, it is often adults who refer young children for an assessment. Therefore, conducting an interview with the referral source is a way to understand the reason for the referral from that individual's perspective. Sattler (2014) is an excellent resource regarding interviewing techniques.

Norm-Referenced Measures

Sattler (2008) described norm-referenced measures (e.g., Wechsler Preschool and Primary Scale of Intelligence–Fourth Edition; Wechsler, 2012) as a necessary method for gathering assessment data on children. Norm-referenced measures are standardized on a norm group (Alfonso & Flanagan, 2009). Standardization implies that the test is administered in a consistent and pre-determined manner so that all examinees are given the same opportunities to respond to test items and that those test items are scored in an objective manner. Doing so reduces the amount of examiner bias and leads to more reliable results (Sattler, 2008). Norm-referenced measures have advantages above and beyond behavioral observations and interviews. First, norm-referenced measures allow practitioners to compare the results of the tested child with those of other young children of similar age and characteristics. Direct comparison allows practitioners to determine whether the young child is below, at, or above expectations on the particular domain that was measured. For example, if a practitioner gives a young child a norm-referenced measure of language abilities, and the child performs significantly below expectations for her or his age, the practitioner may recommend that child for speech and language services. Second, norm-referenced measures allow practitioners to determine not only areas of weakness but also areas of strengths for the child. Third, norm-referenced measures can be completed relatively quickly and provide an aggregate of the domain(s) measured. One particularly promising and popular type of norm-referenced measure that is used in the area of early childhood assessment is rating scales.

Rating Scales

Rating scales (e.g., Behavior Assessment System for Children–Third Edition; Reynolds & Kamphaus, 2015) are used for gathering data from individuals who are familiar with the child's development (Sattler, 2014). Rating scales are standardized instruments that allow practitioners to gather a wealth of objective data within a short period. In addition, rating scales are significantly more cost-effective than are behavioral observations. Similar to interviews, rating scales can capture the perspective of the informant (e.g., parent, caregiver, provider) across a variety of domains. Moreover, rating scales allow practitioners to determine the presence or absence of a behavior or ability as well as a gradation of the occurrence of such behavior or ability. For example, rating scales are typically presented with a statement, followed by a Likert scale rating where the lowest rating suggests that the statement *never* occurs up to the highest rating suggesting that the statement *almost always* occurs (Whitcomb, 2018). The informant (or rater) then reads each statement and marks the most appropriate response.

As with the other methods typically used in the assessment process, there are numerous advantages for the inclusion of rating scales (Whitcomb, 2018). First, as mentioned earlier, rating scales are relatively inexpensive and time-saving tools for gathering adult perceptions of the child's behavior and abilities. Rating scales can be completed by adults familiar with the child so multiple perspectives can be ascertained in a matter of minutes. Second, because of the gradation of a Likert scale, it is possible to obtain data on low-frequency behavior in an efficient manner. For example, it may take several behavioral observations before practitioners are able to observe a low-frequency behavior (e.g., physical aggression toward peers), resulting in lost time and an increased cost of paying for the practitioner's time. Third, rating scales can be used for multiple different types of assessment. For instance, rating scales can be used diagnostically as well as for progress monitoring. Therefore, because of their practical utility, rating scales continue to remain a popular method of assessment for practitioners.

Tests

A second type of norm-referenced measure is tests. Tests involve predetermined questions that are intended to elicit a response (Salvia et al., 2017). Comparable to rating scales, tests are standardized instruments that can provide quantitative information about the examinee's performance in relation to other children of a similar age. In addition, tests are often used within the school setting to assist in making high-stakes decisions for a child. These high-stakes decisions may include whether a child is eligible for special education services and where the best educational placement is for the child. Given the sheer importance and potential life-altering decisions that can be made from test results, it is important to note that not all tests are designed equally well. Therefore, the responsibility rests with practitioners to determine which tests have the best psychometric properties necessary to address the initial referral question(s) (Engler & Alfonso, 2020).

Fortunately, several researchers over the past 20-plus years have worked to identify key psychometric characteristics necessary to evaluate the quality of tests across the five developmental domains addressed in this chapter (see Table 1.1). We reviewed the information found in Table 1.1 and Alfonso and Flanagan (2009) to create Table 1.2, which provides criteria for evaluating the adequacy of the technical characteristics of preschool assessment instruments. These criteria have been used to evaluate adaptive behavior scales (Floyd et al., 2015), language tests for preschoolers (Muldoon et al., 2018), and other early childhood instruments (see Alfonso, Rentz, & Chung, 2010; Alfonso, Wissel, & Lorimer, 2017). Space limitations preclude an in-depth discussion of the technical characteristics as well as explanations of how the criteria to evaluate them were determined. However, we do provide a brief example of how to apply the criteria to a norm-referenced language test for preschoolers—namely, the Preschool Language Scales–Fifth Edition (PLS-5; Zimmerman, Steiner, & Pond, 2011).

REVIEW OF THE TECHNICAL CHARACTERISTICS OF THE PLS-5 FOR 2- TO 5-YEAR-OLDS

The PLS-5 is an individually administered standardized, norm-referenced test used to identify children between the ages of 0 and 7 years, 11 months who have a language delay or disorder. It comprises two standardized scales (Auditory Comprehension [AC] and Expressive Communication [EC]) and three supplemental measures (Language Sample Checklist, Articulation Screener, Home Communication Questionnaire). The AC scale is used to evaluate a child's comprehension of language. The items designed for preschool-aged children are used to assess comprehension of basic vocabulary, concepts, morphology, and early syntax. The EC scale is used to determine how well a child communicates with others. Preschool-age children are asked to name common objects, use concepts that describe objects and express quantity, and use specific prepositions, grammatical markers, and sentence structures. The PLS-5 provides three norm-referenced standard scores that have a mean of 100 and a standard deviation of 15.

Standardization Characteristics

The standardization sample of the PLS-5 included 800 children between the ages of 2 and 5 years (200 children per 1-year age interval), rendering this characteristic *adequate* to *good*. Normative data were collected in 2010, and

TABLE 1.1. Sources That Include Comprehensive Descriptions and Reviews of and Criteria for Evaluating Norm-Referenced Instruments for Preschoolers

Source	Assessment domain(s)	Norm-referenced test characteristics					
		Standardization	Reliability	Norm table age division	Test floors	Item gradients	Validity
Bracken (1987)	Various including cognitive, language, and general development	Not addressed	Median subtest internal consistency ≥ .80; total test internal consistency ≥ .90; total test stability ≥ .90	Not addressed	Average subtest floor ≥ 2 standard deviations below the mean; total test floor ≥ 2 standard deviations below the mean	Each test item is equivalent to no more than one-third standard deviation	Presence or absence of validity evidence in test manual only but no evaluation of the evidence
Alfonso & Flanagan (1999); Flanagan & Alfonso (1995)	Cognitive	Evaluated the size of the normative group, recency of the normative data, and number of demographic variables (see Table 1.2 for specific criteria)	Evaluated total test internal consistency and test-retest as well as test-retest sample characteristics (see Table 1.2 for specific criteria)	Norm tables between 1 and 2 months evaluated as *good*; 3–4 months evaluated as *adequate*; > 4 months evaluated as *inadequate* (see Table 1.2)	Similar to Bracken (1987); see Table 1.2 for application of specific criteria	Same as Bracken (1987); see Table 1.2 for application of specific criteria	Presence or absence of content, criterion-related, and construct validity evidence and authors' evaluation of the evidence (see Table 1.2 for specific criteria)
Bracken & Walker (1997)	Cognitive	Not addressed	Same as Bracken (1987)	Suggested 1- to 2-month intervals but no evaluation according to this criterion	Same as Bracken (1987)	Same as Bracken (1987)	Not addressed

Bradley-Johnson (2001)	Cognitive	Described but no evaluation according to specific criteria	Same as Bracken (1987)	Not addressed	Same as Bracken (1987)	Same as Bracken (1987)	Author's evaluation of content, construct, and criterion validity evidence
Lidz (2003)	Cognitive	Same as Alfonso & Flanagan (1999)	Same as Alfonso & Flanagan (1999)	Recommended Alfonso & Flanagan (1999) but no evaluation according to specific criteria	Not addressed	Recommended Bracken (1987) but no evaluation according to specific criteria	Same as Alfonso & Flanagan (1999)
Saye (2003)	Cognitive	Described but no evaluation according to specific criteria	Same as Bracken (1987)	Recommended Bracken (2000) but no evaluation according to specific criteria	Recommended Bracken (1987) but no evaluation according to specific criteria	Recommended Bracken (1987) but no evaluation according to specific criteria	Author's evaluation of select validity evidence
Ford & Dahinten (2005)	Cognitive	Not addressed	Described but no evaluation according to specific criteria	Not addressed	Described but no evaluation according to specific criteria	Described but no evaluation according to specific criteria	Described but no evaluation of the evidence
Kamphaus (2005)	Cognitive	Described but no evaluation according to specific criteria	Described but no evaluation according to specific criteria	Not addressed	Not addressed	Not addressed	Author's evaluation of select validity evidence
Bradley-Johnson & Johnson (2007)	Cognitive	Described but no evaluation according to specific criteria	Same as Salvia & Ysseldyke (2004)	Described but no evaluation according to specific criteria	Same as Bracken (1987)	Same as Bracken (1987)	Author's evaluation of content, construct, and criterion validity evidence

(continues)

TABLE 1.1. Sources That Include Comprehensive Descriptions and Reviews of and Criteria for Evaluating Norm-Referenced Instruments for Preschoolers (*Continued*)

Source	Assessment domain(s)	Norm-referenced test characteristics					
		Standardization	Reliability	Norm table age division	Test floors	Item gradients	Validity
Vig & Sanders (2007)	Cognitive	Described but no evaluation according to specific criteria	Described but no evaluation according to specific criteria	Not addressed	Not addressed	Not addressed	Described but no evaluation of the evidence
M. E. Williams, Sando, & Soles (2014)	Cognitive	Same as AERA, APA, & NCME (1999); Alfonso & Flanagan (2009); McFadden (1996); Neisworth & Bagnato (2000); Salvia, Ysseldyke, & Bolt, (2013)	Same as Alfonso & Flanagan (2009); Bracken (1987); Salvia et al. (2013)	Not addressed	Same as Bracken (1987)	Same as Bracken (1987)	Described but no evaluation of the evidence
Ellingsen (2016)	Cognitive	Described that norms should be no older than a decade	Same as Lichtenberger (2005)	Not addressed	Described but no evaluation according to specific criteria	Same as Bracken (1987)	Described but no evaluation of the evidence
McCauley & Swisher (1984)	Language	Same as APA (1974); Salvia & Ysseldyke (1981); Weiner & Hoock (1973)	Same as Salvia & Ysseldyke (1981)	Not addressed	Not addressed	Not addressed	Presence or absence of validity evidence in test manual only but no evaluation of the evidence

Study	Category					
Bracken & Pecyna-Rhyner (1991)	Language	Described but no evaluation according to specific criteria	Same as Bracken (1987)	Not addressed	Same as Bracken (1987)	Same as Bracken (1987)	Same as Bracken (1987)
Plante & Vance (1994)	Language	Same as APA (1974); Salvia & Ysseldyke (1981); Weiner & Hoock (1973)	Same as Salvia & Ysseldyke (1981)	Not addressed	Not addressed	Not addressed	Same as McCauley & Swisher (1984)
Wyatt & Seymour (1999)	Language	Described but no evaluation according to specific criteria	Not addressed	Not addressed	Not addressed	Not addressed	Not addressed
Dockrell (2001)	Language	Total sample size reported but no evaluation according to specific criteria	Presence or absence of reliability evidence in test manual but no evaluation of the evidence	Not addressed	Not addressed	Not addressed	Presence or absence of validity evidence in test manual only but no evaluation of the evidence
Brassard & Boehm (2007)	Language	Described but no evaluation according to specific criteria	Described but no evaluation according to specific criteria	Not addressed	Not addressed	Not addressed	Described but no evaluation of the evidence
Nelson & Warner (2007)	Language	Not addressed	Not addressed	Not addressed	Not addressed	Not addressed	Not addressed

(continues)

TABLE 1.1. Sources That Include Comprehensive Descriptions and Reviews of and Criteria for Evaluating Norm-Referenced Instruments for Preschoolers (*Continued*)

Source	Assessment domain(s)	Standardization	Reliability	Norm-referenced test characteristics				
				Norm table age division	Test floors	Item gradients	Validity
Oades-Sese & Alfonso (2003)	Language	Described but no evaluation according to specific criteria	Same as Flanagan & Alfonso (1995)	Described but no evaluation according to specific criteria	Same as Bracken (1987)	Same as Bracken (1987)	Same as AERA, APA, & NCME (1999); Flanagan & Alfonso (1995)
Friberg (2010)	Language	Same as McCauley & Swisher (1984) but added several demographic variables (e.g., age and gender distributions, ethnicity, parental education level)	Same as McCauley & Swisher (1984)	Not addressed	Not addressed	Not addressed	Described but no evaluation of evidence
Kirk & Vigeland (2014)	Language	Same as Andersson (2005); Salvia et al. (2013); Sattler (2008)	Same as Bracken (1987); Nunnally (1978); Salvia et al. (2013)	Not addressed	Not addressed	Not addressed	Author's evaluation of content, construct, and criterion-related evidence

Study	Domain					
Flipsen & Ogiela (2015)	Language	Same as McCauley & Swisher (1984) but added whether test had truncated or full-range norms and if the test authors discussed gender differences	Not addressed	Not addressed	Not addressed	Same as McCauley & Swisher (1984) but added whether diagnostic accuracy data, analyses of formal vowel and phonological processes, and dialect differences were included
Martin (1988)	Behavior and social/emotional	Described but no evaluation according to specific criteria	Not addressed	Not addressed	Not addressed	Author's evaluation of select validity evidence
Wilson & Bullock (1989)	Behavior and social/emotional	Described but no evaluation according to specific criteria	Internal consistency reliability described; test–retest and interrater reliability as per Anastasi (1982)	Not addressed	Not addressed	Presence or absence of validity evidence including content, criterion-related, and construct and authors' evaluation of the evidence
Bracken, Keith, & Walker (1998)	Behavior and social/emotional	Described but no evaluation according to specific criteria	Same as Bracken (1987)	Not addressed	Same as Bracken (1987)	Same as Bracken (1987)

(continues)

TABLE 1.1. Sources That Include Comprehensive Descriptions and Reviews of and Criteria for Evaluating Norm-Referenced Instruments for Preschoolers (*Continued*)

Source	Assessment domain(s)	Norm-referenced test characteristics					
		Standardization	Reliability	Norm table age division	Test floors	Item gradients	Validity
Knoff, Stollar, Johnson, & Chenneville (1999)	Behavior and social/emotional and adaptive behavior	Described but no evaluation according to specific criteria	Described but no evaluation according to specific criteria	Not addressed	Not addressed	Not addressed	Described but no evaluation of the evidence
Floyd & Bose (2003)	Behavior and social/emotional	Same as Flanagan & Alfonso (1995)	Same as Bracken (1987)	Not addressed	Same as Bracken (1987)	Same as Bracken (1987)	Same as AERA, APA, & NCME (1999); Flanagan & Alfonso (1995)
Lidz (2003)	Behavior and social/emotional and adaptive behavior	Described but no evaluation according to specific criteria	Described but no evaluation according to specific criteria	Not addressed	Not addressed	Not addressed	Described but no evaluation of the evidence
Merrell (2003)	Behavior and social/emotional	Described but no evaluation according to specific criteria	Described but no evaluation according to specific criteria	Not addressed	Not addressed	Not addressed	Author's evaluation of select validity evidence
Kamphaus & Frick (2005)	Behavior and social/emotional	Described but no evaluation according to specific criteria	Described but no evaluation according to specific criteria	Not addressed	Not addressed	Not addressed	Described but no evaluation of the evidence
Brassard & Boehm (2007)	Behavior and social/emotional and adaptive behavior	Described but no evaluation according to specific criteria	Described but no evaluation according to specific criteria	Not addressed	Not addressed	Not addressed	Described but no evaluation of the evidence

Study	Domain						
Campbell & James (2007)	Behavior and social/emotional	Not addressed	Described but no evaluation according to specific criteria	Not addressed	Not addressed	Not addressed	Not addressed
Gokiert et al. (2014)	Behavior and social/emotional	≥ 500 individuals included in total sample ≥ 100 individuals included per age group ≥ 3 stratification variables (i.e., socioeconomic status, gender, geographical region, ethnicity/race, education) included	Same as Fallon, Westaway, & Moloney (2008); Reneman, Dijkstra, Geertzen, & Dijkstra (2010); Squires (2003); Sveinbjornsdottir & Thorsteinsson (2008)	Not addressed	Not addressed	Not addressed	Evidence of factor analysis to demonstrate evidence of construct validity, ≥ .7 correlation for convergent validity per Sveinbjornsdottir & Thorsteinsson (2008), statistically significant group difference for criterion validity, content validity described but no evaluation of evidence
Evans & Bradley-Johnson (1988)	Adaptive behavior	Same as Salvia & Ysseldyke (1981)	Same as Aiken (1985)	Not addressed	Not addressed	Not addressed	Authors' evaluation of select validity evidence
Shands et al. (2008)	Adaptive behavior	Described but no evaluation according to specific criteria	Same as Bracken (1987)	Not addressed	Same as Bracken (1987)	Same as Bracken (1987)	Same as Flanagan & Alfonso (1995)

(continues)

TABLE 1.1. Sources That Include Comprehensive Descriptions and Reviews of and Criteria for Evaluating Norm-Referenced Instruments for Preschoolers (*Continued*)

Source	Assessment domain(s)	Norm-referenced test characteristics					
		Standardization	Reliability	Norm table age division	Test floors	Item gradients	Validity
Floyd et al. (2015)	Adaptive behavior	Same as Alfonso & Flanagan (2009)	Same as Bracken (1987); Floyd & Bose (2003)	Same as Kranzler & Floyd (2013)	Same as Bracken (1987)	Not addressed	Same as Alfonso & Flanagan (2009)
Dunn (1999)	Motor	Not addressed	Not addressed	Not addressed	Not addressed	Not addressed	Not addressed
H. G. Williams & Monsma (2007)	Motor	Described but no evaluation according to specific criteria	Not addressed	Not addressed	Not addressed	Not addressed	Not addressed
de Medeiros, Zequinão, Fronza, dos Santos, & Cardoso (2016)	Motor	Not addressed	Described but no evaluation according to specific criteria	Not addressed	Not addressed	Not addressed	Described but no evaluation according to specific criteria

Emmons & Alfonso (2005)	Various (screening)	Described but no evaluation according to specific criteria	Same as Flanagan & Alfonso (1995)	Not addressed	Not addressed	Not addressed	Same as Flanagan & Alfonso (1995)
Brassard & Boehm (2007)	Various (screening)	Described but no evaluation according to specific criteria	Described but no evaluation according to specific criteria	Not addressed	Not addressed	Not addressed	Described but no evaluation of the evidence
Miles, Fulbrook, & Mainwaring-Magi (2018)	Various (screening)	Same as Alfonso & Flanagan (2009); Salvia et al. (2013)	Same as Alfonso & Flanagan (2009); DeThorne & Schaefer (2004); Salvia et al. (2013)	Not addressed	Not addressed	Not addressed	Author's evaluation of select validity evidence

Note. AERA = American Educational Research Association; APA = American Psychological Association; NCME = National Council on Measurement in Education. Although many reviews are included in this table, the list is not exhaustive. Instead, we included only recent or the most often cited journal articles and book chapters that addressed the quality of norm-referenced tests for preschoolers in the following domains: cognitive, language, behavioral and social–emotional functioning, adaptive behavior, and motor skills. The reader is encouraged to review original sources for a more thorough description of the norm-referenced test characteristics. From *Evidence-Based Practice in Infant and Early Childhood Psychology* (pp. 135–141), by B. A. Mowder, F. Rubinson, and A. E. Yasik (Eds.), 2009, Hoboken, NJ: John Wiley & Sons. Copyright 2009 by John Wiley & Sons. Adapted with permission.

TABLE 1.2. Criteria for Evaluating the Adequacy of the Technical Characteristics of Preschool Assessment Instruments

Technical characteristic	Criteria	Evaluative classification
Standardization[a]		
Size of normative group and number of participants at each age/grade interval	200 persons per each 1-year interval and at least 2,000 persons overall	Good
	100 persons per each 1-year interval and at least 1,000 persons overall	Adequate
	Neither criterion above is met	Inadequate
Recency of normative data	Collected in 2009 or later	Good
	Collected between 1999 and 2008	Adequate
	Collected in 1998 or earlier	Inadequate
Age divisions of norm tables	1 to 2 months	Good
	3 to 4 months	Adequate
	Greater than 4 months	Inadequate
Match of the demographic characteristics of the normative group to the U.S. population (e.g., gender, race) with SES included	Normative group represents the U.S. population on five or more important demographic variables	Good
	Normative group represents the U.S. population on three or four important demographic variables with SES included	Adequate
	Neither criterion is met	Inadequate
Reliability		
Internal consistency reliability coefficient (subtests and composites)	Greater than or equal to .90	Good
	.80 to .89	Adequate
	Less than .80	Inadequate
Test–retest reliability coefficient (composites only)	Greater than or equal to .90	Good
	.80 to .89	Adequate
	Less than .80	Inadequate
Test–retest reliability coefficient (subtests only)	Greater than or equal to .80	Adequate
	Less than .80	Inadequate
Test–Retest Sample		
Size and representativeness of test–retest sample	Sample contains at least 100 participants and represents the U.S. population on at least five or more demographic variables	Good
	Sample contains at least 50 participants and represents the U.S. population on three or four demographic variables	Adequate
	Neither criterion is met	Inadequate

TABLE 1.2. Criteria for Evaluating the Adequacy of the Technical Characteristics of Preschool Assessment Instruments (*Continued*)

Technical characteristic	Criteria	Evaluative classification
Age range of the test–retest sample	Spans no more than a 1-year interval	Good
	Spans no more than 2 years	Adequate
	Spans more than 2 years or extends beyond the preschool age range (i.e., 2–5 yrs.), regardless of interval size	Inadequate
Length of test–retest interval[b]	Interval ≤ 3 months	Good
	Interval > 3 and < 6 months	Adequate
	Interval > 6 months	Inadequate
Floors		
Subtests[c]	Raw score of 1 is associated with a standard score greater than 2 standard deviations below the normative mean	Adequate
	Raw score of 1 is associated with a standard score less than or equal to 2 standard deviations below the normative mean	Inadequate
Composites[d]	Composite standard score greater than 2 standard deviations below the normative mean	Adequate
	Composite standard score less than or equal to 2 standard deviations below the normative mean	Inadequate
Item Gradients[e]		
Item gradient violations	No item gradient violations occur *or* all item gradient violations are between 2 and 3 standard deviations below the normative mean *or* the total number of violations is < 5% across the age range of the test	Good
	All item gradient violations occur between 1 and 3 standard deviations below the normative mean *or* the total number of violations is ≥ 5% and ≤ 15% across the age range of the test	Adequate
	All or any portion of item gradient violations occur between the mean and 1 standard deviation below the normative mean *or* the total number of violations is > 15% across the age range of the test	Inadequate

(*continues*)

TABLE 1.2. Criteria for Evaluating the Adequacy of the Technical Characteristics of Preschool Assessment Instruments *(Continued)*

Technical characteristic	Criteria	Evaluative classification
Validity[f]		
Presence and quality of specific forms of validity evidences	Five or six forms of validity evidence and the authors' evaluation of available data	Good
	Four forms of validity evidence and the authors' evaluation of available data	Adequate
	< 4 forms of validity evidence and the authors' evaluation of available data	Inadequate

Note. SES = socioeconomic status. [a]An overall rating is obtained as follows: *good* = all *good*s; *adequate* = *good*s and *adequate*s; *inadequate* = *good*s and/or *adequate*s, and *inadequate*s. [b]The criteria presented here regarding the length of the test–retest interval differ from traditional criteria used with school-age children because young children's abilities change rapidly. [c]If one assumes a scale having a mean of 100 and a standard deviation of 15, a raw score of 1 that is associated with a standard score of ≤ 69 would constitute an adequate floor. [d]Floors are calculated based on the aggregate of the subtest raw scores that comprise the composites, where one item per subtest is scored correctly. [e]An item gradient is defined as the increase in standard score points associated with a 1-point increase in raw score values. An item gradient violation occurs when a 1-point increase in raw score points is associated with a standard score increase of greater than one third of a standard deviation (Bracken, 1987). [f]The standards for validity in *Standards for Educational and Psychological Testing* (American Educational Research Association, American Psychological Association, & National Council on Measurement in Education, 2014) differ from those in the 1999 publication of the same name. Most notably, in the 2014 publication there is one overarching standard or guiding principle for validity, with 25 standards subsumed under three clusters. The third cluster, namely Specific Forms of Validity Evidence, has 15 of the 25 standards subsumed under six forms of validity evidence. These six forms of validity evidence are akin to the five sources of validity evidence found in the 1999 publication and in earlier versions of this table. Ratings of *good* or *adequate* were made only when the available validity evidence was reviewed positively by the authors and corroborated by other reviews in the extant literature. From *Evidence-Based Practice in Infant and Early Childhood Psychology* (pp. 146–148), by B. A. Mowder, F. Rubinson, and A. E. Yasik (Eds.), 2009, Hoboken, NJ: John Wiley & Sons. Copyright 2009 by John Wiley & Sons. Reprinted with permission.

thus this characteristic is *good*. The sample closely approximated the U.S. population (2008 Census data) on the following variables: age, sex, geographic region, race/ethnicity, and education levels. This characteristic is *good*. The norm tables of the PLS-5 are divided into 6-month age blocks for children between the ages of 2 years and 5 years, 11 months, rendering this characteristic *inadequate*.

Reliability

The PLS-5 AC and EC scales have *high* (.90 or greater) internal consistency at the preschool age range with an *adequate* EC scale at ages 2–2 years, 5 months. The Total Language composite has *high* internal consistency across the preschool age range. Test–retest reliability for the AC and EC scales varies. For example, it is *high* or *adequate* except on the AC scale at ages 5–7 years,

11 months, where it is *inadequate* (< .80). The Total Language composite has *high* or *adequate* test–retest reliability across the preschool age range. The size and representativeness of the test–retest sample is *good*, but the age range of the test–retest sample is *inadequate*. Finally, the length of the test–retest interval is *good*.

Test Floors and Item Gradients

The PLS-5 AC and EC scales have *adequate* floors across the preschool age range. The Total Language composite also has an *adequate* floor. The item gradients for the AC and EC scales are *good* at ages 2–5 years, 11 months.

Validity

Validity evidence for the PLS-5 provided in the examiner's manual appears to be *good* based on the quantity and quality of the evidence. That is, the authors of the test include five or six forms of validity evidence including evidence based on (a) test content, (b) response processes, (c) internal structure, (d) relations to tests and score differences between nonclinical and clinical groups, (e) special group studies, and (f) consequences of testing. Some reviewers, however, have questioned the PLS-5's validity. For example, Muldoon et al. (2018) rated the sensitivity and specificity of the PLS-5 *inadequate*. Given that validity is not an all-or-none phenomenon, it is incumbent upon those who use the PLS-5 to understand its validity strengths and limitations to make the best diagnostic and intervention decisions.

SUMMARY

In sum, a well-designed assessment for early childhood assessment typically includes five developmental domains or areas, is fluid, begins with an assessment plan with specific referral questions in mind, and allows practitioners to evaluate assessment data with confidence. Next, it is the responsibility of practitioners to ensure that the assessment process, or gathering of data, includes multiple sources and methods across multiple settings to answer the specific referral question(s). Several of the most commonly used methods for gathering data are behavioral observations, interviews, and norm-referenced rating scales and tests. We have provided a brief description of each method, along with possible uses and strengths. However, it should be noted that along with strengths, each of the methods discussed in this chapter also has weaknesses (see Chapter 2). Therefore, it is the responsibility of practitioners to know and understand the strengths and weaknesses of each method used within the assessment process. If practitioners thoroughly understand the five developmental domains and skills addressed in this chapter, they can apply the best methodology for accurately assessing those areas. This results in a targeted assessment, which can then be used to create intervention strategies to promote future healthy growth and development of young children.

REFERENCES

Aiken, L. R. (1985). *Psychological testing and assessment*. Boston, MA: Allyn & Bacon.

Alfonso, V. C., & Flanagan, D. P. (1999). Assessment of cognitive functioning in preschoolers. In E. V. Nuttall, I. Romero, & J. Kalesnik (Eds.), *Assessing and screening preschoolers* (2nd ed., pp. 186–217). New York, NY: Allyn & Bacon.

Alfonso, V. C., & Flanagan, D. P. (2007). Best practices in the use of the Stanford-Binet Intelligence Scales, Fifth Edition (SB5) with preschoolers. In B. A. Bracken & R. J. Nagle (Eds.), *Psychoeducational assessment of preschool children* (4th ed., pp. 267–296). New York, NY: Routledge.

Alfonso, V. C., & Flanagan, D. P. (2009). Assessment of preschool children: A framework for evaluating the adequacy of the technical characteristics of norm-referenced instruments. In B. Mowder, F. Rubinson, & A. Yasik (Eds.), *Evidence based practice in infant and early childhood psychology* (pp. 129–165). New York, NY: Wiley & Sons.

Alfonso, V. C., Rentz, E. A., & Chung, S. (2010). Review of the Battelle Developmental Inventory-Second Edition. *Journal of Early Childhood and Infant Psychology, 6*, 21–40.

Alfonso, V. C., Ruby, S., Wissel, A. M., & Davari, J. (2020). School psychologists in early childhood settings. In F. C. Worrell, T. L. Hughes, & D. D. Dixson (Eds.), *Cambridge handbook of applied school psychology* (pp. 579–597). Cambridge, England: Cambridge University Press.

Alfonso, V. C., Shanock, A., Muldoon, D., Benway, N., & Oades-Sese, G. (2018, May). *Psychometric integrity of preschool speech/language tests: Implications for diagnosis and progress monitoring of treatment*. Poster presented at the annual meeting of the Association for Psychological Science, San Francisco, CA.

Alfonso, V. C., Wissel, A., & Lorimer, L. (2017). Developmental Test of Visual Perception (3rd ed.). In J. F. Carlson, K. F. Geisinger, & J. L. Jonson, *The twentieth mental measurements yearbook*. Lincoln, NE: Buros Center for Testing.

American Association on Intellectual and Developmental Disabilities. (2010). *Intellectual disability definition, classification, and systems of supports* (11th ed.). Washington, DC: Author.

American Educational Research Association, American Psychological Association, & National Council on Measurement in Education. (1999). *Standards for educational and psychological testing*. Washington, DC: American Educational Research Association.

American Educational Research Association, American Psychological Association, & National Council on Measurement in Education. (2014). *Standards for educational and psychological testing*. Washington, DC: American Educational Research Association.

American Psychological Association. (1974). *Standards for educational and psychological tests*. Washington, DC: Author.

Anastasi, A. (1982). *Psychological testing* (5th ed.). New York, NY: Macmillan.

Andersson, L. (2005). Determining the adequacy of tests of children's language. *Communication Disorders Quarterly, 26*, 207–225. http://dx.doi.org/10.1177/15257401050260040301

Arias, B., Verdugo, M. A., Navas, P., & Gómez, L. E. (2013). Factor structure of the construct of adaptive behavior in children with and without intellectual disability. *International Journal of Clinical and Health Psychology, 13*, 155–166. http://dx.doi.org/10.1016/S1697-2600(13)70019-X

Bauminger, N. (2002). The facilitation of social-emotional understanding and social interaction in high-functioning children with autism: Intervention outcomes. *Journal of Autism and Developmental Disorders, 32*, 283–298. http://dx.doi.org/10.1023/A:1016378718278

Bracken, B. A. (1987). Limitations of preschool instruments and standards for minimal levels of technical adequacy. *Journal of Psychoeducational Assessment, 5*, 313–326. http://dx.doi.org/10.1177/073428298700500402

Bracken, B. A. (2000). Maximizing construct relevant assessment: The optimal pre-school testing situation. In B. A. Bracken (Ed.), *The psychoeducational assessment of preschool children* (2nd ed., pp. 33–44). Boston, MA: Allyn & Bacon.

Bracken, B. A., Keith, L. K., & Walker, K. C. (1998). Assessment of preschool behavior and social-emotional functioning: A review of thirteen third-party instruments. *Journal of Psychoeducational Assessment, 16,* 153–169. http://dx.doi.org/10.1177/073428299801600204

Bracken, B. A., & Nagle, R. J. (2007). *Psychoeducational assessment of preschool children.* New York, NY: Routledge.

Bracken, B. A., & Pecyna-Rhyner, P. M. (1991, November). *Technical adequacy of preschool language and articulation assessments.* Paper presented at the American Speech-Language-Hearing Association's annual conference, Atlanta, GA.

Bracken, B. A., & Walker, K. C. (1997). The utility of intelligence tests for preschool children. In D. P. Flanagan, J. L. Genshaft, & P. L. Harrison (Eds.), *Contemporary intellectual assessment: Theories, tests, and issues* (pp. 484–505). New York, NY: Guilford Press.

Bradley-Johnson, S. (2001). Cognitive assessment for the youngest of children: A critical review of tests. *Journal of Psychoeducational Assessment, 19,* 19–44. http://dx.doi.org/10.1177/073428290101900102

Bradley-Johnson, S., & Johnson, C. M. (2007). Infant and toddler cognitive assessment. In B. A. Bracken & R. J. Nagle (Eds.), *Psychoeducational assessment of preschool children* (4th ed., pp. 325–357). New York, NY: Routledge.

Brassard, M. R., & Boehm, A. E. (2007). *Preschool assessment.* New York, NY: Guilford Press.

Brock, L. L., Rimm-Kaufman, S. E., Nathanson, L., & Grimm, K. R. (2009). The contributions of 'hot' and 'cool' executive functions to children's academic achievement, learning-related behaviors, and engagement in kindergarten. *Early Childhood Research Quarterly, 24,* 337–349. http://dx.doi.org/10.1016/j.ecresq.2009.06.001

Caesar, L. G., & Ottley, S. W. (2020). Assessing communication, language, and speech in preschool children. In V. C. Alfonso, B. A. Bracken, & R. J. Nagle (Eds.), *Psychoeducational assessment of preschool children* (5th ed., pp. 250–282). New York, NY: Routledge.

Campbell, J. M., & James, C. L. (2007). Assessment of social and emotional development. In B. A. Bracken & R. J. Nagle (Eds.), *Psychoeducational assessment of preschool children* (4th ed., pp. 111–135). New York, NY: Routledge.

Costa, L. J., Green, M., Sideris, J., & Hooper, S. R. (2018). First-grade cognitive predictors of writing disabilities in Grades 2 through 4 elementary students. *Journal of Learning Disabilities, 51,* 351–362. http://dx.doi.org/10.1177/0022219417721182

Cristofaro, T. N., & Tamis-LeMonda, C. S. (2012). Mother–child conversations at 36 months and at pre-kindergarten: Relations to children's school readiness. *Journal of Early Childhood Literacy, 12,* 68–97. http://dx.doi.org/10.1177/1468798411416879

de Medeiros, P., Zequinâo, M. A., Fronza, F. C., dos Santos, O. L., & Cardoso, F. L. (2016). Motor assessment instruments and psychometric procedures: A systematic review. *Motricidade, 12,* 64–75. http://dx.doi.org/10.6063/motricidade.6397

DeThorne, L. S., & Schaefer, B. A. (2004). A guide to child nonverbal IQ measures. *American Journal of Speech-Language Pathology, 13,* 275–290. doi:058-0360/04/1304-0275

Dockrell, J. E. (2001). Assessing language skills in preschool children. *Child Psychology and Psychiatry Review, 6,* 74–85. http://dx.doi.org/10.1017/S1360641701002532

Duff, F. J., Reen, G., Plunkett, K., & Nation, K. (2015). Do infant vocabulary skills predict school-age language and literacy outcomes? *The Journal of Child Psychology and Psychiatry, 56,* 848–856. http://dx.doi.org/10.1111/jcpp.12378

Dunn, W. (1999). Assessment of sensorimotor and perceptual development. In E. V. Nuttall, I. Romero, & J. Kalesnik (Eds.), *Assessing and screening preschoolers* (2nd ed., pp. 240–261). Boston, MA: Allyn & Bacon.

DuPaul, G. J., McGoey, K. E., Eckert, T. L., & VanBrakle, J. (2001). Preschool children with attention-deficit/hyperactivity disorder: Impairments in behavioral, social, and school functioning. *Journal of the American Academy of Child & Adolescent Psychiatry, 40*, 508–515. http://dx.doi.org/10.1097/00004583-200105000-00009

Eklund, K., Kilgus, S., von der Embse, N., Beardmore, M., & Tanner, N. (2017). Use of universal screening scores to predict distal academic and behavioral outcomes: A multilevel approach. *Psychological Assessment, 29*, 486–499. http://dx.doi.org/10.1037/pas0000355

Ellingsen, K. M. (2016). Standardized assessment of cognitive development: Instruments and issues. In A. Garro (Ed.), *Early childhood assessment in school and clinical child psychology* (pp. 25–49). New York, NY: Springer. http://dx.doi.org/10.1007/978-1-4939-6349-2_2

Elliott, C. D. (2007). *Differential Ability Scales* (2nd ed.). San Antonio, TX: Harcourt Assessment.

Emmons, M. R., & Alfonso, V. C. (2005). A critical review of the technical characteristics of current preschool screening batteries. *Journal of Psychoeducational Assessment, 23*, 111–127. http://dx.doi.org/10.1177/073428290502300201

Engler, J. R., & Alfonso, V. C. (2020). Cognitive assessment of preschool children: A pragmatic review of theoretical, quantitative, and qualitative characteristics. In V. C. Alfonso, B. A. Bracken, & R. J. Nagle (Eds.), *Psychoeducational assessment of preschool children* (5th ed., pp. 226–249). New York, NY: Routledge.

Evans, L. D., & Bradley-Johnson, S. (1988). A review of recently developed measures of adaptive behavior. *Psychology in the Schools, 25*, 276–287. http://dx.doi.org/10.1002/1520-6807(198807)25:3<276::AID-PITS2310250309>3.0.CO;2-2

Every Student Succeeds Act, Pub.L. 114-95 (2015).

Fallon, A., Westaway, J., & Moloney, C. (2008). A systematic review of psychometric evidence and expert opinion regarding the assessment of faecal incontinence in older community-dwelling adults. *International Journal of Evidence-Based Healthcare, 6*, 225–259.

Flanagan, D. P., & Alfonso, V. C. (1995). A critical review of the technical characteristics of new and recently revised intelligence tests for preschool children. *Journal of Psychoeducational Assessment, 13*, 66–90. http://dx.doi.org/10.1177/073428299501300105

Flipsen, P., Jr., & Ogiela, D. A. (2015). Psychometric characteristics of single-word tests of children's speech sound production. *Language, Speech, and Hearing Services in Schools, 46*, 166–178. http://dx.doi.org/10.1044/2015_LSHSS-14-0055

Floyd, R. G., & Bose, J. E. (2003). Behavior rating scales for assessment of emotional disturbance: A critical review of measurement characteristics. *Journal of Psychoeducational Assessment, 21*, 43–78. http://dx.doi.org/10.1177/073428290302100104

Floyd, R. G., Shands, E. I., Alfonso, V. C., Phillips, J., Autry, B. K., Mosteller, J. A., . . . Irby, S. M. (2015). A systematic review and psychometric evaluation of adaptive behavior scales and recommendations for practice. *Journal of Applied School Psychology, 31*, 83–113. http://dx.doi.org/10.1080/15377903.2014.979384

Ford, L., & Dahinten, S. (2005). Use of intelligence tests in the assessment of preschoolers. In D. P. Flanagan & P. L. Harrison (Eds.), *Contemporary intellectual assessment: Theories, tests, and issues* (2nd ed., pp. 487–503). New York, NY: Guilford Press.

Friberg, J. C. (2010). Considerations for test selection: How do validity and reliability impact diagnostic decisions? *Child Language Teaching and Therapy, 26*, 77–92. http://dx.doi.org/10.1177/0265659009349972

Friend, M., Smolak, E., Liu, Y., Poulin-Dubois, D., & Zesiger, P. (2018). A cross-language study of decontextualized vocabulary comprehension in toddlerhood and kindergarten readiness. *Developmental Psychology, 54*, 1317–1333. http://dx.doi.org/10.1037/dev0000514

Gokiert, R. J., Georgis, R., Tremblay, M., Krishnan, V., Vandenberghe, C., & Lee, C. (2014). Evaluating the adequacy of social-emotional measures in early childhood.

Journal of Psychoeducational Assessment, 32, 441–454. http://dx.doi.org/10.1177/0734282913516718

Goldstein, E. B. (2008). *Cognitive psychology: Connecting mind, research, and everyday experience* (2nd ed.). Belmont, CA: Thompson Wadsworth.

Gridley, B. E., Mucha, L., & Hatfield, B. B. (1995). Best practices in preschool screening. In A. Thomas & J. Grimes (Eds.), *Best practices in school psychology III* (pp. 213–225). Washington, DC: National Association of School Psychologists.

Grissmer, D., Grimm, K. J., Aiyer, S. M., Murrah, W. M., & Steele, J. S. (2010). Fine motor skills and early comprehension of the world: Two new school readiness indicators. *Developmental Psychology, 46,* 1008–1017. http://dx.doi.org/10.1037/a0020104

Harrison, P. L. (2020). Adaptive behavior assessment of preschool children. In V. C. Alfonso, B. A. Bracken, & R. J. Nagle (Eds.), *Psychoeducational assessment of preschool children* (5th ed., pp. 204–225). New York, NY: Routledge.

Harrison, P. L., & Oakland, T. (2015). *Adaptive Behavior Assessment System* (3rd ed.). Torrance, CA: Western Psychological Services.

Harrison, P. L., & Raineri, G. (2007). Adaptive behavior assessment for preschool children. In B. Bracken & R. J. Nagle (Eds.), *Psychoeducational assessment of preschool children* (4th ed., pp. 195–218). New York, NY: Routledge.

Individuals With Disabilities Education Improvement Act, 20 U.S.C. § 1400 (2004).

Jones, D. E., Greenberg, M., & Crowley, M. (2015). Early social-emotional functioning and public health: The relationship between kindergarten social competence and future wellness. *American Journal of Public Health, 105,* 2283–2290. http://dx.doi.org/10.2105/AJPH.2015.302630

Kamphaus, R. W. (2005). *Clinical assessment of child and adolescent intelligence* (2nd ed.). New York, NY: Springer. http://dx.doi.org/10.1007/978-0-387-29149-9

Kamphaus, R. W., & Frick, P. J. (2005). *Clinical assessment of child and adolescent personality and behavior.* New York, NY: Springer.

Kim, S., Im, H., & Kwon, K. A. (2015). The role of home literacy environment in toddlerhood in development of vocabulary and decoding skills. *Child & Youth Care Forum, 44,* 835–852. http://dx.doi.org/10.1007/s10566-015-9309-y

Kirk, C., & Vigeland, L. (2014). A psychometric review of norm-referenced tests used to assess phonological error patterns. *Language, Speech, and Hearing Services in Schools, 45,* 365–377. http://dx.doi.org/10.1044/2014_LSHSS-13-0053

Knoff, H. M., Stollar, S. A., Johnson, J. J., & Chenneville, T. A. (1999). Assessment of social-emotional functioning and adaptive behavior. In E. V. Nuttall, I. Romero, & J. Kalesnik (Eds.), *Assessing and screening preschoolers* (2nd ed., pp. 126–160). Boston, MA: Allyn & Bacon.

Kranzler, J. H., & Floyd, R. G. (2013). *Assessing intelligence in children and adolescents: A practical guide.* New York, NY: Guilford Press.

Lichtenberger, E. O. (2005). General measures of cognition for the preschool child. *Mental Retardation and Developmental Disabilities Research Reviews, 11,* 197–208. http://dx.doi.org/10.1002/mrdd.20076

Lidz, C. S. (2003). *Early childhood assessment.* New York, NY: John Wiley and Sons.

Martin, R. P. (1988). *Assessment of personality and behavior problems.* New York, NY: Guilford Press.

Mascolo, J. T., Alfonso, V. C., & Flanagan, D. P. (Eds.). (2014). *Essentials of planning, selecting, and tailoring interventions for unique learners.* Hoboken, NJ: John Wiley & Sons.

McCauley, R. J., & Swisher, L. (1984). Psychometric review of language and articulation tests for preschool children. *The Journal of Speech and Hearing Disorders, 49,* 34–42. http://dx.doi.org/10.1044/jshd.4901.34

McConnell, S. R., Bradfield, T. A., & Wackerle-Hollman, A. K. (2014). Early childhood literacy screening. In R. J. Kettler, T. A. Glover, C. A. Albers, & K. A. Feeney-Ketter (Eds.), *Universal screening in educational settings* (pp. 141–170). Washington, DC: American Psychological Association.

McFadden, T. U. (1996). Creating language impairments in typically achieving children: The pitfalls of "normal" normative sampling. *Language, Speech, and Hearing Services in Schools, 27,* 3–9.

Merrell, K. W. (2003). *Behavioral, social, and emotional assessment of children and adolescents.* Mahwah, NJ: Erlbaum.

Miles, S., Fulbrook, P., & Mainwaring-Magi, D. (2018). Evaluation of standardized instruments for use in universal screening of very early school-age children: Suitability, technical adequacy, and usability. *Journal of Psychoeducational Assessment, 36,* 99–119. http://dx.doi.org/10.1177/0734282916669246

Monsma, E. V., Miedema, S. T., Brian, A. S., & Williams, H. G. (2020). Assessment of gross motor development in preschool children. In V. C. Alfonso, B. A. Bracken, & R. J. Nagle (Eds.), *Psychoeducational assessment of preschool children* (5th ed., pp. 283–319). New York, NY: Routledge.

Muldoon, D., Benway, N. R., Shanock, A., & Alfonso, V. C. (2018, November). *A review of the psychometric integrity of preschool language tests: Findings and implications for SLPs.* Paper presented at the annual meeting of the American Speech-Language-Hearing Association, Boston, MA.

Neisworth, J. T., & Bagnato, S. J. (2000). Recommended practices in assessment. In S. Sandall, M. E. McLean, & B. J. Smith (Eds.), *DEC recommended practices in early intervention/early childhood special education* (pp. 17–27). Longmont, CO: Sopris West.

Nelson, N. W., & Warner, C. (2007). Assessment of communication, language, and speech: Questions of what to do next? In B. A. Bracken & R. J. Nagle (Eds.), *Psychoeducational assessment of preschool children* (4th ed., pp. 361–395). New York, NY: Routledge.

Neuman, S. B., & Dickinson, D. K. (Eds.). (2011). *Handbook of early literacy research* (Vol. 3). New York, NY: Guilford Press.

Nunnally, J. S. (1978). *Psychometric theories.* New York, NY: McGraw-Hill.

Oades-Sese, G., & Alfonso, V. C. (2003, August). *A critical review of the psychometric integrity of preschool language tests.* Poster presented at the annual meeting of the American Psychological Association, Toronto, Ontario, Canada.

O'Neill, S., Thornton, V., Marks, D. J., Rajendran, K., & Halperin, J. M. (2016). Early language mediates the relations between preschool inattention and school-age reading achievement. *Neuropsychology, 30,* 398–404. http://dx.doi.org/10.1037/neu0000247

Plante, E., & Vance, R. (1994). Selection of preschool language tests: A data-based approach. *Language, Speech, and Hearing Services in Schools, 25,* 15–24. http://dx.doi.org/10.1044/0161-1461.2501.15

Potocki, A., Ecalle, J., & Magnan, A. (2017). Early cognitive and linguistic profiles of different types of 7- to 8-year-old readers. *Journal of Research in Reading, 40,* S125–S140. http://dx.doi.org/10.1111/1467-9817.12076

Ramey, C. T., & Ramey, S. L. (2004). Early learning and school readiness: Can early intervention make a difference? *Merrill-Palmer Quarterly, 50,* 471–491. http://dx.doi.org/10.1353/mpq.2004.0034

Ramey, C. T., Yeates, K. O., & Short, E. J. (1984). The plasticity of intellectual development: Insights from preventive intervention. *Child Development, 55,* 1913–1925. http://dx.doi.org/10.2307/1129938

Reneman, M. F., Dijkstra, A., Geertzen, J. H. B., & Dijkstra, P. U. (2010). Psychometric properties of Chronic Pain Acceptance Questionnaires: A systematic review. *European Journal of Pain, 14,* 457–465. http://dx.doi.org/10.1016/j.ejpain.2009.08.003

Research Excellence and Advancements for Dyslexia Act, H.R. 3033, 114th Cong. (2016).

Reynolds, C. R., & Kamphaus, R. W. (2015). *Behavior Assessment System for Children* (3rd ed.). San Antonio, TX: Pearson.

Salvia, J., & Ysseldyke, J. E. (1981). *Assessment in special and remedial education* (2nd ed.). Boston, MA: Houghton Mifflin.

Salvia, J., & Ysseldyke, J. E. (2004). *Assessment* (9th ed.). Boston, MA: Houghton Mifflin.

Salvia, J., Ysseldyke, J., & Bolt, S. (2013). *Assessment in special education and inclusive education* (12th ed.). Belmont, CA: Wadsworth.

Salvia, J., Ysseldyke, J. E., & Witmer, S. (2017). *Assessment in special and inclusive education* (13th ed.). Boston, MA: Cengage.

Sattler, J. M. (2008). *Assessment of children: Cognitive foundations* (5th ed.). San Diego, CA: Author.

Sattler, J. M. (2014). *Foundations of behavioral, social, and clinical assessment of children* (6th ed.). San Diego, CA: Author.

Saye, K. B. (2003). Preschool intellectual assessment. In C. R. Reynolds & R. W. Kamphaus (Eds.), *Handbook of psychological and educational assessment of children: Intelligence, aptitude, and achievement* (2nd ed., pp. 187–203). New York, NY: Guilford Press.

Schonert-Reichl, K. A., Oberle, E., Lawlor, M. S., Abbott, D., Thomson, K., Oberlander, T. F., & Diamond, A. (2015). Enhancing cognitive and social-emotional development through a simple-to-administer mindfulness-based school program for elementary school children: A randomized controlled trial. *Developmental Psychology, 51*, 52–66. http://dx.doi.org/10.1037/a0038454

Schrank, F. A., McGrew, K. S., & Mather, N. (2014). *Woodcock-Johnson IV Tests of Cognitive Abilities*. Itasca, IL: Riverside.

Shands, E. I., Phillips, J. F., Autry, B. K., Hall, J. A., Floyd, R. G., Alfonso, V. C., & Skinner, M. (2008, February). *A review of the technical characteristics of contemporary adaptive behavior assessment instruments: Preliminary results and conclusions.* Poster presented at the annual meeting of the National Association of School Psychologists, New Orleans, LA.

Shonkoff, J. P., & Phillips, D. A. (Eds.). (2000). *From neurons to neighborhoods: The science of early childhood development.* Washington, DC: The National Academies Press.

Snow, C. E., & Van Hemel, S. B. (Eds.). (2008). *Early childhood assessment: Why, what, and how.* Washington, DC: The National Academies Press.

Sparrow, S. S., Cicchetti, D. V., & Saulnier, C. A. (2016). *Vineland Adaptive Behavior Scales* (3rd ed.). San Antonio, TX: Pearson.

Squires, J. (2003, January). *The importance of early identification of social and emotional difficulties in preschool children.* Retrieved from University of Oregon Early Intervention Program website: https://eip.uoregon.edu/asqse/pdf/ImportEarly_IdenCIR.pdf

Sveinbjornsdottir, S., & Thorsteinsson, E. B. (2008). Adolescent coping scales: A critical psychometric review. *Scandinavian Journal of Psychology, 49*, 533–548. http://dx.doi.org/10.1111/j.1467-9450.2008.00669.x

Vig, S., & Sanders, M. (2007). Cognitive assessment. In M. R. Brassard & A. E. Boehm (Eds.), *Preschool assessment* (pp. 383–419). New York, NY: Guilford Press.

Wechsler, D. (2012). *Wechsler Preschool and Primary Scale of Intelligence* (4th ed.). Bloomington, MN: Pearson.

Weiner, P. S., & Hoock, W. C. (1973). The standardization of tests: Criteria and criticisms. *Journal of Speech and Hearing Research, 16*, 616–626. http://dx.doi.org/10.1044/jshr.1604.616

Whitcomb, S. A. (2018). *Behavioral, social, and emotional assessment of children and adolescents* (5th ed.). New York, NY: Routledge.

Williams, H. G., & Monsma, E. V. (2007). Assessment of gross motor development. In B. A. Bracken & R. J. Nagle (Eds.), *Psychoeducational assessment of preschool children* (4th ed., pp. 397–433). New York, NY: Routledge.

Williams, M. E., Sando, L., & Soles, T. G. (2014). Cognitive tests in early childhood: Psychometric and cultural considerations. *Journal of Psychoeducational Assessment, 32,* 455–476. http://dx.doi.org/10.1177/0734282913517526

Wilson, M. J., & Bullock, L. M. (1989). Psychometric characteristics of behavior rating scales: Definitions, problems and solutions. *Behavioral Disorders, 14,* 186–200. http://dx.doi.org/10.1177/019874298901400305

Wyatt, T. A., & Seymour, H. N. (1999). Assessing the speech and language skills of preschool children. In E. V. Nuttall, I. Romero, & J. Kalesnik (Eds.), *Assessing and screening preschoolers* (2nd ed., pp. 218–239). Boston, MA: Allyn & Bacon.

Zimmerman, I. L., Steiner, V. G., & Pond, R. E. (2011). *Preschool Language Scales* (5th ed.). Bloomington, MN: Pearson.

2

Considerations and Methods in Assessing Early Learning and Social–Emotional Development in Young Children

Robin L. Hojnoski and Kristen N. Missall

Early childhood is a critical period for developing early learning and social–emotional skills. Experiences in social settings provide opportunities for young children to engage in adult- and child-directed activities intended to increase their knowledge and skills in important areas such as language, literacy, numeracy, and science. Young children also increasingly interact with peers and adults in play, problem solving, and learning interactions that require emotional awareness and regulation, as well as in the effective use of prosocial behaviors. Although early learning and social–emotional skills are often addressed as separate domains in educational standards and curricula, research supports complex connections between the two domains and the contexts in which young children learn (see, e.g., Purpura & Schmitt, 2019). Indeed, indicators of early learning and social–emotional development are often used in measuring the larger construct of school readiness (e.g., L. D. Reid & Strobino, 2019; A. J. Reynolds, Richardson, Hayakawa, Englund, & Ou, 2016; Sabol, Bohlmann, & Downer, 2018; see also Chapter 3, this volume). Thus, early childhood is a critical time for establishing positive academic and behavioral trajectories, and effective assessment practices are central to ensuring young children receive necessary early learning and behavioral supports (McCabe & Altamura, 2011).

The purpose of this chapter is to discuss considerations in the assessment of young children and to review approaches to assessment with attention to

http://dx.doi.org/10.1037/0000197-003

Healthy Development in Young Children: Evidence-Based Interventions for Early Education,
V. C. Alfonso and G. J. DuPaul (Editors)

these considerations. We recognize that within each of the domains of early learning and social–emotional development, several specific skills contribute to establishing positive behavioral and academic trajectories that can be examined during the early period of development (see additional chapters in this volume) with implications for applied assessment practices. Here, we focus on the importance of the broader domains of early learning and social–emotional development in young children's engagement in early education settings and their continued success (e.g., Hojnoski & Missall, 2010; Hojnoski, Missall, & Miller Young, 2016). Following this discussion, we propose key considerations in assessment of young children that support a best-practices approach. Finally, we review specific methods of assessment with attention to the key considerations outlined.

EARLY LEARNING AND SOCIAL-EMOTIONAL DEVELOPMENT

Assessment of the domains of early learning and social–emotional development in young children is particularly important given the early emerging variability in performance in these domains, the continuity of performance over time without intervention, and the malleability of specific skills associated with each domain. With regard to early learning, individual differences in children's early literacy and mathematical skills emerge prior to formal schooling (e.g., Hojnoski, Caskie, & Miller Young, 2018; Lambert, Kim, & Burts, 2014; Lonigan & Shanahan, 2009; National Mathematics Advisory Panel, 2008; Norwalk, DiPerna, Lei, & Wu, 2012; see also Chapters 4 and 5, this volume). For example, Hojnoski and colleagues (2018) demonstrated differences in initial mathematical performance as well as growth over time between typically developing children and children with disabilities whereas Norwalk and colleagues (2012) documented different early literacy profiles among children designated as at-risk due to demographic characteristics. These individual differences in early learning trajectories tend to be stable over time in the absence of intervention; thus, children who are low-performing early in their school careers continue to remain low-performing (e.g., Missall et al., 2007; Missall, Mercer, Martínez, & Casebeer, 2012; Morgan, Farkas, & Wu, 2011; Rittle-Johnson, Fyfe, Hofer, & Farran, 2017). Analysis of several large-scale longitudinal data sets indicated that mathematical, reading, and attentional skills at kindergarten entry were strong predictors of later achievement (Duncan et al., 2007); mathematical skills at kindergarten entry as well as growth in mathematical skills from preschool to first grade over time demonstrated the strongest predictive relations with achievement in adolescence (Watts, Duncan, Siegler, & Davis-Kean, 2014).

Individual differences in young children's social–emotional development are reflected in the prevalence rates of behavioral difficulties in young children. Research indicates young children experience clinically significant social–emotional behavioral problems, with general prevalence estimates ranging from as low as 5% to as high as 26% (e.g., Egger & Angold, 2006; Lavigne,

Lebailly, Hopkins, Gouze, & Binns, 2009). Furthermore, even at a young age, behavior problems are internalizing (e.g., anxiety, social withdrawal) and externalizing (e.g., conduct problems, noncompliance) in nature with similar general prevalence estimates (Egger & Angold, 2006; Qi & Kaiser, 2006). Similar to early learning trajectories, social–emotional behavioral problems are likely to persist over time without intervention (e.g., Briggs-Gowan & Carter, 2008; Luby, Si, Belden, Tandon, & Spitznagel, 2009).

For example, in an ethnically and economically diverse sample of more than 1,000 children, parent ratings of child behavior, emotions, and social development during toddlerhood were associated significantly with teacher- and parent-reported behavioral problems as well as symptoms of psychiatric disorders in early elementary school (Briggs-Gowan & Carter, 2008). Research suggests that trajectories of social competence stabilize during the preschool years in the absence of intervening events (Bornstein, Hahn, & Haynes, 2010; Santos, Vaughn, Peceguina, Daniel, & Shin, 2014), with significant consequences for academic and behavioral success (e.g., Brown, Copeland, Sucharew, & Kahn, 2012; Bulotsky-Shearer & Fantuzzo, 2011; McWayne, Green, & Fantuzzo, 2009; National Institute of Child Health and Human Development Early Child Care Research Network, 2004).

Fortunately, research indicates the promise of efforts to support young children's early learning and social–emotional development. In the area of early mathematics, two meta-analyses of interventions conducted in preschool and early elementary school indicate moderate to large effect sizes (Nelson & McMaster, 2019; Wang, Firmender, Power, & Byrnes, 2016). Interventions included comprehensive curriculum and supplemental activities that were implemented in group and individual conditions and varied in duration. Similarly, the National Early Literacy Panel (2008) reviewed a range of interventions conducted to improve young children's early literacy skills, including shared book reading, parent–home programs, and language enhancement interventions. With regard to social–emotional development, several empirically valid strategies have been developed (McCabe & Altamura, 2011), including the use of multitiered systems of support (e.g., Teaching Pyramid; Hemmeter, Ostrosky, & Fox, 2006), structured curriculum (e.g., PATHS [Promoting Alternative THinking Strategies]; Domitrovich, Cortes, & Greenberg, 2007), and comprehensive school- and home-based programs (e.g., Incredible Years; Webster-Stratton & Reid, 2004; for additional details, see Chapter 9, this volume). Finally, during early childhood, comprehensive interventions exist that target early learning and social–emotional development. For example, implementation of the Head Start REDI (Research-based, Developmentally Informed) program resulted in positive effects for participating children on measures of vocabulary, emergent literacy, emotional understanding, social problem solving, social behavior, and learning engagement (Bierman et al., 2008).

Given the importance of establishing positive trajectories of development and the potential for effective programming to do so, effective assessment practices with young children are needed. Such practices should be used to identify young children who may be at risk given their initial level of skill development (e.g., universal screening) and to identify children who fail to demonstrate adequate growth in key skill areas (e.g., formative assessment). Assessment is also needed to better understand children's strengths and needs to inform and evaluate programming and ensure that all children are adequately supported.

ASSESSMENT CONSIDERATIONS

Assessing young children provides opportunities and challenges that must be considered in planning the assessment process, selecting the methods and measures to be used, and conducting the assessment. Certainly, the primary benefit of assessment is the opportunity for early identification of young children who may be struggling in particular areas of development. Related to early identification, assessment is an opportunity to gather information that informs the development of supports, instruction, or intervention to promote healthy growth and development. From a systems perspective, assessing young children is an opportunity to connect families and educators in a partnership to support a child's continued growth and development. One challenge in assessing young children is ensuring sufficient data are collected to accurately represent children's current level of functioning, given rapid development in multiple domains and normative variability in attainment of developmental milestones. Additionally, assessment of young children in particular must account for the influence of context on development, and therefore, assessment across settings (e.g., home, early education program) is needed, which requires additional time, coordination, and resources. We support the use of an ecocultural approach to assessing young children, discussed and defined by Brassard and Boehm (2007) as "an ongoing problem-solving task with the goals of understanding the child within his or her daily environments and planning appropriate instruction or other forms of intervention" (p. 24). Furthermore, we advocate for a multimethod and multisource approach to assessment with young children with deliberate attention to several related issues.

First, assessment with young children must be approached from a developmental perspective, with consideration for individual child characteristics (e.g., age, gender, disability; Brassard & Boehm, 2007) and the unique characteristics of young children (e.g., developmental expectations, autonomy, maturity; Davies, 2011). Consideration must be given to variability in development and behavioral indicators of competence. Practically, this means that multiple samples of the target behavior should be collected over time to increase the reliability of the information gathered and that caution should be used in drawing conclusions based on assessment information. Best practice suggests ongoing or repeated data collection may be most informative and sensitive to changes in setting and child development (Garro, 2016). Finally, the function of behavior must be considered from a developmental perspective. Behaviors that may be maladaptive in form (e.g., screaming) may serve an important function (e.g., communication) that may be linked to a child's present developmental level.

Second, assessment with young children must be highly contextual. Young children's development is influenced greatly by their environment and life experience cumulatively over time as well as in the dynamic interplay found in a single interaction. Children navigate relationships with peers and adults while engaging in early learning and daily routines across different settings (i.e., home, early education, and outside activities). As a result, "children's competencies are likely to vary in meaningful ways depending on where and when they are measured" (Jones, Zaslow, Darling-Churchill, & Halle, 2016, p. 43). Furthermore, development is a transactional process because the environments in which children interact also exert an influence (Rose-Krasnor & Denham, 2009). Thus, to the extent possible, the assessment process must take context into consideration when evaluating competence (Campbell et al., 2016; Johnson, Finlon, & Izard, 2016; Neisworth & Bagnato, 2004). Caregivers, teachers, parents, and other significant family members should be included in the assessment process to gather information about a child's competencies across settings. In addition, information should be gathered about the settings themselves, including type and duration of daily routines and activities, expectations and demands, and environmental features (e.g., size of space, arrangement of space).

Third, assessment of young children should include a focus on strengths as well as areas of concern. Understanding what a child knows or what skills a child already has is important in determining where a child may be on a developmental trajectory in terms of global development in a given domain (e.g., vocabulary) and in terms of key skills to inform instruction (e.g., item counting and cardinality). Identification of strengths can be helpful in designing interventions that build on children's existing capacities (Cress, Lambert, & Epstein, 2016). Furthermore, such an approach reflects not a pathology-focused model but rather a primary prevention and wellness-promotion model, in which one can develop and implement interventions to strengthen existing skills rather than wait for behavioral challenges to develop (LeBuffe & Shapiro, 2004). This proactive approach is more likely to engender collaboration in developing, implementing, and evaluating interventions by reducing a sense of shame, guilt, or blame that caregivers may feel when a deficit approach to assessment is emphasized (LeBuffe & Shapiro, 2004).

Finally, the assessment process must attend to cultural and linguistic diversity factors (e.g., home language, culture, familial and educational experience; see Chapter 13, this volume). More than 25% of children under age 8 years, or about 5.8 million children, have at least one immigrant parent (Williams, 2014). In 2013, children enrolled in Head Start programs spoke 130 different languages (Office of Head Start, 2013). In light of the importance of language to early development, an understanding of culture and language cannot be bypassed in the assessment process. All assessors should be asking questions about primary language, home language, parent education, cultural values and priorities, life experiences, and impact of socioeconomic opportunities.

Cultural factors must be viewed from a strengths-based perspective, and attention should be given to the cultural relevance of the assessment target, the methods, and the outcomes of the assessment process. Child- and family-centered variables must be discussed and analyzed at every step of the assessment process so as to determine what information to collect and how to collect that information as well as determine subsequent actions based on the information collected (Brassard & Boehm, 2007; Elizalde-Utnick, 2007). In general, the assessment process should be guided by best practices in assessing culturally and linguistically diverse children and professional and ethical guidelines related to cultural competence (e.g., American Psychological Association, 2017; National Association of School Psychologists [NASP], 2010; Ortiz, Flanagan, & Dynda, 2008).

METHODS OF ASSESSMENT

Assessment is the process of gathering information to make informed decisions, and such a process must include consideration of the purpose of assessment (e.g., universal screening, diagnosis or eligibility, program planning, progress monitoring). Indeed, the purpose often informs what we assess, how we assess, and what we do with the information gathered (National Research Council [NRC], 2008). Related to the purpose of the assessment, consideration is given to how data will be interpreted or the point of comparison. Broadly, assessment methods can be categorized into different approaches based on the type of comparison made in interpreting the information gathered through the assessment process. Idiographic approaches are those in which information about a child is interpreted in relation to her- or himself from past assessment, whereas with nomothetic, or norm-referenced, approaches, information about a child is interpreted in relation to other children, usually those of the same age. Similarly, with curriculum-referenced approaches, a child's performance is interpreted in relation to a standard or a criterion for success (i.e., the degree to which a child has mastered specific skills; Hallam, Lyons, Pretti-Frontczak, & Grisham-Brown, 2014).

Each approach has advantages and disadvantages, and the selection of one approach over the other should be informed by the purpose of the assessment and the decision to be made. In many cases, information gathered from an idiographic approach (e.g., direct observation of the child in context) is integrated with information gathered from a nomothetic approach (e.g., teacher and parent rating scales, norm-referenced, standardized direct assessment) or a curriculum-referenced approach (e.g., descriptive observations linked to specified criteria). Integrating these approaches promotes a multimethod and multisource assessment of young children that captures different dimensions of constructs of interest (e.g., social–emotional development, early literacy) and leads to a richer and more comprehensive understanding of child strengths and needs.

With young children, four assessment methods are most likely to provide trustworthy (reliable) and meaningful (valid) information: rating scales, interviews, direct observation, and on-demand direct assessment or testing. Although specific tools exist within these methods, the objective in this chapter is not to provide details about specific tools but to broadly discuss methods with attention to the important considerations outlined previously. Indeed, we expect that all assessors carefully evaluate the strengths and weaknesses of specific tools in the context of purpose and use (Salvia, Ysseldyke, & Bolt, 2015; see also Chapter 1, this volume).

Rating Scales

Rating scales are one of the most widely used methods in assessing young children (Major, Seabra-Santos, & Martin, 2015; NRC, 2008). Their use tends to be more in the assessment of social–emotional competence as opposed to early learning; few rating scales specific to early childhood include a large number of items related to early learning competencies. Rating scales can be categorized as omnibus scales that provide an overall score that can be separated into subscores (e.g., Behavioral Assessment System for Children–Third Edition; C. R. Reynolds & Kamphaus, 2015) or behavior-specific scales that measure a discrete domain of behavior (e.g., Preschool Kindergarten Behavior Scales–Second Edition; Busse & Yi, 2013; Merrell, 2002). For young children, scales are designed to be completed by informants (e.g., parents, teachers, caregivers) who are familiar with the child. Informants typically are asked to indicate the degree to which statements describe the child or how often a child exhibits the specific behavior or characteristic using anchors such as *never*, *rarely*, *sometimes*, and *often*.

Advantages of rating scales include (a) ease of administration with no requirements for special setting or materials beyond the forms, which are generally low-cost; (b) the ability to repeat assessment for formative purposes; and (c) objective scoring intended to minimize bias (Salvia et al., 2015). These advantages facilitate the use of rating scales in applied settings and with larger numbers of children (e.g., universal screening) as well as for individual children (Carter, Briggs-Gowan, & Davis, 2004; Caselman & Self, 2008). Despite the advantages of rating scales, there are several important limitations. Because informant reports capture the rater's experience with the child, this method does not directly assess the construct of interest in context. Thus, there is a lack of specificity about situated competence (Campbell et al., 2016). There is also a potential for rater bias, which can stem from how a rater conceptualizes competence across different contexts (Campbell et al., 2016). Differences among raters in their experience with the child, their knowledge of appropriate developmental expectations, the contexts in which the child is interacting, and conceptualizations of the behaviors being assessed as well as rater characteristics can lead to a lack of agreement between informants (e.g., parents and teachers)—a finding that has been documented in the literature (e.g.,

Berg-Nielsen, Solheim, Belsky, & Wichstrom, 2012; Major et al., 2015; Myers, Bour, Sidebottom, Murphy, & Hakman, 2010; Winsler & Wallace, 2002).

In using rating scales, we make several recommendations to address critical issues in the assessment of young children. First, to address developmental concerns, consider rating scales that focus more narrowly on the age range of interest rather than those that include a wide range. Instruments designed specifically for early childhood are likely to include items that are more relevant for an early childhood population and may include a stronger normative group. Fortunately, many rating scales include attention to strengths as well as deficits in the items that comprise the scales. Assessors should ensure their interpretation includes a focus on the child's strengths as well as areas of need. To gain insight into the rater's conceptualization of the behavior as well as the perceived function of the behavior, assessors should supplement quantitative ratings with qualitative information gathered through interviews.

To address the issue of context, rating scale data should be gathered from a number of individuals who interact with the child. Parents, caregivers, and teachers are natural and logical choices; information can also be gathered from extended family, community members, and specialists who may interact with the child on a regular basis. In addition, gathering information across the contexts in which the child interacts can assist in determining whether the child's strengths and needs are setting-specific or generalized across environments. Furthermore, because informant ratings are decontextualized even when collected across multiple individuals, in interpreting rating scale information, assessors should consider the context in which the informant is observing the child and reflect on how any observed differences between informant ratings may reflect differences in context. These differences in context, in turn, may highlight environmental or setting features that support or impede the child's competence.

Finally, assessors should carefully consider the use of rating scales with young children from culturally and linguistically diverse backgrounds. Although some rating scales are available in multiple languages, and linguistic equivalence may be assumed, consideration should also be given to conceptual equivalence (i.e., conceptual meaning of the constructs being assessed), scale equivalence (i.e., all raters share a common understanding of how a specific scale is used as well as a common understanding of the metrics, or anchors), and normative equivalence (i.e., normative standards for a particular behavior across cultural groups; R. Reid, 1995).

Interviews

Interviews can be a useful supplement to rating scales in that they allow the assessor to clarify and expand on areas of strength and need that may have been identified in the rating scale responses. Additionally, interviews with key individuals familiar with the child (e.g., parents, teachers, extended family members) provide information not captured in rating scale items. Interviews can be structured, semistructured, or unstructured; structured and semistructured interviews are often used for diagnostic or research purposes as their uniformity in items and approach address issues of reliability (Marin, Rey, & Silverman, 2013). Unstructured interviews offer greater flexibility in content and approach as the areas addressed may be specific to the individual child and additional areas can be introduced through the interview process and are typically used in clinical assessment. For example, in a teacher interview, information can be gathered about teacher expectations for early skill development, the types of learning activities provided in the classroom, and the teacher's estimate of a child's engagement relative to peers. In a parent interview, parents may discuss daily routines and the ease or challenge of completing tasks (e.g., getting dressed, picking up toys) or a child's relationships with other family members (McWilliam, Casey, & Sims, 2009). In addition, specific approaches to assessment and intervention, such as conjoint behavioral consultation (Sheridan, Kratochwill, & Bergan, 2013) and functional behavioral assessment, use interview protocols that have been evaluated in early childhood settings (e.g., Durán, Bloom, & Samaha, 2013; Sheridan, Clarke, Knoche, & Pope Edwards, 2006).

Advantages of the structured or semistructured approach include the ease of use, standardization, improved reliability, and direct link to diagnosis. However, these advantages lead to the primary disadvantages of this type of interview, that is, a lack of flexibility in interview content and process. Conversely, unstructured interviews, which have flexibility as a primary advantage, lack the standardization and reliability of structured interviews and take additional time to create. Thus, the choice of type of interview largely depends on the purpose of the assessment.

We recommend that structured and semistructured interviews be reserved for diagnostic purposes and that unstructured interviews be routinely incorporated into a multimethod, multisource approach to assessment with young children. Brassard and Boehm (2007) provided an extensive discussion of family assessment that includes attention to interviews, whereas Boone and Crais (1999) provided examples of interview strategies to involve families in assessment and intervention planning. Guidance in developing interviews for classroom teachers can be found in Hojnoski and Wood (2012) and in Wolery, Sigalove Brashers, and Neitzel (2002). To address developmental considerations, interviews should include questions that explore adult expectations of the child in different settings, outline the child's attainment of developmental milestones, obtain a sense of the child's overall health and wellness, and provide for a rich description of the child's strengths and needs across early learning and social–emotional domains. To emphasize context, interviews should include discussion of routines and activities in different settings and the child's degree of participation in these; specific examples can be solicited to provide greater detail about the child's functioning and the conditions surrounding success or challenge. Attention to child strengths can be built into the interview process through explicit questions about what the adult enjoys about the child, an example of the child's positive behavior, or the skills a child already demonstrates. Finally, interviews offer an opportunity to better understand a child's cultural and linguistic background through specific discussion of cultural values, norms, expectations, and practices as well as information about the child's first language development and exposure to other languages. If there are language differences between the assessor and the interviewee, interviews should be conducted with the assistance of an interpreter and following best practices and ethical guidelines (e.g., American Psychological Association, 2017; Brassard & Boehm, 2007; NASP, 2010).

Direct Observation

Whereas rating scales and interviews provide information about the rater's subjective experience with a child, direct observation provides objective information about a child's skills and behavior in context. Direct observation of the child's behavior during naturally occurring events and routines provides contextualized information about child engagement in learning, specific skills, behavior and adaptability, and peer and adult interaction. Direct observation of child development is often described as authentic because of the child-directed, natural context for data collection and can take several forms, including anecdotal notes, narrative records, or systematic recording (e.g., duration, latency, interval-based systems). The form selected largely depends on the purpose of the observation; for example, anecdotal or narrative forms may be useful in initial assessment to gather information about behaviors of concern and the contexts in which they are occurring, whereas systematic direct observation using an approach that best captures the salient features of target behaviors is especially well suited for establishing baseline levels of target behaviors and evaluating change over time (see, for example, Hojnoski, Gischlar, & Missall, 2009).

Perhaps the most significant advantage of direct observation is measurement in the naturally occurring environment (Neisworth & Bagnato, 2004). Through observation of the child in the natural setting, information can be directly gathered about salient dimensions of the target behavior (e.g., frequency, duration, latency, intensity) as well as the context in which the child is interacting. This information can be used to complement other forms of assessment. With regard to early learning skills, directly observing the child engaged in an early learning activity may confirm skills the child has developed in relation to skills that are emerging. Learning-related skills such as task persistence and approaches to learning may also be observed. An important caveat in observing a child's demonstration of early learning skills is that performance must be viewed in the context of the task in which the child is engaged. That is, if the child is working only with numerals 1 through 6 in an activity with dice, we cannot conclude what the child knows about other numerals or set sizes. Similarly, direct observation of social–emotional behavior can provide descriptive information on the specific play-entry strategies and emotional expressions a child uses as well as peer and adult reactions. Direct observation of social–emotional behavior in context also gives insight into how the environment supports the development of social–emotional competence (e.g., opportunities to engage in interactions, scaffolded support for appropriate expression of emotions).

Disadvantages of observation methods include (a) the lack of standardized observation tools with technical adequacy for preschoolers, (b) complexity in selecting and defining observational targets and their properties (i.e., frequency, intensity) as well as in designing systematic direct observation, (c) observation training and monitoring for reliability, (d) reactivity to the observation, and (e) the time involved to conduct multiple observations over time and potentially across settings to ensure adequate samples of behavior over time. From a research perspective, a minimum of 5 data points is suggested per phase (e.g., baseline and intervention), though the precise number required largely depends on the consistency in the observational data (Kratochwill et al., 2010). The amount of data needed may be linked to the purpose of the observations and the availability of supplemental information. For example, if data will be used in establishing baseline levels of a target behavior and evaluating the effect of an intervention, then a larger sample of data will be needed to ensure accurate representation of the child's behavior. If data will be used to add descriptive details to supplement rating scales and teacher interviews only, then a smaller sample may be sufficient.

Developmental considerations in direct observation can be addressed through careful consideration of the behaviors to be observed. Targets should be clearly and operationally defined with examples and nonexamples to increase the reliability of the data obtained; targets should also be developmentally appropriate, that is, meaningful and functional for the individual child of focus. Direct observation inherently includes attention to context, but we recommend explicit attention to context. Focusing on the child and the environment in which the child is operating facilitates a more ecological approach and is consistent with the transactional nature of skill development (Brassard & Boehm, 2007; Denham, 2006; Missall, McConnell, & Cadigan, 2006). Contextual information that describes the setting (e.g., room arrangement, size, access to materials), other individuals (e.g., peers, adults), and the activity or interaction in which the child is engaged (e.g., small-group learning activities, outdoor gross motor play, self-care routines) contributes significantly to an understanding of child competence as it plays out in real-life situations. This information is particularly important in developing interventions and creating environments that support engagement in early learning and appropriate behavior. We also recommend that direct observation procedures include a specific focus on children's strengths; for example, document instances of the child's use of positive behaviors as opposed to focusing exclusively on problem behavior. Finally, with regard to culture and language, these factors must be considered in selecting a target to observe, defining the target, observing the target in context, and interpreting the resulting data because language and culture significantly contribute to children's early learning and social–emotional development.

Testing

We cautiously use the term *testing* to describe a process that largely consists of the use of a specific set of prompts and materials designed to elicit a specific response or behavior and delivered in a standardized manner to an individual child. A child's response to a series of standard prompts is used in determining a score, which, in many instances, is then compared with a normative group. We recognize that *testing* is a controversial term and practice with young children. However, testing with norm-referenced assessments (e.g., Battelle Developmental Inventory–Second Edition; Newborg, 2005) has long been part of early childhood assessment practices, particularly for diagnostic and special education eligibility determination (see McLean, Hemmeter, & Snyder, 2014). Implementation of multitiered systems of support in early childhood has expanded the potential use of testing to universal screening, in which large numbers of children are tested at regular intervals throughout the year, and progress monitoring, in which smaller numbers of children are tested more frequently to evaluate progress toward instructional goals (Buysse & Peisner-Feinberg, 2013; Carta & Miller Young, 2019; Coffee, Ray-Subramanian, Schanding, & Feeney-Kettler, 2013).

There are several advantages to testing, in general. The direct aspect of testing allows for a systematic and structured process for eliciting the target response as compared with direct observation, in which only naturally occurring responses can be observed. Such a process can be helpful in assessing the range of skills and knowledge a child might have; for example, the child's ability to identify numerals across the range of 0 to 20 can be assessed directly. The standardized process and materials allow for intraindividual and interindividual comparisons to be made with more confidence because the testing procedures and materials remain the same across time and children. Finally, published instruments have gone through a development process that generates evidence of technical adequacy (e.g., reliability and validity), allowing consumers to evaluate the quality of the tools for a specific purpose (see Chapter 1, this volume).

These same advantages, however, also serve as disadvantages. For example, a child's response to a specific prompt in direct testing does not provide information about the child's functional use of a skill or knowledge under naturally occurring conditions. Furthermore, information about related skills and knowledge (e.g., creativity, problem solving, critical thinking) is limited. The standardized process and materials limit assessors' ability to make modifications that could provide an understanding of the conditions under which child performance may be maximized—information that is important to instruction and intervention. Test development processes typically generate evidence of reliability and validity, with less evidence supporting the instructional or intervention utility (Snyder, Wixson, Talapatra, & Roach, 2008). Additionally, normative samples are likely limited in their inclusion of children from culturally and linguistically diverse backgrounds, and in general, few assessments have been validated for culturally and linguistically diverse children. The cultural appropriateness of tests is of particular concern given the heavy reliance on receptive and expressive language for item completion of many tests.

We agree with McConnell (2000) that "testing can be assessment but it need not be, and assessment can include testing, but it need not" (p. 44). To qualify as assessment, testing should contribute meaningful information that adds to an understanding of a child's strengths and needs and that informs decisions consistent with the purpose of assessment. To address developmental considerations, tests should be selected carefully to be consistent with the purpose of the assessment. The length of the test should be considered and administration procedures adjusted to accommodate individual differences in attention span and level of engagement. Assessors should establish rapport with young children prior to testing to increase children's comfort level and should attend to children's verbal and nonverbal cues during testing and respond accordingly (e.g., return child to parent/teacher if the child withdraws from the testing interactions).

Understanding what a child knows as demonstrated by test performance is very different from understanding how a child uses that knowledge in daily activities, problem-solving situations, and interpersonal interactions. To address concerns about the decontextualized nature of testing, results from testing should be corroborated (or refuted) by data obtained through rating scales, interviews, and direct observation. Testing inherently includes a focus on "correct and incorrect" and yields a score as well as other indicators of child performance. Assessors should contextualize scores by including descriptions of the child's performance during the testing situation as well as examples of similar performance in the natural setting. Emphasis should be placed on the child's strengths as well as needs with consideration of strengths that extend beyond the child's response to test items (e.g., ability to engage with assessor, compliance with directions, ability to engage in conversation).

Testing with young children from culturally and linguistically diverse backgrounds should be pursued with careful attention to issues of cultural bias as well as the quality of the assessment tools available in terms of their appropriateness, technical adequacy, and instructional utility. In light of the potential significant limitations in testing young children from culturally and linguistically diverse backgrounds, data derived from testing may need to be considered from a more qualitative perspective and supplemented by data obtained from a variety of sources and using a variety of methods.

CONCLUSION

The National Association for the Education of Young Children (2009) and the NRC (2008) have promoted developmentally appropriate practice as one in which assessment is tied to curriculum and intervention in an integrated fashion to inform continuous teaching and learning. Similarly, the position statement on early childhood services by the NASP emphasizes the importance of formative assessment approaches that are grounded in developmental science and are developmentally appropriate to promote data-based decision making and develop effective interventions that address a range of needs in young children (NASP, 2015). Campbell and colleagues (2016) suggested that assessment of any domain of development should be part of a systems approach that includes (a) clear goals and benchmarks for the domain of interest, (b) evidence-based curricula that includes implementation supports, and (c) measures for universal and targeted screening as well as progress monitoring. In line with these recommendations, assessment of young children should be viewed from a systems perspective in which the goal of supporting positive development of all children is clearly articulated; instruction, professional development, and home-based supports are aligned with the goal; assessment methods are consistent with the identified purpose; and all assessment activities are situated within a data-based decision-making framework (e.g., Buysse & Peisner-Feinberg, 2013; Carta & Miller Young, 2019; Coffee et al., 2013).

Research has established indisputably that critical early learning and social–emotional competencies must begin to develop prior to kindergarten entrance. Young children learn key skills in the areas of language, literacy, mathematics, problem solving, and social–emotional interactions that prime, predict, and sustain their uptake of knowledge in formal school and their ability to develop effective relationships. Positive early development has been shown to be critical for continued adaptive and successful development (Duncan et al., 2007; Neuman & Dickinson, 2011; Pace, Alper, Burchinal, Golinkoff, & Hirsh-Pasek, 2019). Effective assessment practices embedded in a systems approach are needed to promote healthy growth and development of all young children.

REFERENCES

American Psychological Association. (2017). *Ethical principles of psychologists and code of conduct* (2002, Amended June 1, 2010, and January 1, 2017). Retrieved from http://www.apa.org/ethics/code/index.aspx

Berg-Nielsen, T. S., Solheim, E., Belsky, J., & Wichstrom, L. (2012). Preschoolers' psychosocial problems: In the eyes of the beholder? Adding teacher characteristics as determinants of discrepant parent–teacher reports. *Child Psychiatry and Human Development, 43,* 393–413. http://dx.doi.org/10.1007/s10578-011-0271-0

Bierman, K. L., Domitrovich, C. E., Nix, R. L., Gest, S. D., Welsh, J. A., Greenberg, M. T., . . . Gill, S. (2008). Promoting academic and social–emotional school readiness: The Head Start REDI program. *Child Development, 79,* 1802–1817. http://dx.doi.org/10.1111/j.1467-8624.2008.01227.x

Boone, H. A., & Crais, E. (1999). Strategies for achieving: Family-driven assessment and intervention planning. *Young Exceptional Children, 3*(1), 2–11. http://dx.doi.org/10.1177/109625069900300101

Bornstein, M. H., Hahn, C. S., & Haynes, O. M. (2010). Social competence, externalizing, and internalizing behavioral adjustment from early childhood through early adolescence: Developmental cascades. *Development and Psychopathology, 22,* 717–735. http://dx.doi.org/10.1017/S0954579410000416

Brassard, M. R., & Boehm, A. E. (2007). *Preschool assessment: Principles and practices.* New York, NY: Guilford Press.

Briggs-Gowan, M. J., & Carter, A. S. (2008). Social–emotional screening status in early childhood predicts elementary school outcomes. *Pediatrics, 121*, 957–962. http://dx.doi.org/10.1542/peds.2007-1948

Brown, C. M., Copeland, K. A., Sucharew, H., & Kahn, R. S. (2012). Social–emotional problems in preschool-aged children: Opportunities for prevention and early intervention. *Archives of Pediatrics & Adolescent Medicine, 166*, 926–932. http://dx.doi.org/10.1001/archpediatrics.2012.793

Bulotsky-Shearer, R. J., & Fantuzzo, J. W. (2011). Preschool behavior problems in classroom learning situations and literacy outcomes in kindergarten and first grade. *Early Childhood Research Quarterly, 26*, 61–73. http://dx.doi.org/10.1016/j.ecresq.2010.04.004

Busse, R. T., & Yi, M. (2013). Behavioral and academic rating scale applications within the problem-solving model. In R. Brown-Chidsey & K. Andren (Eds.), *Assessment for intervention: A problem-solving approach* (pp. 180–198). New York, NY: Guilford Press.

Buysse, V., & Peisner-Feinberg, E. (Eds.). (2013). *Handbook of response to intervention in early childhood*. Baltimore, MD: Paul H. Brookes.

Campbell, S. B., Denham, S. A., Howarth, G. Z., Jones, S. M., Whittaker, J. V., Williford, A. P., . . . Darling-Churchill, K. (2016). Commentary on the review of measures of early childhood social and emotional development: Conceptualization, critique, and recommendations. *Journal of Applied Developmental Psychology, 45*, 19–41. http://dx.doi.org/10.1016/j.appdev.2016.01.008

Carta, J. J., & Miller Young, R. (Eds.). (2019). *Multi-tiered systems of support for young children: Driving change in early education*. Baltimore, MD: Paul H. Brookes.

Carter, A. S., Briggs-Gowan, M. J., & Davis, N. O. (2004). Assessment of young children's social–emotional development and psychopathology: Recent advances and recommendations for practice. *Journal of Child Psychology and Psychiatry, 45*, 109–134. http://dx.doi.org/10.1046/j.0021-9630.2003.00316.x

Caselman, T. D., & Self, P. A. (2008). Assessment instruments for measuring young children's social–emotional behavioral development. *Children & Schools, 30*, 103–115. http://dx.doi.org/10.1093/cs/30.2.103

Coffee, G., Ray-Subramanian, C. E., Schanding, G. T., Jr., & Feeney-Kettler, K. A. (2013). *Early childhood education: A practical guide to evidence-based, multi-tiered service delivery*. New York, NY: Routledge. http://dx.doi.org/10.4324/9780203126875

Cress, C., Lambert, M. C., & Epstein, M. H. (2016). Factor analysis of the preschool behavioral and emotional rating scale for children in Head Start programs. *Journal of Psychoeducational Assessment, 34*, 473–486. http://dx.doi.org/10.1177/0734282915617630

Davies, D. (2011). *Child development: A practitioner's guide* (3rd ed.). New York, NY: Guilford Press.

Denham, S. A. (2006). Social–emotional competence as support for school readiness: What is it and how do we assess it? *Early Education and Development, 17*, 57–89. http://dx.doi.org/10.1207/s15566935eed1701_4

Domitrovich, C. E., Cortes, R. C., & Greenberg, M. T. (2007). Improving young children's social and emotional competence: A randomized trial of the preschool "PATHS" curriculum. *The Journal of Primary Prevention, 28*, 67–91. http://dx.doi.org/10.1007/s10935-007-0081-0

Duncan, G. J., Dowsett, C. J., Claessens, A., Magnuson, K., Huston, A. C., Klebanov, P., . . . Japel, C. (2007). School readiness and later achievement. *Developmental Psychology, 43*, 1428–1446. http://dx.doi.org/10.1037/0012-1649.43.6.1428

Durán, L. K., Bloom, S. E., & Samaha, A. L. (2013). Adaptations to a functional behavior assessment with a Spanish-speaking preschooler: A data-based case study. *Education & Treatment of Children, 36*, 73–95. http://dx.doi.org/10.1353/etc.2013.0009

Egger, H. L., & Angold, A. (2006). Common emotional and behavioral disorders in preschool children: Presentation, nosology, and epidemiology. *Journal of Child Psychology and Psychiatry, 47*, 313–337. http://dx.doi.org/10.1111/j.1469-7610.2006.01618.x

Elizalde-Utnick, G. (2007). Culturally and linguistically diverse preschool children. In G. B. Esquivel, E. C. Lopez, & S. G. Nahari (Eds.), *Handbook of multicultural school psychology: An interdisciplinary perspective* (pp. 497–525). Mahwah, NJ: Erlbaum.

Garro, A. (2016). Early childhood assessment: An integrative framework. In A. Garro (Ed.), *Early childhood assessment in school and clinical child psychology* (pp. 1–24). New York, NY: Springer. http://dx.doi.org/10.1007/978-1-4939-6349-2_1

Hallam, R. A., Lyons, A. N., Pretti-Frontczak, K., & Grisham-Brown, J. (2014). Comparing apples and oranges: The mismeasurement of young children through the mismatch of assessment purpose and the interpretation of results. *Topics in Early Childhood Special Education, 34,* 106–115. http://dx.doi.org/10.1177/0271121414524283

Hemmeter, M. L., Ostrosky, M., & Fox, L. (2006). Social and emotional foundations for early learning: A conceptual model for intervention. *School Psychology Review, 35,* 583–601.

Hojnoski, R. L., Caskie, G. I., & Miller Young, R. (2018). Early numeracy trajectories: Baseline performance levels and growth rates in young children by disability status. *Topics in Early Childhood Special Education, 37,* 206–218. http://dx.doi.org/10.1177/0271121417735901

Hojnoski, R. L., Gischlar, K. L., & Missall, K. N. (2009). Improving child outcomes with data-based decision-making: Collecting data. *Young Exceptional Children, 12,* 32–44. http://dx.doi.org/10.1177/1096250609333025

Hojnoski, R. L., & Missall, K. N. (2010). Social development in preschool classrooms: Promoting engagement, competence, and school readiness. In M. R. Shinn & H. M. Walker (Eds.), *Interventions for achievement and behavior problems in a three-tier model including RTI* (pp. 703–728). Bethesda, MD: National Association of School Psychologists.

Hojnoski, R. L., Missall, K. N., & Miller Young, R. (2016). Defining and measuring early academic development to promote student outcomes. In A. Garro (Ed.), *Early childhood assessment in school and clinical psychology* (pp. 51–72). New York, NY: Springer. http://dx.doi.org/10.1007/978-1-4939-6349-2_3

Hojnoski, R. L., & Wood, B. K. (2012). Challenging behavior and early academic skill development: An integrated approach to assessment and intervention. *Young Exceptional Children, 15,* 29–40. http://dx.doi.org/10.1177/1096250612455033

Johnson, S. R., Finlon, K. J., & Izard, C. E. (2016). The development and validation of the behavior and emotion expression observation system to characterize preschoolers' social and emotional interactions. *Early Education and Development, 27,* 896–913. http://dx.doi.org/10.1080/10409289.2016.1175241

Jones, S. M., Zaslow, M., Darling-Churchill, K. E., & Halle, T. G. (2016). Assessing early childhood social and emotional development: Key conceptual and measurement issues. *Journal of Applied Developmental Psychology, 45,* 42–48. http://dx.doi.org/10.1016/j.appdev.2016.02.008

Kratochwill, T. R., Hitchcock, J., Horner, R. H., Levin, J. R., Odom, S. L., Rindskopf, D. M., & Shadish, W. R. (2010). *Single-case design technical documentation.* Retrieved from What Works Clearinghouse website: https://ies.ed.gov/ncee/wwc/Document/229

Lambert, R. G., Kim, D. H., & Burts, D. C. (2014). Using teacher ratings to track the growth and development of young children using the Teaching Strategies GOLD® assessment system. *Journal of Psychoeducational Assessment, 32,* 27–39. http://dx.doi.org/10.1177/0734282913485214

Lavigne, J. V., Lebailly, S. A., Hopkins, J., Gouze, K. R., & Binns, H. J. (2009). The prevalence of ADHD, ODD, depression, and anxiety in a community sample of 4-year-olds. *Journal of Clinical Child and Adolescent Psychology, 38,* 315–328. http://dx.doi.org/10.1080/15374410902851382

LeBuffe, P. A., & Shapiro, V. B. (2004). Lending "strength" to the assessment of preschool social–emotional health. *California School Psychologist, 9,* 51–61. http://dx.doi.org/10.1007/BF03340907

Lonigan, C. J., & Shanahan, T. (2009). *Developing early literacy: Report of the National Early Literacy Panel. Executive summary.* Jessup, MD: National Institute for Literacy.

Luby, J. L., Si, X., Belden, A. C., Tandon, M., & Spitznagel, E. (2009). Preschool depression: Homotypic continuity and course over 24 months. *Archives of General Psychiatry, 66,* 897–905. http://dx.doi.org/10.1001/archgenpsychiatry.2009.97

Major, S. O., Seabra-Santos, M. J., & Martin, R. P. (2015). Are we talking about the same child? Parent–teacher ratings of preschoolers' social–emotional behaviors. *Psychology in the Schools, 52,* 789–799. http://dx.doi.org/10.1002/pits.21855

Marin, C. E., Rey, Y., & Silverman, W. K. (2013). Interviews. In B. McLeod, A. Jensen-Doss, & T. Ollendick (Eds.), *Diagnostic and behavioral assessment in children and adolescents: A clinical guide* (pp. 103–132). New York, NY: Guilford Press.

McCabe, P. C., & Altamura, M. (2011). Empirically valid strategies to improve social and emotional competence of preschool children. *Psychology in the Schools, 48,* 513–540. http://dx.doi.org/10.1002/pits.20570

McConnell, S. R. (2000). Assessment in early intervention and early childhood special education: Building on the past to project into our future. *Topics in Early Childhood Special Education, 20,* 43–48. http://dx.doi.org/10.1177/027112140002000108

McLean, M., Hemmeter, M. L., & Snyder, P. (2014). *Essential elements for assessing infants and preschoolers with special needs.* Upper Saddle River, NJ: Pearson.

McWayne, C. M., Green, L. E., & Fantuzzo, J. W. (2009). A variable- and person-oriented investigation of preschool competencies and Head Start children's transition to kindergarten and first grade. *Applied Developmental Science, 13,* 1–15. http://dx.doi.org/10.1080/10888690802606719

McWilliam, R. A., Casey, A. M., & Sims, J. (2009). The routines-based interview: A method for gathering information and assessing needs. *Infants & Young Children, 22,* 224–233. http://dx.doi.org/10.1097/IYC.0b013e3181abe1dd

Merrell, K. W. (2002). *Preschool and Kindergarten Behavior Rating Scales (PKBS-2).* Austin, TX: PRO-ED.

Missall, K. N., McConnell, S. R., & Cadigan, K. (2006). Early literacy development: Skill growth and relations between classroom variables for preschool children. *Journal of Early Intervention, 29,* 1–21. http://dx.doi.org/10.1177/105381510602900101

Missall, K. N., Mercer, S. H., Martínez, R. S., & Casebeer, D. (2012). Concurrent and longitudinal patterns and trends in performance on early numeracy curriculum-based measures in kindergarten through third grade. *Assessment for Effective Intervention, 37,* 95–106. http://dx.doi.org/10.1177/1534508411430322

Missall, K., Reschly, A., Betts, J., McConnell, S., Heistad, D., Pickart, M., . . . Marston, D. (2007). Examination of the predictive validity of preschool early literacy skills. *School Psychology Review, 36,* 433–452.

Morgan, P. L., Farkas, G., & Wu, Q. (2011). Kindergarten children's growth trajectories in reading and mathematics: Who falls increasingly behind? *Journal of Learning Disabilities, 44,* 472–488. http://dx.doi.org/10.1177/0022219411414010

Myers, C. L., Bour, J. L., Sidebottom, K. J., Murphy, S. B., & Hakman, M. (2010). Same constructs, different results: Examining the consistency of two behavior-rating scales with referred preschoolers. *Psychology in the Schools, 47,* 205–216. http://dx.doi.org/10.1002/pits.20465

National Association for the Education of Young Children. (2009). *Developmentally appropriate practice in early childhood programs serving children from birth through age 8* [Position statement]. Retrieved from https://www.naeyc.org/resources/position-statements

National Association of School Psychologists. (2010). *Principles for professional ethics.* Retrieved from https://www.nasponline.org/standards-and-certification/professional-ethics

National Association of School Psychologists. (2015). *Early childhood services: Promoting positive outcomes for young children* [Position statement]. Retrieved from https://www.nasponline.org/research-and-policy/policy-priorities/position-statements

National Early Literacy Panel. (2008). *Developing early literacy: Report of the National Early Literacy Panel.* Washington, DC: National Institute for Literacy.

National Institute of Child Health and Human Development Early Child Care Research Network. (2004). Trajectories of physical aggression from toddlerhood to middle childhood: Predictors, correlates, and outcomes. *Monographs of the Society for Research in Child Development, 69*(4), vii, 1–129.

National Mathematics Advisory Panel. (2008). *Foundations for success: The final report of the National Mathematics Advisory Panel.* Jessup, MD: U.S. Department of Education.

National Research Council. (2008). *Early childhood assessment: Why, what, and how.* Washington, DC: The National Academies Press.

Neisworth, J. T., & Bagnato, S. J. (2004). The mismeasure of young children: The authentic assessment alternative. *Infants and Young Children, 17*, 198–212. http://dx.doi.org/10.1097/00001163-200407000-00002

Nelson, G., & McMaster, K. L. (2019). The effects of early numeracy interventions for students in preschool and early elementary: A meta-analysis. *Journal of Educational Psychology, 111*, 1001–1022.

Neuman, S. B., & Dickinson, D. K. (Eds.). (2011). *Handbook of early literacy research* (Vol. 3). New York, NY: Guilford Press.

Newborg, J. (2005). *Battelle Developmental Inventory* (2nd ed.). Rolling Meadows, IL: Riverside.

Norwalk, K. E., DiPerna, J. C., Lei, P. W., & Wu, Q. (2012). Examining early literacy skill differences among children in Head Start via latent profile analysis. *School Psychology Quarterly, 27*, 170–183. http://dx.doi.org/10.1037/spq0000003

Office of Head Start. (2013). *Report to Congress on dual language learners in Head Start and Early Head Start programs.* Washington, DC: U.S. Department of Health and Human Services.

Ortiz, S. O., Flanagan, D. P., & Dynda, A. M. (2008). Best practices in working with culturally diverse children and families. In A. Thomas & J. Grimes (Eds.), *Best practices in school psychology V* (5th ed., pp. 1721–1738). Bethesda, MD: National Association of School Psychologists.

Pace, A., Alper, R., Burchinal, M. R., Golinkoff, R. M., & Hirsh-Pasek, K. (2019). Measuring success: Within and cross-domain predictors of academic and social trajectories in elementary school. *Early Childhood Research Quarterly, 46*, 112–125. http://dx.doi.org/10.1016/j.ecresq.2018.04.001

Purpura, D. J., & Schmitt, S. A. (Eds.) (2019). Cross-domain development of early academic and cognitive skills [Special issue]. *Early Childhood Research Quarterly, 46*.

Qi, C. H., & Kaiser, A. P. (2006). Behavior problems of preschool children from low-income families: A review of the literature. *Topics in Early Childhood Special Education, 23*, 188–216.

Reid, L. D., & Strobino, D. M. (2019). A population-based study of school readiness determinants in a large urban public school district. *Maternal and Child Health Journal, 23*, 325–334. http://dx.doi.org/10.1007/s10995-018-2666-z

Reid, R. (1995). Assessment of ADHD with culturally different groups: The use of behavioral rating scales. *School Psychology Review, 24*, 537–560.

Reynolds, A. J., Richardson, B. A., Hayakawa, M., Englund, M. M., & Ou, S. R. (2016). Multi-site expansion of an early childhood intervention and school readiness. *Pediatrics, 138*, e20154587. http://dx.doi.org/10.1542/peds.2015-4587

Reynolds, C. R., & Kamphaus, R. W. (2015). *Behavior Assessment System for Children* (3rd ed.). Bloomington, MN: Pearson.

Rittle-Johnson, B., Fyfe, E. R., Hofer, K. G., & Farran, D. C. (2017). Early math trajectories: Low-income children's mathematics knowledge from ages 4 to 11. *Child Development, 88*, 1727–1742. http://dx.doi.org/10.1111/cdev.12662

Rose-Krasnor, L., & Denham, S. (2009). Social–emotional competence in early childhood. In K. Rubin, W. Bukowski, & B. Laursen (Eds.), *Handbook of peer interactions, relationships, and groups* (pp. 162–179). New York, NY: Guilford Press.

Sabol, T. J., Bohlmann, N. L., & Downer, J. T. (2018). Low-income ethnically diverse children's engagement as a predictor of school readiness above preschool classroom quality. *Child Development, 89,* 556–576. http://dx.doi.org/10.1111/cdev.12832

Salvia, J., Ysseldyke, J. E., & Bolt, S. (2015). *Assessment in special and inclusive education* (11th ed.). New York, NY: Houghton Mifflin.

Santos, A. J., Vaughn, B. E., Peceguina, I., Daniel, J. R., & Shin, N. (2014). Growth of social competence during the preschool years: A 3-year longitudinal study. *Child Development, 85,* 2062–2073. http://dx.doi.org/10.1111/cdev.12246

Sheridan, S. M., Clarke, B. L., Knoche, L. L., & Pope Edwards, C. (2006). The effects of conjoint behavioral consultation in early childhood settings. *Early Education and Development, 17,* 593–617. http://dx.doi.org/10.1207/s15566935eed1704_5

Sheridan, S. M., Kratochwill, T. R., & Bergan, J. R. (2013). *Conjoint behavioral consultation: A procedural manual.* New York, NY: Springer Science & Business Media.

Snyder, P. A., Wixson, C. S., Talapatra, D., & Roach, A. T. (2008). Assessment in early childhood: Instruction-focused strategies to support response-to-intervention frameworks. *Assessment for Effective Intervention, 34,* 25–34. http://dx.doi.org/10.1177/1534508408314112

Wang, A. H., Firmender, J. M., Power, J. R., & Byrnes, J. P. (2016). Understanding the program effectiveness of early mathematics interventions for prekindergarten and kindergarten environments: A meta-analytic review. *Early Education and Development, 27,* 692–713. http://dx.doi.org/10.1080/10409289.2016.1116343

Watts, T. W., Duncan, G. J., Siegler, R. S., & Davis-Kean, P. E. (2014). What's past is prologue: Relations between early mathematics knowledge and high school achievement. *Educational Researcher, 43,* 352–360. http://dx.doi.org/10.3102/0013189X14553660

Webster-Stratton, C., & Reid, M. J. (2004). Strengthening social and emotional competence in young children—The foundation for early school readiness and success: Incredible Years Classroom Social Skills and Problem-Solving Curriculum. *Infants and Young Children, 17,* 96–113. http://dx.doi.org/10.1097/00001163-200404000-00002

Williams, C. P. (2014, June 5). Building on immigrants' strengths to improve their children's early education [Blog post]. Retrieved from https://www.newamerica.org/education-policy/edcentral/building-immigrants-strengths-improve-childrens-educations

Winsler, A., & Wallace, G. L. (2002). Behavior problems and social skills in preschool children: Parent-teacher agreement and relations with classroom observations. *Early Education and Development, 13,* 41–58. http://dx.doi.org/10.1207/s15566935eed1301_3

Wolery, M., Sigalove Brashers, M., & Neitzel, J. C. (2002). Ecological congruence assessment for classroom activities and routines: Identifying goals and intervention practices in childcare. *Topics in Early Childhood Special Education, 22,* 131–142. http://dx.doi.org/10.1177/02711214020220030101

PREPARING FOR SCHOOL: ENSURING ACADEMIC SUCCESS

3

Addressing Socioeconomic Disparities in School Readiness With Preschool Programming and Professional Development Support

Karen L. Bierman, Michael Sanders, and Leslie C. Ho

The landscape of early childhood education (ECE) has undergone dramatic changes in the United States during the past 2 decades (Lowenstein, 2011), accompanied by fundamental shifts in the way that school readiness is conceptualized (Snow, 2006). Advances in developmental neuroscience research have fueled these changes by revealing the critical importance of early learning experiences for building the neural architecture that supports later learning (Blair & Raver, 2015). In this chapter, we describe the changing environment of ECE and current conceptualizations of school readiness, the developmental research that underlies contemporary approaches, and the implications for ECE practice.

THE CHANGING EARLY CHILDHOOD EDUCATION LANDSCAPE AND CONTEMPORARY CONCEPTUALIZATIONS OF SCHOOL READINESS

In 2015, 38% of American 3-year-olds, 67% of 4-year-olds, and 87% of 5-year-olds were enrolled in some kind of center-based ECE preprimary program (McFarland et al., 2017). In addition to the federal funds that support Head Start programs, most states (43 of 50) now fund prekindergarten programs,

http://dx.doi.org/10.1037/0000197-004
Healthy Development in Young Children: Evidence-Based Interventions for Early Education,
V. C. Alfonso and G. J. DuPaul (Editors)

increasing accessibility for children in low-income families (Friedman-Krauss et al., 2018). These high levels of public interest and investment in ECE reflect a growing body of research that links attendance at a high-quality preschool with a host of positive later outcomes, including enhanced school performance and educational attainment, better social–emotional adjustment, and even improved health (Yoshikawa et al., 2013).

Perhaps, in part, because of increasing attendance at preschool, expectations regarding the skill sets that incoming kindergarten children need and the skills that they will master in kindergarten have also increased (Bassok, Latham, & Rorem, 2016). For example, a recent national survey showed that a majority of teachers (80%) now expect children to learn to read in kindergarten, whereas only 31% did so in 1998 (Bassok et al., 2016). Kindergarten teachers also value the social–emotional skills needed for school success, with more than 75% listing skills such as following directions, taking turns, sharing, and paying attention as critical kindergarten-readiness skills (Bassok et al., 2016; Curby et al., 2017).

Interestingly, parallel to increases in ECE attendance and kindergarten expectations, fundamental shifts have occurred in the conceptualization of school readiness. These shifts extend beyond the increased expectations mentioned previously and represent important changes in our understanding of the nature of the developmental processes that support children's readiness to succeed at school. Initial interest in school readiness and its assessment emerged in the late 1980s through the early 1990s (Snow, 2006). The measures developed then generally reflected a maturationist perspective common at the time that focused on determining whether children had sufficient maturity to manage the demands of formal schooling. Implicit in this conceptualization of school readiness was the notion that children who lacked readiness would not be well-served by schools. In their review of school practices at the time, Prakash, West, and Denton (2003) found that a number of schools used kindergarten-wide screening to make determinations about deviations in the age limits for school entry, with 13% of the schools surveyed using screening to accelerate the early entry of children who were younger than the chronological entry age and 27% of the schools using screening to delay the entry of unready children who met the chronological entry age.

By the early 1990s, schools and policymakers began to move away from this maturationist perspective. Importantly, the National Education Goals Panel report of 1992 identified school readiness as a transactional process involving schools that were ready for children, children who were ready for schools, and parents and communities that could support the child's developmental process (Zuckerman & Halfon, 2003). Rather than assuming school readiness emerges as a product of maturation within the child, this conceptual model focused on the important role that schools, parents, and communities play in providing children with the high-quality support and learning opportunities that build their competencies and fuel their educational success. The National Education Goals Panel also moved away from a unitary conceptualization of school readiness (e.g., a child is or is not ready) to a description that focused on skill development in multiple domains.

By the early 2000s, policymakers had identified school-readiness skills as an important outcome of ECE programs, noting that effective ECE programs should improve child skills at kindergarten entry across multiple domains (Snow, 2006). This focus had compelling longitudinal evidence to support it in two ways. First, accumulating evidence documented that school readiness is quite malleable and is enhanced when children experience high-quality ECE programming. Second, longitudinal research also demonstrated significant links between kindergarten skills and educational success many years later, suggesting that the ECE promotion of early skills had value for later educational attainment (Yoshikawa et al., 2013),

This contemporary conceptualization of school readiness is reflected in the current Head Start definition and approach (U.S. Department of Health and Human Services, Administration for Children and Families, 2018), where school readiness is defined by the skills, knowledge, and attitudes that children possess that fuel their future school success and later learning. Schools and families working together are responsible for providing the opportunities and support for learning that children need to attain those skills, knowledge, and attitudes. Head Start also identifies five key domains for skill development, each contributing to school readiness: (a) social–emotional development; (b) approaches to learning; (c) language and literacy; (d) cognition; and (e) perceptual, motor, and physical development. This overarching framework is intended to support the provision of comprehensive child development and family engagement services that lead to school readiness for young children.

The shifting conceptualization of school readiness and the increased public interest and investment in ECE have been fueled by the developmental neuroscience research that has emerged during the past 2 decades. This research has informed our understanding of how early brain development supports school success and how early childhood experiences affect early brain development.

DEVELOPMENTAL NEUROSCIENCE, THE IMPACT OF ADVERSITY, AND IMPLICATIONS FOR EARLY CHILDHOOD EDUCATION

One well-established finding from developmental research is that a significant gap exists in the kindergarten skill sets of children from families with less versus more socioeconomic advantage (Reardon, 2011). Growing up in poorly resourced, economically disadvantaged environments puts children at risk for compromised development in many areas, including key domains that support school success such as social–emotional adjustment, language skills, and cognitive development (Evans, Gonnella, Marcynyszyn, Gentile, & Salpekar, 2005). In addition, children who start kindergarten with delays in these skill areas are at elevated risk for ongoing school difficulties, including the delayed acquisition of math and reading skills, as well as social and behavioral maladjustment, especially when children are placed in poor-quality class-rooms at school entry. Overall, the gaps associated with family socioeconomic disadvantage do not diminish over time, resulting in long-term disparities in academic achievement, graduation rates, and subsequent employment and well-being (Reardon, 2011).

Advances made in developmental neuroscience research have helped to clarify some of the reasons for these long-term effects of poverty on adaptive development and school attainment. Children growing up in poverty are typically exposed to a host of adverse experiences. These include elevated levels of family mobility and instability, crowded and sometimes unsafe living conditions, chronic stressors, lack of resources, and chaotic, unpredictable home environments, which have shown negative associations with children's social–emotional and cognitive development (Guo & Harris, 2000). Adverse conditions and elevated stress often undermine effective parenting, reducing opportuni-ties for the kind of predictable, sustained, positive interactions with caregivers that promote positive social–emotional, language, and cognitive development (Evans et al., 2005). In addition, low-income families have limited resources, including both less education and less access to high-quality child care and schools compared with more advantaged families (Evans et al., 2005; Masten & Labella, 2016; McLoyd, 1998).

Emerging developmental neuroscience research suggests that exposure to early adversity often undermines the development of key neural structures that support children's capacity for learning. This research has focused spe-cifically on the early development of executive function (EF) skills. EF skills involve a complex set of cognitive processes that help children organize their thinking and behavior with intention and flexibility. These processes include working memory (e.g., being able to hold information in mind and manipu-late it mentally), attention control (e.g., being able to focus selective attention and avoid distractibility), and inhibitory control (e.g., being able to resist impul-sive reactions and plan behavioral responses), all of which enhance goal-oriented learning and problem solving (Hughes & Graham, 2002). These skills develop rapidly during the preschool and early elementary years (ages 3–7) and provide the neural architecture that supports school readiness by increas-ing children's abilities to control their behavior and engage in goal-oriented learning (Blair & Raver, 2015). At school entry, higher levels of EF skills pro-mote the acquisition of reading and math skills (Welsh, Nix, Blair, Bierman, & Nelson, 2010). EF development is often delayed among children growing up in poverty (Noble, McCandliss, & Farah, 2007). Researchers believe that exposure to the chronic stressors that characterize poverty in early childhood overloads stress responses in ways that increase impulsive responding and impede the development of the EF skills that enhance adaptive coping (Blair & Raver, 2015). The impact is associated with delays in the development of the learning behaviors that support academic achievement, reflected in low levels of classroom engagement and elevated teacher-rated attention problems (Bodovski & Youn, 2011).

Fortunately, EF skills are malleable, and evidence is accumulating to show how early intervention and high-quality ECE can remediate or reduce the negative impact of poverty on EF development (Bierman & Torres, 2016; Diamond & Lee, 2011). Combined, this research illustrates the critical need to focus on improving ECE and increasing access to high-quality ECE for all children, and especially for children whose early development may otherwise be compromised by adverse experiences and inadequate positive developmental support.

In the next sections of this chapter, we describe how this developmental research along with policymaker pressures for accountability have increased interest in the impact that different approaches to ECE have on child school-readiness outcomes. Emerging research focused on documenting the child outcomes associated with different kinds of preschool experiences has illuminated new directions for ECE programming with promise for strengthening child school readiness and reducing the gaps associated with family socioeconomic disadvantage.

AN EMERGING FOCUS ON CHILD OUTCOMES TO ASSESS EARLY CHILDHOOD EDUCATION QUALITY

A strong research base supports the link between the quality of ECE programming and its benefits for children (Brown, Scott-Little, Amwake, & Wynn, 2007). At the same time, there is considerable debate about how best to measure ECE quality and about the degree to which different aspects of ECE quality are related to child school-readiness outcomes (Pianta, Barnett, Burchinal, & Thornburg, 2009). Over the past 2 decades, research on this topic has accelerated. In light of the increasing levels of public investments in ECE, policymakers want to ensure that funded ECE programs are preparing children adequately for success in school and reducing the socioeconomic gap in school readiness at kindergarten entry (Brown et al., 2007). Research that examines associations between different aspects of ECE program quality and child school readiness has focused primarily on the preschool years (ages 3–6) with the goal of determining the types of ECE programming that might optimize child success at kindergarten entry.

One domain of quality measurement involves the organizational or structural characteristics of ECE programs such as the level of teacher training, class size, child–teacher ratio, building safety and resources, and general routines of daily programming (Pianta et al., 2009). A second domain of quality measurement focuses on the process characteristics of ECE programming, which involve the nature of interactions between caregivers and children and the way that these interactions support positive learning experiences for children (Pianta et al., 2009). Research comparing associations of ECE structural and process characteristics with child outcomes suggests that process characteristics are of particular importance for boosting school-readiness outcomes, whereas structural characteristics appear important primarily as facilitators of high-quality processes (Pianta et al., 2009). That is, teacher education and training, class size, and adult–child ratios are of benefit primarily when they foster stimulating and sensitive adult–child interactions that support emotional and cognitive development. It is the provision of high-quality teacher–child interactions, including sensitive–warm interactions, instruction and conversation, and responsive feedback, that shows consistent associations with more positive language, academic, and social–behavioral child outcomes in ECE programs (Mashburn et al., 2008).

Although critically important, process measures of classroom quality remain limited in terms of their capacity to predict and promote child school-readiness outcomes. For example, Burchinal and colleagues (2009) conducted a large meta-analysis of program quality features and their associations with child outcomes. Important and statistically significant associations emerged but were modest in level, suggesting that the quality of caregiver–child interactions is one factor promoting child development in ECE settings but that other factors also contribute. Emerging research suggests that, in addition to high-quality teacher–student interactions, intentional instruction may enhance the school readiness of preschool children.

As noted previously, contemporary conceptualizations of school readiness are multidimensional, recognizing the importance of skill acquisition in multiple domains for school success. Accumulating research suggests high-quality preschool instruction is multidimensional as well, with instruction in specific content areas promoting enhanced skill acquisition in the corresponding school-readiness domain (Pianta et al., 2009). Accordingly, efforts to improve child school readiness may hinge on revising and improving the curriculum content of preschool programs as well as promoting high-quality teacher–student interactions, using evidence-based curriculum components, and providing focused professional development support to help teachers implement this programming with high fidelity in the context of positive, responsive teacher–child interactions (Jenkins & Duncan, 2017; Nguyen, Jenkins, & Auger Whitaker, 2018).

Currently, Head Start and many state prekindergarten programs require the use of a whole-child curriculum that is not domain-specific but rather guides teachers in applying a developmental-interaction approach to support learning across multiple domains (Nguyen et al., 2018). According to a 2012 national survey, the most commonly used whole-child curricula are Creative Curriculum for Preschool and HighScope Curriculum (Jenkins & Duncan, 2017). In contrast, content-specific or targeted curricula are designed to increase children's exposure to intentional and explicit learning opportunities in specific content domains, such as math (Clements & Sarama, 2007), literacy (Wasik & Hindman, 2011), or social–emotional learning (Bierman & Motamedi, 2015). These content-specific curricula involve sequenced instruction embedded in stories, games, and activities that progress across the year, building a foundation for within-domain learning with simpler activities at the start of the year that are built on and expanded upon over the course of the year. Teachers are provided with detailed lesson plans and, in the more successful programs, also receive extensive professional development support and coaching in optimal implementation and teaching strategies. As described in more detail in the following sections of this chapter, enriching preschool programs with evidence-based content-specific curriculum components and associated professional development support is proving effective in boosting child school-readiness outcomes in a number of core domains.

EXEMPLAR TARGETED PRESCHOOL CURRICULA PROMOTING SCHOOL-READINESS SKILLS

In this section, we identify several model preschool programs that have proven effective in boosting child school readiness in three of the five domains of school readiness identified by Head Start: (a) language and literacy skills, (b) cognition and numeracy skills, and (c) social–emotional development. In each domain, we highlight a few programs that have strong scientific evidence of efficacy, as documented by randomized controlled trials. For more comprehensive reviews, see Callaghan and Madelaine (2012) and Hall, Simpson, Guo, and Wang (2015) for language and literacy skill programs, Clements and Sarama (2011) for cognition and numeracy programs, and Bierman and Motamedi (2015) for social–emotional learning programs.

Language and Literacy Skills

Opening the World of Learning (OWL; Schickedanz & Dickinson, 2005) is a good example of a targeted preschool curriculum designed to enrich language use in preschool classrooms and provide sequenced learning opportunities that promote emergent literacy skills (Ashe, Reed, Dickinson, Morse, & Wilson, 2009). The full-day programming is divided into teacher-directed and child-initiated activities that are oriented around (a) vocabulary and conceptual learning and (b) code-related learning, both of which contribute in critical ways to establishing later reading skills (Storch & Whitehurst, 2002). In daily Morning Meetings, teachers name and demonstrate with objects that are made available for Center Times, during which child-directed and play-based learning reinforces conceptual knowledge. This is followed by Storybook Time, an interactive instruction format that utilizes repeated exposures of three or four readings to facilitate mastery of new vocabulary and content. As children become familiarized with key words, teachers foster engagement and comprehension by prompting children to help reconstruct story events and read the book using their own words. In Small Group time, teachers lead activities that reinforce previously explored concepts. The Songs, Wordplay, and Letters component of the curriculum teaches phonological awareness, vocabulary, and letter knowledge through engaging, play-based activities. Finally, group discussions focus on either exploring social and emotional issues or introducing conceptual knowledge through short-book reading.

Children who participated in OWL classrooms had significantly improved oral language and code-related skills by the end of preschool and were performing on par with the national average on standardized reading achievement tests in first grade relative to classmates who had not participated in the program (Weiland & Yoshikawa, 2013). Similar gains were found for ethnically diverse, English-language learning, and special needs students (Weiland, 2016; Wilson, Dickinson, & Rowe, 2013). Elements critical to the success of the OWL intervention include strong support for professional development, in-class coaching for teachers, and a curriculum that emphasizes mastery of vocabulary and conceptual knowledge and code-related literacy skills through intentional instruction as well as interactive games (Wilson et al., 2013). Additionally, OWL espouses a classroom interaction style that is characterized by high-quality student–teacher interactions, fostering engaged and flexible responsiveness to individual student needs.

A second example of an evidence-based targeted preschool curriculum promoting language and literacy skills is the Exceptional Coaching for Early Language and Literacy (ExCELL) program. ExCELL is an intensive professional development intervention that trains teachers to promote preschool language development in five domains: interactive book reading, guiding conversations, phonological awareness, alphabet knowledge, and writing (Wasik, 2010). During interactive book reading, teachers ask open-ended questions, define target vocabulary using child-friendly language, and scaffold language learning by drawing connections between words introduced in book reading and their application in other classroom activities (Wasik, Bond, & Hindman, 2006). Teachers are also coached in implementing classroom materials such as story-related props, picture and word cards, and games that naturalistically reinforce target vocabulary in the context of engaging, play-based extension activities used throughout the day in centers and during free play.

In the ExCELL intervention model, conversational support plays a central role in facilitating child mastery of conceptual, vocabulary, and code-related knowledge. Teachers are coached in the use of several key conversational strategies that research has linked with gains in child language and literacy development (Wasik & Hindman, 2011, 2014). For example, teachers are encouraged to make frequent references to target vocabulary words, providing explicit word labels in conversations with students and during activity-related discussions to model the use of new vocabulary words in broad contexts outside of book reading. Additionally, teachers encourage language production by using open-ended questions to initiate conversations, which they extend by building upon children's responses. This is also accomplished by using active listening to respond to child comments and expanding upon the child's utterances. Specifically, teachers are coached to respond to children's simple responses by elaborating upon them, including additional vocabulary and expanded grammatically correct sentences. Teachers who completed the ExCELL professional development program were found to have high-quality, language-rich classroom environments that facilitated significantly greater gains in students' receptive vocabulary and code-related skills compared with usual-practice comparison classrooms (Wasik & Hindman, 2011).

Cognition and Numeracy

Parallel to the emergence of targeted preschool curricula that promote language and literacy skills, mathematics-focused curricula have emerged that promote gains in preschool cognitive reasoning and numeracy skills. A few examples of recent evidence-based mathematics curricula, along with their key findings and primary program components, are presented here.

One widely used evidence-based curriculum targeting mathematics is Building Blocks Pre-K (Clements & Sarama, 2007). This program organizes lessons around topics of interest to young children and utilizes small-group games and activities, along with computer-based games and activities to support the development of (a) spatial and geometric competencies and concepts and (b) numeric and quantitative concepts. There are three mathematical subthemes: patterns and functions, data, and discrete mathematics (classifying, sorting, and sequencing). For example, in the numeracy domain, children learn to compare numbers of different objects and combine objects to increase numbers using simple nonverbal addition games and manipulable objects. Lessons are sequenced so that these activities progress gradually from more basic to more advanced math skills, such as counting objects and doing simple addition. This developmentally sequenced curriculum is based on well-defined learning progressions and has been shown to be more effective at increasing children's number and geometry skills than have usual-practice comparison preschool classrooms (Clements & Sarama, 2008).

The effectiveness of Building Blocks has been tested with two randomized controlled trials (Clements & Sarama, 2007, 2008). In these studies, Building Blocks proved more effective than the usual-practice curriculum in promoting children's mathematical knowledge and reasoning skills. Interestingly, Building Blocks also promoted gains in letter recognition and oral language skills (Sarama, Lange, Clements, & Wolfe, 2012), and the authors hypothesized that strengthening children's conceptual skills enhanced their learning engagement and thereby promoted cross-domain gains in emergent literacy skills along with the direct effects on mathematical skills.

A second example of an evidence-based preschool curriculum targeting numeracy skills is Big Math for Little Kids (BMLK; Lewis Presser, Clements, Ginsburg, & Ertle, 2015). BMLK was developed based on a developmental progression in which preschool children acquire an intuitive sense of mathematics concepts and operations skills even before they can describe their reasoning in words. The program provides sequenced math lessons that utilize play, games, stories, and other engaging children's activities to elicit children's excitement about doing math. The 32-lesson curriculum consists of units that focus on number, shape, patterns/logic, measurement, number operations, and spatial relations and is organized so the same activities are repeated with increasing difficulty over a few days. A randomized controlled trial demonstrated that children who attended child-care programs using BMLK compared with children who attended child-care programs using their usual-practice curriculum showed increased Early Childhood Longitudinal Study–Birth Cohort mathematics assessment scores in kindergarten, gaining the equivalent of an additional 2.9 months of instruction (Lewis Presser et al., 2015).

A third preschool curriculum targeting math is Pre-K Mathematics, developed by Starkey, Klein, and Wakeley (2004). Based on developmental research documenting processes of mathematical knowledge acquisition during the preschool years (ages 3–5), Pre-K Mathematics combines closely related content into units. The seven units, which include 27 small-group activities, are sequential in nature: Enumeration and Number Sense, Arithmetic Reasoning, Spatial Sense, Geometric Reasoning, Pattern Sense and Unit Construction, Non-Standard Measurement, and Logical Relations. Teachers follow detailed lesson plans to teach concepts using concrete materials during small-group instruction, computer-based mathematics activities, and mathematics learning centers. This curriculum was shown to be effective at promoting mathematics knowledge in a randomized controlled trial conducted in 40 Head Start classrooms. Children in classrooms that implemented the intervention showed greater gains in mathematics knowledge compared with children in classrooms that used typical mathematics curriculum as evidenced by significantly higher scores on the Child Mathematics Assessment at the end of the year (Klein, Starkey, Clements, Sarama, & Iyer, 2008).

Finally, a fourth program warrants mention, as it represents a somewhat different approach to mathematics lesson than do the other programs mentioned in this section. The technologically oriented Math Shelf program (Schacter & Jo, 2016) uses a Montessori method approach to teaching mathematics concepts. The program is delivered on an iPad, with the rate of progression tailored to each child's knowledge level and response, thereby personalizing math instruction. Children play a series of games that teach different sequenced mathematics concepts (e.g., beginning with small quantities and one-to-one counting in the first set of games and progressing gradually to more difficult skills using quantities from 10 to 100 as mastery is demonstrated). In a randomized trial, children using this curriculum learned more over the preschool year than did children who participated in their regular mathematics curriculum (Schacter & Jo, 2016).

Social-Emotional Development

Targeted curricula have also been developed to target social–emotional skill development in the preschool years. Social–emotional skills are a central component of school readiness (Bassok et al., 2016). Important preschool skills include getting along and cooperating with others, understanding and managing strong feelings, and solving everyday interpersonal problems. These skills deserve focused attention during the preschool years because they are critical for long-term school and life success (Bierman & Motamedi, 2015; Jones, Greenberg, & Crowley, 2015).

A well-studied example of a content-specific curriculum designed to pro-mote social–emotional learning is the Preschool Promoting Alternative Think-ing Strategies (PATHS) Curriculum (Domitrovich, Greenberg, Cortes, & Kusche, 2005). Preschool PATHS targets four domains of preschool social–emotional skills: (a) friendship skills and prosocial behaviors (e.g., helping, sharing, taking turns), (b) emotional knowledge (e.g., recognizing and labeling core feelings), (c) self-control (e.g., using the turtle technique that guides children when dis-tressed to "tell yourself to stop, take a deep breath to calm down, say the prob-lem and how you feel"), and (d) social problem solving. There are 33 brief (15- to 20-minute) lessons with stories, pictures, and puppets that provide skill instruction, designed for use during circle time, one or two times per week. Teachers introduce and illustrate skill concepts with puppets, pictures, and story examples. Each lesson includes ideas for formal and informal exten-sion activities that teaching staff can use throughout the day to generalize key concepts. For example, the emotion lessons use photographs, stories, and feel-ing face cards to help children learn to identify and label feelings verbally to manage them. Teachers are also encouraged to provide emotion coaching throughout the day, modeling feeling statements themselves when appropri-ate, helping children notice the feelings of peers, and prompting children to describe their own feelings. Teachers are also encouraged to watch for natu-rally occurring teachable moments, such as peer disagreements or conflicts. At these times, teachers are taught to help children stop and calm down (using the turtle technique) and then talk through the problem-solving steps of defin-ing the problem and their feelings, listening to their friend's feelings, and gen-erating ideas for how to solve the problem.

Several randomized trials provide evidence of the efficacy of Preschool PATHS. In the first study, 20 Head Start classrooms were randomized to the intervention (Preschool PATHS) or a usual-practice control group; 287 chil-dren were followed for 1 year, with skills assessed at the start and end of the year. By the end of the year, children who received Preschool PATHS class-rooms outperformed children in the control group on measures of emotion knowledge and emotion-recognition skills and on teacher and parent ratings of social competence (Domitrovich, Cortes, & Greenberg, 2007). In a second study, Preschool PATHS was combined with MyTeachingPartner, a Web-based professional development program (MTP; Hamre, Pianta, Mashburn, & Downer, 2012). Prekindergarten teachers in 233 classrooms were randomly assigned to one of three conditions: (a) PATHS-High, which included the Pre-school PATHS curriculum, access to demonstration videos, and MTP coach-ing; (b) PATHS-Low, which included the Preschool PATHS curriculum and access to demonstration videos, but no MTP coaching; and (c) usual-practice control. Relative to the usual-practice control group, children in both of the other conditions who received Preschool PATHS showed significantly greater improvements in teacher-rated social competencies (frustration tolerance, assertiveness skills, task orientation, social skills). Finally, Preschool PATHS was evaluated in the context of a national randomized study, the Head Start CARES project. It produced heightened levels of emotion knowledge and social problem-solving skills and improved social competence as rated by teachers, as well as stronger learning behaviors (Morris et al., 2014).

FUTURE DIRECTIONS: IMPLICATIONS FOR PRACTICE AND RESEARCH NEEDS

Accumulating research provides strong evidence for the value of high-quality ECE programming in promoting early child skill development and fostering school readiness (Yoshikawa et al., 2013). ECE programming that includes warm, responsive, and intellectually stimulating teacher–child interaction and that utilizes evidence-based skill-focused curricula appears particularly useful in fostering school-readiness skills and closing the gap in school readiness associated with family socioeconomic disadvantage. At the same time, the future poses important challenges.

There are research needs. Although targeted curricula have proven effective in promoting child skills in specific domains such as literacy, numeracy, and social–emotional skills, it remains a challenge to integrate multiple domain-specific curriculum into a cohesive program. A few model studies have illustrated the power of combining two targeted curricula. For example, the Boston Pre-K study used a combination of OWL and Building Blocks Pre-K. Program evaluation demonstrated positive gains for children in the targeted areas of emergent literacy and numeracy skills, along with gains in EF skills (Weiland, 2016; Weiland & Yoshikawa, 2013).

In another example, the Head Start REDI (Research-based, Developmentally Informed) program also combined two targeted curricula, using the Preschool PATHS Curriculum integrated with a literacy intervention that utilized interactive reading, sound games, and alphabet center activities. A randomized trial comparing REDI to usual-practice Head Start showed increases in social–emotional skills (emotional understanding, social problem solving), improvements in emergent literacy skills, and gains in approaches to learning (observed learning engagement and EF skills; Bierman, Domitrovich, et al., 2008; Bierman, Nix, Greenberg, Blair, & Domitrovich, 2008). These studies suggest that two targeted preschool curricula can be combined effectively with positive impact on child outcomes relative to using the kind of whole-child curriculum typically used in Head Start and other programs. However, it seems unlikely that implementing five separate curricula that target the five domains of school readiness would be effective, because of both the practical implementation challenges (e.g., finding time to implement five curriculum programs, managing the teacher burden of learning and implementing five programs with fidelity) and the likelihood that this level of curriculum focus would overstructure the preschool day, undermining teacher's abilities to remain flexible, spontaneous, and child-focused in their program delivery.

Luckily, it does not appear necessary to target all five domains with distinct curricula as emerging evidence suggests cross-domain gains in skill acquisition. For example, the Boston Pre-K study and Head Start REDI project documented improvements in approaches to learning without targeting EF skills or learning engagement directly. In contrast to the domain-specific content areas, such as literacy, numeracy, or social–emotional skills, approaches to learning reflect domain-general skills (attention, memory, inhibitory control) that affect the pace and quality of children's learning capacity across domains. Hence, these skills may benefit from an evidence-based curriculum targeting emergent literacy, numeracy, and/or social–emotional skills.

Positive effects on EF have also been documented using intervention approaches that focus on promoting positive classroom management and teacher–student interaction quality (Raver et al., 2009, 2011). However, additional research is needed to explore programming that integrates multiple targeted curricula to better understand the scope of their effects.

In addition, programming that may foster physical and motor development has garnered relatively little attention. Yet, there is some evidence that certain kinds of physical programming in preschool can promote cross-domain gains in other areas of school readiness as well. For example, Lobo and Winsler (2006) conducted a randomized trial of an 8-week dance program and found positive effects on teacher and parent ratings of child social competence and reduced levels of internalizing and externalizing problems. In another study, Schmitt, McClelland, Tominey, and Acock (2015) found that children attending Head Start who were randomly assigned to an 8-week games program showed greater increases in EF skills than did children in the comparison group. These studies suggest that certain kinds of strategic physical activity programs may foster physical skill development and, at the same time, promote gains in other skill areas such as social–emotional competence and approaches to learning. More research in this area is definitely warranted.

In each of the studies described in this chapter, targeted preschool curricula provided teachers with two types of intervention support that likely each contributed to the benefits observed in child school readiness. These two ingredients were (a) lesson plans that laid out sequenced and intentional learning opportunities for children in specific skill domains provided in the form of engaging stories, games, and activities and (b) professional development and supportive coaching for teachers to help them deliver programming using positive management strategies and with high-quality teacher–student interactions. A key goal for the future is the scaling up of these kinds of model programs to make them more widely available for diverse ECE programs and program staff.

It is also important to note that, although this chapter has focused primarily on how ECE programs can support child school readiness, families play a critical role as well. Child school readiness benefits when parents support early learning at home by engaging in frequent warm and responsive interactions, talking and reading with children, and introducing learning games and activities (Fantuzzo, McWayne, Perry, & Childs, 2004). For children in Head Start, this kind of home-based family involvement is a strong predictor of multiple dimensions of school readiness, including language development, approaches to learning, and social–emotional school readiness (Fantuzzo et al.,

2004). Correspondingly, parent-focused interventions have proven effective in boosting the school readiness of low-income preschool children, adding to the benefits of participation in high-quality ECE. Positive approaches have included the use of parent groups to support positive parent–child interaction and behavior management skills, home routines, and home–school communication (Brotman et al., 2013) and teaching parents to use interactive reading strategies and play learning games at home in ways that are coordinated with center-based ECE (Bierman, Heinrichs, Welsh, Nix, & Gest, 2017). Further research on these kinds of parent support programs is needed, particularly with a focus on scalability and broad diffusion potential.

Finally, additional research is needed to better understand how to promote the sustainability of preschool benefits after children transition into elementary school (Bailey, Duncan, Odgers, & Yu, 2017). Aligning curricula across the prekindergarten to elementary school gap, using parents more effectively as transition supports, and providing booster interventions after the transition have all been suggested as strategies that might maximize the boost to child school success provided by a high-quality ECE program.

SUMMARY

In recent years, ECE programming has become a common interest of educators, policymakers, and the public at large. Increasing numbers of U.S. children are attending center-based ECE programs, and accumulating developmental research suggests that the quality of those ECE experiences can have a long-term impact on child school success and future well-being, particularly for children who face early socioeconomic disadvantage and heightened exposure to adversity. This chapter focused on the shifts that have occurred in the past 2 decades in the conceptualization of school readiness and the corresponding focus on identifying ECE programming that optimizes child school-readiness outcomes. To boost child school-readiness outcomes, future efforts need to focus on supporting the widespread diffusion of evidence-based ECE programming that includes the two critical features of (a) sequenced lesson plans providing intentional learning opportunities for children in specific skill domains and (b) supportive coaching for teachers to enhance high-quality teacher–student interactions and high-fidelity program implementation. Ongoing research is also needed to inform the continued expansion and refinement of school-based and family-focused strategies that can optimize school readiness for all children.

REFERENCES

Ashe, M. K., Reed, S., Dickinson, D. K., Morse, A. B., & Wilson, S. J. (2009). Opening the world of learning: Features, effectiveness, and implementation strategies. *Early Childhood Services: An Interdisciplinary Journal of Effectiveness, 3*, 179–191.

Bailey, D., Duncan, G. J., Odgers, C. L., & Yu, W. (2017). Persistence and fadeout in the impacts of child and adolescent interventions. *Journal of Research on Educational Effectiveness, 10*, 7–39. http://dx.doi.org/10.1080/19345747.2016.1232459

Bassok, D., Latham, S., & Rorem, A. (2016). Is kindergarten the new first grade? *AERA Open, 1*, 1–31. http://ero.sagepub.com/content/spero/2/1/2332858415616358.full.pdf

Bierman, K. L., Domitrovich, C. E., Nix, R. L., Gest, S. D., Welsh, J. A., Greenberg, M. T., . . . Gill, S. (2008). Promoting academic and social–emotional school readiness: The Head Start REDI program. *Child Development, 79*, 1802–1817. http://dx.doi.org/10.1111/j.1467-8624.2008.01227.x

Bierman, K. L., Heinrichs, B. S., Welsh, J. A., Nix, R. L., & Gest, S. D. (2017). Enriching preschool classrooms and home visits with evidence-based programming: Sustained benefits for low-income children. *Journal of Child Psychology and Psychiatry, 58*, 129–137. http://dx.doi.org/10.1111/jcpp.12618

Bierman, K. L., & Motamedi, M. (2015). Social–emotional programs for preschool children. In J. Durlak, C. Domitrovich, R. P. Weissberg, T. Gullotta, & P. Goren (Eds.), *The handbook of social and emotional learning: Research and practice* (pp. 135–150). New York, NY: Guilford Press.

Bierman, K. L., Nix, R. L., Greenberg, M. T., Blair, C., & Domitrovich, C. E. (2008). Executive functions and school readiness intervention: Impact, moderation, and mediation in the Head Start REDI program. *Development and Psychopathology, 20*, 821–843. http://dx.doi.org/10.1017/S0954579408000394

Bierman, K. L., & Torres, M. (2016). Promoting the development of executive functions through early education and prevention programs. In J. A. Griffin, L. S. Freund, & P. McCardle (Eds.), *Executive function in preschool age children: Integrating measurement, neurodevelopment and translational research* (pp. 299–326). Washington, DC: American Psychological Association. http://dx.doi.org/10.1037/14797-014

Blair, C., & Raver, C. C. (2015). School readiness and self-regulation: A developmental psychobiological approach. *Annual Review of Psychology, 66*, 711–731. http://dx.doi.org/10.1146/annurev-psych-010814-015221

Bodovski, K., & Youn, M. (2011). The long term effects of early acquired skills and behaviors on young children's achievement in literacy and mathematics. *Journal of Early Childhood Research, 9*, 4–19. http://dx.doi.org/10.1177/1476718X10366727

Brotman, L. M., Dawson-McClure, S., Calzada, E. J., Huang, K.-Y., Kamboukos, D., Palamar, J. J., & Petkova, E. (2013). Cluster (school) RCT of ParentCorps: Impact on kindergarten academic achievement. *Pediatrics, 131*, e1521–e1529. http://dx.doi.org/10.1542/peds.2012-2632

Brown, G., Scott-Little, C., Amwake, L., & Wynn, L. (2007). *A review of methods and instruments used in state and local school readiness evaluations.* Washington, DC: U.S. Department of Education, Institute of Education Sciences, National Center for Education Evaluation and Regional Assistance, Regional Educational Laboratory Southeast.

Burchinal, M., Kainz, K., Cai, K., Tout, K., Zaslow, M., Martinez-Beck, I., & Rathgeb, C. (2009). *Early care and education quality and child outcomes.* Washington, DC: Office of Planning, Research and Evaluation, Administration for Children and Families, U.S. DHHS, and Child Trends. http://dx.doi.org/10.1037/e573052010-001

Callaghan, G., & Madelaine, A. (2012). Leveling the playing field for kindergarten entry: Research implications for preschool early literacy instruction. *Australasian Journal of Early Childhood, 37*, 13–23. http://dx.doi.org/10.1177/183693911203700103

Clements, D. H., & Sarama, J. (2007). Effects of a preschool mathematics curriculum: Summative research on the Building Blocks project. *Journal for Research in Mathematics Education, 38*, 136–163.

Clements, D. H., & Sarama, J. (2008). Experimental evaluation of the effects of a research-based preschool mathematics curriculum. *American Educational Research Journal, 45*, 443–494. http://dx.doi.org/10.3102/0002831207312908

Clements, D. H., & Sarama, J. (2011). Early childhood mathematics intervention. *Science, 333*, 968–970. http://dx.doi.org/10.1126/science.1204537

Curby, T. W., Berke, E., Alfonso, V. C., Blake, J., DeMarie, D., DuPaul, G. J., . . . Subotnik, R. F. (2017). Kindergarten teacher perceptions of kindergarten readiness: The importance of social–emotional skills. *Perspectives on Early Childhood Psychology and Education, 2*, 115–137.

Diamond, A., & Lee, K. (2011). Interventions shown to aid executive function development in children 4 to 12 years old. *Science, 333*, 959–964. http://dx.doi.org/10.1126/science.1204529

Domitrovich, C. E., Cortes, R. C., & Greenberg, M. T. (2007). Improving young children's social and emotional competence: A randomized trial of the preschool PATHS curriculum. *Journal of Primary Prevention, 28*, 67–91. http://dx.doi.org/10.1007/s10935-007-0081-0

Domitrovich, C. E., Greenberg, M. T., Cortes, R., & Kusche, C. A. (2005). *The Preschool PATHS Curriculum.* Deerfield, MA: Channing-Bete.

Evans, G. W., Gonnella, C., Marcynyszyn, L. A., Gentile, L., & Salpekar, N. (2005). The role of chaos in poverty and children's socioemotional adjustment. *Psychological Science, 16*, 560–565. http://dx.doi.org/10.1111/j.0956-7976.2005.01575.x

Fantuzzo, J., McWayne, C., Perry, M., & Childs, S. (2004). Multiple dimensions of family involvement and their relations to behavioral and learning competencies for urban, low-income children. *School Psychology Review, 33*, 467–480.

Friedman-Krauss, A. H., Barnett, W. S., Weisenfeld, G. G., Kasmin, R., DiCrecchio, N., & Horowitz, M. (2018). *The state of preschool 2017: State preschool yearbook.* New Brunswick, NJ: National Institute for Early Education Research.

Guo, G., & Harris, K. M. (2000). The mechanisms mediating the effects of poverty on children's intellectual development. *Demography, 37*, 431–447. http://dx.doi.org/10.1353/dem.2000.0005

Hall, A. H., Simpson, A., Guo, Y., & Wang, S. (2015). Examining the effects of preschool writing instruction on emergent literacy skills: A systematic review of the literature. *Literacy Research and Instruction, 54*, 115–134. http://dx.doi.org/10.1080/19388071.2014.991883

Hamre, B. K., Pianta, R. C., Mashburn, A. J., & Downer, J. T. (2012). Promoting young children's social competence through the preschool PATHS curriculum and MyTeachingPartner professional development resources. *Early Education and Development, 23*, 809–832. http://dx.doi.org/10.1080/10409289.2011.607360

Hughes, C., & Graham, A. (2002). Measuring executive functions in childhood: Problems and solutions? *Child and Adolescent Mental Health, 7*, 131–142. http://dx.doi.org/10.1111/1475-3588.00024

Jenkins, J. M., & Duncan, G. J. (2017). Do pre-kindergarten curricula matter? In D. Phillips, K. A. Dodge, & Pre-Kindergarten Task Force (Eds.), *The current state of scientific knowledge on pre-kindergarten effects* (pp. 37–44). Washington, DC: Brookings Institution and Duke University.

Jones, D. E., Greenberg, M., & Crowley, M. (2015). Early social–emotional functioning and public health: The relationship between kindergarten social competence and future wellness. *American Journal of Public Health, 105*, 2283–2290. http://dx.doi.org/10.2105/AJPH.2015.302630

Klein, A., Starkey, P., Clements, D., Sarama, J., & Iyer, R. (2008). Effects of a pre-kindergarten mathematics intervention: A randomized experiment. *Journal of Research on Educational Effectiveness, 1*, 155–178. http://dx.doi.org/10.1080/19345740802114533

Lewis Presser, A., Clements, M., Ginsburg, H., & Ertle, B. (2015). Big math for little kids: The effectiveness of a preschool and kindergarten mathematics curriculum. *Early Education and Development, 26*, 399–426. http://dx.doi.org/10.1080/10409289.2015.994451

Lobo, Y. B., & Winsler, A. (2006). The effects of a creative dance and movement program on the social competence of Head Start preschoolers. *Social Development, 15*, 501–519. http://dx.doi.org/10.1111/j.1467-9507.2006.00353.x

Lowenstein, A. E. (2011). Early care and education as educational panacea: What do we really know about its effectiveness? *Educational Policy, 25*, 92–114. http://dx.doi.org/10.1177/0895904810387790

Mashburn, A. J., Pianta, R. C., Hamre, B. K., Downer, J. T., Barbarin, O. A., Bryant, D., . . . Howes, C. (2008). Measures of classroom quality in prekindergarten and children's development of academic, language, and social skills. *Child Development, 79*, 732–749. http://dx.doi.org/10.1111/j.1467-8624.2008.01154.x

Masten, A. S., & Labella, M. H. (2016). Risk and resilience in child development. In L. Balter & C. S. Tamis-LeMonda (Eds.), *Child psychology: A handbook of contemporary issues* (pp. 423–450). New York, NY: Taylor & Francis.

McFarland, J., Hussar, B., de Brey, C., Snyder, T., Wang, X., Wilkinson-Flicker, S., . . . Hinz, S. (2017). *The condition of education 2017*. Washington, DC: National Center for Education Statistics. Retrieved from https://nces.ed.gov/pubsearch/pubsinfo.asp?pubid=2017144

McLoyd, V. C. (1998). Socioeconomic disadvantage and child development. *American Psychologist, 53*, 185–204. http://dx.doi.org/10.1037/0003-066X.53.2.185

Morris, P., Mattera, S. K., Castells, N., Bangser, M., Bierman, K., & Raver, C. (2014). *Impact findings from the Head Start CARES demonstration: National evaluation of three approaches to improving preschoolers' social and emotional competence. Executive summary* (OPRE Report No. 2014-44). New York, NY: U.S. Department of Health and Human Services.

Nguyen, T., Jenkins, J. M., & Auger Whitaker, A. (2018). Are content-specific curricula differentially effective in Head Start or state prekindergarten classrooms? *AERA Open, 4*, 1–17. http://dx.doi.org/10.1177/2332858418784283

Noble, K. G., McCandliss, B. D., & Farah, M. J. (2007). Socioeconomic gradients predict individual differences in neurocognitive abilities. *Developmental Science, 10*, 464–480. http://dx.doi.org/10.1111/j.1467-7687.2007.00600.x

Pianta, R. C., Barnett, W. S., Burchinal, M., & Thornburg, K. R. (2009). The effects of preschool education: What we know, how public policy is or is not aligned with the evidence base, and what we need to know. *Psychological Science in the Public Interest, 10*, 49–88. http://dx.doi.org/10.1177/1529100610381908

Prakash, N., West, J., & Denton, K. (2003). *Schools' use of assessments for kindergarten entrance and placement: 1998–1999*. Washington, DC: National Center for Education Statistics.

Raver, C. C., Jones, S. M., Li-Grining, C., Zhai, F., Bub, K., & Pressler, E. (2011). CSRP's impact on low-income preschoolers' preacademic skills: Self-regulation as a mediating mechanism. *Child Development, 82*, 362–378. http://dx.doi.org/10.1111/j.1467-8624.2010.01561.x

Raver, C. C., Jones, S. M., Li-Grining, C., Zhai, F., Metzger, M. W., & Solomon, B. (2009). Targeting children's behavior problems in preschool classrooms: A cluster-randomized trial. *Journal of Consulting and Clinical Psychology, 77*, 302–316. http://dx.doi.org/10.1037/a0015302

Reardon, S. F. (2011). The widening academic achievement gap between the rich and the poor: New evidence and possible explanations. In G. J. Duncan & R. J. Murnane (Eds.), *Whither opportunity* (pp. 91–116). New York, NY: Russell Sage Foundation.

Sarama, J., Lange, A. A., Clements, D. H., & Wolfe, C. B. (2012). The impacts of an early mathematics curriculum on oral language and literacy. *Early Childhood Research Quarterly, 27*, 489–502. http://dx.doi.org/10.1016/j.ecresq.2011.12.002

Schacter, J., & Jo, B. (2016). Improving low-income preschoolers' mathematics achievement with Math Shelf, a preschool tablet computer curriculum. *Computers in Human Behavior, 55*, 223–229. http://dx.doi.org/10.1016/j.chb.2015.09.013

Schickedanz, J., & Dickinson, D. (2005). *Opening the world of learning*. Iowa City, IA: Pearson.

Schmitt, S. A., McClelland, M. M., Tominey, S. L., & Acock, A. (2015). Strengthening school readiness for Head Start children: Evaluation of a self-regulation intervention. *Early Childhood Research Quarterly, 30*, 20–31. http://dx.doi.org/10.1016/j.ecresq.2014.08.001

Snow, K. L. (2006). Measuring school readiness: Conceptual and practical considerations. *Early Education and Development, 17,* 7–41. http://dx.doi.org/10.1207/s15566935eed1701_2

Starkey, P., Klein, A., & Wakeley, A. (2004). Enhancing young children's mathematical knowledge through a pre-kindergarten mathematics intervention. *Early Childhood Research Quarterly, 19*(1), 99–120. http://dx.doi.org/10.1016/j.ecresq.2004.01.002

Storch, S. A., & Whitehurst, G. J. (2002). Oral language and code-related precursors to reading: Evidence from a longitudinal structural model. *Developmental Psychology, 38,* 934–947. http://dx.doi.org/10.1037/0012-1649.38.6.934

U.S. Department of Health and Human Services, Administration for Children and Families. (2018). *Head Start approach to school readiness—Overview.* Retrieved from https://eclkc.ohs.acf.hhs.gov/school-readiness/article/head-start-approach-school-readiness-overview

Wasik, B. A. (2010). What teachers can do to promote preschoolers' vocabulary development: Strategies from an effective language and literacy professional development coaching model. *The Reading Teacher, 63,* 621–633. http://dx.doi.org/10.1598/RT.63.8.1

Wasik, B. A., Bond, M. A., & Hindman, A. (2006). The effects of a language and literacy intervention on Head Start children and teachers. *Journal of Educational Psychology, 98,* 63–74. http://dx.doi.org/10.1037/0022-0663.98.1.63

Wasik, B. A., & Hindman, A. H. (2011). Improving vocabulary and pre-literacy skills of at-risk preschoolers through teacher professional development. *Journal of Educational Psychology, 103,* 455–469. http://dx.doi.org/10.1037/a0023067

Wasik, B. A., & Hindman, A. H. (2014). Understanding the active ingredients in an effective preschool vocabulary intervention: An exploratory study of teacher and child talk during book reading. *Early Education and Development, 25,* 1035–1056. http://dx.doi.org/10.1080/10409289.2014.896064

Weiland, C. (2016). Impacts of the Boston prekindergarten program on the school readiness of young children with special needs. *Developmental Psychology, 52,* 1763–1776. http://dx.doi.org/10.1037/dev0000168

Weiland, C., & Yoshikawa, H. (2013). Impacts of a prekindergarten program on children's mathematics, language, literacy, executive function, and emotional skills. *Child Development, 84,* 2112–2130. http://dx.doi.org/10.1111/cdev.12099

Welsh, J. A., Nix, R. L., Blair, C., Bierman, K. L., & Nelson, K. E. (2010). The development of cognitive skills and gains in academic school readiness for children from low income families. *Journal of Educational Psychology, 102,* 43–53. http://dx.doi.org/10.1037/a0016738

Wilson, S. J., Dickinson, D. K., & Rowe, D. W. (2013). Impact of an Early Reading First program on the language and literacy achievement of children from diverse language backgrounds. *Early Childhood Research Quarterly, 28,* 578–592. http://dx.doi.org/10.1016/j.ecresq.2013.03.006

Yoshikawa, H., Weiland, C., Brooks-Gunn, J., Burchinal, M., Espinosa, L., Gormley, W., & Zaslow, M. J. (2013). *Investing in our future: The evidence base on preschool.* Washington, DC: Society for Research in Child Development.

Zuckerman, B., & Halfon, N. (2003). School readiness: An idea whose time has arrived. *Pediatrics, 111,* 1433–1436. http://dx.doi.org/10.1542/peds.111.6.1433

4

Coming of Age

Evidence-Based Early Literacy Teaching

Kathleen Roskos and Lisa Lenhart

At one time the thought of preschool literacy did not exist in our conceptualization of literacy education. Not until 1986 did the idea take shape
in Teale and Sulzby's now classic text *Emergent Literacy: Writing and Reading.*
The concept invited a wider perspective on literacy to include early writing
and nascent literacy knowledge, which opened the door to examining children's literacy development before formal beginning reading instruction—
a perspective that now extends to birth. From this perspective, reading, writing,
and oral language skills develop concurrently and interrelatedly in young
children, fostered by literate environments (Dickinson & Neuman, 2006;
Neuman & Dickinson, 2001). Developmental learning of literacy, therefore,
begins very early in life and is foundational in literacy acquisition. The brevity
of the old reading-readiness view was replaced by a longer term view of how
literacy begins and evolves from birth across the lifespan (Cunningham &
Stanovich, 1991). This shift in perspective opened the floodgates of early literacy research and produced a substantial knowledge base on how children
acquire basic literacy concepts and skills before formal schooling.

In this chapter, we acknowledge the tremendous growth in our understanding of literacy development before formal schooling and its impact on
preprimary early literacy education. The field has matured with dramatic
effects on how we view the onset of literacy and its implications for literacy
interactions at home and school. We focus on research knowledge in the preschool developmental period (ages 3–5 years) because it contains the strongest

http://dx.doi.org/10.1037/0000197-005
Healthy Development in Young Children: Evidence-Based Interventions for Early Education,
V. C. Alfonso and G. J. DuPaul (Editors)

evidence on the relationship between early literacy experience and subsequent reading acquisition. We describe the developmental markers most closely associated with learning to read at word and meaning levels. We also discuss the increasing influence of multimedia in early literacy experience and its implications for emerging literacy in young children. Our focus then shifts to early literacy teaching, which is maturing in terms of evidence-based practice and technical expertise and establishing its important role in literacy education.

DEVELOPMENTAL MARKERS OF EARLY LITERACY

The roots of reading skill are found in phonological and orthographic processing, the former involving the discrimination of units in the speech stream (i.e., words, syllables, phonemes) and the latter concerned with identifying printed symbols (i.e., alphabet letters, words; Spear-Swerling, 2004). The cognitive skills embedded in these cognitive processes converge in the alphabetic principle, which is the insight that spoken sounds can be mapped to visual symbols and made meaningful.

Of the two processes, phonological processing is the more researched, and its role is more deeply understood (Kilpatrick, 2015). Several strata of phonological processing are key in learning to read. The most critical is phonological awareness, which involves developing sensitivity to sounds in words and the ability to manipulate them. It demands conscious attention to the sound structure of speech as opposed to its meaning, which is difficult for young children who are highly focused on meaning-making in their environment. Research demonstrates the causal role of phonological awareness in reading acquisition, and this awareness is necessary for grasping the alphabetic principle—that individual sounds in speech (i.e., phonemes) are connected to visual displays of letters (i.e., graphemes; McBride-Chang, 1999). Rapid automatic naming—the ability to rapidly name a sequence of objects, letters, or digits—and phonological memory—the ability to retain spoken information in working memory—are also implicated in phonological awareness because these abilities can support or constrain focused attention to sounds in language (Torgesen, 2002; Wolf, Bally, & Morris, 1986). Phonological awareness is an overarching term that encompasses a general awareness of the sound structure of oral language (e.g., rhymes, alliteration) and also the more precise understanding that spoken words consist of individual sounds (i.e., phoneme awareness) that can be analyzed and manipulated. In the preschool developmental period, the acquisition of phonological awareness is critical, particularly the abilities to distinguish sounds in the environment, recognize and produce rhyming words, segment words in sentences and syllables in words, and recognize repetitions of an initial consonant (Adams, Foorman, Lundberg, & Beeler, 1998).

Orthographic processing—twin to phonological processing—is less researched, and its role in learning to read less clear (Ehri, 2005). The strata of orthographic awareness in reading include rudimentary symbol recognition and rapid retrieval often accompanied by pronunciation (i.e., saying what you see). Early forms involve environmental print that is informed by contextual, often pictorial cues, which then advance to more mature forms of processing that use less contextualized cues of word features (e.g., sounds), configuration, and form (i.e., shape; Both-deVries, 2006; Levin & Bus, 2003).

The convergence of phonological and orthographic processing for purposes of automatic word recognition and fluent reading is the result of myriad literacy-related skills embedded in oral language comprehension, alphabet knowledge, and print awareness. Oral language comprehension or listening comprehension is perhaps the densest skill domain, including semantic, syntactic, and supra-linguistic abilities that coordinate word pronunciation and meaning. Under-standing orally presented information is key to children's success in the classroom. Listening comprehension requires children to integrate oral language abilities, or what they hear, to listen and respond accurately. Perfetti (1987; Perfetti & Stafura, 2014) argued that in the early phases of learning to read, print is more similar to speech than speech is to print; thus, abilities and skills of the more familiar domain (i.e., oral language) are the most useful for problem solving in the less familiar domain (i.e., written language). In brief, children rely on their oral language comprehension skills to make sense of printed words, although their command of linguistic forms is tentative. Their oral language compre-hension is confronted by two word-solving challenges: decoding and decon-textualized word meaning. In each, vocabulary knowledge is key because it coordinates pronouncing and understanding the unknown word to remem-ber it for purposes of comprehension (Kilpatrick, 2015).

Alphabet knowledge is the basic decoding mechanism of the alphabetic principle and a strong predictor of reading proficiency by the end of the primary grades (Ehri & Sweet, 1991; Scarborough, 1998). It consists of knowing letter names and letter sounds and retrieving this information quickly and accurately. Alphabet knowledge starts very early in life, often first introduced in relation to a child's name and singing the alphabet song (Both-deVries, 2006). Specifically, letter-name knowledge is a predictor of future reading and spelling achievement not only in the primary grades but also throughout elementary school, even into adulthood (Mol & Bus, 2011). Saying letter names helps children map phonemes to graphemes, which thus affords phonemic awareness. Children use their letter-name knowledge to learn letter sounds, and when fluent at letter naming, they can pay more attention to sound–symbol mapping and storing this information in memory, thus build-ing skill for single-word reading, that is, decoding words (Both-deVries & Bus, 2008). Early exposure to alphabet knowledge, starting as early as age 2 years, therefore precipitates awareness of the alphabetic principle, which in turn opens the door to decoding words in context.

Closely related is the development of early writing. Early literacy researchers have established an extensive research base describing 3- to 5-year-olds' hypotheses about writing, establishing that early writing behaviors mark the beginning of a learning trajectory that leads to more conventional writing and reading behaviors in the elementary school years (e.g., Clay, 1975; Ferreiro & Teberosky, 1982; Teale & Sulzby, 1986). Writing begins with scribbles that are largely undifferentiated and over time move in a general trajectory toward forms that have more writing-like characteristics, including linearity, appropriate directional patterns, and individual units (Levin & Bus, 2003). Preschoolers construct texts that reflect syntactic and semantic features of a variety of genres such as stories, lists, labels, signs, letters, and e-mails; they naturally combine writing, drawing, and other symbol systems, and their texts reflect flexible interweaving of semiotic systems (Rowe, 2008). The body of research on early writing establishes the importance of encouraging and assessing 3- to 5-year-olds' attempts at writing even before they begin to form conventional letters or spellings for words.

Print awareness combines elements of alphabet letter knowledge, concepts about print, and early spelling. Broadly, it entails knowing the purposes and conventions of print, such as what a word is on a page and its print features as well as an awareness of reading terms (e.g., page), rules (i.e., print conventions), and procedures (e.g., finger pointing). Print knowledge is moderately correlated with reading success, which suggests that it may be a proxy for print exposure and/or other early reading skill domains (e.g., alphabet letter knowledge; Lonigan, Burgess, & Anthony, 2000). In terms of specific abilities and skills related to learning to read, print knowledge is necessarily a large part of early literacy instruction embedded in early book experiences that introduce and expose children to the nature and function of written language—stories, texts, sentences, and words (Justice & Vukelich, 2008).

EARLY LITERACY EXPERIENCE IN A DIGITAL WORLD

According to the Common Sense Census (Rideout, 2017), children under age 2 years spend about 42 minutes, children ages 2 to 4 spend 2 hours and 40 minutes, and children ages 5 to 8 spend nearly 3 hours with screen media daily. Although the American Academy of Pediatrics (2016) recommended that young children spend less time with screens (i.e., 1 hour daily), parents are more concerned about the content of screen media and are eager for advice about the quality of the many educational apps available (Rasmussen, 2018). Quality, in fact, is a serious issue in the educational app market, giving rise to considerable attention among early childhood educators and researchers (see, for example, Barr & Linebarger, 2017).

Across the app spectrum from games to books, the digital book is of particular interest because of the powerful role of storybook reading in early literacy development (Mol & Bus, 2011). Book reading creates a unique opportunity for children to learn and practice the early literacy skills that are essential in learning to read and for enjoying books as future readers (Biemiller, 2003; Holdaway, 1979; Nation, Cocksey, Taylor, & Bishop, 2010; Perfetti, 2007). Shared book reading nurtures a love of books, not to mention a close emotional bond between adults and children (Bus, van IJzendoorn, & Pellegrini, 1995).

Digital books, however, disrupt the shared book reading dynamic, providing new electronic mechanisms that can offload and even strengthen the mediating role of the adult in the young child's literacy experience. These "new age" books have a built-in capacity to automate shared reading in ways that scaffold word learning and story comprehension, sometimes even better than parents can do (Takacs, Swart, & Bus, 2015). Well-designed ebooks can repeatedly and consistently tutor strategies for attending to words, book language, and narration that ready children for the learn-to-read process. For example, when the black cat in *Winnie the Witch* (Thomas, 1987) is turned into a green cat by Winnie's waving of the magic wand and reciting a magic spell, the electronics show, in this order, how Winnie picks up her wand, waves it, uses the spell, and turns the cat from black to green. Although the picture in a traditional book can show the witch with her wand and her green cat, it cannot show *how* Winnie turned the cat to a green cat, which may puzzle the young child and require further explanation by an adult. The electronics, however, concretize events, thus creating a higher probability of comprehension in the absence of adult facilitation. Meaning, in short, is made more accessible.

But does the wizardry of digital books improve young children's literacy readiness over that of paper books? So far the research results are mixed. In their meta-analysis on the effects of digital books on early literacy development, Takacs, Swart, and Bus (2015), for example, found that multimedia features such as animated pictures, music, and sound effects are beneficial for children, whereas hotspots, games, and dictionaries are detrimental, distracting young readers from the story content. Studies focused on parent–child reading and comparing digital and paper books consistently show that children are more engaged with digital books but perhaps at the expense of story comprehension as adult and child spend more time exploring and manipulating the device than talking about the storyline (see, for example, Richter & Courage, 2017). Still other studies indicate that left to their own devices (literally), young children do acquire some important early literacy skills from listening to and browsing digital books on their own, including vocabulary and story comprehension (see, e.g., Segal-Drori, Korat, Shamir, & Klein, 2010). So, although the research is just emerging, it suggests that the important research questions are not whether digital books support early literacy or not, but rather how digital books can do that productively in young children's lives.

Still, educators and parents are justifiably cautious about using digital books on a routine basis. Lisa Guernsey (2017) posed an important question: Who's by their side? At this point in our understanding of the role of digital books in early literacy experience, we are not sure when it is better for children to go solo in browsing digital stories and when it is more beneficial for them to share stories with adults and peers. At best, we have a few broad guidelines that at this time point the way (Vukelich, Enz, Roskos, & Christie, 2019):

- Select digital stories and books that tell a good story, that are age-appropriate, and that engage and appeal to young children.

- Coview a story several times to demonstrate proper device-handling skills, explore digital enhancements, and engage in substantive conversations about the story content.

- Provide easy access to familiar digital stories on devices, so children can choose old favorites and browse independently.

EVIDENCE AND EXPERTISE

At this point in early childhood education, we have a deeper understanding of early literacy development than ever before, which lays the foundation for more robust early literacy teaching. We have a clearer and more comprehensive picture of what young children are capable of knowing and doing as emerging readers and writers, which informs what we can reasonably expect from them at different ages, the learning activities we can and should do with them, assessments we can use to gauge their growth, and criteria for judging whether early literacy programs are appropriate and worthwhile. The early literacy field has made tremendous gains on all of these fronts, as shown by the wide array of articles, books, blogs, and videos on these topics.

Translating what we know about early literacy learning into what we do to teach it is guided by principles derived from professional knowledge. In this section, we describe a set of working principles that reflect early literacy research and also the broader science of learning that synthesizes research on learning and learning contexts across the lifespan (National Academies of Sciences, Engineering, and Medicine, 2018). Our approach is first to ground each principle in the scientific knowledge base, defining its core elements, and then to describe its application in practice—that is, what it looks like in early childhood educational settings, such as Head Start programs, preschools, and prekindergarten classrooms.

Principle 1. Read Books to Children Often

Storybook reading is one of the most powerful sources of complex language-learning processes in young children. It is important not only in the genesis of story comprehension in children ages 0 to 3 years (de Jong & Bus, 2003) but also in developing the precursor skills of emergent literacy, such as print and word awareness (e.g., Goswami, 2001; Whitehurst & Lonigan, 1998). Book language, a necessary prerequisite for literate thought (Paul & Wang, 2006), is more complex and diverse than everyday talk (Montag, Jones, & Smith, 2015). On average, there are 16.3 sophisticated words per 1,000 words in preschool books (Hayes & Ahrens, 1988), 5 times the number of sophisticated vocabulary words that are used in oral conversations (Snow, 1983). Book reading, therefore, fosters active, social, and meaningful involvement with ideas, words, and emotions; it helps children make connections between the known and the new; and it organizes information into meaningful patterns (or text structures) that help children remember story lines and facts.

A substantial body of research describes the strategies of book reading that potentiate young children's emerging literacy concepts and skills from an early age (de Jong & Bus, 2003). It is essential, for example, that adults immediately follow what is read by pointing to a feature on the page when a child initiates looking (Sénéchal, Thomas, & Monker, 1995). Pointing by the child should be accompanied by a verbal label from the adult when children are preverbal, but adults should ask children to provide the label when children are more advanced (DeLoache & DeMendoza, 1987). Young children's engagement in the reading process may be enhanced by giving them control to turn the pages of the book (Martin, 1997). Questions, feedback, and attention-getters are beneficial (Fletcher & Finch, 2015), and routines, as described by Ninio and Bruner (1978), are beneficial to help children practice using labels (i.e., referencing, evoking responses, and pointing).

Interactive Book Reading

In educational programs, book reading pedagogy is referred to as *interactive book reading* or, in colloquial terms, *shared book reading*. The framework for interactive reading provides the opportunity for children to participate actively and respond (Morrow & Gambrell, 2001). The teacher reads aloud, explicitly modeling skills of proficient readers (e.g., fluency, expression), and uses three types of scaffolding or support: (a) before-reading activities that arouse children's interest and curiosity in the book about to be read and help children make predictions, (b) during-reading prompts and questions that keep children actively engaged with the text being read, and (c) after-reading questions and activities such as retellings that give children an opportunity to discuss and respond to the books that have been read (Roskos, Tabors, & Lenhart, 2009; Vukelich, Enz, Roskos, & Christie, 2019).

What It Looks Like

Interactive read-alouds can vary on the bases of teacher objectives and student needs, but they should integrate instructional strategies before, during, and after reading. Table 4.1 provides a brief example of the framework in action during the first day of a read-aloud. It is important for the teacher to ask open-ended questions to help children build connections to the text. Giving children (even very young children) the chance talk about their thinking is mentally stimulating and ensures their full participation. Sometimes, in subsequent readings, teachers involve children even more during the reading phase by using a pointer to point to individual words and letting the children take turns reading text.

Principle 2. Provide an Interactive Language and Literacy Environment for Learning

We know that young children thrive in environments that support and nurture their interactions with the world around them—people, other children, toys, and material objects. Learning how to use language and, later on, print to negotiate the world depends heavily on the environment that surrounds

TABLE 4.1. Example of Interactive Reading

Interactive Reading Procedure: Read-Aloud Day 1		
Read-aloud phase	Teacher guidance	Instructional purpose
Before reading	"Look at the cover of the book. I wonder what it is going to be about?"	Arouse interest Make predictions
	"The little raccoon in this story has a problem. Look at the picture. What do you think the problem might be?"	Match text to picture Make predictions
During reading	"I wonder what will happen next?"	Alert to story sequence Encourage active engagement
	"I wonder how the little raccoon is feeling?"	Make inferences
After reading	"I noticed the author put some little pictures along the side of the page. I wonder why?"	Read like a writer Alert to author's purpose
	"Has anything like this ever happened to you?"	Make connections beyond text

children. Children's environmental surround, of course, is not static. Rather, it consists of dynamically changing contexts that push and shape children's growth, including their language and literacy development (Bronfenbrenner, 1995; National Academies of Sciences, Engineering, and Medicine, 2018). Language is at the very heart of these contexts, and indeed it is a mechanism that rouses children's minds to life (Tharp & Gallimore, 1988). Creating environments where children can experience substantial quality language and exposure to print over time, therefore, is foundational in early literacy pedagogy. The classic study by Hart and Risley (1995, 2003), for example, demonstrated the power of talk in shaping future literacy achievement as children growing up in households with more interactive talk develop into better readers by the end of the primary grades. Relatedly, children exposed to more books and print from early on are more successful literacy achievers (Mol & Bus, 2011).

Rich Environment for Talking, Reading, Writing, and Singing

Creating a conducive environment in educational settings where robust language and literacy experiences occur regularly requires thoughtful planning. It involves more than decoration; it is a matter of design (see Neuman & Roskos, 1997, 2007; Vukelich et al., 2019; see also Chapters 2 and 3, this volume). The design of the physical environment brings into play the basic elements of space, light, color, and sound to create appealing work and play spaces that accommodate solo and group activity and avoid crowding (i.e., about 25 square feet per child). It takes into consideration design features of signage, materials, storage, and overall appeal. Signage, for example, should be bold with sufficient white space; it should be functional. Activity settings should provide enough varied materials accompanied by well-organized storage that also teaches (e.g., close to the point of use, labels with picture and print). Appeal involves manipulating color and light to attract children into activity spaces and incorporating culturally relevant and familiar artifacts to stimulate talk and interaction.

Design of the social environment is equally deliberate, creating predictability via adult presence, routines, and good use of time. It establishes a positive tone that is encouraging and comforting and that promotes children's active participation in the learning environment; for very young children it should be homelike. The language and literacy of the social environment "tutor" content and knowledge about the world; they support and expand language use for purposes of learning.

The design considerations that yield a rich physical and social environment for talking, reading, writing, and singing can be summed up in the "four As" of environmental design for learning:

- appealing spaces that are inviting to young children;
- access to supports (e.g., adults, children, language, print);
- abundant, varied materials that engage and teach; and
- ample time to work and play.

Physical Environment

Examples of spaces in the physical environment that support early literacy activity and also teach are provided in Figures 4.1 and 4.2. Figure 4.1 shows a space where children constructed a water wall to illustrate what they are learning about pipes and water flow through pipes. In addition to the child-made structure, the space displays a printed ad dictated by the children, titled "We Need

FIGURE 4.1. Build a Water Wall

FIGURE 4.2. Explore Parts of a Wheel

From "Our Wheels Project: Finding the Extraordinary Within the Ordinary," by J. Cowan, 2015, *Early Childhood Research and Practice*, *17*, p. 11. Copyright 2015 by Owl Child Care Services of Ontario. Reprinted with permission.

a Plumber," that describes several serious water problems. Figure 4.2 illustrates an activity center with hands-on resources to aid exploring the parts of a wheel (e.g., axle, hub, rim, tube), including pictures, books, and signage.

Social Environment

Because their own names are immensely important to young children, having them write (or attempt to write) their names at sign-in as part of the morning routine is one way to embed writing in an authentic way. For example, the sign-in sheet could be located just outside the door of the classroom. Children sign in and then line up to be greeted by a friend. The greeter stands next to a chart that has three choices written on it—a hug, handshake, or fist bump—and students point to the greeting they want and say it. The practice encourages positive interactions between classmates and incorporates print. By pointing to the word (e.g., handshake) and saying it, students experience that print has meaning and represents the spoken word.

Principle 3. Promote Literacy Play

Play is a way to learn at any age, but it is especially useful for young children for whom so much is new and unexamined. Classic Piagetian and Vygotskian theories explain the critical role of play in the early years as a mechanism for language acquisition, symbolic thinking, and concept formation (Henricks, 2019). Vygotskian theory in particular places a premium on early childhood pretend play as a zone of proximal development for scaffolding language use toward higher-order thinking that supports early literacy skills (e.g., narrative comprehension).

Syntheses of research indicate a positive relationship between play activity in the early childhood period and early literacy development (Roskos & Christie, 2013). It's quite clear, for example, that play environments that are deliberately enriched with literacy materials increase the incidence of emerging literacy behaviors and skills, such as pretending to read, scribbling, reciting the alphabet, and recognizing words. Several studies document this finding among preschool children across early childhood settings (Christie & Stone, 1999; Morrow, 1990; Neuman & Roskos, 1992). There is enough evidence, as well, to assume an isomorphism between pretend play language and oral narratives that undergirds the oral language processes needed for early literacy. Studies reveal that thematic fantasy paradigm training improves story comprehension, showing gains in specific story comprehension (i.e., understanding the reenacted story) and generalized story comprehension (i.e., understanding other stories), which implies that the training may improve children's knowledge of narrative story structure (Pellegrini, 1984; Saltz & Johnson, 1974; Silvern, Taylor, Williamson, Surbeck, & Kelley, 1986).

Finally, a growing body of studies shows that learning centers as play-based activity settings afford a broad spectrum of literacy learning opportunities that can help young children learn relevant early literacy skills (e.g., name writing; Johnson, Christie, & Wardle, 2005). Quasiexperimental studies show the benefits of guided pretend play for vocabulary learning (Han, Moore, Vukelich, & Buell, 2010), for reading and writing words (Vukelich, 1991, 1994), for developing syntactic complexity of spoken language (Vedeler, 1997), and for using meta-linguistic verbs in play talk (Galda, Pellegrini, & Cox, 1989). Combining game play with storybook reading has also been found to help children learn new vocabulary words (Hassinger-Das et al., 2016; LaGamba, 2018; Lenhart, Roskos, Brueck, & Liang, 2019; Roskos & Burstein, 2011).

Literacy-Enriched Play That Teaches

The actual practice of teaching literacy in play involves an instructional framework referred to as *contingent teaching*, in which the teacher leads and follows the child's lead or what Bruner (2008) referred to as "leading from behind":

- Plan for play activity that supports emerging reading and writing skills.
- Give children ideas and language for complex social play.
- Connect play themes and topics to children's experience.
- Hand over responsibility for play activity to children.

Using a contingent teaching approach, teaching techniques such as topic play, story drama, puppet play, and play planning have been found to support children's emergent literacy development and learning (Roskos, 2019). Story drama, for example, develops working memory, language, and narrative skills essential in learning to read words and to follow story lines. The instructional procedure is straightforward: (a) select a predictable book with a good story;

(b) read the book several times, highlighting elements of setting, character, and plot; (c) model key roles; (d) use the classroom as a stage for scenes, select props, and assign roles; and (e) read aloud the story as the children reenact it. The key to using play activity effectively in the literacy curriculum in the pre-school years is to organize activity around a contingent teaching framework that bridges the known with the new yet allows children to take control of their own play experiences.

What It Looks Like

In Ms. Madrid's prekindergarten classroom, the children decide to enact one of their favorite stories, *The Three Billy Goats Gruff.* After listening to the story a few times and discussing the characters and plot with the children, Ms. Madrid models a few of the roles (e.g., children liked the troll the best). After some discussion about props (e.g., horns, troll mask, sign to bridge), they designate spaces in the classroom that represent the setting of the story (e.g., the meadow, the bridge, under the bridge, the hill). They take turns practicing roles (e.g., the goats, the troll). Then they enact the story as Ms. Madrid narrates it, moving from space to space. They enjoyed it so much, they reenacted it again. When asked to retell the story, children demonstrated recall of story setting, characters (e.g., names, voice, motivation), sequence of events, and resolution, thus developing their comprehension of story structure. The alliteration of *trip, trap, trip, trap* was especially memorable.

Principle 4. Personalize Early Literacy Learning

In one sense, a personalized approach to nurturing young children's early literacy knowledge and skills seems nothing new. Historically, a child-centered approach to teaching is a basic tenet of early childhood education with the aim of accommodating developmental, cultural, and linguistic diversity. Yet the concept of personalization is more nuanced than the traditional one of respect for individual differences. Personalization in the 21st century includes the feature of customization, which means tailoring or fitting learning activities to a particular learner's needs and preferences. New technologies afford per-sonalization that is more effective and efficient than in the past. Apps, for example, use intelligent tutoring systems that can quickly respond to learn-ers' psychological states as well as their background knowledge to personalize instruction. Well-designed apps, in brief, can quickly adapt to young learners' skill levels and pace, thus tutoring them without an adult present. Rather than being a threat to early literacy teaching, digital books, tools, and media are promising newcomers to pedagogy that can expand young children's oppor-tunities to learn language and literacy skills leading to literacy achievement (see, for example, Roskos, 2017; Wohlwend, 2015).

Tailoring Literacy Activity to the Learner

How to tailor literacy learning activities to suit each child involves integrating new technology tools with the tried-and-true methods of the past. The goal is a good match between what the child needs to grow and learning activities that help build and advance the child's early literacy skills. An important first step is to become familiar with quality digital tools, such as e-books and apps, that can be integrated with more traditional materials, such as paper books, puzzles, games, and writing tools. Several sites (e.g., Common Sense Media at https://www.commonsensemedia.org, Reading Rockets at https://www.readingrockets.org, local libraries) are helpful resources in selecting quality digital materials. The next important step is to provide learning activities that increase exposure to written language and that scaffold emergent literacy skills using multimedia in differentiated ways. When kindergarten teacher Mr. Munoz, for example, models and incorporates the Puppet Pal app into a unit on fantasy, he expands how different children might experience fantasy differently using multimedia to create imaginative stories that combine narration, sound, pictures, and animation.

What It Looks Like

A small group of children needs additional practice on phonological awareness, an important early literacy skill. The teacher decides to use a digital book for her lesson, but before she does, she carefully assesses the content and technical features and any reading aids that are a part of the book. She does this to determine if any features included in the book could be distractors, such as sounds or animation that could take attention away from the content of the book. Once convinced the selection is appropriate and having identified the enhancements she will highlight, she introduces the book by reading the name of the title and author and showing the children the home page icon, the back/forward icons, and any special features on the menu or toolbar. As she begins reading, she swipes the pages to turn them and demonstrates how the digital enhancements, such as tapping an object, reinforce the story line. This helps children to use these digital features on their own when they reread the e-book. The first time through, she models the use of the digital book but soon lets the children swipe to turn the page or tap to hear the words and book language. She then lets the children practice reading the story on their own devices, after adjusting digital enhancements to better suit children's needs. Luka, for example, is already an accomplished reader, so he can read the story without narration, whereas Sofia is easily distracted by the music, so the teacher turns off that feature for Sofia. This multisensory approach (i.e., seeing, hearing, doing, touching) gives children multiple ways of learning and, when coupled with the engaging nature of the digital book, can provide specialized and personalized instruction in a targeted area.

Principle 5. Promote Authentic Early Literacy Activities and Experiences

Early literacy instruction that engages young children and gets them to use their minds well is the key to early literacy learning that is sustained over time. This involves literacy teaching that pulls children into higher order thinking, deeper knowledge of book content, robust vocabulary, substantive conversations, and collaboration with one another at an early age (Katz & Chard, 2000; see http://projectapproach.org/about/project-approach). The best way to do this is to embed reading and writing in the pursuit of topics and themes that are of high interest and appeal to young children—an approach with a long history in early childhood education. Grounded in the science of learning (National Academies of Sciences, Engineering, and Medicine, 2018), the overarching teaching goal is to provide activities and learning environments that nurture problem solving, sustain a focus on a significant topic, encourage dialogue, and connect to children's real-life experiences. Throughout, children learn language and literacy skills, and they use language and literacy skills to learn.

Using Language and Literacy for Real

What does authentic early literacy learning mean? It means using the physical and mental tools of literacy to explore and investigate real and imaginary worlds. For the young child, it means engaging in inquiry by learning from digital and paper books and games, gathering information, using symbol systems to record information, and playing with one another to consolidate and express what is learned. How do teachers teach to promote authentic preschool literacy experience? They design learning activities that ask children to construct knowledge by organizing information and considering alternatives, to show understanding by explaining and communicating ideas, and to grapple with concepts and problems they are likely to encounter in life by making thoughtful choices and listening and collaborating with others. The design of authentic early literacy units and learning activities requires considerable knowledge and some discipline of thought on the teacher's part. There is no lack of planning guidance in early childhood teaching. Among the sources available, Understanding by Design is one of the more comprehensive (Wiggins & McTighe, 2005). The design process begins with the end goals in mind (i.e., expectations) and performance tasks that assess children's developing knowledge and skills followed by a scope and sequence of activities that lead to achieving expectations. Learning activities, in short, align with assessments and desired outcomes to increase opportunity for constructing knowledge, demonstrating depth of knowledge, and communicating ideas and experiences to others in multimodal ways—the hallmarks of authentic learning experience.

What It Looks Like

In her Head Start classroom, Ms. Jamison is planning a topic study on *Water Pipes and Pumps* (Dodge et al., 2002). Instead of planning by first considering activities children will do, she first identifies what they will learn aligned to early learning standards. She targets the following language and literacy indicators of the Head Start Child Development and Learning Framework among other domain indicators (e.g., science):

- comprehends increasingly complex and varied vocabulary,
- uses increasingly complex and varied vocabulary,

- retells stories or information from books,
- identifies beginning sounds in words,
- shows awareness of words as a unit of print, and
- uses scribbles, shapes, pictures, and letters to represent objects, stories, experiences, or ideas.

Next, she identifies assessments that measure children's progress in these skill areas, deciding (a) an oral language checklist of language interactions in different settings (e.g., whole group, play), (b) a vocabulary task that asks children to point to or name photos of terms related to the unit, and (c) a drawing/writing sample of play plans. Play plans, she reasons, will provide her with solid information about children's emerging awareness of words and the alphabetic principle. Given the busy schedule, she plans to assess only a sample of students each week—a few high-performing, typical, and lower-performing children (three to four in each grouping). This approach gives her a fairly accurate picture of how the whole class is doing.

As a final step, she selects and sequences key instructional activities each week that will engage children and exercise their speaking, listening, reading, and writing skills. Here are a few of the learning activities she plans to do:

- observe the flow of water in gutters, hoses, and pipes to understand factors that affect water flow;
- map the locations and routes of pipes in the school and at home;
- talk with the custodian about the functions of pipes in various areas of the school building;
- measure pipes;
- make three-dimensional models of water systems; and
- weight containers of water.

CONCLUSION

There was a time when parents and early childhood teachers were not expected (or even encouraged) to work with children to develop early literacy knowledge and skills. As a result, children often entered kindergarten without knowing the alphabet, without being able to write their name, and without being able to count, although many were quite capable of doing so, and some even did so. After conducting her landmark studies on children who read early, Durkin (1966) reflected:

> One outstanding impression left by many of the interviews had to do with the uneasy concern of parents about their role as educators of the preschool child in matters like reading and writing. . . . There was an expression almost of guilt feelings as parents told about ways their children learned to read. These parents also asked many questions about warnings that had come from PTA meetings, from the teachers of older children in the family, and from newspaper and magazine articles telling parents that preschool reading would only lead to problems and confusion when school instruction began. (p. 57)

She went on to share one mother's confession about early reading at home: "[We] try to encourage learning and we had discouraged reading . . . but now I'll get him books from the library if he wants them and forget what people say, and they have said plenty" (Durkin, 1966, p. 57).

Today's teachers and parents are far more informed about emergent literacy and young children's capabilities of learning the rudiments of reading and writing at an early age. Evidence from a substantial and growing body of research shows that young children and even very young children are capable of so much more than we thought prior to school. Furthermore, we know there is much parents and teachers can do to ensure children arrive at school with the necessary skills and developmental abilities that will prepare them for early reading instruction.

How to teach reading to young children in the preschool years is also far better understood than it once was. Although reading to children is a tradition in early reading pedagogy, research now shows the tremendous benefits of lots of deliberate interactive reading in preschool settings that purposefully teaches the roots of conventional reading, such as word awareness, word meanings, and text structure. It demonstrates the power of language and literacy-rich environments to teach children about book reading—how it works and its many pleasures. It highlights the critical importance of literacy-related play that nurtures story comprehension and vocabulary. And increasingly, research points to the importance of personalizing children's early learning, especially in supporting their efforts to grasp difficult literacy skills, such as the concept of a word. Finally, and perhaps key to advancing early literacy pedagogy, is emerging evidence that the integration of early literacy instruction in authentic learning experiences is more transferable and enduring for children on the oft-challenging road to reading in elementary school.

REFERENCES

Adams, M. J., Foorman, B. R., Lundberg, I., & Beeler, T. (1998). The elusive phoneme: Why phonemic awareness is so important and how to help children develop it. *American Educator, 22*, 18–29.

American Academy of Pediatrics. (2016). *New recommendations for children's media use.* Retrieved from https://www.aap.org/en-us/about-the-aap/aap-press-room/Pages/American-Academy-of-Pediatrics-Announces-New-Recommendations-for-Childrens-Media-Use.aspx

Barr, R., & Linebarger, D. N. (Eds.). (2017). *Media exposure during infancy and early childhood: The effects of content and context on learning and development.* New York, NY: Springer. http://dx.doi.org/10.1007/978-3-319-45102-2

Biemiller, A. (2003, May). Using stories to promote vocabulary. In *Fostering early narrative competency: Innovations in instruction.* Symposium conducted at the meeting of the International Reading Association, Orlando, FL.

Both-deVries, A. C. (2006). *It's all in the name: Early writing from imitating print to phonetic writing* (Unpublished doctoral dissertation). Leiden University, Amsterdam, The Netherlands.

Both-deVries, A. C., & Bus, A. G. (2008). Name writing: A first step to phonetic writing? Does the name have a special role in understanding the symbolic function of writing? *Literacy, Teaching and Learning, 12*, 37–55.

Bronfenbrenner, U. (1995). Developmental ecology through space and time: A future perspective. In P. Moen, G. Elder, & K. Luscher (Eds.), *Examining lives in context* (pp. 619–647). Washington, DC: American Psychological Association. http://dx.doi.org/10.1037/10176-018

Bruner, J. (2008). Culture and mind: Their fruitful incommensurability. *Ethos, 36*, 29–45. http://dx.doi.org/10.1111/j.1548-1352.2008.00002.x

Bus, A. G., van IJzendoorn, M. H., & Pellegrini, A. D. (1995). Joint book reading makes for success in learning to read: A meta-analysis on intergenerational transmission of literacy. *Review of Educational Research, 65*, 1–21. http://dx.doi.org/10.3102/00346543065001001

Christie, J. F., & Stone, S. J. (1999). Collaborative literacy activity in print-enriched play centers: Exploring the "zone" in same-age and multi-age groupings. *Journal of Literacy Research, 31*(2), 109–131. http://dx.doi.org/10.1080/10862969909548042

Clay, M. M. (1975). *What did I write? Beginning writing behaviour.* Auckland, New Zealand: Heinemann.

Cunningham, A., & Stanovich, K. (1991). Tracking the unique effects of print exposure in children: Associations with vocabulary, general knowledge, and spelling. *Journal of Educational Psychology, 83*, 264–274. http://dx.doi.org/10.1037/0022-0663.83.2.264

de Jong, M. T., & Bus, A. G. (2003). How well suited are electronic books to supporting literacy? *Journal of Early Childhood Literacy, 3*, 147–164. http://dx.doi.org/10.1177/14687984030032002

DeLoache, J. S., & DeMendoza, O. A. (1987). Joint picture book interactions of mothers and 1-year-old children. *British Journal of Developmental Psychology, 5*, 111–123. http://dx.doi.org/10.1111/j.2044-835X.1987.tb01047.x

Dickinson, D., & Neuman, S. (Eds.). (2006). *Handbook of early literacy research* (Vol. 2). New York, NY: Guilford Press.

Dodge, D. T., Berke, K., Rudick, S., Baker, H., Sparling, J., Lewis, I., & Teaching Strategies, Inc. (2002). *The creative curriculum.* Bethesda, MD: Teaching Strategies.

Durkin, D. (1966). *Children who read early.* New York, NY: Teachers College Press.

Ehri, L. (2005). Learning to read words. *Scientific Studies of Reading, 9*, 167–188. http://dx.doi.org/10.1207/s1532799xssr0902_4

Ehri, L., & Sweet, J. (1991). Fingerpoint reading of memorized text: What enables beginning readers to process the print? *Reading Research Quarterly, 26*, 442–462. http://dx.doi.org/10.2307/747897

Ferreiro, E., & Teberosky, A. (1982). *Literacy before schooling.* Portsmouth, NH: Heinemann.

Fletcher, K. L., & Finch, W. H. (2015). The role of book familiarity and book type on mothers' reading strategies and toddlers' responsiveness. *Journal of Early Childhood Literacy, 15*, 73–96. http://dx.doi.org/10.1177/1468798414523026

Galda, L., Pellegrini, A. D., & Cox, S. (1989). A short-term longitudinal study of preschoolers' emergent literacy. *Research in the Teaching of English, 23*, 292–309.

Goswami, U. (2001). Early phonological development and the acquisition of literacy. In S. B. Neuman & D. Dickinson (Eds.), *Handbook of early literacy research* (pp. 111–125). New York, NY: Guilford Press.

Guernsey, L. (2017). Who's by their side? Questions of context deepen the research on children and media: Commentary on Chapter 1. In R. Barr & D. Linebarger (Eds.), *Media exposure during infancy and early childhood* (pp. 25–32). Cham, Switzerland: Springer International. http://dx.doi.org/10.1007/978-3-319-45102-2_2

Han, M., Moore, N., Vukelich, C., & Buell, M. (2010). Does play make a difference? How plain intervention affects the vocabulary learning of at-risk preschoolers. *American Journal of Play, 3*, 82–104.

Hart, B., & Risley, T. (1995). *Meaningful differences in the everyday experience of young American children.* Baltimore, MD: Paul H. Brookes.

Hart, B., & Risley, T. R. (2003). The early catastrophe: The 30 million word gap by age 3. *American Educator, 4*(9), 4–9.

Hassinger-Das, B., Ridge, K., Parker, A., Golinkoff, R. M., Hirsh-Pasek, K., & Dickinson, D. K. (2016). Building vocabulary knowledge in preschoolers through shared book reading and gameplay. *Mind, Brain and Education, 10,* 71–80. http://dx.doi.org/10.1111/mbe.12103

Hayes, D. P., & Ahrens, M. G. (1988). Vocabulary simplification for children: A special case of 'motherese'? *Journal of Child Language, 15,* 395–410. http://dx.doi.org/10.1017/S0305000900012411

Henricks, T. S. (2019). Classic theories of play. In P. K. Smith & J. L. Roopnarine (Eds.), *The Cambridge handbook of play: Developmental and disciplinary perspectives* (pp. 361–382). New York, NY: Cambridge University Press.

Holdaway, D. (1979). *The foundations of literacy.* Sydney, Australia: Ashton Scholastic.

Johnson, J., Christie, J., & Wardle, F. (2005). *Play, development, and early education.* Boston, MA: Pearson/Allyn and Bacon.

Justice, L. M., & Vukelich, C. (2008). *Achieving excellence in preschool literacy instruction.* New York, NY: Guilford Press.

Katz, L. G., & Chard, S. (2000). *Engaging young children's minds: The project approach* (2nd ed.). Stamford, CT: Ablex.

Kilpatrick, D. A. (2015). *Essentials of assessing, preventing and overcoming reading difficulties.* Hoboken, NJ: John Wiley & Sons.

LaGamba, E. (2018, April). *An investigation of read alouds, classroom interactions, and guided play as supports for vocabulary learning in preschool* (Unpublished doctoral dissertation). University of Pittsburgh, Pittsburgh, PA.

Lenhart, L. A., Roskos, K. A., Brueck, J., & Liang, X. (2019). Does play help children learn words? Analysis of a book play approach using an adapted alternating treatment design. *Journal of Research in Childhood Education, 33,* 290–306. http://dx.doi.org/10.1080/02568543.2019.1577776

Levin, I., & Bus, A. G. (2003). How is emergent writing based on drawing? Analyses of children's products and their sorting by children and mothers. *Developmental Psychology, 39,* 891–905. http://dx.doi.org/10.1037/0012-1649.39.5.891

Lonigan, C. J., Burgess, S. R., & Anthony, J. L. (2000). Development of emergent literacy and early reading skills in preschool children: Evidence from a latent-variable longitudinal study. *Developmental Psychology, 36,* 596–613. http://dx.doi.org/10.1037/0012-1649.36.5.596

Martin, L. E. (1997). Early book reading: How mothers deviate from printed text for young children. *Reading Research and Instruction, 37,* 137–160. http://dx.doi.org/10.1080/19388079809558260

McBride-Chang, C. (1999). The ABCs of the ABCs: The development of letter-name and letter-sound knowledge. *Merrill-Palmer Quarterly, 45,* 285–308.

Mol, S. E., & Bus, A. G. (2011). To read or not to read: A meta-analysis of print exposure from infancy to early adulthood. *Psychological Bulletin, 137,* 267–296. http://dx.doi.org/10.1037/a0021890

Montag, J. L., Jones, M. N., & Smith, L. B. (2015). The words children hear: Picture books and the statistics for language learning. *Psychological Science, 26,* 1489–1496. http://dx.doi.org/10.1177/0956797615594361

Morrow, L. (1990). Preparing the classroom environment to promote literacy during play. *Early Childhood Research Quarterly, 5,* 537–554. http://dx.doi.org/10.1016/0885-2006(90)90018-V

Morrow, L., & Gambrell, L. (2001). Literature-based instruction in the early years. In S. B. Neuman & D. Dickinson (Eds.), *Handbook of early literacy research* (pp. 348–360). New York, NY: Guilford Press.

Nation, K., Cocksey, J., Taylor, J. S. H., & Bishop, D. V. M. (2010). A longitudinal investigation of early reading and language skills in children with poor reading comprehension. *Journal of Child Psychology and Psychiatry, 51,* 1031–1039.

National Academies of Sciences, Engineering, and Medicine. (2018). *How people learn II: Learners, contexts, and cultures*. Washington, DC: The National Academies Press.

Neuman, S. B., & Dickinson, D. (Eds.). (2001). *The handbook of early literacy research* (Vol. 1). New York, NY: Guilford Press.

Neuman, S., & Roskos, K. (1992). Literacy objects as cultural tools: Effects on children's literacy behaviors in play. *Reading Research Quarterly, 27*, 202–225. http://dx.doi.org/10.2307/747792

Neuman, S. & Roskos, K. (1997). Literacy knowledge in practice: Contexts of participation for young writers and readers. *Reading Research Quarterly, 32*(1), 10–33.

Neuman, S. B., & Roskos, K. (2007). *Nurturing knowledge: Building a foundation for school success by linking early literacy to math, science, art and social studies*. New York, NY: Scholastic.

Ninio, A., & Bruner, J. (1978). The achievement and antecedents of labelling. *Journal of Child Language, 5*, 1–15. http://dx.doi.org/10.1017/S0305000900001896

Paul, P. V., & Wang, Y. (2006). Literate thought and multiple literacies. *Theory Into Practice, 45*, 304–310. http://dx.doi.org/10.1207/s15430421tip4504_3

Pellegrini, A. D. (1984). Identifying causal elements in the thematic-fantasy play paradigm. *American Educational Research Journal, 21*, 691–701. http://dx.doi.org/10.3102/00028312021003691

Perfetti, C., & Stafura, J. (2014). Word knowledge in a theory of reading comprehension. *Scientific Studies of Reading, 18*(1), 22–37. http://dx.doi.org/10.1080/10888438.2013.827687

Perfetti, C. A. (1987). Language, speech, and print: Some asymmetries in the acquisition of literacy. In R. Horowitz & S. J. Samuels (Eds.), *Comprehending oral and written language* (pp. 355–369). New York, NY: Academic Press.

Perfetti, C. A. (2007). Reading ability: Lexical quality to comprehension. *Scientific Studies of Reading, 11*, 357–383. http://dx.doi.org/10.1080/10888430701530730

Rasmussen, E. (2018, October 19). *Screen time and kids: Insights from a new report*. Retrieved from http://www.pbs.org/parents/expert-tips-advice/2017/10/screen-time-kids-insights-new-report

Richter, A., & Courage, M. L. (2017). Comparing electronic and paper storybooks for preschoolers: Attention, engagement, and recall. *Journal of Applied Developmental Psychology, 48*, 92–102. http://dx.doi.org/10.1016/j.appdev.2017.01.002

Rideout, V. (2017). *The Common Sense census: Media use by kids age zero to eight*. San Francisco, CA: Common Sense Media.

Roskos, K. (2017). First principles of teaching reading with e-books in the primary grades. In N. Kucirkova & G. Falloon (Eds.), *Apps, technology and young learners* (pp. 27–38). New York, NY: Routledge.

Roskos, K. (2019). Play-literacy knowns and unknowns in a changing world. In P. K. Smith & J. L. Roopnarine (Eds.), *Cambridge handbook of play: Developmental and disciplinary perspectives* (pp. 528–545). Cambridge, England: Cambridge University Press.

Roskos, K., & Burstein, K. (2011). Assessment of the design efficacy of a preschool vocabulary instruction technique. *Journal of Research in Early Childhood, 25*, 268–287.

Roskos, K., & Christie, J. (2013). Gaining ground in understanding the play-literacy relationship. *American Journal of Play, 6*(1), 82–97.

Roskos, K., Tabors, P., & Lenhart, L. (2009). *Oral language and literacy in preschool* (2nd ed.). Newark, DE: International Reading Association.

Rowe, D. W. (2008). Development of writing abilities in childhood. In C. Bazerman (Ed.), *Handbook of research on writing* (pp. 401–419). New York, NY: Erlbaum.

Saltz, E., & Johnson, J. (1974). Training for thematic-fantasy play in culturally disadvantaged children: Preliminary results. *Journal of Educational Psychology, 66*, 623–630. http://dx.doi.org/10.1037/h0036930

Scarborough, H. (1998). Early identification of children at risk for reading disabilities: Phonological awareness and some promising predictors. In B. K. Shapiro, P. J. Accado, & A. J. Capute (Eds.), *Specific reading disability: A view of the spectrum* (pp. 75–120). Timonium, MD: York Press.

Segal-Drori, O., Korat, O., Shamir, A., & Klein, P. S. (2010). Reading electronic and printed books with and without adult instruction: Effects on emergent reading. *Reading and Writing, 23*, 913–930. http://dx.doi.org/10.1007/s11145-009-9182-x

Sénéchal, M., Thomas, E., & Monker, J. (1995). Individual differences in 4-year-old children's acquisition of vocabulary during storybook reading. *Journal of Educational Psychology, 87*, 218–229. http://dx.doi.org/10.1037/0022-0663.87.2.218

Silvern, S., Taylor, J., Williamson, P., Surbeck, E., & Kelley, M. (1986). Young children's story recall as a product of play, story familiarity, and adult intervention. *Merrill-Palmer Quarterly, 32*, 73–86.

Snow, C. E. (1983). Literacy and language: Relationships during preschool years. *Harvard Educational Review, 53*(2), 165–189. http://dx.doi.org/10.17763/haer.53.2.t6177w39817w2861

Spear-Swerling, L. (2004). A road map for understanding reading disability and other reading problems: Origins, prevention, and intervention. In N. J. Unrau & R. Ruddell (Eds.), *Theoretical models and processes of reading* (5th ed., pp. 517–573). Newark, DE: International Reading Association.

Takacs, Z. K., Swart, E. K., & Bus, A. G. (2015). Benefits and pitfalls of multimedia and interactive features in technology-enhanced storybooks: A meta-analysis. *Review of Educational Research, 85*, 698–739. http://dx.doi.org/10.3102/0034654314566989

Teale, W. H., & Sulzby, E. (1986). *Emergent literacy: Writing and reading.* Norwood, NJ: Ablex.

Tharp, R., & Gallimore, R. (1988). *Rousing minds to life: Teaching, learning and schooling in social context.* New York, NY: Cambridge University Press.

Thomas, V. (1987). *Winnie the witch.* Oxford, England: Oxford University Press.

Torgesen, J. K. (2002). The prevention of reading difficulties. *Journal of School Psychology, 40*, 7–26. http://dx.doi.org/10.1016/S0022-4405(01)00092-9

Vedeler, L. (1997). Dramatic play: A format for 'literate' language? *British Journal of Educational Psychology, 67*, 153–167. http://dx.doi.org/10.1111/j.2044-8279.1997.tb01234.x

Vukelich, C. (1991, December). *Learning about the functions of writing: The effects of three play interventions on children's development and knowledge about writing.* Paper presented at the meeting of the National Reading Conference, Palm Springs, CA.

Vukelich, C. (1994). Effects of play interventions on young children's reading of environmental print. *Early Childhood Research Quarterly, 9*, 153–170. http://dx.doi.org/10.1016/0885-2006(94)90003-5

Vukelich, C., Enz, B., Roskos, K., & Christie, J. (2019). *Helping young children learn language and literacy* (5th ed.). New York, NY: Pearson.

Whitehurst, G. J., & Lonigan, C. J. (1998). Child development and emergent literacy. *Child Development, 69*, 848–872. http://dx.doi.org/10.1111/j.1467-8624.1998.tb06247.x

Wiggins, G., & McTighe, J. (2005). *Understanding by design* (2nd ed.). Alexandria, VA: Association for Supervision and Curriculum Development.

Wohlwend, K. E. (2015). One screen, many fingers: Young children's collaborative literacy play with digital puppetry apps and touchscreen technologies. *Theory Into Practice, 54*, 154–162. http://dx.doi.org/10.1080/00405841.2015.1010837

Wolf, M., Bally, H., & Morris, R. (1986). Automaticity, retrieval processes, and reading: A longitudinal study in average and impaired readers. *Child Development, 57*, 988–1000. http://dx.doi.org/10.2307/1130373

5

Early Number Knowledge and Skills

Gena Nelson and Michèle M. M. Mazzocco

Adults' perceptions of children's mathematical thinking, including children's thinking about numbers, are often focused on school mathematics. This misperception leads, unfortunately, to excluding mathematics from early childhood programs and neglecting to expose children to mathematics learning opportunities before the school-age years (Ginsburg, Lee, & Boyd, 2008). Teachers, parents, and even children themselves may view preschoolers as too young to learn math. This restrictive view of mathematics as an academic subject contrasts with the fact that we use mathematics daily, beginning in infancy and throughout our lives; it further contrasts with the developmental science evidence that very young children have intuitive perceptions of number, ratio, space, and time that become more refined during the preschool years (e.g., Halberda & Feigenson, 2008).

In this chapter, we focus specifically on young children's early number knowledge and skills and on why it is essential that early childhood educators and caregivers[1] provide children with a numeracy-enriched learning environment. We avoid the term *number sense* because of the inconsistency with which the term is used across disciplines of educational psychology, cognitive science, developmental science, and mathematics education (Berch, 2005; Dehaene,

---

[1]Throughout this chapter, the term *caregivers* collectively refers to parents and other family members, child-care professionals, and others in a child caregiver role.

Preparation of this chapter was supported by NSF Grant 1644748 awarded to M. Mazzocco, and Heising-Simons Award 2018-0680 which supports the Development and Research in Early Mathematics Education (DREME) Network of which M. Mazzocco is a member.

http://dx.doi.org/10.1037/0000197-006
Healthy Development in Young Children: Evidence-Based Interventions for Early Education,
V. C. Alfonso and G. J. DuPaul (Editors)

2011), but we do attend to skills that are collectively referred to as number sense across these disciplines. We focus on children's awareness and recognition of quantity, their gradual understanding of the relations between quantities and how symbols are used to represent quantities, and their ability to use numbers and number words across a range of contexts. In this way, we demonstrate children's intuitive sense of number yet also acknowledge the complexity that children gradually overcome when acquiring number knowledge and skills. Importantly, we do not view number knowledge as something that is either present or absent but instead describe the many facets of number knowledge that emerge throughout the early years. Finally, we address the importance of individuals' perception of their own numerical abilities beginning in early childhood.

WHY FOCUS ON NUMBER SKILLS?

Math is more than number, but our focus on early number skills stems from longitudinal studies showing that children with low number knowledge at kindergarten (Jordan, Kaplan, Ramineni, & Locuniak, 2009; Mazzocco & Thompson, 2005) or first grade (Geary, Hoard, Nugent, & Bailey, 2013) continue to underperform in mathematics throughout school and that later underperformance in mathematics is linked to early low numeracy (Geary, Hoard, Nugent, & Bailey, 2012; Mazzocco, Murphy, Brown, Rinne, & Herold, 2013). In later life, mathematics achievement is associated with outcomes such as postsecondary school enrollment and completion (Lee, 2012), job earnings (Rose & Betts, 2004), and assessing health care information (Peters, Hibbard, Slovic, & Dieckmann, 2007). These links between school mathematics and later quality-of-life indicators are correlational, complex, and likely indirect, but we cannot ignore the fact that quality of life is potentially at stake when numeracy skills are neglected. Early childhood educators and caregivers play a critical role by providing children with meaningful opportunities to develop and apply numeracy skills, and they also serve as important role models for healthy dispositions toward mathematics in general. In the sections that follow, we provide readers with knowledge and instructional practices to help them have a positive impact on children's development of number concepts and skills.

NUMBER CONCEPTS IN EARLY CHILDHOOD

A preschooler was overheard explaining to a colleague of ours that he did not do math because he was "only 4." The colleague did not miss the opportunity to point out the contrary, noting, "You said you are 4 years old. You used a number word. That's math!" She then cleverly maneuvered the conversation toward a more skillful level of number knowledge—a skill that exceeds mere number word recitation by focusing on number relations—by asking,

"When you have a birthday, how old will you be then?"

"Five," the child replied.

"Five?" my colleague replied, with a feigned look of astonishment. "*You know what comes right after four! You're doing math!*"

In this section, we demonstrate that *number* is a complex concept that emerges early and becomes more sophisticated throughout early childhood. Although we acknowledge a wide range in the timing of emerging number concepts, we describe how (and roughly when) children typically develop number skills informally (without instruction, such as in the conversation in the above example) and formally. Informal and formal learning occurs across a variety of instructional settings, such as home, preschool, or child care centers, even if the informal skills are emphasized. Importantly, both types of learning opportunities can be intentional, and research indicates that formal (Jordan et al., 2009) and informal (LeFevre et al., 2009) learning opportunities are both associated with later success with school mathematics.

EARLY NONSYMBOLIC AND SYMBOLIC NUMBER SKILLS

We begin our review of number skills with early nonverbal, nonsymbolic skills such as instant and accurate recognition of small quantities and the comparison of approximate large quantities. Following a review of nonsymbolic skills, we discuss skills that demonstrate children's understanding of the connections between quantities and number words and other symbols. We also provide recommendations for parents and caregivers to build children's early nonverbal or symbolic number skills.

Early Nonsymbolic (Nonverbal) Number Skills

When do children first demonstrate numerical skills? Many adults might assume this occurs when children begin to count, but infants have an innate perception of number even before they learn to speak (Wynn, 1992). Infants can represent quantities and compare how many items are in two sets well enough to choose the more numerous set. Developmental scientists refer to these skills as *nonverbal* or *nonsymbolic* because the skills do not require use or knowledge of number words, general quantifiers such as *more*, or other symbols such as digits. For instance, infants are capable of representing very small sets of items and can reliably discriminate between them (Xu & Spelke, 2000). Ten- to 12-month-olds will reliably choose the container with the more numerous set of crackers if two containers hold one versus two, two versus three, or one versus three crackers, but these same infants will choose randomly if one of the sets of crackers exceeds three, even if one set is very small (e.g., one versus four; Feigenson, Carey, & Hauser, 2002). These findings demonstrate that very young children can represent number and that their cognitive system for representing a small exact number is constrained to sets of less than four. Young children can even carry out nonverbal addition or subtraction on these small numbers, as suggested by their surprise at mathematically impossible events. In one study, infants observed an adult carefully place two dolls behind a screen, one at a time, before removing the screen. Infants were more likely to show surprise when removal of the screen revealed one doll, compared with when two dolls were revealed (Wynn, 1992). We infer from this sort of evidence that children's expectation (i.e., that two dolls should be present) is based on their ability to add and that children can differentiate one from two, long before they acquire the words *one* and *two*. These early studies of nonverbal arithmetic (e.g., Wynn, 1992) were conducted with infants under 6 months of age!

Infants' capacity with small numbers reflects the cognitive process of *subitizing*, the instantaneous and accurate enumeration of a small quantity (e.g., children may recognize the quantity 3 on a die without counting) that occurs without counting. Subitizing is an automatic process that differs from deliberate counting (Wynn, 1990). This original use of the term *subitize* refers to an innate capacity that is observed in infants, nonhuman animals, and even nonprimates. Many cognitive scientists believe that subitizing supports the infant's innate ability to discriminate sets of one, two, or three items, does not depend on knowledge of number words or symbols, and likely underlies some of the capacities described in the previous paragraph.

Infants' nonverbal numerical skills are not, however, limited to sets of less than four. With larger numbers, infants can differentiate large approximate quantities, and their ability to differentiate the quantity of two sets improves throughout childhood (Halberda & Feigenson, 2008). Specifically, what improves are the conditions under which children reliably detect a difference in numerosities; in infancy, differences in sets are often not detectable unless the quantities being compared differ by a very large ratio, such as 2:1 (e.g., 20 vs. 10 squares). However, the ratios at which a comparison is reliably accurate diminish from infancy to early adulthood; some adults can reliably detect the larger of two sets of items that differ by a 1.1:1 ratio (20 vs. 18; Halberda, Ly, Wilmer, Naiman, & Germine, 2012). Importantly, large individual differences are seen at all ages, and in early childhood, these individual differences in nonverbal numerical comparison skills are predictive of mathematics (but not reading) scores at kindergarten (Libertus, Feigenson, & Halberda, 2011; Mazzocco, Feigenson, & Halberda, 2011).

Numerous other studies also demonstrate that young children recognize, compare, and operate on quantity even before they can count out exact sets of objects. One question that researchers continue to explore is whether these intuitive numerical capacities play a role in formal number knowledge and skills, such as counting. Educators and caregivers may question whether these findings matter. At a minimum, the findings matter because they show us that young children are numerical thinkers and provide evidence to justify the efforts early childhood practitioners take to create numeracy-enriched informal learning environments, such as play opportunities to compare stacks of blocks or bunches of flowers on a nature walk. Although early math researchers largely disagree on the relative importance of nonverbal, nonsymbolic number skills or their appropriateness as targets of learning opportunities, they generally agree that early symbolic skills are very important (e.g., De Smedt, Noël, Gilmore, & Ansari, 2013; Mazzocco & Thompson, 2005). We turn to these symbolic skills next.

Early Symbolic Number Skills

Subitizing, as we described in the previous section, refers to the immediate and accurate recognition of a very small set. As with the term *number sense*, the term *subitizing* is used inconsistently by scientists and educators. In this chapter, we use the term as originally intended, to convey the innate nonverbal ability to accurately discriminate sets of one, two, or three items without use or even knowledge of number words. As a cognitive process, subitizing is nonsymbolic and nonverbal; once we introduce number words and numerals (i.e., digits) and link these symbols to familiar arrangements of three or more items (e.g., the array of three or five dots on a die), this type of *identifying quantity* is symbolic (i.e., using verbal number words or digits) and does not engage the same basic cognitive process characteristic of subitizing. Moreover, recognizing sets that exceed three (e.g., six dots on a die) and associating them with a specific number word (e.g., *six*) may happen quickly, but it is not truly instantaneous and does not conform to other characteristic properties of subitizing. As a contrast to our use of the term *subitizing*, we refer to the learned (rather than innate) capacity to rapidly recognize and label set sizes as *fluent quantity identification*. *Fluent* here refers to a skill that is practiced and overlearned, and identification relies on use of formal symbols such as number words or digits. (We acknowledge that some scholars include these skills in their definition of subitizing.)

Like some innate number skills, number words or digits are representations of number, a key predictor of overall mathematics achievement (Schneider et al., 2018). But before children learn exact word meanings, they learn the general idea that number words refer to how many—and this concept emerges and evolves from experience. Educators and caregivers can create many opportunities for children to hear and respond to another child's or adult's use of number words, such as "Please give me one of your cookies" or "You added two more blocks to your tower." Educators and caregivers can foster children's development of early number knowledge and skills simply by providing children with more opportunities to explore their own understanding of number, without necessarily focusing on whether the child's response is exactly correct. For instance, saying "five comes after three" is true, even if four comes immediately afterward. In reply to a response such as this one, acknowledge what is accurate and build from it (e.g., "Five does come after three, because it's more than three, isn't it? When we count, we count three, four, then five!").

Recommendations for Building Early Nonverbal or Symbolic Number Skills

Even an allegedly simple task of naming a small set involves different levels of number skills (i.e., innate to learned) or knowledge (i.e., emerging knowledge or emerging fluency), and there are different ways to help children develop these skills. Children benefit from opportunities to learn the precursors to formal number skills, and we provide a few examples of such opportunities in this section. These examples represent some of the numeracy activities that are observed, to different degrees, in home environments and are associated with later mathematics (e.g., LeFevre et al., 2009). Educators and caregivers should keep in mind that these and other examples throughout the chapter may be adapted for children of varying ages and abilities.

Practice Nonsymbolic and Symbolic Numerical Skills

If subitizing is innate, is it counterintuitive to target subitizing for instruction? Should educators and caregivers attend to children who appear not to have these intuitive skills and offer opportunities to strengthen them? Most studies of preschoolers' nonsymbolic comparison skills use visual arrays of images that are carefully controlled for item size, set size, and even ratio between set sizes (e.g., Hyde, Khanum, & Spelke, 2014). Preschoolers are asked which is more, and more complex research designs are used with preverbal infants. But this experimental measure of numerical ability is not necessarily ideal for practice; studies on this approach are limited, and the findings are mixed. Instead, early childhood educators and caregivers can begin by referring to quantities in everyday scenarios, commenting on whether there are more blocks, books, crackers, or trees in one set compared with another and creating opportunities to practice counting the sets. It may be useful to consider the following points when focusing on sets during these opportunities, whether objects are real or pictured, such as in counting books (Ward, Mazzocco, Bock, & Prokes, 2017):

- Compare sets of items clearly grouped in two distinct sets. For example, it may be difficult for a child to comprehend which is more if two groups of objects overlap with each other.

- Pay attention to object sizes (Sophian, 2000). If you have eight grapes and two bananas, you might be correct in saying "there are more grapes," but the child may think there are more bananas because two bananas are more food than eight grapes!

- For beginning learners or children who are nonverbal, remember that by simply using number words and other quantifiers such as *more* when speaking to children, adults may help children acquire concepts of number and math vocabulary (e.g., Levine, Suriyakham, Rowe, Huttenlocher, & Gunderson, 2010). These are precursors to counting and comparing number words and digits.

- Support children's understanding of what number words mean. For instance, use conversational or questioning strategies in authentic learning settings (e.g., a park, zoo, car ride) with objects that are naturally available. For example, "There are birds on that bench. I see one, two, three; there are three" or "How many cups are still on the table?" (These are examples of the type of "math talk" that is associated with later math skills; Levine et al., 2010.) In these situations, however, educators and caregivers should keep in mind whether children can inhibit visual distractions (e.g., other items near or on the table).

- Young children learn the meaning of small number words more readily if adults specify what items they are referring to before specifying how many items there are. That is, saying, "See the birds on the bench. There are three" increases the chance that a child knows *three* applies to the birds, compared to saying only, "Look at the three birds on the bench" (Ramscar, Dye, Popick, & O'Donnell-McCarthy, 2011).

BRIDGING EARLY NONVERBAL SKILLS AND CONVENTIONAL MATH

The number skills discussed in this section typically develop as children have more exposure to, and interaction with, their environment when they receive mathematics instruction at school entry (Purpura & Lonigan, 2013). Number skills such as counting or understanding relations between numbers support the more complex mathematics skills of problem solving and computation. Moreover, relatively low performance on early number skills in kindergarten is associated with continued poor mathematics knowledge and skills throughout elementary school (Jordan et al., 2009; Judge & Watson, 2011; Mazzocco & Thompson, 2005). This is why early numeracy environments play an important role before school entry (e.g., LeFevre et al., 2009).

Counting

As children interact with adults, peers, and their environment, they begin to understand that counting is more than reciting words. But this shift from word reciting to understanding counting principles is gradual (Purpura, Baroody, & Lonigan, 2013). Typically, around 2 to 3 years of age, children use quantifiers, such as *more* or *some*. When they first learn words from a count sequence, the sequence may be inaccurate, and the number words may be spoken without meaning. Children may count or even label objects without an understanding that the function of counting is to inform us of how many (Clements & Sarama, 2004). Caregivers should expect that errors will occur and recognize that these errors may nevertheless reflect partial understanding (Johnson, Turrou, McMillan, Raygoza, & Franke, 2019); for example, a child may understand that *four* refers to how many, even without knowledge of exactly how many. Because understanding the purpose of counting is foundational for formal math (Geary et al., 2012), it is important that preschoolers have many opportunities to acquire the five principles of counting (Gelman & Gallistel, 1978). Initially, children count without adherence to these principles, so watching children's counting behavior helps educators and caregivers recognize individual children's level of number understanding.

- One-to-one correspondence: Children show an understanding of this principle when they assign one, and only one, counting word to each item in a set. If a child is presented with six blocks and asked to count the blocks, the child will tap/point to and count each and every block once, "one, two, three, four, five, six," without skipping or double counting any of the blocks.

• Stable order: Children who know that number words or symbols must be used in the same order when counting understand the stable-order principle. A child might recite the number words in the correct order when counting a set of items without correctly applying one-to-one correspondence, which could lead to over- or undercounting.

• Cardinality: Children who understand the cardinal number principle will understand that the last number in the counting sequence represents the total number of objects in the set. If a child who counts five toy cars is then asked, "How many cars do you have?" the child without an understanding of cardinality will count the set of cars all over again. The child who knows the cardinal principle will immediately reply, "Five." However, if a child recounts, it is important to determine whether the child has misunderstood your prompt or misinterpreted your question "So how many are there?" as a signal to count all over. An alternative assessment is to cover the items counted before asking, "So how many are there?" (Clements & Sarama, 2004).

• Order irrelevance: Children who have developed the order-irrelevance principle understand that objects themselves can be counted in any order (e.g., left to right, right to left, top to bottom, or in no particular order) with no effect on the total.

• Abstraction: Children demonstrate the abstraction principle by applying the previously described principles to a set of uncommon items or nontangible items. Children who understand abstraction may count the different types of food on their dinner plate (i.e., not all food is the same, but it can still be counted) or things they cannot see or physically manipulate, such as the number of knocks they hear at the door.

Long before children master these counting principles, they are likely to accurately recite the count sequence from one to 10, or even higher, exhibiting the ability to produce a memorized sequence of numbers. However, if you ask a child to count on from five and the child cannot count without starting from one (which is common among preschoolers), this reflects an immature understanding of the number line or of number relations. Knowledge of the verbal counting sequence typically improves throughout the preschool years, when children accurately count a small set of objects and gradually determine that the number words spoken during counting represent how many objects are in the set. This understanding of cardinality may not occur until 4 to 5 years of age. This knowledge about counting is an important precursor to understanding number relations (which we address in the next section), so providing ample opportunities to practice counting is warranted.

Recommendations for Practicing Counting Skills

Educators and caregivers can encourage the development of counting skills in a variety of ways, including the following:

- Recognize that counting errors may still reveal what children currently know about number. Pay attention! A child might know that number words mean how many without knowing what exact quantity the number word means.

- Provide opportunities to count and label small sets of tangible objects; keep in mind that young children may need the one-to-one counting process modeled before counting activities and that children understand the concept of *one* before they understand the concept of *two*, which they typically understand before they grasp the concept of *three* (e.g., Wagner, Chu, & Barner, 2018).

- Provide opportunities to work with tangible objects (e.g., blocks) or pictures (e.g., animals on a page of a book) that can easily and physically be tracked—this supports one-to-one correspondence and cardinality (Alibali & DiRusso, 1999).

- When children lack one-to-one correspondence and miscount, help them self-regulate purposeful counting. Intentionally create and use preconstructed frames (e.g., an egg carton for counting small objects) or use tongs to help children slow down and attend to only one item per count word.

- As children learn numbers larger than five, access to four, five, and 10 frames may help organize their counting and reduce the cognitive demand of that counting may impose on many beginning learners (McGuire, Kinzie, & Berch, 2012). Educators and caregivers should model how to use the frames, putting only one object per square of the frame. Note that some board games are a playful use of 10 frames, and the research on home numeracy environments supports using board games to increase children's mathematics knowledge and skills (Cheung & McBride, 2017; Ramani & Scalise, 2020).

- Incorporate meaningful counting activities throughout the day, including time that is not regularly scheduled for math (e.g., lunch, circle time, literacy block, lining up at transition time) to practice counting and labeling objects with number words to determine the total number of items. For example, ask children to count the number of crackers on their lunch plate or create a graph that shows the number of children who selected milk versus juice for a snack. These opportunities allow for natural discussions about math to occur between children from simple adult prompts, such as "With your table partners, decide who has the most crackers." Use calendar time to talk about numbers; however, be sure to incorporate number activities during other times as well, especially because the calendar does not represent the base-10 system and can confuse young counters.

- Educators and caregivers can incorporate numeracy activities during book reading. Children can count, add, subtract, and compare numbers in many books. Books also provide opportunities to refer to numbers' ordinal properties, such as what happened first, next, and last or first, second, and third. Research also indicates that reading books with a focus on number concepts promotes mathematics understanding in both formal and informal learning environments (Hendrix, Hojnoski, & Missall, 2019).

- When children understand that a number word always refers to the same quantity (that *eight* always refers to eight things), they can reliably map number words to those quantities. Provide children with opportunities to map numbers to sets and become fluent with quantity identification. On paper plates, place patterns of dots such as two rows of five dots or three rows of three dots and ask, "How many dots?" When children respond, encourage them to describe their grouping strategies and how they know the quantity is three, five, six, and so on. Not only do these activities help children to gradually associate specific labels (i.e., number words) with specific quantities, but for children who have not yet learned number words, doing these activities with very small set sizes (e.g., one, two, and three) may support their understanding of the general principle that number words refer to specific quantities. This helps children gradually make sense of the number words they hear daily and link their intuitive sense of quantity to formal number words (Van de Walle, Karp, & Bay-Williams, 2013).

- Once children demonstrate mastery of basic counting skills, they may practice more complex counting skills that develop into early elementary school, such as counting on and skip counting. Young children may need to continue to use tangible items for counting on and skip counting, but educators and caregivers can gradually remove those tools so that children become automatic in their counting.

NUMBER RELATIONS

Number relations refers to knowledge of how two or more numerals or sets are connected and related to each other and may also refer to the association between numbers on the mental or a physical number line (National Research Council [NRC], 2009; Purpura & Lonigan, 2013). In other words, "numbers do not exist in isolation" (NRC, 2009, p. 30). Knowledge that numbers are part of a coherent system helps children master place value and can support understanding of equality. By the end of kindergarten, children are expected to identify which number or set is greater than, less than, or the same as another number or set (National Governors Association Center for Best Practices and Council of Chief State School Officers [NGA & CCSSO], 2010). Older children who cannot explain why two numbers that are added are the same as the sum (e.g., explaining why two plus two is the same as four) exhibit poor understanding of number relations, even if they can accurately retrieve basic facts from memory.

Recommendations for Teaching Number Relations

Following are a few suggestions for ways educators and caregivers can integrate practicing number relations into daily activities:

- While on a walk, at the park, in the grocery store, or in the car or bus, ask children to identify objects in their environment that are greater than or less than a given quantity. Educators and caregivers might say to children, "I see bicycles on the street. I see three bicycles over there, and one more bicycle over here; one more than three is four." At the grocery store, parents might say to children, "There are two boxes of cereal in the cart, but we need to buy four boxes of cereal. How many more boxes do we need to add to the cart to have four?" Similar questions can be applied in any setting with any number or type of objects.

- Extend children's thinking by asking questions such as "How do you know there are more red flowers than yellow flowers in the garden?" and "How might you show me that there are fewer carrots on your plate compared with my plate?" or "How do you know there are four?"

- Have children predict "what comes next" or "what came first" or who is older (e.g., the 3- or 4-year-old) and how much older.

- Play linear board games to help young children develop an understanding of the number line. You can create the board games and adjust the range of numbers included on the board based on children's current level of performance. For detailed instruction on how to create a research-based and effective number line board game (Siegler & Ramani, 2009), see https://www.parentingscience.com/preschool-math-games.html.

Ordinality

Numbers do not always specify how many. *Ordinality* refers to ordinal properties of numbers, which concern a position in a sequence. For instance, home addresses have an ordinal value rather than a cardinal value. A house at 10 Maple Drive in not necessarily larger than a house at 5 Maple Drive, but we know something about the relative position of these homes based on this ordinal sequence of street addresses. Children use ordinal values when describing the first or second person in line or being in the last row or being the third person at bat during a game. All of these uses of number words pertain to sequences or orders. Ordinal number skill requires quantification (e.g., the quantity 1 is related to the ordinal position first) and comparison (e.g., the second person in a grocery line is closer to the checkout than is the fourth person in line) in ways that differ from how traditional counting and comparison tasks are presented. Understanding how many or how much does not automatically translate to understanding in what order, with an understanding of ordinality usually developing after an understanding of cardinality

(Lyons & Beilock, 2013). By the end of kindergarten, children are expected to understand, compare, and order ordinal numbers (National Council of Teachers of Mathematics [NCTM], 2006), although the research demonstrates that ordinality skills do not fully mature in some children until after first grade (Lyons, Price, Vaessen, Blomert, & Ansari, 2014). Skill with understanding ordinal numbers in the beginning of kindergarten has been linked with broad mathematics achievement at the end of kindergarten (Methe, Hintze, & Floyd, 2008).

Recommendations for Enhancing Understanding of Ordinality

Because using and practicing ordinality may differ compared with traditional counting activities, it is important that educators and caregivers provide children with explicit practice opportunities. Educators and caregivers can refer to ordinal numbers during everyday routines, such as when lining up or cooking; the following are a few examples:

- Use ordinal numbers when describing situations and asking children questions so that children can make connections between ordinal numbers and cardinal numbers, such as "Which car is first in line at the stoplight?" or "How do you know that the green car is second in line?"

- Create opportunities for children to demonstrate their understanding of ordinal numbers such as creating patterns with colored blocks. Provide instructions such as "The first block in the pattern is blue" and "The next block in the pattern is purple." To extend, ask children questions after the pattern is built such as "Which block in the pattern is green—the second block or the third block?"

- Recognize that ordinality is not limited to consecutive numbers. The values three, five, and eight are in order from smallest to biggest, even though they are not the right counting sequence. This concept can be confusing for young children and not mastered by some children until about 8 years of age (e.g., Lyons et al., 2014).

COMPOSING AND DECOMPOSING NUMBERS

Before children are taught how to add and subtract formally with abstract symbols (e.g., $2 + 3 = 5$), they first learn and explore how numbers are put together (i.e., composed) and taken apart (i.e., decomposed). As we discussed, infants have skills in this area, but not symbolically. When children understand that numbers can be represented as part–whole relations, they understand that the quantity six, for example, can be deconstructed into two sets of three, or sets of five and one, and so on. According to national standards, children are expected to compose and decompose numbers up to 10 and record their work with drawings or equations by the end of kindergarten (NGA & CCSSO, 2010). First graders with stronger composing and decomposing skills perform significantly better on measures of broad mathematics later in elementary school compared with children who did not perform well with composing and decomposing in first grade (Geary, Bailey, & Hoard, 2009; Kiss, Nelson, & Christ, 2019), and children with persistent mathematics difficulties continue to perform poorly on decomposition skills even at sixth grade (Mazzocco & Hanich, 2010). Thus, for children to master other mathematics skills such as computation later on, it is essential that they develop strong number relations knowledge, such as understanding how to compose and decompose numbers.

Recommendations for Introducing Composing and Decomposing

Below is an example of how to introduce and encourage the understanding of part–part–whole relationships with developing composing and decomposing skills. The goal of the activity is for children to practice making combinations that comprise a number, such as five or 10.

1. Provide children with sets of objects such as blocks, counting chips, or beans or small toys children play with such as plastic building bricks.

2. Model the activity for children. Say, "We are going to practice making groups of five with these blocks. Here's one way I can make five." (Point to each block while counting.) "One, two, three, four blocks. I have four blocks. How many more blocks do I need to make five?" Allow children to respond and provide explicit feedback such as "Yes, we need one more block because five is one more than four" or "Three more blocks might be too many. Let's try and see what happens when we add four blocks and three blocks."

3. For children who are struggling or are beginning learners, consider using five frames and 10 frames. Educators and parents can create five and 10 frames on handheld whiteboards or scratch paper (see Figure 5.1). For example, using a five frame, you may fill two frames with a counting chip and ask, "How many more chips do I need to make the number five? Let's count and see how many more chips we need to make five." Then, you may provide the child with feedback such as "Yes, two chips and three chips is the same as five chips!"

FIGURE 5.1. Example of a Five Frame

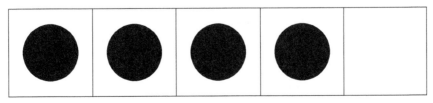

This example of a five frame may be filled with any counters, such as counting chips, rocks, or bottle caps. This frame can easily be drawn on a whiteboard or piece of paper so that children may fill the frame with objects and track their counting.

4. If a child creates an incorrect model (e.g., adds one block instead of two blocks), discuss what other number the model works for and how to change the model to work for the target number. If the child is correct, use explicit feedback such as "Yes, three and two more is the same as five" instead of only nonspecific feedback such as "Good job."

5. To make the task more challenging, educators and caregivers can ask children to create models of the same number (e.g., five) using different combinations of objects. For example, a child may use two different colors of blocks to make a group of five (three green, two blue). An educator or caregiver can expand on this activity by asking, "What is another way you can make a group of five?" or "Show me how to make a group of five with one green block and some yellow blocks." Educators and caregivers can also ask children to create a story or a sentence to go along with their models. Model for the child, "Four green chips and one yellow chip is the same as five chips." This extension also allows educators and caregivers to measure informally whether the child understands the part–part–whole relationship.

PLACE VALUE

All numbers in our counting system, regardless of their value, are created using only 10 digits (0, 1, 2, 3, 4, 5, 6, 7, 8, 9). This system is often referred to as the base-10 counting system because it uses 10 unique digits that are grouped repeatedly by 10 to make subsequent groups of numbers (NRC, 2009). We need only 10 digits to represent all numbers in a counting sequence because of *place value*, which refers to understanding that the value of an individual digit in a multidigit number depends on its position (i.e., place) within the respective number. Conceptual understanding of place value is essential for developing strong computational skills in childhood (Dietrich, Huber, Dackermann, Moeller, & Fischer, 2016), and among adults, it supports interpreting, using, and manipulating multidigit numbers in everyday occurrences (e.g., estimating grocery costs). According to recommendations from the NCTM, children should develop a solid understanding of place value by the end of second grade (NCTM, 2006).

Place-value understanding requires an integration of new and sometimes difficult-to-construct concepts of grouping by 10s (the base-10 concept) with procedural knowledge of how groups are recorded in our place-value scheme, how numbers are written, and how they are spoken. Importantly, learners must understand the word *grouping* (Van de Walle et al., 2013, p. 193).

Despite these recommendations, as many as 27% of second graders continue to have difficulty understanding place-value concepts (Gervasoni & Sullivan, 2007). Moreover, children at risk for mathematical learning difficulties may develop an understanding of the place-value system at a slower rate compared with typically developing children (Landerl, 2013), and linking verbal number words (e.g., twenty-seven) with the standardized approach for representing digits according to place value (e.g., reading "27") is not as simple as repeating the digit names from left to right as "two seven." Children who show persistent place-value difficulties through third grade are more likely to underperform on paper-and-pencil mathematics calculations at eighth grade and to make atypical calculation errors (Mazzocco et al., 2013). Because many children experience difficulty with place value, it is essential that educators and caregivers support children's understanding of the concept.

Recommendations for Teaching and Practicing Place Value

Children can practice grouping and place-value skills long before conceptual understanding of place value is required for efficient and accurate multidigit computation. Below are a few suggestions:

- Practice grouping objects into sets of 10. For example, at home, parents can prompt children to group objects such as blocks, small toy cars, coins, and books into sets of 10. By grouping items into sets of 10, children will gain an understanding of number combinations that sum to 10 even without the use of formal notation (e.g., 8 + 2 = 10).

- Once children can fluently identify number combinations that add to 10 (an instructional goal for most children in kindergarten), ask them to decompose numbers 11 to 19 into tens and ones (e.g., one ten and three ones makes 13). Children should fluently decompose numbers 11 to 19 in this way by the end of kindergarten (NGA & CCSSO, 2010).

- For children in kindergarten who need a challenge, allow them to count large quantities of objects and track groups of tens and ones. For example, place a large bowl of lima beans, paper clips, or buttons in front of a group of children and first ask them to estimate how many are in the bowl. Then, discuss with them why grouping the objects into groups of 10 can help them keep track and accurately count the total number of objects. Have children count the objects, placing each group of 10 lima beans into a different cup. Once children are finished grouping the lima beans, discuss how many groups of 10 and how many ones there are in total. Even if children are not able to accurately count to larger numbers such as 76, educators and caregivers can still discuss with children the number of groups of 10 and the number of remaining ones.

- When a child counts to the end of a decade, such as ". . . 37, 38, 39," and pauses, instead of answering "What comes next?" with "40," the adult can model, "Hmmm, what comes after three? Four! So, after 39 comes 40." This labeling helps children understand the structure of the base-10 system.

Many of these number concepts and skills may be learned in formal learning settings, but as we demonstrated in our examples throughout the chapter, educators and caregivers may also promote healthy numeracy learning environments. The skills described in this chapter lay the foundation for success with mathematics later in life, and early childhood educators and caregivers may access a variety of resources (see Exhibit 5.1) and instructional strategies to meet the needs of children who are at any learning stage.

WHO IS A MATH PERSON?

We have emphasized early number skills that we expect all young children to acquire provided they have numeracy-enriched learning environments. In addition to the benefits of opportunities to learn about number (and math in general), children benefit from developing a positive sense of themselves as competent numerical thinkers. Have you ever heard someone claim to be bad at math, to never use math, or to find math boring or too hard? Such claims reflect negative dispositions toward math, whereas positive dispositions reflect a sense of self as competent and math as a useful set of skills and knowledge that can be achieved with effort (Mathematics Learning Study Committee, Center for Education, Division of Behavioral and Social Sciences and Education,

---

EXHIBIT 5.1

Resources for Educators and Caregivers

Following are sample resources for early childhood educators and caregivers that support efforts to promote healthy numeracy environments:

- Development and Research in Early Math Education (https://dreme.stanford.edu). This network-created website focuses on resources related to early math learning. It includes a blog that focuses on topics related to early math, extending beyond only number skills (e.g., measurement, spatial reasoning), as well as specific information for families and family support professionals (https://familymath.stanford.edu).

- Institute of Education Sciences and What Works Clearinghouse. These organizations publish practice guides for educators working with children, including children with disabilities, in content areas such as math (see *Teaching Math to Young Children* [Frye et al., 2013]) literacy, science, and behavior: https://ies.ed.gov/ncee/wwc/PracticeGuides

- National Association for the Education of Young Children (NAEYC; https://www.naeyc.org). The NAEYC is a national organization with the mission of connecting practice, policy, and research. State chapters of the organization often provide training and workshops for educators and parents on a variety of topics.

- National Research Council (NRC). The NRC provides a free downloadable report of a summary of research on early childhood math learning. The report highlights recommendations for teaching early childhood math learning broadly: https://www.nap.edu/catalog/12519/mathematics-learning-in-early-childhood-paths-toward-excellence-and-equity

- Erikson Institute (https://www.erikson.edu) Early Math Collaborative. This organization provides professional development and continuing education opportunities for early childhood educators as well as updates related to research and policy.

- The Division for Early Childhood of the Council for Exceptional Children (https://www.dec-sped.org). This organization has information on current policy and initiatives and holds regional institutes focused on early childhood education, particularly related to disability.

NRC, 2001). Developing a positive math disposition is an important compo-
nent to building mathematics success (Gunderson, Park, Maloney, Beilock, &
Levine, 2018; Mathematics Learning Study Committee, Center for Education,
Division of Behavioral and Social Sciences and Education, NRC, 2001; Thomaes,
Tjaarda, Brummelman, & Sedikides, 2019). Educators and caregivers can help
children build a positive disposition toward mathematics in the following ways:

- Model your own positive disposition even if this means building one yourself!

- Avoid negative comments about math, such as stating you are bad at math
  or that math is too hard, unnecessary, or only for certain people.

- Be a math detective—find the math in what you are already doing, build
  on it, and help children discover that math is useful, fun, and achiev-
  able with effort; part of being a math detective is recognizing the diverse
  mathematical thinking of the children you are with.

CONSIDERATIONS FOR YOUNG CHILDREN AT RISK
FOR MATHEMATICAL LEARNING DIFFICULTIES

Throughout this chapter, we recommend various instructional practices that
educators and caregivers can use to promote healthy numeracy environments for young children. The aforementioned instructional practices are
appropriate to use with any child, but in this section of the chapter, we focus
on children who are at risk for mathematical learning difficulties.

Because there are many reasons why math may be difficult for some individuals (Murphy, Mazzocco, Hanich, & Early, 2007), we avoid a single description of children with math difficulties. Math difficulties may be tied specifically
to difficulties with number (e.g., Berch, 2005) related to instructional opportunities or lack thereof, characteristics of a child's numerical thinking, or a combination of child and instructional characteristics (Bodovski & Farkas, 2007;
Connor et al., 2018; Geary, 2013). Educators and caregivers may benefit from
a basic understanding of the types of difficulties children may experience with
learning number knowledge and skills, so we provide a brief overview of these
difficulties and offer recommendations for instructional practices for children
who may be at risk for low number knowledge at kindergarten to second grade.

The Trouble With Numbers

Throughout this chapter, we referenced findings that kindergartners and first
graders with low number knowledge are more likely to experience persistent
math difficulties throughout their school years. Thus, it is important to focus
on the factors that may underlie a child's low number knowledge at kindergarten or soon after.

First and foremost, young children who have weak number knowledge
relative to their peers may have lacked adequate learning opportunities. They
may have arrived in kindergarten without understanding the purpose of

counting, the meaning of number words, how numbers are related to each other, and the reasons why numbers are so useful. Compared with literacy-enriched learning opportunities, preschool children in general experience fewer numeracy-enriched learning opportunities in home (Skwarchuk, 2009) and prekindergarten (Farran, Meador, Christopher, Nesbitt, & Bilbrey, 2017) settings, as reviewed by Jordan and Levine (2009).

Second, but less frequently, young children with a weak number knowledge may have *dyscalculia*, a specific learning disability characterized by a lack of an intuitive understanding of number, inefficient number processing, difficulty learning basic facts and procedures for solving problems, and chronic low achievement in mathematics (Butterworth, 2011). Dyscalculia occurs in about 5% of the population (e.g., Shalev, Auerbach, Manor, & Gross-Tsur, 2000), but because math difficulties are more prevalent than dyscalculia, dyscalculia is not a primary cause of lack of kindergarten readiness. Dyscalculia is not typically diagnosed in early childhood, but children with weak early number knowledge may benefit from the numeracy-enriched opportunities described in this chapter regardless of whether that weakness is due to lack of opportunity or weak innate number skills. Indeed, numeracy-enriched learning environments may benefit all young children.

Finally, children's difficulty with number or mathematics may be secondary to difficulties in other areas, such as underdeveloped executive function or visuospatial skills. We next address each of these influences on the development of early number skills.

Number Skills and Executive Function Skills

Executive function (EF) *skills* are deliberate, goal-oriented skills such as focused attention, cognitive flexibility, and working memory (see Chapters 3 and 6, this volume). Working memory is the mental workspace where we manage and organize incoming information, a real-time mechanism that supports information processing that is subject to a limited capacity. There are developmental and individual differences in how much information a person can attend to, process, and manipulate mentally at one time in working memory. These EF skills are critical in math because they allow students to keep track of their work (e.g., count without error), carry out and track multistep problems, mentally manipulate or compare numbers (e.g., with decomposition), and think flexibly about approaches to solutions.

Without strong EF skills, children may struggle with math, including number skills. They might use inefficient strategies, such as continuing to count with their fingers at a point when fact retrieval has been mastered by most of their peers. (However, finger counting is appropriate in very early childhood.) Finger counting beyond an appropriate age or difficulty following multiple steps in mathematics problems may reflect EF difficulties, such as difficulty holding information from the first step to the next step (Geary, 2004).

Not surprisingly, mathematics achievement and EF scores are positively correlated (Mazzocco & Kover, 2007). Weak EF skills may manifest as poor mathematics skills even among children who have a solid understanding of number concepts and fluent number skills performance. Perhaps, however, a child with very good EF skills and poor number skills will also use finger counting or have difficulty with multiple steps not because of poor EF skills per se but because of the little cognitive energy remaining after exerting a great deal of effort thinking about the number relations. For example, when children lack fluency with number skills, their reliance on effortful calculation over retrieval overtaxes their working memory (e.g., as reviewed by Raghubar, Barnes, & Hecht, 2010). Educators and caregivers can modify math activities to strengthen math and EF skills by including turn-taking, asking children to reflect on their process or solution, or asking children to identify multiple solution strategies for the same problem (Joswick, Clements, Sarama, Banse, & Day-Hess, 2019).

Visuospatial Skills

Mathematical information is often visual, particularly with regard to under-standing geometry and measurement. What does this have to do with number? Number and space concepts are related to each other; even a number line represents quantity not only by ordinal position but also by spatial extent—how far down the number line a digit is represented. Visuospatial processes may support using algorithms in calculations and using representations to solve word problems; just as number knowledge and skills develop from basic number recognition to being able to compose and decompose numbers, children gradually learn to visually represent, compose/decompose, and transpose and mentally rotate shapes—all skills with a strong visual problem-solving component (Sarama & Clements, 2009). Opportunities to engage in such skills, beginning with shape sorters and puzzles, help children navigate and represent the space in their environment (Verdine, Golinkoff, Hirsh-Pasek, & Newcombe, 2014).

EVIDENCE-BASED PRACTICES FOR CHILDREN AT RISK FOR MATH LEARNING DIFFICULTIES

The practices described in this section of the chapter may be used with any child; however, research indicates that these practices are particularly useful for children at risk for math learning difficulties (as reviewed by Gersten et al., 2009).

Use Explicit and Systematic Instruction

Explicit and systematic instruction includes several components (Archer & Hughes, 2011), but each component does not need to be present in every activity. Components that may be relevant in early childhood include but are not limited to these steps:

- Break down concepts into smaller, more manageable, parts.
- Model and demonstrate concepts and activities.
- Use a variety of clear examples, and relevant and appropriate nonexamples to introduce or practice a skill or concept.

- Provide feedback that is corrective and specific and that also addresses what is accurate about the child's solution or strategy.

Provide Opportunities to Develop Fluency

When children develop fluency, they are able to recall or produce information quickly and accurately to perform a task. Many children, especially children at risk for developing learning difficulties, benefit from brief but regular bursts of fluency-building practice, such as approximately 10 minutes of daily activities, including speeded practice, once children reach about first grade (Fuchs et al., 2013). Although fluency is typically thought of as automatic retrieval of basic facts, it is important for other number combination or even comparison skills, too. For young children, fluency-building activities may include counting small sets of objects, discerning which group of objects is more or less, and accurately reciting the names of numerals. Fluency building can be incorporated with games or technology.

Use Multiple Representations

Representations are tools for illustrating and communicating about ideas, strategies, and solutions (Gersten et al., 2009). Eventually, children should understand and apply different representations of the same concept (e.g., that "•••" and "3" represent the same concept). Some children who are at risk of math learning difficulties have a weak understanding of the relations between abstract symbols (e.g., numerals) and concrete (e.g., blocks) or pictorial (e.g., number lines, simple drawings) representations. Educators and caregivers may use concrete and visual representations to scaffold the learning of new skills until children are ready to use abstract symbols. In order to encourage children to eventually use multiple mathematical representations, educators and caregivers can model for children how to use different representations, such as blocks, number spaces on a board game, and numerals.

Increase Opportunities for Practice

Educators and caregivers should build in time and meaningful opportunities for extra practice because children with or at risk for math learning difficulties may require many more practice opportunities to master the same skill compared with typically developing peers (Gersten et al., 2008). In a preschool setting, this may mean that educators align practice opportunities for mathematics skills with other activities, such as during literacy or free-play activities. For example, if a child is interested in bugs, an educator could develop an activity in which the child records information in a table with tallies about how many bugs are on each page of the book. From there, partner activities could be developed and modeled for children to help them answer questions such as "Which page of the book has the most bugs? The least number of bugs? Did any page of the book have more than five bugs? If so, how many pages?" The goal is to avoid assuming that a child's success with one skill will readily persist, and to instead provide children with repeated opportunities to strengthen their emerging knowledge and skills.

CONCLUSION

In this chapter, we summarized research on the development of number knowledge and skills and provided practical recommendations for educators and caregivers in early childhood settings to promote healthy numeracy learning environments in early childhood. We conveyed the message that not all children learn at the same rate and that although the development of number knowledge and skills occurs gradually, it begins in infancy. We emphasized that all children deserve a numeracy-enriched environment and illustrated how numeracy-enriched environments can be embedded in existing routines at home and in preschool settings. Educators and caregivers can use the instructional strategies and suggested resources provided in this chapter to promote an understanding of number knowledge and skills for all learners and promote positive dispositions toward mathematics not only in the children they support but also in themselves.

REFERENCES

Alibali, M. W., & DiRusso, A. A. (1999). The function of gesture in learning to count: More than keeping track. *Cognitive Development, 14,* 37–56. http://dx.doi.org/10.1016/S0885-2014(99)80017-3

Archer, A. L., & Hughes, C. A. (2011). Exploring the foundations of explicit instruction. In A. L. Archer & C. A. Hughes (Eds.), *Explicit instruction: Effective and efficient teaching* (pp. 1–22). New York, NY: Guilford Press.

Berch, D. B. (2005). Making sense of number sense: Implications for children with mathematical disabilities. *Journal of Learning Disabilities, 38,* 333–339. http://dx.doi.org/10.1177/00222194050380040901

Bodovski, K., & Farkas, G. (2007). Mathematics growth in early elementary school: The roles of beginning knowledge, student engagement, and instruction. *The Elementary School Journal, 108,* 115–130. http://dx.doi.org/10.1086/525550

Butterworth, B. (2011). Foundational numerical capacities and the origins of dyscalculia. *Space, Time and Number in the Brain, 14,* 249–265. http://dx.doi.org/10.1016/B978-0-12-385948-8.00016-5

Cheung, S. K., & McBride, C. (2017). Effectiveness of parent–child number board game playing in promoting Chinese kindergarteners' numeracy skills and mathematics interest. *Early Education and Development, 28,* 572–589. http://dx.doi.org/10.1080/10409289.2016.1258932

Clements, D. H., & Sarama, J. (2004). Learning trajectories in mathematics education. *Mathematical Thinking and Learning, 6,* 81–89. http://dx.doi.org/10.1207/s15327833mtl0602_1

Connor, C. M., Mazzocco, M. M. M., Kurz, T., Crowe, E. C., Tighe, E. L., Wood, T. S., & Morrison, F. J. (2018). Using assessment to individualize early mathematics instruction. *Journal of School Psychology, 66,* 97–113. http://dx.doi.org/10.1016/j.jsp.2017.04.005

Dehaene, S. (2011). *The number sense: How the mind creates mathematics.* New York, NY: Oxford University Press.

De Smedt, B., Noël, M. P., Gilmore, C., & Ansari, D. (2013). How do symbolic and non-symbolic numerical magnitude processing skills relate to individual differences in children's mathematical skills? A review of evidence from brain and behavior. *Trends in Neuroscience and Education, 2,* 48–55. http://dx.doi.org/10.1016/j.tine.2013.06.001

Dietrich, J. F., Huber, S., Dackermann, T., Moeller, K., & Fischer, U. (2016). Place-value understanding in number line estimation predicts future arithmetic performance. *British Journal of Developmental Psychology, 34,* 502–517. http://dx.doi.org/10.1111/bjdp.12146

Farran, D. C., Meador, D., Christopher, C., Nesbitt, K. T., & Bilbrey, L. E. (2017). Data-driven improvement in prekindergarten classrooms: Report from a partnership in an urban district. *Child Development, 88,* 1466–1479.

Feigenson, L., Carey, S., & Hauser, M. (2002). The representations underlying infants' choice of more: Object files versus analog magnitudes. *Psychological Science, 13,* 150–156. http://dx.doi.org/10.1111/1467-9280.00427

Frye, D., Baroody, A. J., Burchinal, M., Carver, S. M., Jordan, N. C., & McDowell, J. (2013). *Teaching math to young children: A practice guide* (NCEE 2014-4005). Washington, DC: National Center for Education Evaluation and Regional Assistance, Institute of Education Sciences, U.S. Department of Education. Retrieved from https://ies.ed.gov/ncee/wwc/PracticeGuide/18

Fuchs, L. S., Geary, D. C., Compton, D. L., Fuchs, D., Schatschneider, C., Hamlett, C. L., . . . Changas, P. (2013). Effects of first-grade number knowledge tutoring with contrasting forms of practice. *Journal of Educational Psychology, 105,* 58–77. http://dx.doi.org/10.1037/a0030127

Geary, D. C. (2004). Mathematics and learning disabilities. *Journal of Learning Disabilities, 37,* 4–15. http://dx.doi.org/10.1177/00222194040370010201

Geary, D. C. (2013). Early foundations for mathematics learning and their relations to learning disabilities. *Current Directions in Psychological Science, 22,* 23–27. http://dx.doi.org/10.1177/0963721412469398

Geary, D. C., Bailey, D. H., & Hoard, M. K. (2009). Predicting mathematical achievement and mathematical learning disability with a simple screening tool: The number sets test. *Journal of Psychoeducational Assessment, 27,* 265–279. http://dx.doi.org/10.1177/0734282908330592

Geary, D. C., Hoard, M. K., Nugent, L., & Bailey, D. H. (2012). Mathematical cognition deficits in children with learning disabilities and persistent low achievement: A five-year prospective study. *Journal of Educational Psychology, 104,* 206–223. http://dx.doi.org/10.1037/a0025398

Geary, D. C., Hoard, M. K., Nugent, L., & Bailey, D. H. (2013). Adolescents' functional numeracy is predicted by their school entry number system knowledge. *PLoS ONE, 8*(1), e54651. http://dx.doi.org/10.1371/journal.pone.0054651

Gelman, R., & Gallistel, C. R. (1978). *The child's understanding of number.* Cambridge, MA: Harvard University Press.

Gersten, R., Beckmann, S., Clarke, B., Foegen, A., Marsh, L., Star, J. R., & Witzel, B. (2009). *Assisting students struggling with mathematics: Response to intervention (RTI) for elementary and middle schools* (NCEE 2009-4060). Washington, DC: National Center for Education Evaluation and Regional Assistance, Institute of Education Sciences, U.S. Department of Education. Retrieved from https://eric.ed.gov/?id=ED504995

Gersten, R., Compton, D., Connor, C. M., Dimino, J., Santoro, L., Linan-Thompson, S., & Tilly, W. D. (2008). *Assisting students struggling with reading: Response to intervention and multi-tier intervention for reading in the primary grades. A practice guide* (NCEE 2009-4045). Washington, DC: National Center for Education Evaluation and Regional Assistance, Institute of Education Sciences, U.S. Department of Education. Retrieved from https://ies.ed.gov/ncee/wwc/PracticeGuide/3

Gervasoni, A., & Sullivan, P. (2007). Assessing and teaching children who have difficulty learning arithmetic. *Educational and Child Psychology, 24,* 40–53.

Ginsburg, H., Lee, J., & Boyd, J. (2008). Mathematics education for young children: What it is and how to promote it. *Society for Research in Child Development Social Policy Report, 22*(1), 1–24. http://dx.doi.org/10.1002/j.2379-3988.2008.tb00054.x

Gunderson, E. A., Park, D., Maloney, E. A., Beilock, S. L., & Levine, S. C. (2018). Reciprocal relations among motivational frameworks, math anxiety, and math achievement in early elementary school. *Journal of Cognition and Development, 19,* 21–46. http://dx.doi.org/10.1080/15248372.2017.1421538

Halberda, J., & Feigenson, L. (2008). Developmental change in the acuity of the "Number Sense": The Approximate Number System in 3-, 4-, 5-, and 6-year-olds and adults. *Developmental Psychology, 44,* 1457–1465. http://dx.doi.org/10.1037/a0012682

Halberda, J., Ly, R., Wilmer, J. B., Naiman, D. Q., & Germine, L. (2012). Number sense across the lifespan as revealed by a massive Internet-based sample. *Proceedings of the National Academy of Sciences of the United States of America, 109,* 11116–11120. http://dx.doi.org/10.1073/pnas.1200196109

Hendrix, N. M., Hojnoski, R. L., & Missall, K. N. (2019). Shared book reading to promote math talk in parent–child dyads in low-income families. *Topics in Early Childhood Special Education, 39,* 45–55. http://dx.doi.org/10.1177/0271121419831762

Hyde, D. C., Khanum, S., & Spelke, E. S. (2014). Brief non-symbolic, approximate number practice enhances subsequent exact symbolic arithmetic in children. *Cognition, 131,* 92–107. http://dx.doi.org/10.1016/j.cognition.2013.12.007

Johnson, N. C., Turrou, A. C., McMillan, B. G., Raygoza, M. C., & Franke, M. L. (2019). "Can you help me count these pennies?": Surfacing preschoolers' understandings of counting. *Mathematical Thinking and Learning, 21,* 237–264. http://dx.doi.org/10.1080/10986065.2019.1588206

Jordan, N. C., Kaplan, D., Ramineni, C., & Locuniak, M. N. (2009). Early math matters: Kindergarten number competence and later mathematics outcomes. *Developmental Psychology, 45,* 850–867. http://dx.doi.org/10.1037/a0014939

Jordan, N. C., & Levine, S. C. (2009). Socioeconomic variation, number competence, and mathematics learning difficulties in young children. *Developmental Disabilities Research Reviews, 15*(1), 60–68. http://dx.doi.org/10.1002/ddrr.46

Joswick, C., Clements, D. H., Sarama, J., Banse, H. W., & Day-Hess, C. A. (2019). Double impact: Mathematics and executive function. *Teaching Children Mathematics, 25*(7), 416–426.

Judge, S., & Watson, S. M. (2011). Longitudinal outcomes for mathematics achievement for students with learning disabilities. *The Journal of Educational Research, 104,* 147–157. http://dx.doi.org/10.1080/00220671003636729

Kiss, A. J., Nelson, G., & Christ, T. J. (2019). Predicting third-grade mathematics achievement: A longitudinal investigation of the role of early numeracy skills. *Learning Disability Quarterly, 42,* 161–174. http://dx.doi.org/10.1177/0731948718823083

Landerl, K. (2013). Development of numerical processing in children with typical and dyscalculic arithmetic skills—a longitudinal study. *Frontiers in Psychology, 4,* 459. http://dx.doi.org/10.3389/fpsyg.2013.00459

Lee, J. (2012). College for all: Gaps between desirable and actual P–12 math achievement trajectories for college readiness. *Educational Researcher, 41,* 43–55. http://dx.doi.org/10.3102/0013189X11432746

LeFevre, J. A., Skwarchuk, S. L., Smith-Chant, B. L., Fast, L., Kamawar, D., & Bisanz, J. (2009). Home numeracy experiences and children's math performance in the early school years. *Canadian Journal of Behavioural Science, 41,* 55–66. http://dx.doi.org/10.1037/a0014532

Levine, S. C., Suriyakham, L. W., Rowe, M. L., Huttenlocher, J., & Gunderson, E. A. (2010). What counts in the development of young children's number knowledge? *Developmental Psychology, 46,* 1309–1319. http://dx.doi.org/10.1037/a0019671

Libertus, M. E., Feigenson, L., & Halberda, J. (2011). Preschool acuity of the approximate number system correlates with school math ability. *Developmental Science, 14,* 1292–1300. http://dx.doi.org/10.1111/j.1467-7687.2011.01080.x

Lyons, I. M., & Beilock, S. L. (2013). Ordinality and the nature of symbolic numbers. *The Journal of Neuroscience, 33,* 17052–17061. http://dx.doi.org/10.1523/JNEUROSCI. 1775-13.2013

Lyons, I. M., Price, G. R., Vaessen, A., Blomert, L., & Ansari, D. (2014). Numerical predictors of arithmetic success in grades 1-6. *Developmental Science, 17,* 714–726. http://dx.doi.org/10.1111/desc.12152

Mathematics Learning Study Committee, Center for Education, Division of Behavioral and Social Sciences and Education, National Research Council. (2001). *Adding it up: Helping children learn mathematics* (J. Kilpatrick, J. Swafford, & B. Findell, Eds.). Washington, DC: National Academy Press.

Mazzocco, M. M., Feigenson, L., & Halberda, J. (2011). Preschoolers' precision of the approximate number system predicts later school mathematics performance. *PLoS ONE, 6*(9), e23749. http://dx.doi.org/10.1371/journal.pone.0023749

Mazzocco, M. M., & Hanich, L. B. (2010). Math achievement, numerical processing, and executive functions in girls with Turner syndrome: Do girls with Turner syndrome have math learning disability? *Learning and Individual Differences, 20,* 70–81. http://dx.doi.org/10.1016/j.lindif.2009.10.011

Mazzocco, M. M., & Kover, S. T. (2007). A longitudinal assessment of executive function skills and their association with math performance. *Child Neuropsychology, 13*(1), 18–45. http://dx.doi.org/10.1080/09297040600611346

Mazzocco, M. M., Murphy, M. M., Brown, E. C., Rinne, L., & Herold, K. H. (2013). Persistent consequences of atypical early number concepts. *Frontiers in Psychology, 4,* 486. http://dx.doi.org/10.3389/fpsyg.2013.00486

Mazzocco, M. M., & Thompson, R. E. (2005). Kindergarten predictors of math learning disability. *Learning Disabilities Research & Practice, 20,* 142–155. http://dx.doi.org/ 10.1111/j.1540-5826.2005.00129.x

McGuire, P., Kinzie, M. B., & Berch, D. B. (2012). Developing number sense in pre-K with five-frames. *Early Childhood Education Journal, 40,* 213–222. http://dx.doi.org/ 10.1007/s10643-011-0479-4

Methe, S. A., Hintze, J. M., & Floyd, R. G. (2008). Validation and decision accuracy of early numeracy skill indicators. *School Psychology Review, 37,* 359–373.

Murphy, M. M., Mazzocco, M. M., Hanich, L. B., & Early, M. C. (2007). Cognitive characteristics of children with mathematics learning disability (MLD) vary as a function of the cutoff criterion used to define MLD. *Journal of Learning Disabilities, 40,* 458–478. http://dx.doi.org/10.1177/00222194070400050901

National Council of Teachers of Mathematics. (2006). *Curriculum focal points for prekindergarten through grade 8 mathematics: A quest for coherence.* Reston, VA: Author.

National Governors Association Center for Best Practices and Council of Chief State School Officers. (2010). *Common Core State Standards–Math.* Washington, DC: Author.

National Research Council. (2009). *Mathematics learning in early childhood: Paths toward excellence and equity.* Washington, DC: The National Academies Press.

Peters, E., Hibbard, J., Slovic, P., & Dieckmann, N. (2007). Numeracy skill and the communication, comprehension, and use of risk-benefit information. *Health Affairs, 26,* 741–748. http://dx.doi.org/10.1377/hlthaff.26.3.741

Purpura, D. J., Baroody, A. J., & Lonigan, C. J. (2013). The transition from informal to formal mathematical knowledge: Mediation by numeral knowledge. *Journal of Educational Psychology, 105,* 453–464. http://dx.doi.org/10.1037/a0031753

Purpura, D. J., & Lonigan, C. J. (2013). Informal numeracy skills: The structure and relations among numbering, relations, and arithmetic operations in preschool. *American Educational Research Journal, 50,* 178–209. http://dx.doi.org/10.3102/ 0002831212465332

Raghubar, K. P., Barnes, M. A., & Hecht, S. A. (2010). Working memory and mathematics: A review of developmental, individual difference, and cognitive approaches.

Learning and Individual Differences, 20(2), 110–122. http://dx.doi.org/10.1016/j.lindif.2009.10.005

Ramani, G., & Scalise, N. (2020). It's more than just fun and games: Play-based mathematics activities for Head Start families. *Early Childhood Research Quarterly, 50*(Pt. 3), 78–89.

Ramscar, M., Dye, M., Popick, H. M., & O'Donnell-McCarthy, F. (2011). The enigma of number: Why children find the meanings of even small number words hard to learn and how we can help them do better. *PLoS ONE, 6*(7), e22501. http://dx.doi.org/10.1371/journal.pone.0022501

Rose, H., & Betts, J. R. (2004). The effect of high school courses on earnings. *The Review of Economics and Statistics, 86*, 497–513. http://dx.doi.org/10.1162/003465304323031076

Sarama, J., & Clements, D. H. (2009). Composition and decomposition of shapes. In *Early childhood mathematics education research: Learning trajectories for young children* (pp. 247–270). New York, NY: Routledge. http://dx.doi.org/10.4324/9780203883785-9

Schneider, M., Merz, S., Stricker, J., De Smedt, B., Torbeyns, J., Verschaffel, L., & Luwel, K. (2018). Associations of number line estimation with mathematical competence: A meta-analysis. *Child Development, 89*, 1467–1484.

Shalev, R. S., Auerbach, J., Manor, O., & Gross-Tsur, V. (2000). Developmental dyscalculia: Prevalence and prognosis. *European Child & Adolescent Psychiatry, 9*, S58–S64. http://dx.doi.org/10.1007/s007870070009

Siegler, R. S., & Ramani, G. B. (2009). Playing linear number board games—but not circular ones—improves low-income preschoolers' numerical understanding. *Journal of Educational Psychology, 101*, 545–560. http://dx.doi.org/10.1037/a0014239

Skwarchuk, S. L. (2009). How do parents support preschoolers' numeracy learning experiences at home? *Early Childhood Education Journal, 37*, 189–197. http://dx.doi.org/10.1007/s10643-009-0340-1

Sophian, C. (2000). From objects to quantities: Developments in preschool children's judgments about aggregate amount. *Developmental Psychology, 36*, 724–730. http://dx.doi.org/10.1037/0012-1649.36.6.724

Thomaes, S., Tjaarda, I. C., Brummelman, E., & Sedikides, C. (2019). Effort self-talk benefits the mathematics performance of children with negative competence beliefs. *Child Development*. Advance online publication. http://dx.doi.org/10.1111/cdev.13347

Van de Walle, J. A., Karp, K. S., & Bay-Williams, J. M. (2013). *Elementary and middle school mathematics: Teaching developmentally* (8th ed.). Bloomington, MN: Pearson.

Verdine, B. N., Golinkoff, R. M., Hirsh-Pasek, K., & Newcombe, N. S. (2014). Finding the missing piece: Blocks, puzzles, and shapes fuel school readiness. *Trends in Neuroscience and Education, 3*, 7–13. http://dx.doi.org/10.1016/j.tine.2014.02.005

Wagner, K., Chu, J., & Barner, D. (2018). Do children's number words begin noisy? *Developmental Science, 22*, e12752. http://dx.doi.org/10.1111/desc.12752

Ward, J. M., Mazzocco, M. M., Bock, A. M., & Prokes, N. A. (2017). Are content and structural features of counting books aligned with research on numeracy development? *Early Childhood Research Quarterly, 39*, 47–63. http://dx.doi.org/10.1016/j.ecresq.2016.10.002

Wynn, K. (1990). Children's understanding of counting. *Cognition, 36*, 155–193. http://dx.doi.org/10.1016/0010-0277(90)90003-3

Wynn, K. (1992). Addition and subtraction by human infants. *Nature, 358*, 749–750. http://dx.doi.org/10.1038/358749a0

Xu, F., & Spelke, E. S. (2000). Large number discrimination in 6-month-old infants. *Cognition, 74*, B1–B11. http://dx.doi.org/10.1016/S0010-0277(99)00066-9

6

Self-Regulation in Young Children

A Skill Set for Lifetime Success

Amanda M. Dettmer, Amanda B. Clinton, and Heather A. Mildon

JOCELYN'S DIFFICULTIES WITH SELF-REGULATION: A TYPICAL DAY IN PRE-K

On this, the first snowy day of the school year, Jocelyn's preschool class job was recess bell helper. When her assignment was initially announced at circle time, Jocelyn became exceedingly happy, romping around her area of the carpet and crawling atop the teaching assistant's back in celebration. Her focus then shifted to Miss Maria; Jocelyn played first with her hair and next with her earring, despite being reminded to focus. Jocelyn then spied her slap band bracelet nearby in a cubby. Slapping it noisily onto her wrist once, she found immediate delight in repeatedly slapping it off and on, distracting her classmates.

Later, after 30 minutes of recess time on the freshly snow-covered playground, Ms. Watson reviewed Jocelyn's bell-ringing job duty with her. She was to ring the handheld brass school bell loudly six times for her classmates to hear, then promptly join them in line outside the door. Jocelyn rang the bell proudly from the top of the sledding hill, her wide smile indicating her satisfaction with her performance. Classmates began walking and running to the lineup area. Reluctant to return to the classroom, Jocelyn stayed atop the sledding hill while continuing to ring the bell. After three requests from her teacher to join the class, Jocelyn grudgingly moved toward the line, and Ms. Watson reclaimed the

(continues)

---

http://dx.doi.org/10.1037/0000197-007
Healthy Development in Young Children: Evidence-Based Interventions for Early Education,
V. C. Alfonso and G. J. DuPaul (Editors)

school bell. Jocelyn cried and whined as she slowly made her way into the school and down the hallway well behind her peers.

Suddenly, Jocelyn realized she had lost a hair bow, which added to the upset. Jocelyn stopped and dropped to the floor calling, "My hair bow! My hair bow!" as the adults helped by backtracking and looking for it without her. Nearby classes sent students to close their doors to buffer Jocelyn's loud wails coming from the hall. Jocelyn remained there, lying in the middle of the hallway floor, refusing to walk toward class, crying, and ignoring adult prompts about choices for quite some time.

SELF-REGULATION: SETTING UP CHILDREN FOR SUCCESS

As we saw in Jocelyn's case, lack of self-regulation can be frustrating for teachers, at the least. At the most, it can hinder children's abilities to learn. *Self-regulation* is defined as the ability to manage one's emotions and behavior in accordance with the demands of the situation (Child Mind Institute, n.d.). In preschool-age children, self-regulation often translates into *not* having a tantrum when things don't go their way or when unexpected things happen. As children grow, self-regulation enables them to engage in goal-directed behaviors including planning, focusing attention, remembering instructions, and juggling multiple tasks while also controlling impulses. In this way, children's brains act not as the brakes on behavior but as the air traffic control tower (Center on the Developing Child, 2012). In other words, children's brains do not simply stop certain behaviors (e.g., tantrums) from occurring but orchestrate multiple actions and reactions to filter distractions, prioritize tasks, set and achieve goals, and control impulses (Center on the Developing Child, 2012).

Self-regulatory skills, such as attention, organization, and self-monitoring, are important for young children to develop because these skills contribute to their growing independence. Decades of research have shown that self-regulation is central to school readiness, transition to kindergarten, school performance, and children's abilities to master new information in the classroom (for a review, see Zelazo, Blair, & Willoughby, 2016). Self-regulation also enables children to have stronger friendships and relationships with others and allows them to cope better with typical daily disappointments and stresses. Children's self-regulation also predicts their future likelihood of social and academic success (Eisenberg, Valiente, & Eggum, 2010; Zimmerman, 1995) and health and wealth (Graziano, Calkins, & Keane, 2010; Moffitt et al., 2011).

It is important to remember that self-regulation is not all-or-nothing: It exists on a continuum of abilities and expression. It is equally important to remember that children are not born with self-regulation skills and that these skills are not age dependent. Children are born with the potential to develop them. Self-regulation develops gradually, and these skills can be taught or enhanced (Center on the Developing Child, 2012). Thus, teachers can play a pivotal role in setting children up for success. In fact, educators have long been influenced by psychologists and other scientists who recognize the role of educators in optimal child development. Lev Vygotsky (1978) theorized that children can be taught to think independently about how to solve problems with scaffolding, with the zone of proximal development being the area where the most sensitive instruction should occur. Long before Vygotsky, Maria Montessori (1949/1967) described her concept of inner discipline after conducting careful observations of children who were allowed freedom in environments that suited their needs. She observed that after a period of continued concentrated work of their own choice, children grew inner discipline and peace (a process she called *normalization*; Montessori, 1949/1967). More recently, Albert Bandura's (1993) theories of self-efficacy declared that teachers' beliefs in their personal efficacy to motivate and promote learning affect the learning environments they create and the level of academic progress their students achieve.

JOSHUA'S ADJUSTMENT TO KINDERGARTEN: BRAIN DEVELOPMENT AMID CHRONIC STRESS AND ADVERSE CHILDHOOD EXPERIENCES

From the first day of kindergarten, Joshua had shown that regulating his emotions was challenging. In class with his twin brother, Jacob, he was prone to making noises, rolling on the carpet, or touching and prodding other students—most often his brother—instead of attending to the lessons. When classwork proved difficult, Joshua crumpled his paper or scribbled furiously across the page, pressing ever harder with his pencil until he broke the lead. The angst and anxiety within him were showing through his behavior, but the cause would not become known until midyear. Joshua and his three siblings were living with the daily fear that their father would abuse their mother. Their home hours included angry voices, yelling, and physical aggression. At 5 years of age, Joshua's escalated behaviors at school were influenced by his emotions resulting from conflict at home.

MECHANISMS OF SELF-REGULATION

A later section of this chapter is devoted to describing programs and methods that teachers and schools have implemented that result in greater self-regulation among students. First, however, it is important to understand the neurobiology behind self-regulation—that is, how the brain is involved in self-regulation and what factors contribute to (or hinder) children's ability to self-regulate. Only then are we able to understand how and why the programs discussed later are effective.

The Brain

Self-regulation skills depend on three types of brain function: working memory, mental flexibility, and self-control. These functions must operate in coordination with each other for optimal self-regulation. *Working memory* governs our ability to retain and manipulate pieces of information over short periods. *Mental flexibility* helps us either sustain or shift attention in response to different demands or apply different rules in different settings. *Self-control* enables us to resist impulsive actions or responses (Center on the Developing Child, 2012).

Comparative psychology—the scientific behavioral study of nonhuman animals, as well as neuroscience research with human and nonhuman animals— has revealed brain regions responsible for self-regulation skills. Most of these brain regions are in the frontal lobes, the areas that lie immediately behind the forehead (see Figure 6.1). A particular part of the frontal lobes, the prefrontal cortex (PFC), contains brain regions that are known in primates (human and nonhuman alike) to regulate impulsive responses, apply different rules to different situations, hold information in mind, and filter out distractions (Zelazo et al., 2016). We also know, through research studies with humans and animals, that the PFC does not fully develop until late in adolescence or even early adulthood (Diamond, 2002; Zelazo et al., 2013). In fact, basic sensory and motor areas develop first, and areas associated with more complex functions—such as self-regulation or executive function (EF)—develop

FIGURE 6.1. Brain Regions in the Prefrontal Cortex (PFC) Are Responsible for Orchestrating Self-Regulation Skills and Behaviors

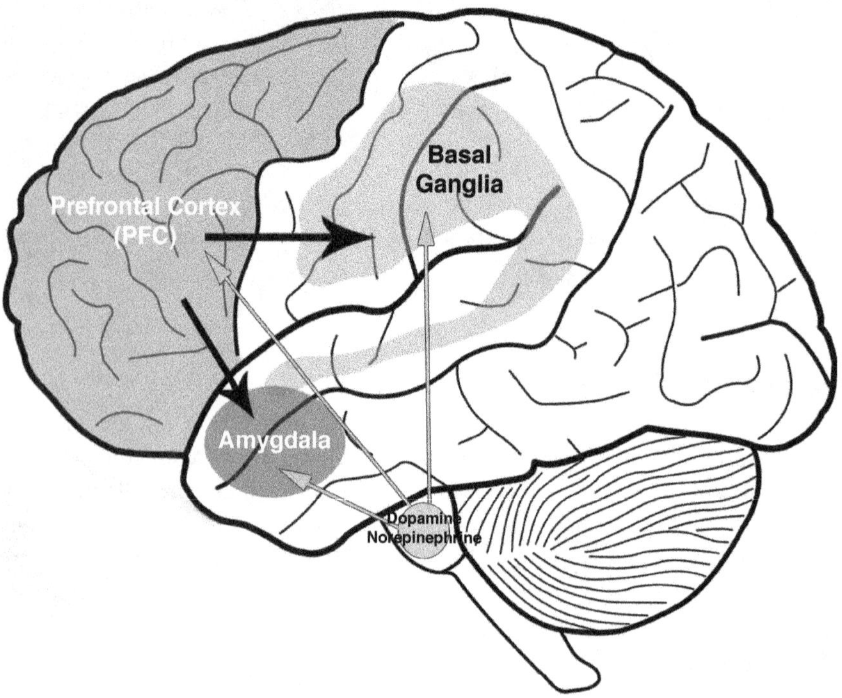

The PFC has strong connections to other brain regions, including the basal ganglia and the amygdala. In addition, the PFC, basal ganglia, and amygdala are affected by variations in neurotransmitters released by the brain, particularly dopamine and norepinephrine.

later, on top of and around the sensory and motor areas (Zelazo et al., 2016). Therefore, we can expect that very young children are still developing the brain regions responsible for self-regulation; they're building the components that will become their air traffic control tower.

Decades of research have also taught us that many experiential factors can support or inhibit children's brain growth, which has a direct impact on their abilities to develop self-regulation skills. These factors include environment, socioeconomic status (SES), and relationships; all of these can be and often are interrelated (e.g., Petrill & Deater-Deckard, 2004). The reason these experiences support or inhibit children's brain growth, particularly areas related to self-regulation, is because the PFC is highly connected with, and coordinates activity in, many other brain regions. These regions include the basal ganglia, areas deep inside the brain that are important for learning patterns and routines, and the amygdala, which is crucial for emotional and stress-related responses (see Figure 6.1). The PFC is also sensitive to changes in the levels of neurotransmitters, which are chemicals released between brain cells (neurons) that transmit information. In particular, brain cells in the PFC respond to changes in dopamine and norepinephrine (Xing, Li, & Gao, 2016). Dopamine is a chemical that helps control the brain's reward centers and also regulates movement and emotional responses. Norepinephrine is a hormone released in response to stress that affects some parts of the brain that control attention and responses to stimuli. We know from research in monkeys that when individuals are attentive and engaged—meaning, they are experiencing typical, healthy, and moderate levels of arousal or stress—there is more activity in the PFC regions that are responsible for working memory and suppressing competing information. However, when stimuli are uncontrollable and overwhelming, brain activity in the PFC is reduced while activity in areas responsible for more reactive and automatic responses (i.e., the amygdala) is increased (Arnsten, 2009; Arnsten, Raskind, Taylor, & Connor, 2015). Varying levels of dopamine and norepinephrine are responsible for these changes in brain activity, and various experiences can result in varying levels of these neurotransmitters, thereby affecting brain development.

The Environment

Children experience a variety of environments in their everyday lives. Where and how they spend the majority of their waking hours matter. The quality of their homes, day care centers, and classrooms can have tremendous impacts on children's brain development and, ultimately, their ability to acquire self-regulation skills. Children thrive when they grow up in stable home environments with high-quality parenting, attend day cares with high-quality caregiving, or go to schools with high-quality teacher interactions and curricula. Their brains are primed for success: They experience situations that enable optimal brain development, including later self-regulation skills (Center on the Developing Child, 2016). What determines high quality? For preschool-age children, some examples of high-quality interactions are stimulating experiences (e.g., exposure to a rich and diverse vocabulary and opportunities to explore and manipulate the environment), responsive caregiving (e.g., serve-and-return or reciprocal interactions with parents and care providers), and effective teaching (e.g., age-appropriate curricula providing engaging activities that achieve well-defined goals; Center on the Developing Child, 2016). Conversely, when children grow up in environments that are unstable, neglectful, or abusive, they do not receive the same opportunities for optimal brain development. Why? Because in such environments, children's stress-response systems are persistently activated—sometimes very strongly so, depending on the situation—and this chronic activation can result in permanent disruptions to brain circuits during periods of critical development that are required for developing self-regulation skills (National Scientific Council on the Developing Child, 2007). These brain circuits include the PFC, amygdala, and basal ganglia (see Figure 6.1).

Scientists refer to such experiences as *adverse childhood experiences*, or ACEs (Centers for Disease Control and Prevention, 2019). Some ACEs, such as childhood abuse or neglect, are more salient or obvious. Other ACEs are less obvious but can still have long-term negative effects on children's brain and behavioral development: Caregiver mental illness and systemic racism are some examples. In addition, low SES, which is strongly associated with ACEs, is related to suboptimal development and adult health and productivity (Currie, 2009). Together, ACEs and low SES are strong risk factors for reduced school engagement, increased likelihood of juvenile delinquency, and poor physical and mental health outcomes (Bethell, Newacheck, Hawes, & Halfon, 2014; Campbell, Walker, & Egede, 2016; Nurius, Green, Logan-Greene, Longhi, & Song, 2016).

However, there is hope. Children who experience ACEs are not necessarily irreparably damaged. Although ACEs can be clearly detrimental to brain development and to the development of self-regulation skills, the good news is that these skills can be learned and improved by training and practice (Center on the Developing Child, 2012). Thus, even if children experience suboptimal home environments, poverty, or other types of chronic stress, teachers and school administrators have a unique opportunity to provide positive experiences by means of which children can cultivate self-regulation skills and, ultimately, have a greater likelihood of future successes. The key to cultivating self-regulation in young children, as is seen in the following section, is well-timed and well-targeted scaffolding and support.

MAX'S SELF-REGULATION IN PRESCHOOL: CELEBRATING PROGRESS

Max's self-regulation skills had grown significantly since he started preschool 5 months ago. He once showed defiance and impulsivity by ignoring adult requests, hollering at top volume when a peer came near, or hauling off and hitting someone who took his toy away. More recently, Max had chosen to comply with adult directions, was frequently engaging in parallel play with peers, and was heard using words such as "Please give it back" in response to a peer taking a toy before he was finished.

Kendra, Max's teacher, was thrilled with his progress in self-regulation and executive function skills. She attributed his growth to the combination of explicit social–emotional learning (SEL) skills instruction, SEL infusion into daily lessons, and his growing confidence as a member of the safe, responsive community she and her students created through their use of daily classroom rituals and routines. Kendra observed that the rehearsal and verbal mediation experiences she employed in class had given Max the practice he needed to internalize his new skills and apply them more consistently.

Max's parents, too, were pleased with his growing ability to self-regulate. They expressed appreciation for the SEL tips and tools Kendra and her kindergarten team had shared with them, describing with wonder how Max used the language at home to redirect the behavior of their dog, Scout, or his little sister, Margaret.

PROGRAMS AND TREATMENTS THAT BOOST SELF-REGULATION SKILLS

Educators and parents familiar with children similar to Max who demonstrate underdeveloped self-regulation skills are eager to find effective means of helping these children develop the knowledge and skills they need to thrive. Specifically, adults seek ways to support children's ability to manage their emotions, thoughts, and behaviors across contexts. This is important because, as previously detailed, the ability to synchronize one's actions with the demands of a particular setting or task contributes to positive long-term outcomes, such as academic success and positive peer relationships (Davis, Solberg, de Baca, & Gore, 2014) and mental and physical health (Jones, Greenberg, & Crowley, 2015).

A number of school-based prevention and intervention programs promoting and advancing the development of self-regulation skills in preschool-age children are available to professionals (McClelland, Acock, & Morrison, 2006; Sklad, Diekstra, Ritter, Ben, & Gravesteijn, 2012). Some of these incorporate psychoeducational materials for parents as well. The most widely utilized programs boast solid evidence of their effectiveness in teaching knowledge and skills related to self-regulation, such as impulse control and emotion recognition and management. Although programs that emphasize self-regulation training may often be termed *social problem-solving* or *social skills* programs, they actually integrate components that contribute to regulated cognitive, emotional, and behavioral functioning for children to practice as individuals as well as to apply in group settings, such as the classroom. Before we delve into specific programs, however, it is first important to understand the continuum along which such programs are designed.

The Prevention and Intervention Continuum

Programs aimed at addressing potentially problematic self-regulatory skills in childhood are typically categorized in terms of their developmental continuum and their instructional approach (Adelman & Taylor, 1994; Mrazek & Haggerty, 1994). As originally described by Caplan in 1964, a developmental continuum includes primary, secondary, and tertiary prevention, which may also be referred to as Tier I, II, and III prevention. Instructional approaches are classified in terms of universal, selective, and indicated prevention interventions (National Collaborating Center for Mental Health, Social Care Institute for Excellence, 2013). Specific examples of the continuum of prevention and intervention programs are reviewed in subsequent paragraphs.

Primary prevention efforts represent the first level of the developmental continuum system of categorization. Self-regulation-focused programs and curricula that fall into this category would be directed at children—often those noted to be at-risk—who have not begun to demonstrate overt symptomatology (O'Connell, Boat, & Warner, 2009). In effect, primary prevention aims to avoid the onset of problems where there is potential for them to occur. In terms of self-regulation for young children specifically, primary prevention efforts build on existing abilities and continue to teach increasingly more advanced aspects of self-regulation skills. Secondary prevention programs are designed to address emerging problems or even to allow for early diagnosis of a critical issue in order to treat it in an efficient and effective manner and, ultimately, avoid the development of a more serious behavioral or learning problem (Mytton, DiGuiseppi, Gough, Taylor, & Logan, 2007). For young children, secondary prevention efforts addressing self-regulation skills may include preventive interventions developed for application in small groups. Fewer children in a group allows for targeted efforts that are determined by initial screening data or posttest results from evaluations that are conducted subsequent to primary prevention program implementation. The tertiary level of the developmental continuum of prevention categories focuses on addressing behavioral issues that have already emerged and limiting related behaviors that might emerge subsequently. For young children, this would likely include individualized interventions (Tobin & Sugai, 2005).

The developmental continuum approach that classifies the degree of need for prevention serves as a complement to the instructional approach to self-regulation programs for young children. Gordon (1987) developed instructional approach categories from a risk–benefit point of view. That is, this alternative threefold approach attempted to weigh the potential risk of a child being identified as demonstrating significant self-regulatory problems and the benefit of implementing a preventive intervention. This approach provided a more empirically sound option because, developmentally speaking, many mental, emotional, and behavioral symptoms are risk factors for later disability, and, as such, all treatments could be considered preventative (O'Connell et al., 2009). Universal prevention strategies and programs represent the least intensive level of the instructional approach classification and are commonly employed in school settings by nature of their design for classroom-based application. These are aimed at the general population and, in slight contrast to primary prevention programs, are applied to groups that are not preselected. Many universal programs are, however, applied to at-risk populations. In the case of universal prevention strategies, the entire early childhood population would be the target of a universal program designed to increase self-regulation skills. Programs that incorporate self-regulation training for preschool children are frequently adopted by school systems and applied to all of their students across grades because they have good evidence of their effectiveness, are easy for teachers to apply, and provide key skills that are associated with positive learning outcomes in math, reading, and other areas (McClelland et al., 2006). Selective prevention efforts are defined as strategies targeted to subgroups of children recognized as being at elevated risk for self-regulation difficulties, whereas indicated prevention is aimed at those who have been individually screened and identified at high risk for a self-regulation disorder (O'Connell et al., 2009).

Some such programs are described next. These programs range from short-term, finite interventions to curriculum-based, pedagogical practices.

Critical Skills of Focus in Self-Regulation Training

The concept of self-regulation manifests in different ways across the lifespan. Children often inquire as to why they cannot do precisely what they feel like doing when they feel like doing it. At an adult level, the self-regulation questions are typically framed in terms of how one makes responsible decisions—such as going to work or eating a healthy meal—when one may be disinclined to do so. According to Albert Bandura (1991), self-regulation is an active process in which humans (a) monitor their own behavior, the influences of their behavior, and the consequences of their behaviors; (b) judge their behavior in relation to their personal standards and broader, more contextual standards; and (c) react to how they think and feel about their behavior. Self-regulation is more advanced than self-control in that it refers to reducing the frequency of strong impulses and the mechanism of controlling oneself. Self-regulation incorporates cognitive, emotional, and behavioral components and is often taught in school settings where children are engaged in socially and academically challenging tasks that require the processes outlined by Bandura.

In terms of the school context, self-regulation is particularly critical in learning because of its influence on motivation and achievement, notably for preschool-age children (Hubert, Guimard, Florin, & Tracy, 2015). In terms of classroom success, several key approaches are crucial in self-regulation. First, children who are self-regulated are aware of their own learning strategies in terms of planning, monitoring, and modifying their thinking as needed pending the task at hand (Corno, 1986; Zimmerman & Martinez Pons, 1986). Similarly, children must be able to manage and control the effort they put into new learning in terms of persistence on challenging tasks as well as attention, focus, and engagement (Corno, 1986). Finally, academically focused self-regulation incorporates specific cognitive strategies that enhance learning, such as rehearsal, elaboration, and organization (Weinstein & Mayer, 1986).

EMPOWERING YOUNG LEARNERS WITH SKILLS FOR SUCCESS

The four-teacher pre-K team had a combined 45 years of classroom experience between them, which explained why they were baffled to find themselves struggling to manage classroom behavior this year. They agreed that behavior management had never before been so challenging.

After a particularly difficult week that included student behaviors such as hiding under tables, disrupting during circle time, and emotional escalations due to peer conflicts during explorations, the team determined they needed to make a change. They reviewed the social–emotional learning resources available in their district and selected the Second Step Early Learning curriculum as one they might try. Their goal was to empower themselves while equipping their students with tools for self-regulation and developing their foundational learning skills.

Team members each completed the online training module to familiarize themselves with the curriculum, then collaboratively planned weekly themes, daily lessons, and school–home communication as part of their classroom instruction for the next 9 weeks. Teachers embarked on a plan–do–study–act cycle in their classrooms in which they compared the current number of classroom behavioral incidences or office discipline referrals with the counts recorded after 9 weeks of daily focus on social–emotional learning skills through Second Step kindergarten curriculum lessons.

Their efforts paid off! At the end of the 9 weeks, teachers reported being able to teach their lessons without interruption more often. They noticed students were listening more attentively, seemed more engaged, and were getting along better with their peers. Although some students continued to struggle to manage their behavior, the teachers were encouraged to see that their focus on explicit instruction in social–emotional skills was having a positive impact on the daily experience and student learning in their classrooms.

Classroom-Based Self-Regulation Training Programs and Curricula

Relatively few programs and curricula exist that address self-regulation directly and uniquely for very young children, such as preschoolers. However, self-regulation training is frequently incorporated into the more general framework of social–emotional learning programs designed for young children (Tominey & McClelland, 2011). This section reviews training programs and curricula that are specific to increasing self-regulation skills in young children. It also highlights programs that incorporate self-regulation into a broader set of social skills, because the latter approach is commonly utilized.

Recent data indicate that the dynamic nature of self-regulation requires attending to the social–emotional aspects of managing one's behaviors as well as the cognitive components. As such, it appears that a more integrated approach could have the greatest impact (Wagener, 2013).

The programs outlined next represent distinct approaches to teaching self-regulation. Universal prevention curricula oriented toward teaching and reinforcing skills considered fundamental to effective self-regulation offer a series of scripted lessons and supportive materials that are presented to children over the course of weeks or months during the school year. Such programs include Second Step Early Learning (SSEL; Committee for Children, 2011), which offers a focus on self-regulation within a larger social–emotional learning package and game-based behavioral regulation training activities designed for teachers to incorporate into their lessons, which are a series of classroom activities. Conversely, pedagogical practices refer to classroom-wide curricula and practices of teaching throughout an entire year or years, often in a theoretical framework, that enhance self-regulation skills. Such programs include Montessori, Tools of the Mind, and the Chicago School Readiness Project (CSRP).

Short-Term Programs

This section describes evidence-based educational philosophies, curricula, and methods of instruction that are typically schoolwide, and which, by the nature of their teaching practices, provide self-regulation practice for young children. Not all of these practices focus explicitly on SEL.

Second Step Early Learning Program

The Early Learning SSEL Program, published by Committee for Children (2011), is a universal prevention program designed to increase school readiness for preschool children ages 4 to 5 years. Rooted in social–emotional learning, SSEL is promoted as a violence prevention program, but that is primarily because prosocial abilities and well-developed self-regulation reduce impulsive behaviors, such as those associated with aggression. SSEL is a scripted curriculum that includes tools and tips to share with parents. SSEL consists of five units focusing on skills for learning, empathy, emotion management, friendship skills and problem solving, and transitioning to kindergarten, respectively. Lessons are presented by teachers during short, daily activities of 5 to 7 minutes each over the course of 28 weeks during the school year.

A key component of the SSEL Program is its focus on training EF skills, such as impulse control and socially just decision making, in addition to broader social skill instruction. The SSEL Program has been demonstrated to enhance social interactions by improving self-regulatory abilities, notably EFs (Wenz-Gross, Yoo, Upshur, & Gambino, 2018). As such, critical self-regulatory skills, including behavioral inhibition, cognitive control (e.g., attention/focus and working memory), and task persistence along with socially oriented decision making, have all been shown to improve in young children when they receive the SSEL lessons (Blair & Raver, 2014; Razza, Martin, & Brooks-Gunn, 2015).

Game-Based Behavioral Self-Regulation Training Program

The idea of game-based behavioral self-regulation training resulted from an acknowledged need for preschool-oriented self-regulation teaching tools that were effective at improving children's skills while also being economically afford- able. These play-based activities emphasize cognitive control and behavioral maturity resulting from advancements in long-term attention, metacognition, emotion identification and inhibition of emotional reactions, perspective taking, reasoning, and behavior control (Sezgin & Demiriz, 2019). The methods may employ role playing, movement games, or music games integrated into class- room activities several times per week over the course of about 8 weeks (Schmitt, McClelland, Tominey, & Acock, 2015; Sezgin & Demiriz, 2019). Examples include activities such as Head, Shoulders, Knees and Toes, Red Light–Green Light, and the Freeze Game (see *5 Incredibly Fun GAMES to Teach Self-Regulation* at https://youtu.be/H_O1brYwdSY). Rules, guidance, reminders, and role defini- tion all support the process of internalizing habits that enhance self-regulation. Evaluation of play-based self-regulation training programs in which children are studied before and after an 8-week intervention indicates significant improvement in self-regulation and behavior control (Schmitt et al., 2015; Sezgin & Demiriz, 2019), with one study finding gains particularly for children who started the year with low self-regulation skills (Tominey & McClelland, 2011). However, research on these approaches is limited. Notably, sample sizes are rather small, and the students were not followed beyond the end of the training programs.

Pedagogical Practices

This section describes evidence-based educational philosophies and methods of instruction that are typically schoolwide and last one school year or more and that integrate self-regulation practice for young children into instructional methodology. A common trait of the three practices described here is their com- bination of intensive teacher-training/professional development programs with a comprehensive curriculum.

Montessori

The Montessori method was developed by Dr. Maria Montessori in the first half of the 20th century (Montessori, 1949/1967) after her rigorous close observa- tions of children in relatively free environments. The method focuses on the "whole child" approach, integrating social and cognitive growth to promote independent functioning. The classroom is a "prepared environment" that is designed to allow children's independent work and discovery. High-fidelity Montessori classrooms are filled with unique materials that are designed for children to learn practical life skills, sensory development, literacy and math competence, and cultural appreciation (Montessori, 1914). A central tenet of the Montessori method is that, with proper support from the prepared envi- ronment and the guide (the teacher), children are capable of developing themselves (Montessori, 1949/1967). Montessori classrooms occur in mixed

3-year age groups, so preschoolers (ages 3–4 years) are in the same class with kindergarteners; these classrooms are called "primary classrooms" (Montessori, 1949/1967).

In studies of Montessori primary students who were enrolled via a randomized lottery system, benefits for EF and self-regulation are evident. Across the school year, 3-year-olds in a Montessori public preschool improved on tasks measuring inhibitory control and cognitive flexibility (Phillips-Silver & Daza, 2018). However, it should be noted that there was no control-group comparison for this study, meaning there was no comparison with children attending traditional public schools. Comparing young 70 children who entered Montessori at 3 years through the end of their primary class at 6 years with 71 similarly aged children in other public and private schools, Lillard and colleagues (2017) found that Montessori children scored higher on EF tasks at age 4. However, EF was not significantly different across all ages combined. In another study of 5-year-olds, the 30 public Montessori children performed better on a card-sorting test of EF at the end of kindergarten than did the 25 control children (Lillard & Else-Quest, 2006). And in a study of three private preschools—one classic Montessori (strict adherence to Montessori, including all Montessori materials), one supplemented Montessori (many, but not entirely, Montessori materials supplemented with conventional preschool materials), and one conventional Montessori (no Montessori materials)—the 36 preschoolers in classic Montessori made better gains from fall to spring in an EF task than did the 95 supplemented Montessori or the 41 conventional Montessori preschoolers (Lillard, 2012).

Tools of the Mind
The Tools of the Mind Program was developed by Drs. Elena Bodrova and Deborah Leong in 1993 (see Bodrova & Leong, 2007). Tools of the Mind, which is based on Vygotsky's theory (1978) that active learning is socially mediated, consists of a kit of 40 EF activities for pre-K and kindergarten-age children. Intentional, make-believe play-based engagement options outlined in Tools of the Mind specifically aim to train young children in skills such as inhibiting acting out of character, remembering their own and others' roles, and flexibly adjusting as their friends improvise. Children also practice using self-regulating private speech to verbally walk themselves through decisions, focusing their attention on critical tasks, and applying deliberate memory techniques (Bodrova & Leong, 2007). Having initially developed Tools of the Mind as a curriculum add-on, Bodrova and Leong realized that supports, trainings, and challenges to EFs had to be consistent—part of what children do every day. Consequently, Tools of the Mind exercises are interwoven into all academic activities throughout the day (Diamond & Lee, 2011).

Tools of the Mind has been implemented in diverse classrooms in the United States and Canada (Solomon et al., 2018). Numerous scientific studies have examined the efficacy of Tools of the Mind; although results have been mixed, the overall trends suggest that the curriculum enhances EF skills. A randomized controlled trial (RCT) of 147 pre-K students showed that those randomly assigned to Tools of the Mind versus a district curriculum performed better on EF tasks requiring them to flexibly switch mindsets and attentional focus (Diamond, Barnett, Thomas, & Munro, 2007). However, a larger trial of approximately 800 pre-K students found no differences in EF compared with control or business-as-usual teaching curricula (Wilson & Farran, 2012), meaning that Tools of the Mind was no better or no worse than business as usual in that study. In a Canadian study of pre-K students, children with high levels of initial hyperactivity or inattention showed the greatest improvements on EF after Tools of the Mind (Solomon et al., 2018). Additionally, pre-K teachers who applied the Tools of the Mind activities in their classrooms further reported that their students showed fewer problem behaviors and experienced a more positive classroom environment (Barnett, Yarosz, Thomas, & Hornbeck, 2006). In a large RCT of kindergarten students, random assignment to Tools of the Mind resulted in improved EF, reasoning ability, and control of attention at the end of kindergarten that increased into the first grade (Blair & Raver, 2014). Importantly, many of these positive effects of Tools of the Mind for kindergarten students were specific to high-poverty schools, suggesting that this curriculum may be promising for closing the achievement gap.

Chicago School Readiness Project

CSRP is a federally funded RCT intervention that was launched in 2003 to target low-income preschool-age children living in Chicago, with the aim of improving children's chances of success in school. CSRP was implemented in Head Start classrooms, and children from the original sample are now being followed through high school (The Institute of Human Development and Social Change, n.d.). From the start, CSRP's focus was not on academics but rather on developing verbally skilled strategies for emotion regulation and on coaching teachers in stress reduction throughout the school year (Diamond & Lee, 2011). The classroom-based mental health intervention aims to improve teachers' behavior management of preschoolers' dysregulated behavior (Li-Grining & Haas, 2010). Teachers are provided with 30 hours of training in strategies to provide their classrooms with more effective regulatory support and better management (e.g., strategies such as rewarding positive behavior and redirecting negative behavior). They also receive weekly coaching via classroom-based mental health consultants (MHCs; Li-Grining & Haas, 2010; Raver et al., 2008). MHCs also provided direct child-focused consultations with children expressing the most severe externalizing behavior (Li-Grining & Haas, 2010; Raver et al., 2008).

RCTs examined Head Start classrooms assigned to receive either CSRP or lower-intensity support services including an extra teacher's aide in the classroom instead of an MHC. In 18 of 35 Head Start classrooms receiving CSRP, teachers provided better managed and more emotionally supportive classrooms than did control teachers. Moreover, EFs of 4-year-old students improved over the year, significantly more so in CSRP versus control classrooms. CSRP children also improved in vocabulary, letter naming, and math significantly more than did controls. Importantly, these improvements were mediated largely by improvements of EFs (Raver et al., 2011). This means that the improvements in academic outcomes resulting from CSRP very likely emerged because of improvements in EFs resulting from CSRP.

Longer-term studies of CSRP have also shown promising effects. One RCT found that EFs in the spring of preschool predicted math and reading achievement 3 years later (Li-Grining, Raver, & Pess, 2011). A recent study tracked students 10 to 11 years after they completed CSRP in preschool. Researchers found promising outcomes for CSRP children, who as adolescents performed better on games testing EF and on academic achievement (as measured by student-reported grade point average; Watts, Gandhi, Ibrahim, Masucci, & Raver, 2018).

JOSHUA'S ENDING: CLASSROOM-BASED SELF-REGULATION SKILL TRAINING

How did Joshua's kindergarten story end? His difficulty with self-regulation continued through the middle of the school year, escalating to even more frequent and intense behavioral episodes. Joshua joined a highly structured, targeted intervention group aiming to grow student knowledge and skill in self-regulation and prosocial behaviors in a small-group setting. Explicit instruction in skills for learning, empathy, recognizing and managing emotions, and building friendships featured prominently. A strong emphasis was placed on the application of skills through game-based self-regulation training, along with role playing and literacy connections.

Joshua exited his intervention group in the spring, then began spending full days in his kindergarten classroom. He brought with him a new and growing skill set that enabled him to identify his emotions and handle frustration. He had learned how to react to situations in a safe manner while working to consider others' perspectives. Many of the prosocial strategies and self-management techniques Joshua learned were also taught to his classroom teachers and peers to smooth his transition and ensure he was well-supported within the larger group setting. Joshua's increased ability to delay an upset reaction had prepared him to respond to peers and adults in a socially acceptable manner that kept him in class and learning. His mother expressed gratitude for helping Joshua recognize and process his emotions, stating that the experience of supporting Joshua in working through his behavior had helped her begin to address the relationship challenges at home.

CONCLUSION

Self-regulation has been defined as children's ability to manage their emotions and behavior amid demanding or unpredictable circumstances. Although all children have the potential to develop healthy self-regulation skills, challenging home lives, ACEs, or growing up in low-income settings can be barriers to their development. Children struggling with self-regulation within school settings may have difficulty developing positive peer relationships, often experiencing barriers to learning and achievement. Educators charged with supporting children in developing proficiency with self-regulation should first learn about the brain's role in development, along with factors contributing to or creating barriers to healthy development. As illustrated in this chapter, classroom-based self-regulation training programs and curricula can make a difference in increasing young children's self-regulation skills, with an integrated approach likely having the most significant impact. Children who receive short-term intervention program instruction that allows practice of self-regulation skills or who are members of classrooms in which pedagogical approaches that enhance self-regulation are used over the course of the school year are positioned to develop healthy self-regulation skills that will serve them well in school and in life.

REFERENCES

Adelman, H. S., & Taylor, L. (1994). *On understanding intervention in psychology and education*. Westport, CT: Praeger.

Arnsten, A. F. (2009). Stress signalling pathways that impair prefrontal cortex structure and function. *Nature Reviews Neuroscience, 10*, 410–422. http://dx.doi.org/10.1038/nrn2648

Arnsten, A. F., Raskind, M. A., Taylor, F. B., & Connor, D. F. (2015). The effects of stress exposure on prefrontal cortex: Translating basic research into successful treatments for post-traumatic stress disorder. *Neurobiology of Stress, 1*, 89–99. http://dx.doi.org/10.1016/j.ynstr.2014.10.002

Bandura, A. (1991). Social cognitive theory of self-regulation. *Organizational Behavior and Human Decision Processes, 50*, 248–287. http://dx.doi.org/10.1016/0749-5978(91)90022-L

Bandura, A. (1993). Perceived self-efficacy in cognitive development and functioning. *Educational Psychologist, 2*, 117–148. http://dx.doi.org/10.1207/s15326985ep2802_3

Barnett, W. S., Yarosz, D. J., Thomas, J., & Hornbeck, A. (2006). *Educational effectiveness of a Vygotskian approach to preschool education: A randomized trial*. Rutgers, NJ: National Institute for Early Education Research.

Bethell, C. D., Newacheck, P., Hawes, E., & Halfon, N. (2014). Adverse childhood experiences: Assessing the impact on health and school engagement and the mitigating role of resilience. *Health Affairs, 33*, 2106–2115. http://dx.doi.org/10.1377/hlthaff.2014.0914

Blair, C., & Raver, C. C. (2014). Closing the achievement gap through modification of neurocognitive and neuroendocrine function: Results from a cluster randomized controlled trial of an innovative approach to the education of children in kindergarten. *PLoS ONE, 9*(11), e112393. http://dx.doi.org/10.1371/journal.pone.0112393

Bodrova, E., & Leong, D. J. (2007). *Tools of the Mind: The Vygotskian approach to early childhood education* (2nd ed.). New York, NY: Merrill/Prentice Hall.

Campbell, J. A., Walker, R. J., & Egede, L. E. (2016). Associations between adverse childhood experiences, high-risk behaviors, and morbidity in adulthood. *American Journal of Preventive Medicine, 50*, 344–352. http://dx.doi.org/10.1016/j.amepre.2015.07.022

Caplan, G. (1964). *Principles of prevention psychiatry*. Oxford, England: Basic Books.

Center on the Developing Child. (2012). *Executive function* (InBrief). Retrieved from https://developingchild.harvard.edu/resources/inbrief-executive-function

Center on the Developing Child. (2016). *From best practices to breakthrough impacts: A science-based approach to building a more promising future for young children and families*.

Retrieved from https://developingchild.harvard.edu/resources/from-best-practices-to-breakthrough-impacts

Centers for Disease Control and Prevention. (2019, May 14). *Adverse childhood experiences (ACEs).* Retrieved from https://www.cdc.gov/violenceprevention/childabuseandneglect/acestudy/index.html

Child Mind Institute. (n.d.). *How can we help kids with self-regulation?* Retrieved from https://childmind.org/article/can-help-kids-self-regulation

Committee for Children. (2011). *Find lifelong success with social-emotional learning.* Retrieved from https://www.cfchildren.org/programs/social-emotional-learning

Corno, L. (1986). The metacognitive control components of self-regulated learning. *Contemporary Educational Psychology, 11,* 333–346. http://dx.doi.org/10.1016/0361-476X(86)90029-9

Currie, J. (2009). Healthy, wealthy, and wise: Socioeconomic status, poor health in childhood, and human capital development. *Journal of Economic Literature, 47*(1), 87–122. http://dx.doi.org/10.1257/jel.47.1.87

Davis, A., Solberg, V. S., de Baca, C., & Gore, T. H. (2014). Use of social emotional learning skills to predict future academic success and progress toward graduation. *Journal of Education for Students Placed at Risk, 19*(3–4), 169–182. http://dx.doi.org/10.1080/10824669.2014.972506

Diamond, A. (2002). Normal development of prefrontal cortex from birth to young adulthood: Cognitive functions, anatomy, and biochemistry. In D. Struss & R. Knight (Eds.), *Principles of frontal lobe function* (pp. 466–503). New York, NY: Oxford University Press. http://dx.doi.org/10.1093/acprof:oso/9780195134971.003.0029

Diamond, A., Barnett, W. S., Thomas, J., & Munro, S. (2007). Preschool program improves cognitive control. *Science, 318,* 1387–1388. http://dx.doi.org/10.1126/science.1151148

Diamond, A., & Lee, K. (2011). Interventions shown to aid executive function development in children 4 to 12 years old. *Science, 333,* 959–964. http://dx.doi.org/10.1126/science.1204529

Eisenberg, N., Valiente, C., & Eggum, N. D. (2010). Self-regulation and school readiness. *Early Education and Development, 21,* 681–698. http://dx.doi.org/10.1080/10409289.2010.497451

Gordon, R. (1987). An operational classification of disease prevention. In J. A. Steinberg & M. M. Silverman (Eds.), *Preventing mental disorders* (pp. 20–26). Rockville, MD: Department of Health and Human Services.

Graziano, P. A., Calkins, S. D., & Keane, S. P. (2010). Toddler self-regulation skills predict risk for pediatric obesity. *International Journal of Obesity, 34,* 633–641. http://dx.doi.org/10.1038/ijo.2009.288

Hubert, B., Guimard, P., Florin, A., & Tracy, A. (2015). Indirect and direct relationships between self-regulation and academic achievement during the nursery/elementary school transition of French students. *Early Education and Development, 26,* 685–707. http://dx.doi.org/10.1080/10409289.2015.1037624

The Institute of Human Development and Social Change. (n.d.). *Chicago School Readiness Project.* Retrieved from https://steinhardt.nyu.edu/ihdsc/csrp

Jones, D. E., Greenberg, M., & Crowley, M. (2015). Early social-emotional functioning and public health: The relationship between kindergarten social competence and future wellness. *American Journal of Public Health, 105,* 2283–2290. http://dx.doi.org/10.2105/AJPH.2015.302630

Li-Grining, C., & Haas, K. (2010, March). *Academic outcomes of the Chicago School Readiness Project in first grade: Do children's approaches to learning mediate treatment effects on academic skills?* Paper presented at the Spring Conference of the Society for Research on Educational Effectiveness, Chicago, IL.

Li-Grining, C. P., Raver, C. C., & Pess, R. A. (2011, March). *Academic impacts of the Chicago School Readiness Project: Testing for evidence in elementary school.* Paper presented at the biennial meeting of the Society for Research in Child Development, Montreal, QC, Canada.

Lillard, A. S. (2012). Preschool children's development in classic Montessori, supplemented Montessori, and conventional programs. *Journal of School Psychology, 50,* 379–401. http://dx.doi.org/10.1016/j.jsp.2012.01.001

Lillard, A. S., & Else-Quest, N. (2006). The early years: Evaluating Montessori. *Science, 313,* 1893–1894.

Lillard, A. S., Heise, M. J., Richey, E. M., Tong, X., Hart, A., & Bray, P. M. (2017). Montessori preschool elevates and equalizes child outcomes: A longitudinal study. *Frontiers in Psychology, 8,* 1783. http://dx.doi.org/10.3389/fpsyg.2017.01783

McClelland, M. M., Acock, A. C., & Morrison, F. J. (2006). The impact of kindergarten learning-related skills on academic trajectories at the end of elementary school. *Early Childhood Research Quarterly, 21,* 471–490. http://dx.doi.org/10.1016/j.ecresq.2006.09.003

Moffitt, T. E., Arseneault, L., Belsky, D., Dickson, N., Hancox, R. J., Harrington, H., . . . Caspi, A. (2011). A gradient of childhood self-control predicts health, wealth, and public safety. *Proceedings of the National Academy of Sciences of the United States of America, 108,* 2693–2698. http://dx.doi.org/10.1073/pnas.1010076108

Montessori, M. (1914). *U.S. Patent No. 1,103,369.* Washington, DC: U.S. Patent and Trademark Office.

Montessori, M. (1967). *The absorbent mind.* New York, NY: Holt, Rinehart, and Winston. (Original work published 1949)

Mrazek, P., & Haggerty, R. J. (Eds.). (1994). *Reducing risks for mental disorders: Frontiers for preventive intervention research.* Washington, DC: National Academy Press.

Mytton, J., DiGuiseppi, C., Gough, D., Taylor, R., & Logan, S. (2007). School-based secondary prevention programmes for preventing violence [Review]. *Evidence-Based Child Health: A Cochrane Review Journal, 2,* 814–891. http://dx.doi.org/10.1002/ebch.127

National Collaborating Center for Mental Health, Social Care Institute for Excellence. (2013). *Antisocial behavior and conduct disorders in children and young people: Recognition, intervention and management* (NICE Clinical Guidelines, No. 158). Leicester, England: British Psychological Society. Retrieved from https://www.ncbi.nlm.nih.gov/books/NBK299074

National Scientific Council on the Developing Child. (2007). *The science of early childhood development: Closing the gap between what we know and what we do.* Retrieved from https://developingchild.harvard.edu/resources/the-science-of-early-childhood-development-closing-the-gap-between-what-we-know-and-what-we-do

Nurius, P. S., Green, S., Logan-Greene, P., Longhi, D., & Song, C. (2016). Stress pathways to health inequalities: Embedding ACEs within social and behavioral contexts. *International Public Health Journal, 8,* 241–256.

O'Connell, M., Boat, T., & Warner, K. (Eds.). (2009). *National Research Council (US) and Institute of Medicine (US) Committee on the Prevention of Mental Disorders and Substance Abuse Among Children, Youth and Young Adults: Research advances and promising interventions.* Washington, DC: The National Academies Press.

Petrill, S. A., & Deater-Deckard, K. (2004). Task orientation, parental warmth and SES account for a significant proportion of the shared environmental variance in general cognitive ability in early childhood: Evidence from a twin study. *Developmental Science, 7*(1), 25–32. http://dx.doi.org/10.1111/j.1467-7687.2004.00319.x

Phillips-Silver, J., & Daza, M. T. (2018). Cognitive control at age 3: Evaluating executive functions in an equitable Montessori preschool. *Frontiers in Education, 3,* 106.

Raver, C. C., Jones, S. M., Li-Grining, C. P., Metzger, M., Champion, K. M., & Sardin, L. (2008). Improving preschool classroom processes: Preliminary findings from a randomized trial implemented in Head Start settings. *Early Childhood Research Quarterly, 23*(1), 10–26. http://dx.doi.org/10.1016/j.ecresq.2007.09.001

Raver, C. C., Jones, S. M., Li-Grining, C., Zhai, F., Bub, K., & Pressler, E. (2011). CSRP's Impact on low-income preschoolers' preacademic skills: Self-regulation as a mediating mechanism. *Child Development, 82*(1), 362–378. http://dx.doi.org/10.1111/j.1467-8624.2010.01561.x

Razza, R. A., Martin, A., & Brooks-Gunn, J. (2015). Are approaches to learning in kindergarten associated with academic and social competence similarly? *Child & Youth Care Forum, 44*, 757–776. http://dx.doi.org/10.1007/s10566-015-9307-0

Schmitt, S. A., McClelland, M. M., Tominey, S. L., & Acock, A. C. (2015). Strengthening school readiness for Head Start children: Evaluation of a self-regulation intervention. *Early Childhood Research Quarterly, 30*, 20–31. http://dx.doi.org/10.1016/j.ecresq.2014.08.001

Sezgin, E., & Demiriz, S. (2019). Effect of play-based educational programme on behavioral self-regulation skills of 48–60 month-old children. *Early Child Development and Care, 189*, 1100–1113. http://dx.doi.org/10.1080/03004430.2017.1369972

Sklad, M., Diekstra, R., Ritter, M., Ben, J., & Gravesteijn, C. (2012). Effectiveness of school-based universal social-emotional, and behavioral programs: Do they enhance students' development in the area of skill, behavior and adjustment? *Psychology in the Schools, 49*, 892–909. http://dx.doi.org/10.1002/pits.21641

Solomon, T., Plamondon, A., O'Hara, A., Finch, H., Goco, G., Chaban, P., . . . Tannock, R. (2018). A cluster randomized-controlled trial of the impact of the *Tools of the Mind* curriculum on self-regulation in Canadian preschoolers. *Frontiers in Psychology, 8*, 2366. http://dx.doi.org/10.3389/fpsyg.2017.02366

Tobin, T. J., & Sugai, G. (2005). Prevention problem behaviors: Primary, secondary and tertiary level prevention interventions for young children. *Journal of Early and Intensive Behavior Intervention, 2*(3), 125–144. http://dx.doi.org/10.1037/h0100309

Tominey, S. L., & McClelland, M. M. (2011). Red light, purple light: Findings from a randomized trial using circle time games to improve behavioral self-regulation in preschool. *Early Education and Development, 22*, 489–519. http://dx.doi.org/10.1080/10409289.2011.574258

Vygotsky, L. (1978). Interaction between learning and development. *Readings on the Development of Children, 23*(3), 34–41.

Wagener, U. (2013). Young children's self-regulated learning: A reflection on Pintrich's model from a microanalytic perspective. *Journal of Cognitive Education and Psychology, 12*, 306–322. http://dx.doi.org/10.1891/1945-8959.12.3.306

Watts, T. W., Gandhi, J., Ibrahim, D. A., Masucci, M. D., & Raver, C. C. (2018). The Chicago School Readiness Project: Examining the long-term impacts of an early childhood intervention. *PLoS ONE, 13*(7), e0200144. http://dx.doi.org/10.1371/journal.pone.0200144

Weinstein, C. E., & Mayer, R. E. (1986). The teaching of learning strategies. In M. Wittrock (Ed.), *Handbook of research on teaching* (pp. 315–327). New York, NY: Macmillan.

Wenz-Gross, M., Yoo, Y., Upshur, C. C., & Gambino, A. (2018). Pathways to kindergarten readiness: The roles of Second Step Early Learning Curriculum and social emotional, executive functioning, preschool academic and task behavior skills. *Frontiers in Psychology, 9*(1886), 1–19. http://dx.doi.org/10.3389/fpsyg.2018.01886

Wilson, S. J., & Farran, D. C. (2012, March). *Experimental evaluation of the Tools of the Mind preschool curriculum.* Paper presented at the spring conference of the Society for Research on Educational Effectiveness, Washington, DC.

Xing, B., Li, Y. C., & Gao, W. J. (2016). Norepinephrine versus dopamine and their interaction in modulating synaptic function in the prefrontal cortex. *Brain research, 1641*(Pt. B), 217–233. http://dx.doi.org/10.1016/j.brainres.2016.01.005

Zelazo, P. D., Anderson, J. E., Richler, J., Wallner-Allen, K., Beaumont, J. L., & Weintraub, S. (2013). II. NIH Toolbox Cognition Battery (CB): Measuring executive function and attention. *Monographs of the Society for Research in Child Development, 78*(4), 16–33. http://dx.doi.org/10.1111/mono.12032

Zelazo, P. D., Blair, C. B., & Willoughby, M. T. (2016). *Executive function: Implications for education* (NCER 2017-2000). Washington, DC: National Center for Education Research, Institute of Education Sciences, U.S. Department of Education. Retrieved from https://ies.ed.gov/ncer/pubs/20172000/pdf/20172000.pdf

Zimmerman, B. J. (1995). Self-efficacy and educational development. In A. Bandura (Ed.), *Self-efficacy in changing societies* (pp. 202–231). New York, NY: Cambridge University Press. http://dx.doi.org/10.1017/CBO9780511527692.009

Zimmerman, B. J., & Martinez Pons, M. (1986). Development of a structured interview for assessing student use of self-regulated learning strategies. *American Educational Research Journal, 23*, 614–628. http://dx.doi.org/10.3102/00028312023004614

7

The Utility of Play for Later Academic Achievement

Darlene DeMarie and Jennifer Bugos

David Elkind (2007) wrote that play, work, and love should complement one another, and when they work together, development and learning are optimized. Yet, in the United States in recent years, children's time for play has been shortened or even sometimes even eliminated to give children more allocated time for learning specific academic skills. In this chapter, we detail different types of play that not only benefit young children's academic achievement but also provide a foundation for their lifelong learning. In addition to detailing research that supports these claims, we provide examples of activities within classrooms.

CHILDREN'S OPPORTUNITIES FOR PLAY

In the foreword to *A Mandate for Playful Learning in Preschool: Presenting the Evidence* by Hirsh-Pasek, Golinkoff, Berk, and Singer (2009), Ed Ziegler (2009) explained the historical roots of the false dichotomy between play and learning. The Soviet Union's launching of the satellite Sputnik in the late 1950s and the No Child Left Behind Act (2001) during George W. Bush's presidency pushed trends that emphasized children's mastery of academic (e.g., literacy, math) cognitive skills, while ignoring children's socioemotional skill development. In recent years, parents seem to be increasingly concerned that their children have more early academic learning so they can become high achievers when they enter elementary school (Ziegler, 2009). And the current multimillion-dollar educational toy industry is geared to teach children

http://dx.doi.org/10.1037/0000197-008
Healthy Development in Young Children: Evidence-Based Interventions for Early Education,
V. C. Alfonso and G. J. DuPaul (Editors)

academic skills, which often are taught in isolation (i.e., child isolation from others and skill isolation within content).

In addition to these trends, children, especially those from certain groups, have fewer opportunities during preschool and primary school for spontaneous, creative, or outdoor play (Ginsburg, American Academy of Pediatrics Committee on Communications, & American Academy of Pediatrics Committee on Psychosocial Aspects of Child and Family Health, 2007). Jarrett's (2019) review of research showed how recess impacted children's learning, social development, and health. However, Jarrett, Sutterby, DeMarie, and Stenhouse (2015) noted play opportunities are not equitable across different groups. Children whose families have lower socioeconomic status (SES) do not have as many play opportunities as do those from families who have higher SES. The playgrounds in these children's neighborhoods tend to be of lower quality (Allen, Hill, Tranter, & Sheehan, 2013), the children have fewer opportunities for recess within their school schedule (Barros, Silver, & Stein, 2009), and they typically attend schools where they have less playful learning from an early age (DeMarie, 2010). Children with physical challenges may not have access to playgrounds (Burke, 2013). And those children who are from racially underrepresented groups are more likely to lose recess at schools, even if recess is offered to other children. However, there is mounting evidence that having recess helps children not only physically but also socially and emotionally (Jarrett, 2013).

So why should teachers or parents care about children's play? Does play benefit young children's academic skill development, or is play something that takes away from children's academic learning? In this chapter, we provide examples from research that support ways children's play and learning complement one another. And these benefits often extend beyond the child's early years.

Why would people assume children need early academic learning to be successful in school? If you ask parents, they probably think schools require children to enter kindergarten with that knowledge. Do teachers agree that knowing academic skills is the most important part of readiness for school? A cited study in the following section explored kindergarten teachers' perspectives about what made children ready for kindergarten.

WHAT ARE THE MOST IMPORTANT SKILLS FOR CHILDREN ENTERING KINDERGARTEN?

The results of a recent survey sent to a national sample of kindergarten teachers (Curby et al., 2017) revealed that kindergarten teachers did not consider academic skills the most important skills for children to have to be considered ready for kindergarten. The survey asked kindergarten teachers to rate the importance of different skills for children's readiness for kindergarten. The teachers ranked the eight items from 1 (*most important*) to 8 (*least important*). The four highest ranked items all were socioemotional skills:

- getting along with others (*M* rank = 2.15),
- knowing how to solve basic social problems (*M* rank = 2.97),

- understanding basic emotions (e.g., anger, sadness; *M* rank = 3.20), and
- calming themselves down when they're upset (*M* rank = 3.26).

On the other hand, teachers' mean rankings of the four academic items all were lower than their rankings of the socioemotional items. The academic items were as follows:

- knowing upper- and lowercase letters (*M* rank = 4.24),
- counting to 20 (*M* rank = 5.43),
- knowing how to read simple sentences (*M* rank = 7.20), and
- knowing how to add single-digit numbers (*M* rank = 7.64).

Thus, what teachers considered the most important skills for children's kindergarten readiness were those not typically taught via direct instruction of academic skills in isolation.

Other studies investigated changes in children's school readiness from 1998 to 2010 (Latham, 2015). The findings revealed that in more recent years, children had higher skill levels and were more likely to be ready for academic skills when they entered kindergarten. However, the same studies revealed decreases in children's approaches to learning and, specifically, in children's self-control in more recent years.

So, how do we optimize children's early childhood experiences, so they can learn academic skills while also learning important socioemotional skills? And is it possible for children to learn any of these important skills while they play?

The section that follows contains a definition of play. We then discuss children's executive functioning (EF) skills that probably impact children's academic achievement. We explain the key EF skills identified in previous research (i.e., inhibition, working memory, and attentional shifting), how they usually are assessed in research, and how children use them during play. We then explain different types of play. The subsequent sections detail the benefits of specific types of play for young children's later academic skill development. We present an example of play that typically does not directly include adults and work toward play that has more adult presence. Illustrations are provided of play that engages children and that also teaches them skills that lead to their future academic success.

WHAT IS CONSIDERED PLAY?

There is not a consensus on the definition of *play* (Pellegrini, 2009). Elkind (2007) defined it as children's "inborn disposition for learning, curiosity, imagination, and fantasy" (p. ix). Hirsh-Pasek and Golinkoff (2003) reported Catherine Garvey and Kenneth Rubin's five elements of play:

- Play is pleasurable and enjoyable for the individual.
- Play involves active engagement of the individual.
- Play contains some type of make-believe.
- Play is not an activity that has extrinsic goals.
- Play is spontaneous and voluntary.

Hirsh-Pasek and colleagues (2009) mentioned additional qualities from other authors, noting that play

- "has a private reality,"
- "is . . . all-engrossing,"
- "is non-literal," and
- "can contain a certain element of make-believe." (p. 26)

Hirsh-Pasek and colleagues (2009) then explained when play is used for instruction, the requirements that play not have extrinsic goals, be spontaneous, and have a private reality could be relaxed.

Our general definition of play is an activity that promotes a child's continued engagement by choice, with or without materials. That activity may or may not involve a teacher, a parent, or another child. It is something the child chooses to continue to do, whether it was the child's idea or someone else led the child to participate in that activity. For example, a teacher may suggest a child play a number board game with other children. If the child plays the game and chooses to keep playing it and enjoys that activity, we would say the child is playing. At the same time, a teacher may select the materials to place in the classroom to encourage children's dramatic play. Again, if children choose to engage in the dramatic play center and do or do not use those materials, we would identify their activity as playing.

Different types of play have different benefits, so it is important that we note how types of play are proposed to impact children's future academic achievement. Although the benefits of play may not be observed immediately, different types of play may provide varied experiences needed for optimal learning and development in subsequent years.

Before we discuss specific types of play, it is important to provide background on skills that probably are enhanced by play and that may be a cause of children's later academic success.

EXECUTIVE FUNCTIONING SKILLS THAT PROBABLY IMPACT CHILDREN'S ACADEMIC ACHIEVEMENT

Cooper-Kahn and Foster (2013) defined *executive function* as "an umbrella term for the mental processes that serve a supervisory role in thinking and behavior" and claimed these processes "work together to direct and coordinate our efforts to achieve a goal" (p. 7). Within the past decade, results of numerous studies suggest there are anywhere from one to three core factors of young children's EF. The three dominant, interrelated EF factors most visible in the literature include inhibitory control or inhibition, working memory or updating, and cognitive flexibility or attentional shifting (Diamond, 2013; Miyake et al., 2000). The two that have the greatest support to date for relations to children's early academic achievement are inhibition and working memory (Nguyen & Duncan, 2019).

Inhibitory Control or Inhibition

The most common tasks used to assess young children's inhibition are forms of the go/no-go task. Children must do something or say something, except when other conditions are present. For example, one of the eight tasks of the computerized version of the EF Touch battery (Willoughby, Blair, Wirth, Greenberg, & The Family Life Project Investigators, 2010) is labeled the pig task. Young children are told to point (on the touchscreen) to animals presented on the screen, except if the animal is a pig. Thus, when they see a pig, because it is an animal, they may be inclined to touch the pig. However, they must inhibit pointing, because they were told to not point to animals that were pigs.

An example evident in children's play is seen in the Simon Says game. Children do whatever the leader says and does, but only when the request is preceded by the words "Simon says" (e.g., The leader says, "Simon says 'Touch your toes,'" so the children follow and touch their toes). Alternatively, if the leader does not begin with the words "Simon says," the children must inhibit their behavior of doing what the leader says and does (e.g., The leader says, "Touch your nose," and the children must resist touching their nose and instead must keep their hands touching their toes).

Working Memory

Tasks used to assess young children's working memory require that children hold certain information in mind while processing information in some way. An example of a task used to assess children's verbal working memory is the backward digit span. Children must hold a string of digits (5, 8, 3, 7) in mind while saying them backwards (e.g., 7, 3, 8, 5; Wechsler, 2014).

The same elements are required when we assess children's visual working memory. For example, in the houses task of the EF battery (Willoughby et al., 2010), children see houses with colored circles and animals in them. After the screen is no longer visible, children are asked to name the colors or to name the animals they had seen within the previously visible houses. Thus, children must store all the house information in memory while selecting those relevant to report.

Working memory skills are an important part of learning to decode words in early reading. For example, before children can read certain words automatically, they must say each letter sound in the order of presentation, then hear the sounds in that order in memory while blending them to figure out the word. For example, the child sees the word *cat*, says the sounds /k/, /ă/, and /t/, and then says "cat." At the same time, beginning readers read each word in the sentence individually (e.g., "The cat sat on the rug"), and they must remember each of the words they already read as they work to understand the sentence, the paragraph, and, finally, the story.

Working memory skills also are needed when children play in dramatic play centers. They must keep their own role in mind (e.g., I am the teacher who is teaching arithmetic) while enacting actions that typify that role and also considering what others do (e.g., pupils are misbehaving), which may require other actions (e.g., raising a hand to the mouth to signify being quiet). Actions typical of the character they are portraying must be retrieved and enacted while processing the others' ongoing activity.

Cognitive Flexibility or Attentional Shifting

A third factor identified in EF research is cognitive flexibility, also known as attentional shifting. Something a child did previously is no longer the appropriate response, and the child must use a different response. For example, in the card-sorting task, a child is told to sort cards by one characteristic (e.g., color). Then the child is told to sort by a different characteristic (e.g., size). Therefore, for the first sort, the large brown horse would be placed in the pile with other brown things, which also may contain a small brown monkey and a small brown box. However, for the next sort, sorting by size, the large brown horse would be placed on the pile with the large green dinosaur. It would not be appropriate to place the large brown horse with the small brown monkey. Thus, the child's attention must shift from one characteristic of the items to a different characteristic.

One type of play that requires attentional shifting is a game that requires a change of directions. For instance, in games such as Duck, Duck, Goose or Closet Key, children must switch between watching the player selecting the goose and moving when it is their turn to run around the circle away from getting tagged. This scenario creates an immediate attention shift from a steady chanting of a game to capturing the player running around the circle.

EXECUTIVE FUNCTIONS AS PREDICTORS OF CHILDREN'S ACADEMIC ACHIEVEMENT

Many studies show children's math achievement is related to their EF skills (Blair, Ursache, Greenberg, Vernon-Feagans, & Family Life Project Investigators, 2015; Bull, Espy, & Wiebe, 2008; Bull & Scerif, 2001; Fuhs & McNeil, 2013; Fuhs, Nesbitt, Farran, & Dong, 2014; Geary, 2011; Ng, Tamis-LeMonda, Yoshikawa, & Sze, 2015; Schmitt, Geldhof, Purpura, Duncan, & McClelland, 2017; Schmitt, Pratt, & McClelland, 2014). There also is support that EF skills relate to children's reading achievement, especially during their early school years (e.g., McKinnon & Blair, 2019; Meixner, Warner, Lensing, Schiefele, & Elsner, 2019). Some studies found relations between children's EF and early math and reading achievement (e.g., Blair & Razza, 2007; Montoya et al., 2019).

This advantage of better EF skills and early academic achievement may continue into the adolescent years (Watts, Duncan, Siegler, & Davis-Kean, 2014). Thus, young children's EF may provide them with the necessary foundation and building blocks for later academic skill learning (Blair & Raver, 2015; McClelland et al., 2007). In fact, some claim that EF skill deficits are detrimental to children's success in reading, math, and science across elementary school, and children's working memory is especially important (e.g., Morgan et al., 2019).

One example of research by Bull et al. (2008) revealed inhibition and working memory tasks all correlated significantly with math assessments each year through the end of the third year of primary school. The strongest correlation was between math achievement and visuospatial working memory span.

Achievement in reading was a bit different. Whereas all cognitive tasks predicted early reading achievement, inhibition and backward digit span (i.e., the verbal working memory task) did not predict reading achievement by the end of the third year of primary school. Bull and colleagues (2008) concluded,

> Better executive functions skills (inhibition and planning) in preschool already provide children with a building block for math and reading resulting in better academic skills early in development, an advantage that is maintained throughout their first three years of formal schooling. (p. 221)

There also is some evidence not only that EF skills predict later math achievement but that math achievement also predicts later EF skills (Nesbitt, Fuhs, & Farran, 2019). Thus, EF skills and math achievement may have a bidirectional relationship across development.

The following sections elaborate on different types of play that relate to areas of children's academic achievement. Examples of children's play, the research supporting its link to EF or academic skills, and other direct or indirect outcomes are detailed. We present examples from dramatic play, number board games, and music activities.

DRAMATIC PLAY EXPERIENCES

As Cohen (2006) noted, "Pretend play seems to be a key skill in social and cognitive development" (p. 10). Pretend play sometimes is labeled *dramatic play* or *sociodramatic play*, and when children engage in these forms of play, their play affords them opportunities for expressing language and for practicing writing. Through this play, children recreate stories that may or may not resemble experiences they have had directly. Research conducted with children in kindergarten in Jordan found that introducing dramatic play enhanced children's writing behaviors (see Ihmeideh, 2015), including creating letterlike forms, drawings, and other symbolic representations. Those who engaged in dramatic play also had more favorable attitudes toward writing.

Teachers' roles can vary, but typically teachers are the ones who prepare the play space for children based on their previous observations of the children's play in that space. In a cyclic manner, teachers observe children's play, introduce new materials, learn from what they see children doing with those new materials, and plan what to introduce into that space next. Although teachers can facilitate play by selecting appropriate materials for the play space, they should try not to control play as it ensues. However, a very shy child or a child whose home language differs from the dominant culture may need additional teacher support to feel comfortable engaging in play with others (Scrafton & Whitington, 2015).

Suppose a teacher observed children pretending to be at a restaurant. The teacher might decide to add menus from local restaurants, a small tablet, and writing utensils to the play space to prompt children to use their emerging literacy skills (Alghamdi, DeMarie, & Alanazi, in press). If the class has children from other countries, the teacher might place items appropriate within children's home cultures (e.g., chopsticks) to engage the children in dialogue and learning about their respective cultural differences.

As the children pretend to be at the restaurant, one child might pretend to be the waiter and ask, "Can I take your order?"

A second child might reply, "I want a hamburger," and another child might say, "I want a burrito." As they play their roles, they probably will engage in conversation about why they ordered these items or what they want to put on those items. This helps them to learn about their choices and their cultural diversity (Scrafton & Whitington, 2015).

The child who pretended to be the waiter might tell the cook the items children ordered. To do this, the child would need to either write them down (i.e., a literacy task) or maintain those items in memory. Next, the cook would need to keep the items ordered in mind, while pretending to prepare them. This would require working memory (i.e., holding items in mind while processing the sequence of steps to prepare them). Then after pretending to cook the items, the waiter, when serving the items, would need to remember which child ordered each item.

In the process of creating dramatic play scenarios, children may also learn a sense of story. Their actions and words support a proper sequence of activities. The cook cannot make the food without knowing what the children chose to order. Likewise, children cannot eat the food before it is served. If teachers photograph children's play activities, they later can challenge the children to put the photographs into the proper sequence and retell the story from the photographs. Teachers also can create a book for children to choose to read from the children's words and photographs. Activities like these introduce children to sequencing and the symbolic meaning of print. This back-and-forth sequence of events—children's play, then optional activities based on play, then children's choice to interact with those materials created for them—all help to encourage children to practice academic skills in meaningful contexts.

PLAY WITH NUMBER BOARD GAMES

Whereas teachers' involvement in dramatic play activities typically is minimal, when children play number board games, more teacher support is needed, especially at first. Although the teacher demonstrates and supports children's number board play, children's choice to continue to play reinforces and supports their skills for later math learning.

The early foundational knowledge that is essential for math achievement is learned during early childhood (Ramani, Daubert, & Scalise, 2019). Longitudinal research revealed that the numerical knowledge children had at age 4 predicted their math skills at age 15, even when controlling for other factors such as IQ and SES (Watts, Duncan, Siegler, & Davis-Kean, 2014). However, young children from families with lower income have skills that typically lag those of children from families with middle income (Geary, 1994). So how do children acquire this foundational knowledge at the age of 4 years? Does teaching children to count to 10 and to identify the numerals 1 to 10 suffice for laying an appropriate foundation for their later math achievement in school?

The answer most likely is no. In addition to these rote memory activities (e.g., learning to count and to identify numbers), children need to understand the magnitude of these numbers and how the numbers' quantities relate to one another. Additionally, research shows there are playful ways for children to learn the foundational skills for their later math achievement. Playing linear board games such as Chutes and Ladders is one of these ways.

Siegler and Booth (2004) explained the benefits of children playing numerical board games such as Chutes and Ladders. When children spin the spinner, it lands on a number. Then they move their token that many spaces. In the process, children will hear or say more numbers for larger numbers (e.g., "1, 2, 3, 4, 5, 6, 7" for "7") than for smaller numbers (e.g., "1, 2" for "2"). Not only did they hear or say more numbers, but they also had more discrete moves, had more time that elapsed before their token landed on the appropriate space, and had more distance covered by their token on the board. These are all cues to the relative size of each of the numbers.

The benefits of board games were demonstrated in experimental research by Siegler and Ramani (2008) with children whose families were from lower-SES backgrounds. In this research, 4-year-old preschool children were randomly assigned to play either a linear, numerical board game or a similar game with colored squares instead of numbered squares for 1 hour. The children's number estimation skills were assessed by providing them with a number line that had only the number *0* at one end and the number *10* at the other end, with no numbers in between those numbers. Children were shown a number and were asked to point to the place on the number line where that number would be. Siegler and Ramani then measured the distance between the location chosen by the child and the location where the number would be located if there were equal intervals between all numbers.

The results showed that those children who played the number board game for four 15- to 20-minute periods within a 2-week period not only showed improvement in counting and number identification but also improved significantly more in their number estimation skills than did the children who played the color square game. Those children who played linear board games also showed significant improvement in numerical magnitude comparisons (e.g., "Which number is larger: 8 or 2?"), and the gains remained 9 weeks after they had played the number board game.

In another study, children who played linear numerical board games improved significantly more than did children who played circular board games (Siegler & Ramani, 2009). In addition, Ramani, Siegler, and Hitti (2012) found children who were in Head Start classrooms (i.e., came from lower-SES backgrounds) made significant gains when playing number board games in small groups or with a paraprofessional. In their review of research, Schneider et al. (2017) concluded that the effects of this type of intervention in experimental research may be greater for children who come from families with lower SES. Thus, this type of play seems to promote skills needed for children's later math achievement, and the impact of this play may be greater for children from families with certain demographics.

Play that is guided by adults is just as important as free play (Hirsh-Pasek et al., 2009). In fact, guided play can enhance children's learning while still not controlling the spontaneous enjoyment of that play. In the next section, we explore the benefits of children's engagement with musical play.

ENGAGEMENT WITH MUSICAL PLAY

Multimodal music programs utilize musical play by fostering vocal development, bimanual coordination (i.e., instrumental performance), and creative improvisation. Preliminary research has shown that a multimodal music program can enhance working memory through including a variety of musical tasks that facilitate attention and concentration in young children (Bugos & DeMarie, 2017). Because young children have difficulty attending for long periods, components of each piece of a multimodal music program promote attention and enhance areas of EF through a variety of musical play tasks.

Children flourish in an environment that includes a variety of opportunities to engage in musical play. Musical play can consist of vocal and instrumental improvisational activities, singing games, music listening exercises, and folk dances. An example of a vocal improvisational activity for young preschoolers may include the substitution of their names to simple songs with repetition that include so-mi-la pitches such as "Bounce High, Bounce Low" or "Rain, Rain, Go Away." Bilateral facilitation of Curwen hand signs (i.e., standard hand signs representing pitches of a scale that were developed by John Curwen) enables the children to place the pitch on an imaginary pitch ladder, kinesthetically feeling the concept of pitch while receiving feedback regarding their pitch accuracy.

Behavioral research supports the inclusion of body movements in singing games at very early ages. Children from 5 to 24 months old were found to demonstrate rhythmic movement by listening to music as compared with other stimuli such as speech (Zentner & Eerola, 2010). There seems to be a natural connection between music and movement from a very early age. Musically engaging activities for preschool children include synchronizing their bodies to the underlying rhythmic structure without requiring a visual of the sound source (Gruhn et al., 2012). Children learn to make coordinated and controlled movements by feeling the underlying steady beat and distinguishing this beat from other rhythmic characteristics (e.g., rhythm of the words) or rhythmic ostinatos (i.e., repeated patterns).

Children learn to imitate melodic pitch patterns. On the playground, children often sing the minor third interval sol-mi-sol-mi-sol-mi as if to say, "You can't catch me." Singing is a naturally playful activity and can be implemented while keeping rhythms through movements such as jumping rope or playing nonpitched percussion instruments (e.g., drums, maracas). Children copy pitch patterns using hand signs to develop fluency and memory for solfege (i.e., every note of a scale is given its own unique syllable). After practice, young children can take turns creating phrases using melodic patterns that the class copies. Singing games often include pentatonic folk songs (e.g., "There's a Hole in the Bucket"), familiar songs (e.g., "Farmer in the Dell," "Blue Bird," "London Bridges," "Closet Key," "This Old Man"), and nursery rhymes that may take the form of mini-operas (e.g., "The Three Bears," "Old King Cole," "Humpty Dumpty") in which children can sing the songs and act out the mini-opera with props. Children who serve as actors in the mini-opera are encouraged to sing the parts, just as any opera would include a sung libretto.

Engagement with creative musical activities enhances critical thinking (Kelstrom, 1998). Improvisational activities or games can provide children the freedom to play with new musical ideas. Children are encouraged through creative improvisation to complete songs such as "Going on a Picnic" and to generate various food items that they might take with them on a picnic. Children must attend to the temporal requirements of the song and add the sung word(s) on the correct beat(s). Working memory for melodies and rhythms can be strengthened through repetition of simple songs and singing games.

Inhibition of melody or rhythms at inappropriate times contributes to enhanced EF skills (Bowmer, Mason, Knight, & Welch, 2018; Bugos & DeMarie, 2017). A short-term multimodal training program that focused upon creative improvisational activities with mallet-based percussion instruments enhanced areas of EF for children from families of migrant farm workers (Bugos & DeMarie, 2017). Another study found support that 8 weeks of vocal music and listening activities in the Creative Futures program increased inhibitory control of preschool children in London (Bowmer et al., 2018). These experimental data revealed that a short-term music program can increase inhibitory behavior in preschoolers.

Musical play experiences place complex demands upon attention that may be responsible for academic and cognitive performance. Researchers who implemented an early childhood music program with singing games as an intervention for a group of Head Start children found enhanced academic and cognitive performance posttraining (Neville et al., 2008). Neville and colleagues (2008) attributed differences in performance to the attentional demands of music training in selective attention. There are many implications from this research such as including musical play programs for children who experience high levels of adversity as these children are most susceptible to deficits in selective attention as well as extending musical interventions to children with attentional deficits (Giuliano et al., 2018).

CONCLUSION

In this chapter, we reviewed research related to different types of children's play and each one's relation to children's later academic achievement. We provided examples of different play activities that required minimal to more direct adult involvement and showed that play benefits the development of children's EF skills (i.e., inhibition, working memory, and attentional flexibility). When teachers observe children's play, they can learn about different children's cultures. Play can bring groups together to share experiences and learn how to take turns and how to cooperate with one another. According to kindergarten teachers, these socioemotional skills are the most important skills for children to have for them to be considered ready for kindergarten.

This chapter emphasized the value of children's play and how it facilitates EF and academic skill development. Play and learning are certainly not opposites! Bjorklund (2018) noted, "Contemporary psychologists have long acknowledged that play has both immediate and deferred benefits for a young organism" (p. 2,297). He recommended we consider framing development using an evolutionary perspective. With that perspective, "Play evolved as a means for young animals to acquire important physical, social and cognitive skills" (Bjorklund, 2018, p. 2,297). Perhaps Bjorklund's suggestion that evolutionary theory may become a new metatheory for cognitive development will happen in the future. Then people would understand why play should never be eliminated from children's school experiences.

REFERENCES

Alghamdi, R. S., DeMarie, D., & Alanazi, D. (in press). Teacher–child interactions in play that enhance young children's learning: Stories from three countries. *International Journal of the Child*.

Allen, E. M., Hill, A. L., Tranter, E., & Sheehan, K. (2013). Playground safety and quality in Chicago. *Pediatrics, 131,* 233–241.

Barros, R. M., Silver, E. J., & Stein, R. E. K. (2009). School recess and group classroom behavior. *Pediatrics, 123,* 431–436. http://dx.doi.org/10.1542/peds.2007-2825

Bjorklund, D. F. (2018). A metatheory for cognitive development (or "Piaget is dead" revisited). *Child Development, 89,* 2288–2302. http://dx.doi.org/10.1111/cdev.13019

Blair, C., & Raver, C. C. (2015). School readiness and self-regulation: A developmental psychobiological approach. *Annual Review of Psychology, 66,* 711–731. http://dx.doi.org/10.1146/annurev-psych-010814-015221

Blair, C., & Razza, R. P. (2007). Relating effortful control, executive function, and false belief understanding to emerging math and literacy ability in kindergarten. *Child Development, 78,* 647–663. http://dx.doi.org/10.1111/j.1467-8624.2007.01019.x

Blair, C., Ursache, A., Greenberg, M., Vernon-Feagans, L., & Family Life Project Investigators. (2015). Multiple aspects of self-regulation uniquely predict mathematics but not letter-word knowledge in the early elementary grades. *Developmental Psychology, 51,* 459–472. http://dx.doi.org/10.1037/a0038813

Bowmer, A., Mason, K., Knight, J., & Welch, G. (2018). Investigating the impact of a musical intervention on preschool children's executive function. *Frontiers in Psychology, 9*, 2389. http://dx.doi.org/10.3389/fpsyg.2018.02389

Bugos, J., & DeMarie, D. (2017). The effects of a short-term music program on preschool children's executive functions. *Psychology of Music, 45*, 855–867. http://dx.doi.org/10.1177/0305735617692666

Bull, R., Espy, K. A., & Wiebe, S. A. (2008). Short-term memory, working memory, and executive functioning in preschoolers: Longitudinal predictors of mathematical achievement at age 7 years. *Developmental Neuropsychology, 33*, 205–228. http://dx.doi.org/10.1080/87565640801982312

Bull, R., & Scerif, G. (2001). Executive functioning as a predictor of children's mathematics ability: Inhibition, shifting and working memory. *Developmental Neuropsychology, 19*, 273–293. http://dx.doi.org/10.1207/S15326942DN1903_3

Burke, J. (2013). Just for the fun of it: Making playgrounds accessible to all children. *World Leisure Journal, 55*(1), 83–95. http://dx.doi.org/10.1080/04419057.2012.759144

Cohen, D. (2006). *The development of play* (3rd ed.). New York, NY: Routledge. http://dx.doi.org/10.4324/9780203133774

Cooper-Kahn, J., & Foster, M. (2013). *Boosting executive skills in the classroom: A practical guide for educators.* San Francisco, CA: John Wiley & Sons.

Curby, T. W., Berke, E., Alfonso, V., Blake, J., DeMarie, D., DuPaul, G. J., . . . Subotnik, R. F. (2017). Kindergarten teacher perceptions of kindergarten readiness: The importance of social–emotional skills. *Perspectives on Early Childhood Psychology and Education, 2*, 115–137.

DeMarie, D. (2010). Successful versus unsuccessful schools through the eyes of children: The use of interviews, autophotography, and picture selection. *Early Childhood Research & Practice, 12*(2). Retrieved from http://ecrp.illinois.edu/v12n2/demarie.html

Diamond, A. (2013). Executive functions. *Annual Review of Psychology, 64*, 135–168. http://dx.doi.org/10.1146/annurev-psych-113011-143750

Elkind, D. (2007). *The power of play: Learning what comes naturally.* Philadelphia, PA: Da Capo Press.

Fuhs, M. W., & McNeil, N. M. (2013). ANS acuity and mathematics ability in preschoolers from low-income homes: Contributions of inhibitory control. *Developmental Science, 16*(1), 136–148. http://dx.doi.org/10.1111/desc.12013

Fuhs, M. W., Nesbitt, K. T., Farran, D. C., & Dong, N. (2014). Longitudinal associations between executive functioning and academic skills across content areas. *Developmental Psychology, 50*, 1698–1709. http://dx.doi.org/10.1037/a0036633

Geary, D. C. (1994). *Children's mathematics development: Research and practical applications.* Washington, DC: American Psychological Association. http://dx.doi.org/10.1037/10163-000

Geary, D. C. (2011). Cognitive predictors of achievement growth in mathematics: A 5-year longitudinal study. *Developmental Psychology, 47*, 1539–1552. http://dx.doi.org/10.1037/a0025510

Ginsburg, K. R., American Academy of Pediatrics Committee on Communications, & American Academy of Pediatrics Committee on Psychosocial Aspects of Child and Family Health. (2007). The importance of play in promoting healthy child development and maintaining strong parent-child bonds. *Pediatrics, 119*, 182–191. http://dx.doi.org/10.1542/peds.2006-2697

Giuliano, R. J., Karns, C. M., Roos, L. E., Bell, T. A., Peterson, S., Skowron, E. A., . . . Pakulak, E. (2018). Effects of early adversity on neural mechanisms of distractor suppression are mediated by sympathetic nervous system activity in preschool-aged children. *Developmental Psychology, 54*, 1674–1686. http://dx.doi.org/10.1037/dev0000499

Gruhn, W., Haussmann, M., Herb, U., Minkner, C., Rottger, K., & Gollhofer, A. (2012). The development of motor coordination and musical abilities in preschool children. *Arts BioMechanics, 1*(2), 89–103.

Hirsh-Pasek, K., & Golinkoff, R. M. (2003). *Einstein never used flashcards: How our children really learn—and why they need to play more and memorize less.* Emmaus, PA: St. Martin's Press.

Hirsh-Pasek, K., Golinkoff, R. M., Berk, L. E., & Singer, D. G. (2009). *A mandate for playful learning in preschool: Presenting the evidence.* New York, NY: Oxford University Press.

Ihmeideh, F. (2015). The impact of dramatic play center on promoting the development of children's early writing skills. *European Early Childhood Education Research Journal, 23,* 250–263. http://dx.doi.org/10.1080/1350293X.2014.970848

Jarrett, O. S. (2013, November). *A research-based case for recess.* U.S. Play Coalition. Retrieved from https://www.schoolfamily.com/images/articles/a-research-based-case-for-recess.pdf

Jarrett, O. S. (2019). *A research-based case for recess: Position paper 2019.* Retrieved from https://usplaycoalition.org/wp-content/uploads/2019/08/Need-for-Recess-2019-FINAL-for-web.pdf

Jarrett, O., Sutterby, J., DeMarie, D., & Stenhouse, V. (2015). Play for all children: Access to quality play experiences as a social justice issue. In A. J. Mashburn, J. LoCasale-Crouch, & K. C. Pears (Eds.), *Spotlight on early childhood: Special issue on play* (pp. 98–106). Washington, DC: National Association for the Education of Young Children.

Kelstrom, J. M. (1998). The untapped power of music: Its role in the curriculum and its effect on academic achievement. *NASSP Bulletin, 82*(597), 34–43. http://dx.doi.org/10.1177/019263659808259707

Latham, S. (2015). Changes in school readiness of America's entering kindergarteners (1998–2010). In A. J. Mashburn, J. LoCasale-Crouch, & K. C. Pears (Eds.), *Kindergarten transition and readiness* (pp. 111–138). Cham, Switzerland: Springer International.

McClelland, M. M., Cameron, C. E., Connor, C. M., Farris, C. L., Jewkes, A. M., & Morrison, F. J. (2007). Links between behavioral regulation and preschoolers' literacy, vocabulary, and math skills. *Developmental Psychology, 43,* 947–959. http://dx.doi.org/10.1037/0012-1649.43.4.947

McKinnon, R. D., & Blair, C. (2019). Bidirectional relations among executive function, teacher–child relationships, and early reading and math achievement: A cross-lagged panel analysis. *Early Childhood Research Quarterly, 46,* 152–165. http://dx.doi.org/10.1016/j.ecresq.2018.03.011

Meixner, J. M., Warner, G. W., Lensing, N., Schiefele, U., & Elsner, B. (2019). The relation between executive functions and reading comprehension in primary-school students: A cross-lagged-panel analysis. *Early Childhood Research Quarterly, 46,* 62–74. http://dx.doi.org/10.1016/j.ecresq.2018.04.010

Miyake, A., Friedman, N. P., Emerson, M. J., Witzki, A. H., Howerter, A., & Wager, T. D. (2000). The unity and diversity of executive functions and their contributions to complex "Frontal Lobe" tasks: A latent variable analysis. *Cognitive Psychology, 41,* 49–100. http://dx.doi.org/10.1006/cogp.1999.0734

Montoya, M. F., Susperreguy, M. I., Dinarte, L., Morrison, F. J., San Martín, E., Rojas-Barahona, C. A., & Förster, C. E. (2019). Executive function in Chilean preschool children: Do short-term memory, working memory and response inhibition contribute differentially to early academic skills? *Early Childhood Research Quarterly, 46,* 187–200. http://dx.doi.org/10.1016/j.ecresq.2018.02.009

Morgan, P. L., Farkas, G., Wang, Y., Hillemeier, M. M., Oh, Y., & Maczuga, S. (2019). Executive function deficits in kindergarten predict repeated academic difficulties across elementary school. *Early Childhood Research Quarterly, 46*(1), 20–32. http://dx.doi.org/10.1016/j.ecresq.2018.06.009

Nesbitt, K. T., Fuhs, M. W., & Farran, D. C. (2019). Stability and instability in the co-development of mathematics, executive function skills, and visual-motor integration from prekindergarten to first grade. *Early Childhood Research Quarterly, 46,* 262–274. http://dx.doi.org/10.1016/j.ecresq.2018.02.003

Neville, H., Andersson, A., Bagdade, O., Bell, T., Currin, J., Fanning, J., & Sabourin, L. (2008). Effects of music training on brain and cognitive development in under-privileged 3- to 5-year-old children: Preliminary results. In B. Rich & C. Asbury (Eds.), *Learning, arts, and the brain: The Dana Consortium report on arts and cognition* (pp. 105–106). New York, NY: Dana Press.

Ng, F. F.-Y., Tamis-LeMonda, C., Yoshikawa, H., & Sze, I. N.-L. (2015). Inhibitory control in preschool predicts early math skills in first grade: Evidence from an ethnically diverse sample. *International Journal of Behavioral Development, 39,* 139–149. http://dx.doi.org/10.1177/0165025414538558

Nguyen, T., & Duncan, G. (2019). Kindergarten components of executive functions and third grade achievement: A national study. *Early Childhood Research Quarterly, 46,* 49–61. http://dx.doi.org/10.1016/j.ecresq.2018.05.006

No Child Left Behind Act of 2001, 20 U.S.C. § 6319 (2011).

Pellegrini, A. D. (2009). *The role of play in human development.* New York, NY: Oxford University Press. http://dx.doi.org/10.1093/acprof:oso/9780195367324.001.0001

Ramani, G. B., Daubert, E. N., & Scalise, N. R. (2019). Role of play and games in building children's foundational numerical knowledge. In D. C. Geary, D. B. Berch, & K. M. Koepke (Eds.), *Cognitive foundations for improving mathematical learning: Vol. 5. Mathematical cognition and learning* (pp. 69–90). San Diego, CA: Elsevier Academic Press. http://dx.doi.org/10.1016/B978-0-12-815952-1.00003-7

Ramani, G. B., Siegler, R. S., & Hitti, A. (2012). Taking it to the classroom: Number board games as a small group learning activity. *Journal of Educational Psychology, 104,* 661–672. http://dx.doi.org/10.1037/a0028995

Schmitt, S. A., Geldhof, G. J., Purpura, D. J., Duncan, R., & McClelland, M. M. (2017). Examining the relations between executive function, math, and literacy during the transition to kindergarten: A multi-analytic approach. *Journal of Educational Psychology, 109,* 1120–1140. http://dx.doi.org/10.1037/edu0000193

Schmitt, S. A., Pratt, M. E., & McClelland, M. M. (2014). Examining the validity of behavioral self-regulation tools in predicting preschoolers' academic achievement. *Early Education and Development, 25,* 641–660. http://dx.doi.org/10.1080/10409289.2014.850397

Schneider, M., Beeres, K., Coban, L., Merz, S., Schmidt, S. S., Stricker, J., & De Smedt, B. (2017). Associations of non-symbolic and symbolic numerical magnitude processing with mathematical competence: A meta-analysis. *Developmental Science, 20*(3), e12372. http://dx.doi.org/10.1111/desc.12372

Scrafton, E., & Whitington, V. (2015). The accessibility of socio-dramatic play to culturally and linguistically diverse Australian preschoolers. *European Early Childhood Education Research Journal, 23,* 213–228. http://dx.doi.org/10.1080/1350293X.2015.1016806

Siegler, R. S., & Booth, J. L. (2004). Development of numerical estimation in young children. *Child Development, 75,* 428–444. http://dx.doi.org/10.1111/j.1467-8624.2004.00684.x

Siegler, R. S., & Ramani, G. B. (2008). Playing linear numerical board games promotes low-income children's numerical development. *Developmental Science, 11,* 655–661. http://dx.doi.org/10.1111/j.1467-7687.2008.00714.x

Siegler, R. S., & Ramani, G. B. (2009). Playing linear number board games—but not circular ones—improves low-income preschoolers' numerical understanding. *Journal of Educational Psychology, 101,* 545–560. http://dx.doi.org/10.1037/a0014239

Watts, T. W., Duncan, G. J., Siegler, R. S., & Davis-Kean, P. E. (2014). What's past is prologue: Relations between early mathematics knowledge and high school achievement. *Educational Researcher, 43,* 352–360. http://dx.doi.org/10.3102/0013189X14553660

Wechsler, D. (2014). *Wechsler Intelligence Scale for Children* (5th ed.). San Antonio, TX: NCS Pearson.

Willoughby, M. T., Blair, C. B., Wirth, R. J., Greenberg, M., & The Family Life Project Investigators (2010). The measurement of executive function at age 3 years: Psychometric properties and criterion validity of a new battery of tasks. *Psychological Assessment, 22,* 306–317. http://dx.doi.org/10.1037/a0018708

Zentner, M., & Eerola, T. (2010). Rhythmic engagement with music in infancy. *Proceedings of the National Academy of Science, 107,* 5768–5773. http://dx.doi.org/10.1073/pnas.1000121107

Ziegler, E. (2009). Foreword. In K. Hirsh-Pasek, R. M. Golinkoff, L. E. Berk, & D. G. Singer (Eds.), *A mandate for playful learning in preschool: Presenting the evidence* (pp. ix–xiii). New York, NY: Oxford University Press.

8

Leveraging the Developmental Strengths of Young Children in Context

Rebecca Bulotsky-Shearer, Jenna Futterer, Jhonelle Bailey, and Chelsea Morris

Approximately 44% (10.1 million) of our nation's children under 6 years of age live within 200% of the federal poverty level, and 21% (4.8 million) live at or below the federal poverty level (National Center for Children in Poverty, 2016). Poverty and its associated ecological risks to health, well-being, and educational success disproportionately affect many young children, particularly those from racial and ethnic minority backgrounds (Crosnoe et al., 2010; Duncan & Magnuson, 2011; Gillanders, Iruka, Ritchie, & Cobb, 2012) and are associated with inequities in early learning opportunities. However, despite experiencing elevated risks associated with living in poverty, many young children show resilient outcomes and subsequent positive developmental and educational trajectories (Masten, 2001).

Factors within the child and within key proximal contexts that promote resilience are conceptualized within the bioecological framework. In this model, within-child ontogenetic (biological and developmental) capacities interact dynamically with the opportunities present in proximal contexts, such as the home, school, and community contexts, to promote positive development and early school success (Bronfenbrenner & Morris, 1998). The processes through which this nested system influences children are bidirectional or transactional over time (Sameroff, 2009). Not only are children influenced by the environment, but the environment is responsive to individual characteristics of children (Bronfenbrenner & Morris, 1998).

In accord with this model, many early childhood researchers have turned to a strength-based, or resiliency-oriented, perspective to identify within-child

http://dx.doi.org/10.1037/0000197-009
Healthy Development in Young Children: Evidence-Based Interventions for Early Education,
V. C. Alfonso and G. J. DuPaul (Editors)

and external factors embedded in naturally occurring learning contexts that support positive outcomes for children (e.g., Lamb-Parker, LeBuffe, Powell, & Halpern, 2008; Luthar, Cicchetti, & Becker, 2000). Early childhood programs and elementary classrooms are among the earliest opportunities to promote positive development for all children. In addition to providing rich opportunities for learning, early childhood programs serve as one of the earliest mechanisms for identification of children in need of developmental and/or behavioral intervention (Zigler & Bishop-Josef, 2006). For example, as a two-generation, comprehensive program, federally funded Head Start is child- and family-centered and promotes child health, socioemotional development, and family well-being, thus recognizing the importance of collaborations among foundational ecological systems that touch children. In this way, families and early childhood providers can work together to understand critical junctures in a child's educational trajectory that will set her on a course for positive school success.

The purpose of this chapter is to highlight research on within-child (i.e., internal developmental capacities) and external (i.e., contextual factors within the home, community, and school setting) strengths that influence the development of young children's academic, socioemotional, and behavioral skills. We provide an overview of these factors within the bioecological framework, followed by a summary of our own research conducted within Head Start programs. The overarching goal is to illustrate the importance of family–school, teacher–child, and child-initiated peer play interactions as critical contexts for supporting engagement in learning, particularly for children from ethnic, racial, and linguistically diverse low-income backgrounds. Furthermore, evidence-based, practical suggestions to support these relational contexts as key contributors to early school success, particularly related to the transition to kindergarten, are emphasized throughout.

WITHIN-CHILD DEVELOPMENTAL STRENGTHS AND CAPACITIES

During the first 5 years of life, children experience rapid change in multiple developmental domains. Five major school-readiness domains are recognized as foundational to prepare children for kindergarten: language and literacy, cognition, approaches to learning, physical/motor skills, and social–emotional development (National Education Goals Panel, 1998; U.S. Department of Health and Human Services, Administration on Children, Youth, and Families/Head Start Bureau, 2003). These developmental skills emerge not in isolation but dynamically within the child over time (Snow, 2007). In this integrative view of school readiness, all domains are interrelated and develop in transaction with the opportunities and demands present in proximal ecological contexts, such as the home, school, and community (Downer & Myers, 2009). Here, we provide an overview of readiness skills that prepare children for kindergarten, highlighting domain-general and foundational socioemotional skills that support children's engagement in learning.

A series of studies has identified profiles of developmental skills comprising school readiness within early childhood samples. These dimensions of school-readiness skills have been analyzed using data from the Early Childhood Longitudinal Study–Kindergarten Cohort and the Head Start Family and Child Experiences Study (FACES). Researchers found that children demonstrating strengths across multiple readiness dimensions were more likely to succeed in preschool, kindergarten, and longitudinally into first grade than were those with strengths in only one or two areas (Hair, Halle, Terry-Humen, Lavelle, & Calkins, 2006; Halle, Hair, Wandner, & Chien, 2012). In the FACES 2000 cohort, McWayne, Hahs-Vaughn, Cheung, and Wright (2012) also identified multiple patterns of socioemotional and academic strengths associated with later academic achievement outcomes.

Increasing recognition is being paid to the foundational role of socioemotional skills, approaches to learning, and executive function skills (e.g., self-control, self-regulation) in children's successful engagement in learning opportunities within home (e.g., parent–child interactions) and classroom (e.g., task engagement, peer interactions, teacher–child interactions) settings. Termed *soft skills* by researchers and policymakers (Heckman, 2011), these developmental capacities form the foundations of social and academic school readiness. They support children's ability to engage with learning tasks and in social interactions with others, such as teachers and peers, that support learning (Duncan & Magnuson, 2011; Thompson & Raikes, 2007). During early childhood, engagement in learning is relational, and children develop within the context of relationships (National Scientific Council on the Developing Child, 2004). To take advantage of the learning opportunities present at home and school, children must develop these socioemotional and regulatory skills (Raver & Zigler, 1997). In the following paragraphs, we review the importance of self-regulation and social competence as within-child developmental skills that support engagement within early learning contexts.

Self-Regulation

In particular, self-regulation has gained considerable attention as a developmental skill that supports engagement in learning and children's positive engagement in social interactions within early learning environments. Indeed, self-regulation is a central task of the preschool years and undergoes tremendous growth during the early childhood period (2–5 years of age; Blair & Raver, 2012; see also Chapter 6, this volume). Defined as the skills to manage emotions, focus attention, and inhibit or activate behavior in response to environmental demands, self-regulation is a core contributor to early school success (Blair & Raver, 2012; Cadima, Doumen, Verschueren, & Buyse, 2015; Rimm-Kaufman, Curby, Grimm, Nathanson, & Brock, 2009). Children's early self-regulation skills are associated with concurrent and long-term literacy, vocabulary, mathematics, socioemotional, and behavioral skills (McClelland, Acock, & Morrison, 2006; Ursache, Blair, & Raver, 2012). Self-regulation is believed to have a greater influence on a student's academic performance than intelligence has (Duckworth & Seligman, 2005; McClelland et al., 2006).

Self-regulation skills are thought to be built upon neurological and bio-logical foundations. All children are born with the genetic potential to develop self-regulation skills. However, very young children have immature nervous systems that rely on input to develop (e.g., experience, practice, and inter-actions with others; Blair, 2002). As the neurological system is provided infor-mation about the external world, experience builds the architecture of the brain. Development of neural connected systems that manage, integrate, and regulate information requires experience and practice through consistent, sen-sitive, responsive caregiver interactions. When a child experiences cumulative or repeated stress and trauma, her ability to develop foundational brain con-nections that support successful self-regulation skills may be compromised (Blair & Raver, 2012; Shonkoff, Richter, van der Gaag, & Bhutta, 2012).

The sympathetic nervous system (which could be visualized as the gas pedal of a vehicle) and the parasympathetic nervous system (the brake pedal) work together to maintain regulation and balance. The ability to step on the gas to manage complex or difficult situations successfully as well as know when to hit the brakes is critical to individual growth and learning; young children cannot be ready for academic or social learning without emotional self-regulation. If the child has been unable to develop or has not yet fully developed a mature regulatory response to stress, an increased reliance on adult intervention and/or an increase in challenging behavior is likely to occur (Blair, 2002; Blair & Raver, 2012; Dunn, 1997). During this period of escalation, the child's mind-set shifts toward failure and frustration, away from organization and planning of thoughts, and skills are impaired, working memory suffers, and capability of solving the problem decreases.

Preschool children from low-income families are more likely to have diffi-culty with self-regulation compared with their demographically advantaged peers (Blair & Raver, 2012; Tominey & McClelland, 2011). Children who dis-play challenging behavior often have core deficits in self-regulation that place them at significant risk for school failure. These difficulties in self-regulation interfere with the ability to inhibit impulsive behavior, manage strong emotions, and/or shift and maintain attention and thinking within the early childhood classroom (Bulotsky-Shearer, Bell, & Domínguez, 2012; Rimm-Kaufman, Pianta, & Cox, 2000). Often, delays in self-regulation result in behavior problems in the classroom that look like disruptive or impulsive behavior such as running when walking is expected, not being able to stay seated during circle time, or grabbing toys or materials. These behaviors prevent children from fully engaging in learning opportunities and are challenging for teachers to manage (Graziano et al., 2015). Below, we discuss ways in which teachers and families can help children develop more adaptive behavior and self-regulatory skills before behavior problems resulting from poor regulation become more stable, disrupt learning, and lead to negative school consequences such as expulsion from preschool (Gilliam, 2005).

Connecting Science to Practice

The early childhood period is a critical window for intervention when self-regulation skills are most malleable. Caregivers can support self-regulated behavior especially for those children with a low threshold for stress and challenge, who often rely more on caregivers to help them self-regulate. By learning strategies for deescalation (e.g., breaks, adjusted expectations, positive behavior supports), caregivers can be prepared to support young children when they are having difficulty responding to the classroom environment. Examples of interventions within early childhood settings that support self-regulation skills include Red Light Purple Light (Tominey & McClelland, 2011), Check-In/Check-Out (Green, 2016), Tools of the Mind (resources available at https://toolsofthemind.org/learn/resources), and the story of Tucker the Turtle available through the Center on the Social and Emotional Foundations for Early Learning (http://csefel.vanderbilt.edu/resources/strategies.html).

Social Competence

In addition to self-regulation, social competence is a foundational skill that emerges during the early childhood period and supports learning with early childhood contexts. In the past 2 decades, peer social competence has been leveraged in a series of strengths-based studies of preschool children enrolled in Head Start. In this research, social competence, as observed through peer play interactions, is conceptualized as domain-general skills that support learning in other school-readiness domains (Bulotsky-Shearer, Manz, et al., 2012; Bulotsky-Shearer, McWayne, Mendez, & Manz, 2016; Wentzel, 2005). Children who develop positive and prosocial skills through their engagement within naturally occurring peer play experiences, at home and in the classroom, show concurrent strengths in language, approaches to learning, executive function, and academic achievement in literacy and mathematics during early childhood (Bulotsky-Shearer, Bell, Romero, & Carter, 2012; Fantuzzo, Manz, Atkins, & Meyers, 2005; Mendez & Fogle, 2002; see also Chapter 7, this volume) as well as longitudinally into first grade (e.g., higher reading, mathematics, social studies achievement, better work habits; McWayne, Green, & Fantuzzo, 2009) and third grade (e.g., higher mathematics and reading achievement; Hampton & Fantuzzo, 2003; Sekino, 2006).

PROXIMAL CONTEXTS THAT SUPPORT SCHOOL READINESS: FAMILY AND SCHOOLS

In a bioecological, strengths-based framework, within-child developmental capacities are considered the foundation of school readiness that are nurtured dynamically in the opportunities present in early contexts and experiences (Bronfenbrenner & Morris, 1998). The primary developmental context for children is the family, and several aspects of family and parenting within the home environment support children's early development, learning, and transition to kindergarten. For example, parental warmth, sensitivity, and support for a child's autonomy and parents' active participation in and promotion of a child's learning is associated with positive socioemotional and cognitive development (Bornstein & Tamis-LeMonda, 1989; Hirsh-Pasek & Burchinal, 2006; National Institute of Child Health and Human Development, Early Child Care Research Network, 2002; National Scientific Council on the Developing Child, 2004).

Key to understanding opportunities to support positive development for families from low-income backgrounds is identifying and leveraging those strengths that are commensurate with family culture, home language, and ethnic identity (Barrueco, Smith, & Stephens, 2015; Cabrera & The Society for Research in Child Development, Ethnic and Racial Issues Committee, 2013; García Coll et al., 2002). To identify and leverage those strengths within diverse families, a series of studies, using a within-group perspective, highlighted the unique positive parenting practices that Black and Latino parents bring to support children's development and learning (McWayne, Mattis, Green Wright, Limlingan, & Harris, 2017; McWayne, Melzi, Schick, Kennedy, & Mundt, 2013). For example, through McWayne and Mattis's Project P.E.A.R.L.S. (Parents Enhancing Academic Readiness through Lessons about Strengths), several nuanced dimensions of positive parenting were derived through qualitative interviews with Black low-income families. These dimensions included fostering a connected and competent self, religious/spiritual practices and values, Black cultural pride, involvement at school, and behavioral guidance and responsiveness. These positive parenting practices and beliefs were associated with improved socioemotional outcomes for preschool children (McWayne, Mattis, & Hyun, 2018). In other samples of Black preschool children enrolled in Head Start, positive parenting practices were associated with lower aggressive and hyperactive behaviors (Carpenter & Mendez, 2013).

Family engagement is also an important context to support children's early learning. Consistent findings from several recent meta-analyses suggested that children are better prepared and more successful in school when their parents are involved in their children's academic activities, have open communication with their children about schoolwork at home, and have high expectations for children's achievement (Castro et al., 2015; Jeynes, 2012). Family engagement is a protective factor for racial and ethnic minority low-income children (Jeynes, 2003).

In alignment with the ecological model, family engagement is recognized as a multidimensional construct during early childhood (Epstein, 2001; McWayne, Campos, & Owsianik, 2008; Sheridan, Knoche, Edwards, Bovaird, & Kupzyk, 2010). Through research conducted in school district Head Start programs in the northeastern United States, a multidimensional measure of family engagement was developed in collaboration with families, the Family Involvement Questionnaire (Fantuzzo, Tighe, & Childs, 2000). The Family Involvement Questionnaire has been used to find that three dimensions of involvement (home-based, school-based, and home–school communication) are positively associated with children's outcomes. Home-based involvement measures specific ways in which parents promote learning in the home and community for their children, such as providing materials and space for children to do homework, reading books together, and going to the library (Gadsden, 2013). School-based involvement is defined by the activities that parents are involved in at school such as volunteering, participating in school events, and meeting with teachers. Home–school conferencing comprises communication across home and school settings, such as parents and teachers talking or sharing information about children's progress or difficulties (Fantuzzo et al., 2013). For Head Start children, home-based engagement is associated with higher school-readiness skills, such as approaches to learning, receptive vocabulary skills, and lower conduct problems (Fantuzzo, McWayne, Perry, & Childs, 2004). When families reinforce the importance of education and high expectations are set, this is a strong influence on their children's motivation to learn and succeed in school. Parents' participation in school is associated with higher academic achievement, literacy skills, social skills, and positive parenting practices (Arnold, Zeljo, Doctoroff, & Ortiz, 2008; Powell, Son, File, & San Juan, 2010; Toldson & Lemmons, 2013).

Opportunities to Connect Science to Practice

As a two-generation model, Head Start programs recognize parents as children's first teachers and support family engagement in learning (U.S. Department of Health and Human Services, 2015). The Parent, Family, and Community Engagement Framework (National Center on Parent, Family, and Community Engagement, 2018) provides an opportunity for Head Start staff, families, and children to build positive relationships through mutual respect, focusing on the strengths of all contributors and promoting inclusiveness and cultural and linguistic responsiveness. Head Start staff work with families to promote family well-being and positive parent–child relationships so that families feel empowered as lifelong educators, advocates, and leaders. Other national early childhood organizations such as the National Association for the Education of Young Children's (NAEYC) developmentally appropriate practice guidelines advocate for family partnerships as integral to children's early school success and transition (NAEYC, 2009). In addition, the Division for Early Childhood of the Council for Exceptional Children has recommended practices that encourage building trusting and respectful partnerships with families, intended to build on current family strengths and capacities, and that are culturally and linguistically sensitive (Division for Early Childhood, 2014).

Home–School Collaboration

A key dimension of family engagement is the connection that parents and teachers make to enhance children's learning across home and school contexts. When the child enters a preschool setting, home–school collaboration reflects the development of positive relationships between the home and the early education program, more specifically through parent–professional partnerships (Sheridan et al., 2010). Active parent engagement is the foundation of these relationships, as parents are substantial contributors and collaborators in a child's development (Sheridan et al., 2010). By creating a home–school collaboration that consists of meaningful partnerships across developmental contexts within the preschool years, stability and transitions are improved across systems (Early, Pianta, Taylor, & Cox, 2001; Ramey & Ramey, 1999).

Partnerships are particularly important for low-income families, as families from low-income backgrounds may face barriers in forming positive relationships with school personnel and are less likely to visit their child's school (Toldson & Lemmons, 2013). Research suggests that for these families, there may be barriers to engagement due to language differences and/or distrust or lack of comfort when interacting with public school systems (Barrueco et al., 2015). Alternatively, when parents perceive their child's teacher as valuing them as a meaningful partner, they become more involved and visit the school more frequently (Sheridan et al., 2010; Toldson & Lemmons, 2013). Children in programs serving low-income families that implement effective strategies to improve parent engagement show higher socioemotional skills, such as ability to think and act independently, develop positive social bonds, and exhibit less anxious and dependent behavior (Sheridan et al., 2010). This home–school connection is critical in the preschool years, especially for children and families in low-income communities, to pave a path toward successful transition to kindergarten and future school success.

Opportunities to Connect Science to Practice

There are evidence-based interventions that effectively enhance the home–school collaboration during early childhood. These include relationship-based interventions that foster family–school partnerships, defined as "intentional and ongoing relationships between school and family designed to directly or indirectly enhance children's learning and development, and/or address the obstacles that impede it" (Christenson & Sheridan, 2001, p. 38).

One example of a relationship-based early childhood intervention showing positive impacts for low-income families with children from birth to 5 years is the Getting Ready program (Sheridan, Marvin, Knoche, & Edwards, 2008). The intervention establishes parent–child and parent–professional relationships and encourages the sharing and brainstorming of ideas to help the child meet academic and behavioral expectations (Sheridan et al., 2008). Children showed gains in literacy skills (e.g., language use, reading, and writing abilities) whereas parents showed improvements in the quality of parent–child interactions (e.g., enhanced quality of warmth and sensitivity) and support of children's learning (Knoche et al., 2012; Sheridan, Knoche, Kupzyk, Edwards, & Marvin, 2011). Certainly, as early as possible, it is important for early childhood programs to devote resources to train and support teachers to implement strategies that engage families through relationship-based models such as the collaborative (i.e., conjoint) consultation practices used in Getting

Ready. For example, triadic strategies that involved the teacher, parent, and child are encouraged during parent–child interactions to support parents to actively participate and respond sensitively to a child's cues and developmental needs. Teachers praise parents, model appropriate interaction strategies, and suggest and reinforce positive skills demonstrated by parents. In this way, parents and teachers may feel more comfortable reaching out and communicating with one another to support the child's learning and development (McWayne, 2015).

IMPROVING TEACHER–STUDENT INTERACTIONS

One of the most proximal supports for within-child developmental skills is the opportunity for children to engage in learning within the classroom and to form close relationships with teachers and peers. Positive teacher–child relationships, also known as quality teacher–child interactions, influence development in all domains, including children's motivation to learn, socioemotional and behavioral skills, and development of positive peer relationships (La Paro, Pianta, & Stuhlman, 2004). When children develop socioemotional skills and positive approaches to learning, they are more likely to engage and succeed in school (Fantuzzo, Perry, & McDermott, 2004; Nix, Bierman, Domitrovich, & Gill, 2013).

The Teaching Through Interactions Framework

Following a line of research on high-quality teacher–child interactions, the Teaching Through Interactions (Hamre, 2014; Hamre et al., 2013) framework underscores the importance of early childhood teachers engaging in high-quality interactions with children in three domains: emotional support, classroom organization, and instructional support. *Emotional support* is the extent to which the teacher creates a warm and respectful environment and attends to the child's needs, whether socially or academically. For example, emotionally supportive teachers recognize when children are upset, acknowledge their feelings, and comfort them in an appropriate way (La Paro et al., 2004). High emotional support is associated with the development of social skills and self-regulated behavior in preschool and kindergarten (Burchinal et al., 2008; Hamre, 2014). *Classroom organization* is the degree to which the teacher communicates consistent behavioral expectations, develops routines, maximizes learning time, and promotes children's engagement and interest in learning with varied activities, centers, and materials. When teachers effectively and proactively manage children's behavior and attention, children stay on task and exhibit better behavioral and cognitive control (Rimm-Kaufman et al., 2009). Last, *instructional support* is the extent to which the teacher deepens children's higher analysis and reasoning skills, concept knowledge, and language skills and engages in language-rich conversations with children. High instructional support is associated with greater academic gains in language, literacy, and mathematics during preschool (Hamre, Hatfield, Pianta, & Jamil, 2014).

Through the quality of the emotional support, classroom organization, and instructional support teachers provide within the classroom, children's experiences and successes are enhanced within and outside the school setting (McClelland et al., 2006; Vandell et al., 2010). High-quality teacher–child interactions may be even more important for the socioemotional, behavioral, and academic skill development of children from low-income families (Birch & Ladd, 1997; Brophy-Herb, Lee, Nievar, & Stollak, 2007; Burchinal, Peisner-Feinberg, Pianta, & Howes, 2002; Hamre, 2014). For example, highly emotionally supportive classrooms are a protective factor for children's approaches to learning when they enter preschool displaying externalizing behavior problems (Domínguez, Vitiello, Fuccillo, Greenfield, & Bulotsky-Shearer, 2011). Relatedly, for children with low language skills displaying behavior problems, sensitive and stimulating teacher–child interactions are protective in promoting positive classroom behavior in Head Start children (Qi, Zieher, Lee Van Horn, Bulotsky-Shearer, & Carta, 2019) and in first grade (Hamre & Pianta, 2005).

Opportunities to Connect Science to Practice

There are several opportunities within the classroom to enhance the quality of teacher–child interactions to support children's early learning and development. Interventions that support early childhood educators to improve the quality of their teacher–child interactions are important particularly for children who are at risk for behavior problems (Brennan, Shaw, Dishion, & Wilson, 2012; Bulotsky-Shearer & Fantuzzo, 2011). The pyramid model for supporting social emotional competence (Fox, Dunlap, Hemmeter, Joseph, & Strain, 2003; Hemmeter, Ostrosky, & Fox, 2006) is an evidence-based intervention framework that promotes social, emotional, and behavioral development of young children ages birth to 5 years. It is designed to be developmentally appropriate and utilized in a variety of early childhood programs, such as Head Start, Early Head Start, and child-care programs (Fox & Hemmeter, 2009). The Pyramid model is a tiered framework (see Figure 9.1 in Chapter 9, this volume), with foundational Tier 1 practices related to nurturing and responsive relationships and high-quality, supportive environments that promote socio-emotional competencies of all children (Hemmeter, Snyder, Fox, & Algina, 2016). At Tier 2, more targeted strategies teach socioemotional skills, such as friendship, social skills, emotional literacy, and social problem solving. Tier 3 comprises developing individual behavior intervention plans to address children with persistent challenging behavior. Several training resources and materials are available for both teachers and parents at http://csefel.vanderbilt.edu.

Another professional development intervention is MyTeachingPartner (MTP), a web-mediated coaching program that provides teachers with access to resources to learn to observe, implement, and integrate into their daily practice high-quality teaching based on the Classroom Assessment Scoring System (Pianta, La Paro, & Hamre, 2008) Teaching through Interactions Framework

(Kinzie et al., 2006). Teachers who participate in MTP have access to (a) a video library of exemplary interactions (e.g., high-quality emotionally supportive, well-organized, and instructionally supportive teacher–child interactions); (b) online didactic course content to improve knowledge, skills, and application of effective interactions; and (c) web-mediated individualized coaching and reflective supervision sessions using guided video review. In guided video review, teachers analyze their own interactions with students in the classroom to improve the quality of their interactions (see https://curry.virginia.edu/myteachingpartner). In efficacy trials, teachers participating in MTP improved the quality of their interactions in comparison with a control group (Early, Maxwell, Ponder, & Pan, 2017).

PEER INTERACTIONS AS CONTEXT FOR SUPPORTING DEVELOPMENT AND LEARNING

As a naturally occurring, developmentally appropriate context, social interaction with peers through play is a primary mechanism through which preschool children learn (Fisher, Hirsh-Pasek, Golinkoff, Singer, & Berk, 2011; Zigler, Singer, & Bishop-Josef, 2004; see also Chapter 7, this volume). Developmentally appropriate practices in early childhood delineate that "play is an important vehicle for developing self-regulation as well as promoting language, cognition, and social competence" (NAEYC, 2009, p. 14). This notion is supported by constructivist theorists Piaget (1932) and Vygotsky (1978), who asserted that child-initiated playful exploration of the environment provides enriching opportunities for developing skills that support a child's readiness for future education, socialization, and adjustment in the child's society and culture.

A series of research studies conducted with racial and ethnic minority preschool children from low-income backgrounds demonstrated the importance of positive peer interactions through play in supporting academic and social, emotional, and regulatory skills that prepare children for kindergarten (Bulotsky-Shearer, Manz, et al., 2012; Bulotsky-Shearer et al., 2016). Employing a strength-based, within-group approach, Fantuzzo, Mendez, and Tighe (1998) initiated a series of studies to develop and validate dimensions of peer play interaction for Head Start children. In collaboration with parents and teachers, on the basis of observations of children in the Head Start classroom, behaviors that differentiated between successful and unsuccessful engagement in peer play interactions were identified and used to create a 32-item rating scale for use by parents and teachers: the Penn Interactive Peer Play Scale (PIPPS), parent version (Fantuzzo, Mendez, & Tighe, 1998) and PIPPS, teacher version (Fantuzzo, Coolahan, Mendez, McDermott, & Sutton-Smith, 1998). Research using the PIPPS has helped to identify children demonstrating strengths and those who display behavioral needs experienced within early learning contexts within three dimensions of peer play interactions: play interaction, play disruption, and play disconnection.

Peer Play Interactions and Learning

Play interactions with peers are naturally occurring opportunities within the home and early childhood classroom that support learning. Interactive play skills are characterized as prosocial and cooperative behaviors (Fantuzzo, Coolahan, et al., 1998). As children develop more prosocial interactive play skills in the home and school context, they are more autonomous, have more positive approaches to learning, and have higher receptive vocabulary skills, whereas more disconnected and disconnected play behaviors are negatively associated with expressive and receptive vocabulary skills (Fantuzzo & McWayne, 2002; Fantuzzo, Sekino, & Cohen, 2004; McWayne et al., 2009; Mendez & Fogle, 2002). Additionally, when play trajectories of preschool children were observed, those who had higher initial levels of peer play skill were rated higher by kindergarten teachers as having greater academic skills and more autonomy and independence (Eggum-Wilkens et al., 2014).

Certain child-level or within-child factors interact dynamically with the opportunities present in classrooms, related to positive play interactions (Bulotsky-Shearer et al., 2016). As children's school-readiness skills emerge dynamically over time, several within-child developmental competencies are associated concurrently with children's ability to engage in positive peer interactions. These include self-regulation, positive engagement, attention, initiation, cognitive flexibility, and approaches to learning in the classroom (Coolahan, Fantuzzo, Mendez, & McDermott, 2000; Fantuzzo & McWayne, 2002; Fantuzzo et al., 2005; Mendez, Fantuzzo, & Cicchetti, 2002). Children in Head Start classrooms who show strengths in these competencies, in concert with adaptable temperament and strong language skills, are likely to play effectively with peers (Mendez, Fantuzzo, & Cicchetti, 2002).

However, some children may display disruptive or disconnected play behaviors when engaging with peers. Disruptive play behaviors are characterized by aggressive behaviors that interfere with peer interactions, whereas disconnected play is characterized by more withdrawn behaviors that inhibit initiation of peer interactions (Fantuzzo, Coolahan, Mendez, McDermott, & Sutton-Smith, 1998). Disruptive and disconnected peer play behaviors are associated with lower expressive vocabulary, receptive vocabulary, and mathematics scores during preschool (Fantuzzo, Sekino, & Cohen, 2004; Mendez & Fogle, 2002) and longitudinally into third grade (Sekino, 2006). In a kindergarten study, children disconnected from peers in preschool concurrently displayed greater inattentive, withdrawn, and passive behavior, required more prompts from the teacher to join play, and earned lower grades (Hampton & Fantuzzo, 2003).

Opportunities to Connect Science to Practice

There are many opportunities for interactive peer play to be supported in early childhood classrooms. One mechanism is through high-quality teacher–child interactions. For example, a recent study found that the positive associations between interactive play in the beginning of the year and mathematics skills in the spring were strengthened for children in classrooms with high levels of instructional support (Bulotsky-Shearer, Bell, Carter, & Dietrich, 2014). This finding suggests that teachers were able to scaffold cognitive concepts and academic skills through guided play and cooperative peer learning activities that promoted higher-level thinking and conceptual mathematical skill development. This enhanced discovery approach integrates cognitive problem solving, language, and mathematics learning within child-directed play through adult scaffolding and gentle guidance (Hassinger-Das, Hirsh-Pasek, & Golinkoff, 2017; Weisberg, Hirsh-Pasek, & Golinkoff, 2013). For example, teachers can intentionally deepen children's learning of language and literacy skills through props, pretend play themes, books, songs, and games encouraging expressive language and literacy skills, such as rhyming (Stanton-Chapman & Hadden, 2011). To do so, early childhood educators may need professional development support and additional training to engage children in peer-mediated learning experiences, especially when children display disruptive or disconnected peer play behaviors (see Bulotsky-Shearer et al., 2016).

In a recent study, negative associations between disruptive and disconnected peer play in preschool and language and literacy skills were not found to be moderated by high-quality teacher–child interactions (Bulotsky-Shearer, Bell, Carter, & Dietrich, 2014). In other words, high disruptive or disconnected peer play early in the year predicted lower literacy outcomes in the spring, regardless of whether children experienced high-quality instructional, well-organized, or emotionally supportive classrooms. In another study, however, high classroom organization mitigated the negative relationship between negative peer engagement in the fall and disruptive play outcomes in the spring (Bulotsky-Shearer et al., 2020). For all children, but particularly for those children with social difficulties with peers, training to support teachers to teach friendship skills intentionally is available through the pyramid model (Fox et al., 2003; Hemmeter et al., 2006) in a variety of engaging formats (e.g., scripted social skills stories, Book Nook; see http://csefel.vanderbilt.edu/resources/strategies.html for more information). In addition, those children who are disconnected in play may need more intensive support to engage with peers. The pyramid model is a good resource for Tier 2 social skills and friendship skills; for example, using the book *The Rainbow Fish* from the Book Nook (http://csefel.vanderbilt. edu/booknook/rainbow_fish.pdf) provides opportunities for children to discuss how a fish has trouble getting along with others and learns how to make friends. In addition, recognizing and praising friendship skills by being a "super friend" is an effective way to introduce and reinforce these skills within early childhood classrooms (see http://csefel.vanderbilt.edu/modules-archive/module1/handouts/4.pdf).

Peer-mediated interventions may also be helpful; some are developed to engage typically developing children with children with disabilities (e.g., autism; for review, see Carter, Sisco, & Chung, 2012) or children with socially withdrawn behavior (Fantuzzo et al., 2005). The play buddy intervention, also known as resilient peer treatment, was developed with the use of the

PIPPS measure to support the social skills of socially withdrawn, maltreated preschool children (Fantuzzo et al., 1996). When the play buddy intervention was implemented in a Head Start classroom, participating children were paired with a resilient peer demonstrating interactive peer play strengths. Children in the paired play condition gained in their level of collaborative peer interactions in free play, compared with those in the control condition. Finally, the Front Porch Broadcast Series, available on the Office of Head Start Early Childhood Learning and Knowledge Center website (https://eclkc.ohs.acf. hhs.gov/school-readiness/article/front-porch-broadcast-series), offers a series of webinars focused on the adult's role in supporting peer relationships and provides additional resources for early childhood practitioners (see https:// eclkc.ohs.acf.hhs.gov/video/adults-role-supporting-peer-relationships).

SUMMARY AND IMPLICATIONS FOR EARLY CHILDHOOD SYSTEMS

Over the past decade, we have seen our nation increasing its investment in early learning programs, with more attention paid to the importance of early childhood (ages birth to 5) as a critical opportunity for intervention when developmental trajectories are most malleable and, therefore, the cost–benefit of early intervention is greatest (Heckman, 2006). For example, the Administration for Children and Families recently awarded more than $140 million to support the expansion of Early Head Start–Child Care Partnerships, and the U.S. Department of Education recently funded 46 states and U.S. territories with preschool development grants to mobilize early childhood programs and public schools toward greater system alignment from ages birth to 8 years (U.S. Department of Education, Office of Early Learning, 2018). As we consider our next steps as practitioners, policymakers, and researchers to support the early school success of our nation's most vulnerable children, several key takeaways should be acknowledged.

First, children living in low-income families today are growing up in complex ecological systems and represent increased racial, ethnic, cultural, and linguistic diversity (National Center for Children in Poverty, 2016). Systems that touch children must align to support the developmental needs and capacities of children within the broader contexts. For example, although developmental science underscores the importance of promoting the development of the whole child in context, many early childhood programs such as state prekindergarten programs focus on discrete skills that are tested upon kindergarten entry (e.g., language and literacy) and curricular approaches that are not aligned with practices that support the whole child (Zigler & Bishop-Josef, 2006). Head Start, our nation's largest comprehensive early childhood intervention program, is an effective dual-generation model that historically has prioritized the health, well-being, socioemotional, and academic development of children within the context of their families, culture, and community. Integrating holistic approaches within early childhood programs and school systems that identify and embrace the strengths within the child and leverage natural contributors to a child's development within the family and home culture and within classrooms is a promising approach (Fantuzzo, McWayne, & Bulotsky, 2003).

Another key message is that early childhood programs can promote positive adaptation and development for all young children through enhancing collaborative and positive relationships within the home and school and across the home and school. An important relational context for socioemotional development and learning is the peer context, a key mechanism that fosters enjoyable and engaged learning experiences that sustain children's motivation and persistence through formal schooling (e.g., Bulotsky-Shearer et al., 2016). Those children who are not engaged with peers or who do not have opportunities for productive interactions are vulnerable to being left out and fall behind over time.

Finally, understanding points of intervention where the strengths of families and schools can be leveraged and where collaborative dialogue and connections can be made is critical to moving the field forward for our nation's most vulnerable children. Inequitable access to high-quality learning environments and resources sets up not only children and parents for failure but educators as well. Starting a real dialogue among teachers, parents, and administrators within early childhood programs that are focused on the success of the child is a step in the right direction.

REFERENCES

Arnold, D. H., Zeljo, A., Doctoroff, G. L., & Ortiz, C. (2008). Parent involvement in preschool: Predictors and the relation of involvement to preliteracy development. *School Psychology Review, 37*(1), 74–90.

Barrueco, S., Smith, S., & Stephens, S. (2015). *Supporting parent engagement in linguistically diverse families to promote young children's learning: Implications for early care and education policy.* New York, NY: Child Care & Early Education Research Connections. Retrieved from https://www.researchconnections.org/childcare/resources/30185/pdf

Birch, S. H., & Ladd, G. W. (1997). The teacher–child relationship and children's early school adjustment. *Journal of School Psychology, 35*(1), 61–79. http://dx.doi.org/10.1016/S0022-4405(96)00029-5

Blair, C. (2002). School readiness. Integrating cognition and emotion in a neurobiological conceptualization of children's functioning at school entry. *American Psychologist, 57*(2), 111–127. http://dx.doi.org/10.1037/0003-066X.57.2.111

Blair, C., & Raver, C. C. (2012). Child development in the context of adversity: Experiential canalization of brain and behavior. *American Psychologist, 67,* 309–318. http://dx.doi.org/10.1037/a0027493

Bornstein, M. H., & Tamis-LeMonda, C. S. (1989). Maternal responsiveness and cognitive development in children. *New Directions for Child and Adolescent Development, 1989*(43), 49–61. http://dx.doi.org/10.1002/cd.23219894306

Brennan, L. M., Shaw, D. S., Dishion, T. J., & Wilson, M. (2012). Longitudinal predictors of school-age academic achievement: Unique contributions of toddler-age aggression, oppositionality, inattention, and hyperactivity. *Journal of Abnormal Child Psychology, 40,* 1289–1300. http://dx.doi.org/10.1007/s10802-012-9639-2

Bronfenbrenner, U., & Morris, P. A. (1998). The ecology of developmental processes. In W. Damon & R. M. Lerner (Eds.), *Handbook of child psychology: Theoretical models of human development* (pp. 993–1028). Hoboken, NJ: John Wiley & Sons.

Brophy-Herb, H. E., Lee, R. E., Nievar, M. A., & Stollak, G. (2007). Preschoolers' social competence: Relations to family characteristics, teacher behaviors and classroom climate. *Journal of Applied Developmental Psychology, 28*(2), 134–148. http://dx.doi.org/10.1016/j.appdev.2006.12.004

Bulotsky-Shearer, R. J., Bell, E. R., Carter, T. M., & Dietrich, S. L. (2014). Peer play interactions and learning for low-income preschool children: The moderating role of classroom quality. *Early Education and Development, 25,* 815–840. http://dx.doi.org/10.1080/10409289.2014.864214

Bulotsky-Shearer, R. J., Bell, E. R., & Domínguez, X. (2012). Latent profiles of problem behavior within learning, peer, and teacher contexts: Identifying subgroups of children at academic risk across the preschool year. *Journal of School Psychology, 50,* 775–798. http://dx.doi.org/10.1016/j.jsp.2012.08.001

Bulotsky-Shearer, R. J., Bell, E. R., Romero, S., & Carter, T. (2012). Preschool interactive peer play mediates problem behavior and learning for low income children. *Journal of Applied Developmental Psychology, 33,* 53–65. http://dx.doi.org/10.1016/j.appdev.2011.09.003

Bulotsky-Shearer, R. J., & Fantuzzo, J. W. (2011). Preschool behavior problems in classroom learning situations and literacy outcomes in kindergarten and first grade. *Early Childhood Research Quarterly, 26*(1), 61–73. http://dx.doi.org/10.1016/j.ecresq.2010.04.004

Bulotsky-Shearer, R. J., Fernandez, V., Bichay-Awadalla, K., Bailey, J., Futterer, J., & Huaqing Qi, C. (2020). Teacher-child interaction quality moderates social risks associated with problem behavior in preschool classroom contexts. *Journal of Applied Developmental Psychology, 67.* Advance online publication. http://dx.doi.org/10.1016/j.appdev.2019.101103

Bulotsky-Shearer, R. J., Manz, P., Mendez, J., McWayne, C., Sekino, Y., & Fantuzzo, J. (2012). Peer play interactions and readiness to learn: A protective influence for African American preschool children from low-income households. *Child Development Perspectives, 6,* 225–231. http://dx.doi.org/10.1111/j.1750-8606.2011.00221.x

Bulotsky-Shearer, R. J., McWayne, C., Mendez, J., & Manz, P. (2016). Preschool peer play interactions, a developmental context for learning for all children: Revisiting issues of equity and opportunity. In K. Sanders & A. Wishard Guerra (Eds.), *Attachment peers & child care in the 21st century: Where we have been and where we are headed* (pp. 179–202). New York, NY: Oxford University Press.

Burchinal, M., Howes, C., Pianta, R., Bryant, D., Early, D., Clifford, R., & Barbarin, O. (2008). Predicting child outcomes at the end of kindergarten from the quality of pre-kindergarten teacher–child interactions and instruction. *Applied Developmental Science, 12,* 140–153. http://dx.doi.org/10.1080/10888690802199418

Burchinal, M. R., Peisner-Feinberg, E., Pianta, R., & Howes, C. (2002). Development of academic skills from preschool through second grade: Family and classroom predictors of developmental trajectories. *Journal of School Psychology, 40,* 415–436. http://dx.doi.org/10.1016/S0022-4405(02)00107-3

Cabrera, N., & The Society for Research in Child Development, Ethnic and Racial Issues Committee. (2013). Positive development of minority children. *Social Policy Report, 27*(2), 1–15.

Cadima, J., Doumen, S., Verschueren, K., & Buyse, E. (2015). Child engagement in the transition to school: Contributions of self-regulation, teacher–child relationships and classroom climate. *Early Childhood Research Quarterly, 32,* 1–12. http://dx.doi.org/10.1016/j.ecresq.2015.01.008

Carpenter, J. L., & Mendez, J. (2013). Adaptive and challenged parenting among African American mothers: Parenting profiles relate to head start children's aggression and hyperactivity. *Early Education and Development, 24*(2), 233–252. http://dx.doi.org/10.1080/10409289.2013.749762

Carter, E. W., Sisco, L. G., & Chung, Y. (2012). Peer-mediated support strategies. In P. A. Prelock & R. McCauley (Eds.), *Treatment of autism spectrum disorders: Evidence-based intervention strategies for communication and social interactions* (pp. 221–254). Baltimore, MD: Paul H. Brookes.

Castro, M., Expósito-Casas, E., López-Martín, E., Lizasoain, L., Navarro-Asencio, E., & Gaviria, J. L. (2015). Parental involvement on student academic achievement: A meta-analysis. *Educational Research Review, 14*, 33–46. http://dx.doi.org/10.1016/j.edurev.2015.01.002

Christenson, S. L., & Sheridan, S. M. (2001). *Schools and families: Creating essential connections for learning.* New York, NY: Guilford Press.

Coolahan, K., Fantuzzo, J., Mendez, J., & McDermott, P. (2000). Preschool peer interactions and readiness to learn: Relationships between classroom peer play and learning behaviors and conduct. *Journal of Educational Psychology, 92*, 458–465. http://dx.doi.org/10.1037/0022-0663.92.3.458

Crosnoe, R., Leventhal, T., Wirth, R. J., Pierce, K. M., & Pianta, R. C., & The NICHD Early Child Care Research Network. (2010). Family socioeconomic status and consistent environmental stimulation in early childhood. *Child Development, 81*, 972–987. http://dx.doi.org/10.1111/j.1467-8624.2010.01446.x

Division for Early Childhood. (2014). *DEC recommended practices in early intervention/early childhood special education 2014.* Retrieved from http://www.dec-sped.org/recommendedpractices

Domínguez, X., Vitiello, V. E., Fuccillo, J. M., Greenfield, D. B., & Bulotsky-Shearer, R. J. (2011). The role of context in preschool learning: A multilevel examination of the contribution of context-specific problem behaviors and classroom process quality to low-income children's approaches to learning. *Journal of School Psychology, 49*, 175–195. http://dx.doi.org/10.1016/j.jsp.2010.11.002

Downer, J., & Myers, S. (2009). Application of a developmental/ecological model to family-school partnerships. In S. L. Christenson & A. L. Reschly (Eds.), *Handbook of school–family partnerships* (pp. 3–29). New York, NY: Routledge and Taylor & Francis.

Duckworth, A. L., & Seligman, M. E. (2005). Self-discipline outdoes IQ in predicting academic performance of adolescents. *Psychological Science, 16*, 939–944. http://dx.doi.org/10.1111/j.1467-9280.2005.01641.x

Duncan, G. J., & Magnuson, K. (2011). The nature and impact of early achievement skills, attention skills, and behavior problems. In G. J. Duncan & R. J. Murnane (Eds.), *Whither opportunity* (pp. 47–70). New York, NY: Russell Sage.

Dunn, W. (1997). The impact of sensory processing abilities on the daily lives of young children and their families: A conceptual model. *Infants and Young Children, 9*(4), 23–35. http://dx.doi.org/10.1097/00001163-199704000-00005

Early, D. M., Maxwell, K. L., Ponder, B. D., & Pan, Y. (2017). Improving teacher–child interactions: A randomized controlled trial of Making the Most of Classroom Interactions and My Teaching Partner professional development models. *Early Childhood Research Quarterly, 38*, 57–70. http://dx.doi.org/10.1016/j.ecresq.2016.08.005

Early, D. M., Pianta, R. C., Taylor, L. C., & Cox, M. J. (2001). Transition practices: Findings from a national survey of kindergarten teachers. *Early Childhood Education Journal, 28*, 199–206. http://dx.doi.org/10.1023/A:1026503520593

Eggum-Wilkens, N. D., Fabes, R. A., Castle, S., Zhang, L., Hanish, L. D., & Martin, C. L. (2014). Playing with others: Head Start children's peer play and relations with kindergarten school competence. *Early Childhood Research Quarterly, 29*, 345–356. http://dx.doi.org/10.1016/j.ecresq.2014.04.008

Epstein, J. L. (2001). *School, family, and community partnerships: Preparing educators and improving schools.* Boulder, CO: Westview Press.

Fantuzzo, J., Coolahan, K., Mendez, J., McDermott, P., & Sutton-Smith, B. (1998). Contextually-relevant validation of peer play constructs with African American

Head Start children: Penn interactive peer play scale. *Early Childhood Research Quarterly, 13*, 411–431. http://dx.doi.org/10.1016/S0885-2006(99)80048-9

Fantuzzo, J., Gadsden, V., Li, F., Sproul, F., McDermott, P., Hightower, D., & Minney, A. (2013). Multiple dimensions of family engagement in early childhood education: Evidence for a short form of the Family Involvement Questionnaire. *Early Childhood Research Quarterly, 28*, 734–742. http://dx.doi.org/10.1016/j.ecresq.2013.07.001

Fantuzzo, J., Manz, P., Atkins, M., & Meyers, R. (2005). Peer-mediated treatment of socially withdrawn maltreated preschool children: Cultivating natural community resources. *Journal of Clinical Child and Adolescent Psychology, 34*, 320–325. http://dx.doi.org/10.1207/s15374424jccp3402_11

Fantuzzo, J., & McWayne, C. (2002). The relationship between peer-play interactions in the family context and dimensions of school readiness for low-income preschool children. *Journal of Educational Psychology, 94*(1), 79–87. http://dx.doi.org/10.1037/0022-0663.94.1.79

Fantuzzo, J., McWayne, C., & Bulotsky, R. (2003). Forging strategic partnerships to advance mental health science and practice for vulnerable children. *School Psychology Review, 32*, 17–37.

Fantuzzo, J., McWayne, C. M., Perry, M. A., & Childs, S. (2004). Multiple dimensions of family involvement and their relations to behavioral and learning competencies for urban, low-income children. *School Psychology Review, 33*, 467–480.

Fantuzzo, J., Mendez, J., & Tighe, E. (1998). Parental assessment of peer play: Development and validation of the parent version of the Penn Interactive Peer Play Scale. *Early Childhood Research Quarterly, 13*, 659–676. http://dx.doi.org/10.1016/S0885-2006(99)80066-0

Fantuzzo, J., Perry, M. A., & McDermott, P. (2004). Preschool approaches to learning and their relationship to other relevant classroom competencies for low-income children. *School Psychology Quarterly, 19*, 212–230. http://dx.doi.org/10.1521/scpq.19.3.212.40276

Fantuzzo, J., Sekino, Y., & Cohen, H. L. (2004). An examination of the contributions of interactive peer play to salient classroom competencies for urban Head Start children. *Psychology in the Schools, 41*, 323–336. http://dx.doi.org/10.1002/pits.10162

Fantuzzo, J., Sutton-Smith, B., Atkins, M., Meyers, R., Stevenson, H., Coolahan, K., . . . Manz, P. (1996). Community-based resilient peer treatment of withdrawn maltreated preschool children. *Journal of Consulting and Clinical Psychology, 64*, 1377–1386. http://dx.doi.org/10.1037/0022-006X.64.6.1377

Fantuzzo, J., Tighe, E., & Childs, S. (2000). Family Involvement Questionnaire: A multivariate assessment of family participation in early childhood education. *Journal of Educational Psychology, 92*, 367–376. http://dx.doi.org/10.1037/0022-0663.92.2.367

Fisher, K., Hirsh-Pasek, K., Golinkoff, R. M., Singer, D. G., & Berk, L. (2011). Playing around in school: Implications for learning and educational policy. In A. D. Pellegrini (Ed.), *Oxford library of psychology. The Oxford handbook of the development of play* (pp. 341–360). New York, NY: Oxford University Press.

Fox, L., Dunlap, G., Hemmeter, M. L., Joseph, G. E., & Strain, P. S. (2003). The Teaching Pyramid: A model for supporting social competence and preventing challenging behavior in young children. *Young Children, 58*, 48–52.

Fox, L., & Hemmeter, M. L. (2009). A program-wide model for supporting social emotional development and addressing challenging behavior in early childhood settings. In W. Sailor, G. Dunlap, G. Sugai, & R. Horner (Eds.), *Handbook of positive behavior support* (pp. 177–202). New York, NY: Springer. http://dx.doi.org/10.1007/978-0-387-09632-2_8

Gadsden, V. L. (2013). *Evaluating family and neighborhood context for PreK-3 (Report commissioned by the Foundation for Child Development)*. New York, NY: Foundation for Child Development.

García Coll, C., Akiba, D., Palacios, N., Bailey, B., Silver, R., DiMartino, L., & Chin, C. (2002). Parental involvement in children's education: Lessons from three immigrant groups. *Parenting: Science and Practice, 2,* 303–324. http://dx.doi.org/10.1207/S15327922PAR0203_05

Gillanders, C., Iruka, I., Ritchie, S., & Cobb, C. T. (2012). Restructuring and aligning early education opportunities for cultural, language, and ethnic minority children. In R. Pianta, W. Barnett, L. Justice, & S. Sheridan (Eds.), *Handbook of early childhood education* (pp. 111–136). New York, NY: Guilford Press.

Gilliam, W. S. (2005). *Prekindergarteners left behind: Expulsion rates in state prekindergarten systems.* New York, NY: Foundation for Child Development.

Graziano, P. A., Slavec, J., Ros, R., Garb, L., Hart, K., & Garcia, A. (2015). Self-regulation assessment among preschoolers with externalizing behavior problems. *Psychological Assessment, 27,* 1337–1348. http://dx.doi.org/10.1037/pas0000113

Green, K. (2016). Implementing check-in/check-out in family childcare centers: An intervention for children with attention seeking behaviors. *Young Exceptional Children, 21*(4), 1–12.

Hair, E., Halle, T., Terry-Humen, T., Lavelle, B., & Calkins, J. (2006). Children's school readiness in the ECLS-K: Predictions to academic, health, and social outcomes in first grade. *Early Childhood Research Quarterly, 21,* 431–454. http://dx.doi.org/10.1016/j.ecresq.2006.09.005

Halle, T. G., Hair, E. C., Wandner, L. D., & Chien, N. C. (2012). Profiles of school readiness among four-year-old Head Start children. *Early Childhood Research Quarterly, 27,* 613–626. http://dx.doi.org/10.1016/j.ecresq.2012.04.001

Hampton, V. R., & Fantuzzo, J. W. (2003). The validity of the Penn Interactive Peer Play Scale with urban, low-income kindergarten children. *School Psychology Review, 32*(1), 77–91.

Hamre, B., Hatfield, B., Pianta, R., & Jamil, F. (2014). Evidence for general and domain-specific elements of teacher-child interactions: Associations with preschool children's development. *Child Development, 85,* 1257–1274. http://dx.doi.org/10.1111/cdev.12184

Hamre, B. K. (2014). Teachers' daily interactions with children: An essential ingredient in effective early childhood programs. *Child Development Perspectives, 8,* 223–230. http://dx.doi.org/10.1111/cdep.12090

Hamre, B. K., & Pianta, R. C. (2005). Can instructional and emotional support in the first-grade classroom make a difference for children at risk of school failure? *Child Development, 76,* 949–967. http://dx.doi.org/10.1111/j.1467-8624.2005.00889.x

Hamre, B. K., Pianta, R. C., Downer, J. T., DeCoster, J., Mashburn, A. J., Jones, S. M., . . . Hamagami, A. (2013). Teaching through interactions: Testing a developmental framework of teacher effectiveness in over 4,000 classrooms. *The Elementary School Journal, 113,* 461–487. http://dx.doi.org/10.1086/669616

Hassinger-Das, B., Hirsh-Pasek, K., & Golinkoff, R. M. (2017). The case of brain science and guided play. *YC Young Children, 72*(2), 45–50.

Heckman, J. J. (2006). Skill formation and the economics of investing in disadvantaged children. *Science, 312*(5782), 1900–1902. http://dx.doi.org/10.1126/science.1128898

Heckman, J. J. (2011). The economics of inequality: The value of early childhood education. *American Educator, 35*(1), 31–35.

Hemmeter, M. L., Ostrosky, M., & Fox, L. (2006). Social and emotional foundations for early learning: A conceptual model for intervention. *School Psychology Review, 35,* 583–601.

Hemmeter, M. L., Snyder, P. A., Fox, L., & Algina, J. (2016). Evaluating the implementation of the Pyramid Model for promoting social-emotional competence in early childhood classrooms. *Topics in Early Childhood Special Education, 36,* 133–146. http://dx.doi.org/10.1177/0271121416653386

Hirsh-Pasek, K., & Burchinal, M. (2006). Mother and caregiver sensitivity over time: Predicting language and academic outcomes with variable-and person-centered approaches. *Merrill-Palmer Quarterly, 52*, 449–485. http://dx.doi.org/10.1353/mpq.2006.0027

Jeynes, W. (2012). A meta-analysis of the efficacy of different types of parental involvement programs for urban students. *Urban Education, 47*, 706–742. http://dx.doi.org/10.1177/0042085912445643

Jeynes, W. H. (2003). A meta-analysis: The effects of parental involvement on minority children's academic achievement. *Education and Urban Society, 35*, 202–218. http://dx.doi.org/10.1177/0013124502239392

Kinzie, M. B., Whitaker, S. D., Neesen, K., Kelley, M., Matera, M., & Pianta, R. C. (2006). Innovative web-based professional development for teachers of at-risk preschool children. *Journal of Educational Technology & Society, 9*, 194–204.

Knoche, L. L., Edwards, C. P., Sheridan, S. M., Kupzyk, K. A., Marvin, C. A., Cline, K. D., & Clarke, B. L. (2012). Getting ready: Results of a randomized trial of a relationship-focused intervention on the parent–infant relationship in rural early head start. *Infant Mental Health Journal, 33*, 439–458. http://dx.doi.org/10.1002/imhj.21320

Lamb-Parker, F., LeBuffe, P., Powell, C. G., & Halpern, E. (2008). A strength-based, systemic mental health approach to support children's social and emotional development. *Infants & Young Children, 21*, 45–55. http://dx.doi.org/10.1097/01.IYC.0000306372.40414.a7

La Paro, K. M., Pianta, R. C., & Stuhlman, M. (2004). The classroom assessment scoring system: Findings from the prekindergarten year. *The Elementary School Journal, 104*, 409–426. http://dx.doi.org/10.1086/499760

Luthar, S. S., Cicchetti, D., & Becker, B. (2000). The construct of resilience: A critical evaluation and guidelines for future work. *Child Development, 71*, 543–562. http://dx.doi.org/10.1111/1467-8624.00164

Masten, A. S. (2001). Ordinary magic. Resilience processes in development. *American Psychologist, 56*, 227–238. http://dx.doi.org/10.1037/0003-066X.56.3.227

McClelland, M. M., Acock, A. C., & Morrison, F. J. (2006). The impact of kindergarten learning-related skills on academic trajectories at the end of elementary school. *Early Childhood Research Quarterly, 21*, 471–490. http://dx.doi.org/10.1016/j.ecresq.2006.09.003

McWayne, C., Campos, R., & Owsianik, M. (2008). A multidimensional, multilevel examination of mother and father involvement among culturally diverse Head Start families. *Journal of School Psychology, 46*, 551–573. http://dx.doi.org/10.1016/j.jsp.2008.06.001

McWayne, C. M. (2015). Family–school partnerships in a context of urgent engagement: Rethinking models, measurement, and meaningfulness. In S. M. Sheridan & E. M. Kim (Eds.), *Foundational aspects of family-school partnership research* (pp. 105–124). Cham, Switzerland: Springer International Publishing. http://dx.doi.org/10.1007/978-3-319-13838-1_6

McWayne, C. M., Green, L. E., & Fantuzzo, J. W. (2009). A variable- and person-oriented investigation of preschool competencies and Head Start children's transition to kindergarten and first grade. *Applied Developmental Science, 13*(1), 1–15. http://dx.doi.org/10.1080/10888690802606719

McWayne, C. M., Hahs-Vaughn, D., Cheung, K., & Wright, L. E. G. (2012). National profiles of school readiness skills for Head Start children: An investigation of stability and change. *Early Childhood Research Quarterly, 27*, 668–683. http://dx.doi.org/10.1016/j.ecresq.2011.10.002

McWayne, C. M., Mattis, J. S., Green Wright, L. E., Limlingan, M. C., & Harris, E. (2017). An emic, mixed-methods approach to defining and measuring positive parenting among low-income Black families. *Early Education and Development, 28*, 182–206. http://dx.doi.org/10.1080/10409289.2016.1208601

McWayne, C. M., Mattis, J. S., & Hyun, S. (2018). Profiles of culturally salient positive parenting practices among urban-residing Black Head Start families. *Cultural Diversity & Ethnic Minority Psychology, 24*, 414–428. http://dx.doi.org/10.1037/cdp0000164

McWayne, C. M., Melzi, G., Schick, A. R., Kennedy, J. L., & Mundt, K. (2013). Defining family engagement among Latino Head Start parents: A mixed-methods measurement development study. *Early Childhood Research Quarterly, 28*, 593–607. http://dx.doi.org/10.1016/j.ecresq.2013.03.008

Mendez, J. L., Fantuzzo, J., & Cicchetti, D. (2002). Profiles of social competence among low-income African American preschool children. *Child Development, 73*, 1085–1100. http://dx.doi.org/10.1111/1467-8624.00459

Mendez, J. L., & Fogle, L. M. (2002). Parental reports of preschool children's social behavior: Relations among peer play, language competence, and problem behavior. *Journal of Psychoeducational Assessment, 20*, 370–385. http://dx.doi.org/10.1177/073428290202000405

National Association for the Education of Young Children (NAEYC). (2009). *Developmentally appropriate practice in early childhood programs serving children from birth through age 8: Position Statement*. Washington, DC: Author.

National Center for Children in Poverty. (2016). *Basic facts about low-income children: Children under 18 years, 2016*. Retrieved from http://www.nccp.org/publications/pub_1194.html

National Center on Parent, Family, and Community Engagement. (2018). *Head Start parent, family, and community engagement framework*. Retrieved from https://eclkc.ohs.acf.hhs.gov/sites/default/files/pdf/pfce-framework.pdf

National Education Goals Panel. (1998). *Ready schools*. Washington, DC: Government Printing Office. Retrieved from http://govinfo.library.unt.edu/negp/reports/readysch.pdf

National Institute of Child Health and Human Development, Early Child Care Research Network. (2002). Child-care structure → process → outcome: Direct and indirect effects of child-care quality on young children's development. *Psychological Science, 13*, 199–206. http://dx.doi.org/10.1111/1467-9280.00438

National Scientific Council on the Developing Child. (2004). *Young children develop in an environment of relationships* (Working Paper No. 1). Retrieved from https://developingchild.harvard.edu/wp-content/uploads/2004/04/Young-Children-Develop-in-an-Environment-of-Relationships.pdf

Nix, R. L., Bierman, K. L., Domitrovich, C. E., & Gill, S. (2013). Promoting children's social-emotional skills in preschool can enhance academic and behavioral functioning in kindergarten: Findings from Head Start REDI. *Early Education and Development, 24*, 1000–1019. http://dx.doi.org/10.1080/10409289.2013.825565

Piaget, J. (1932). *The moral development of the child*. London, England: Kegan Paul.

Pianta, R. C., La Paro, K. M., & Hamre, B. K. (2008). *Classroom Assessment Scoring System™: Manual K-3*. Baltimore, MD: Paul H. Brookes.

Powell, D. R., Son, S. H., File, N., & San Juan, R. R. (2010). Parent-school relationships and children's academic and social outcomes in public school pre-kindergarten. *Journal of School Psychology, 48*, 269–292. http://dx.doi.org/10.1016/j.jsp.2010.03.002

Qi, C. H., Zieher, A., Lee Van Horn, M., Bulotsky-Shearer, R., & Carta, J. (2019). Language skills, behaviour problems, and classroom emotional support among preschool children from low-income families. *Early Child Development and Care*. Advance online publication. http://dx.doi.org/10.1080/03004430.2019.1570504

Ramey, S. L., & Ramey, C. T. (1999). The transition to school for "at-risk" children. In R. C. Pianta & M. J. Cox (Eds.), *The transition to kindergarten* (pp. 217–251). Baltimore, MD: Paul H. Brookes.

Raver, C. C., & Zigler, E. F. (1997). Social competence: An untapped dimension in evaluating Head Start's success. *Early Childhood Research Quarterly, 12*, 363–385. http://dx.doi.org/10.1016/S0885-2006(97)90017-X

Rimm-Kaufman, S. E., Curby, T. W., Grimm, K. J., Nathanson, L., & Brock, L. L. (2009). The contribution of children's self-regulation and classroom quality to children's adaptive behaviors in the kindergarten classroom. *Developmental Psychology, 45*, 958–972. http://dx.doi.org/10.1037/a0015861

Rimm-Kaufman, S. E., Pianta, R. C., & Cox, M. J. (2000). Teachers' judgments of problems in the transition to kindergarten. *Early Childhood Research Quarterly, 15*, 147–166. http://dx.doi.org/10.1016/S0885-2006(00)00049-1

Sameroff, A. J. (Ed.). (2009). *The transactional model of development: How children and contexts shape each other*. Washington, DC: American Psychological Association. http://dx.doi.org/10.1037/11877-000

Sekino, Y. (2006). *Investigation of the relationship between preschool peer play and third-grade outcomes for low-income urban students* (Doctoral dissertation). Retrieved from http://repository.upenn.edu/dissertations/AAI3246236

Sheridan, S. M., Knoche, L. L., Edwards, C. P., Bovaird, J. A., & Kupzyk, K. A. (2010). Parent engagement and school readiness: Effects of the Getting Ready intervention on preschool children's social–emotional competencies. *Early Education and Development, 21*(1), 125–156. http://dx.doi.org/10.1080/10409280902783517

Sheridan, S. M., Knoche, L. L., Kupzyk, K. A., Edwards, C. P., & Marvin, C. A. (2011). A randomized trial examining the effects of parent engagement on early language and literacy: The Getting Ready intervention. *Journal of School Psychology, 49*, 361–383. http://dx.doi.org/10.1016/j.jsp.2011.03.001

Sheridan, S. M., Marvin, C., Knoche, L., & Edwards, C. P. (2008). Getting ready: Promoting school readiness through a relationship-based partnership model. *Early Childhood Services: An Interdisciplinary Journal of Effectiveness, 2*(3), 149–172.

Shonkoff, J. P., Richter, L., van der Gaag, J., & Bhutta, Z. A. (2012). An integrated scientific framework for child survival and early childhood development. *Pediatrics, 129*, e460–e472. http://dx.doi.org/10.1542/peds.2011-0366

Snow, K. L. (2007). Integrative views of the domains and child function: Unifying school readiness. In R. C. Pianta, M. J. Cox, & K. L. Snow (Eds.), *School readiness and the transition to kindergarten in the era of accountability* (pp. 197–216). Baltimore, MD: Paul H. Brookes.

Stanton-Chapman, T. L., & Hadden, D. S. (2011). Encouraging peer interactions in preschool classrooms: The role of the teacher. *Young Exceptional Children, 14*(1), 17–28. http://dx.doi.org/10.1177/1096250610395458

Thompson, R. A., & Raikes, H. A. (2007). The social and emotional foundations of school readiness. In D. F. Perry, R. K. Kaufman, & J. Knitzer (Eds.), *Social and emotional health in early childhood: Building bridges between services and systems* (pp. 13–36). Baltimore, MD: Paul H. Brookes.

Toldson, I. A., & Lemmons, B. P. (2013). Social demographics, the school environment, and parenting practices associated with parents' participation in schools and academic success among Black, Hispanic, and White students. *Journal of Human Behavior in the Social Environment, 23*(2), 237–255. http://dx.doi.org/10.1080/10911359.2013.747407

Tominey, S. L., & McClelland, M. M. (2011). Red Light, Purple Light: Findings from a randomized trial using circle time games to improve behavioral self-regulation in preschool. *Early Education and Development, 22*, 489–519. http://dx.doi.org/10.1080/10409289.2011.574258

Ursache, A., Blair, C., & Raver, C. C. (2012). The promotion of self-regulation as a means of enhancing school readiness and early achievement in children at risk for school failure. *Child Development Perspectives, 6*(2), 122–128. http://dx.doi.org/10.1111/j.1750-8606.2011.00209.x

U.S. Department of Education, Office of Early Learning. (2018). Preschool development grants. Retrieved from https://www2.ed.gov/programs/preschooldevelopmentgrants/index.html

U.S. Department of Health and Human Services. (2015). Program performance standards for the operation of Head Start programs by grantee and delegate agencies, 45 C.F.R. Part 1302.50 [Washington, DC: U.S. GOP]. *Federal Register, 80,* 35479–35481.

U.S. Department of Health and Human Services, Administration on Children, Youth, and Families/Head Start Bureau. (2003). *The Head Start path to positive child outcomes.* Washington, DC: Author.

Vandell, D. L., Belsky, J., Burchinal, M., Steinberg, L., Vandergrift, N., & The NICHD Early Child Care Research Network. (2010). Do effects of early child care extend to age 15 years? Results from the NICHD study of early child care and youth development. *Child Development, 81,* 737–756. http://dx.doi.org/10.1111/j.1467-8624.2010.01431.x

Vygotsky, L. (1978). Interaction between learning and development. *Readings on the Development of Children, 23*(3), 34–41.

Weisberg, D. S., Hirsh-Pasek, K., & Golinkoff, R. M. (2013). Guided play: Where curricular goals meet a playful pedagogy. *Mind, Brain, and Education, 7*(2), 104–112. http://dx.doi.org/10.1111/mbe.12015

Wentzel, K. R. (2005). Peer relationships, motivation, and academic performance at school. In A. Elliot & C. Dweck (Eds.), *Handbook of competence and motivation* (pp. 279–296). New York, NY: Guilford Press.

Zigler, E. F., & Bishop-Josef, S. J. (2006). The cognitive child vs. the whole child: Lessons from 40 years of Head Start. In D. G. Singer, R. M. Golinkoff, & K. Hirsh-Pasek (Eds.), *Play = learning: How play motivates and enhances children's cognitive and social emotional growth* (pp. 15–35). New York, NY: Oxford University Press.

Zigler, E. F., Singer, D. G., & Bishop-Josef, S. J. (Eds.). (2004). *Children's play: The roots of reading.* Washington, DC: ZERO TO THREE/National Center for Infants, Toddlers and Families.

HIGH-QUALITY LEARNING ENVIRONMENTS

Principles and Practices That Promote Positive Guidance in Early Childhood

George J. DuPaul and Courtney L. Cleminshaw

In light of the prevalence of emotion and behavior disorders among young children, there is a clear need for early childhood educators to address children's challenging behaviors in an effective fashion. Unfortunately, early educators typically rely on reactive and punitive behavior management strategies that have limited impact, particularly on long-term development of children's self-regulation. In contrast, research has supported the efficacy of proactive approaches that seek to prevent challenging behaviors and positively reinforce children's appropriate actions. In addition, teachers can support children's use of problem solving to regulate behavior and communicate needs (e.g., Kreibich, Chen, & Reichle, 2015). The purpose of this chapter is to describe methods for teachers to prevent children's challenging behaviors and promote growth in self-regulation skills in the context of a multitiered system of support (MTSS). First, we discuss the prevalence of emotion and behavior difficulties in young children, impairment in functioning associated with those difficulties, and the importance of addressing these difficulties in early childhood settings. Next, we describe an MTSS and how this can be applied in early childhood settings. Details regarding specific, effective classwide (Tier 1), small-group (Tier 2), and individual (Tier 3) intervention strategies are provided. We conclude with recommendations regarding the assessment of behavior change and the use of outcome data to make ongoing intervention decisions.

http://dx.doi.org/10.1037/0000197-010
Healthy Development in Young Children: Evidence-Based Interventions for Early Education,
V. C. Alfonso and G. J. DuPaul (Editors)

ADDRESSING EMOTION AND BEHAVIOR DIFFICULTIES
IN EARLY CHILDHOOD SETTINGS

Young children exhibit relatively high rates of emotion, self-regulation, and behavior control difficulties. Epidemiological studies in the United States and Europe have found that rates of diagnosable psychiatric disorders in 3- to 5-year-olds ranged from 7.1% (Wichstrøm et al., 2012) to 21.4% (Lavigne et al., 1996). Thus, up to one in five preschoolers may exhibit significant symptoms of emotion and behavior disorders. Rates vary as a function of diagnostic criteria, respondent (e.g., parent or teacher report), diagnostician (e.g., psychologist or pediatrician), and consideration of impairment beyond display of symptomatic behaviors. Although overall rates of disorder have varied across investigations, studies are consistent in finding highest prevalence for attention-deficit/hyperactivity disorder (ADHD) and oppositional defiant disorder (ODD), higher risk for disorder among boys, relatively strong associations across disorders (i.e., comorbidity), and very low rates of mental health service receipt (Carter et al., 2010; Egger & Angold, 2006; Lavigne, LeBailly, Hopkins, Gouze, & Binns, 2009; Wichstrøm et al., 2012). Other than the relatively low rate of internalizing disorders (i.e., anxiety and depression) among young children, prevalence rates and demographic patterns are quite similar to those found among school-age children (Egger & Angold, 2006). It is important to note that these prevalence figures do not take into account children who may exhibit challenging behaviors or poor self-regulation skills that do not meet diagnostic thresholds. Thus, early childhood educators are likely to work with one or more children with emotion and behavior difficulties each school year.

Challenging behaviors frequently are associated with impairment in development of early social and academic skills. Young children with emotion and behavior disorders exhibit lower levels of social competence and higher rates of familial conflict (Carter et al., 2010), greater negative affect and poorer effortful control (Martel, Gremillion, & Roberts, 2012), and delays in early academic skills (DuPaul, McGoey, Eckert, & VanBrakle, 2001). Thus, children may experience significant problems transitioning to elementary school and typically enter school lagging behind their peers in academic and social functioning. In fact, functional impairment is arguably a more important target for intervention than are symptomatic behaviors given the critical importance of development in behavioral self-regulation, early literacy and numeracy, and interpersonal relationship skills.

Recent years have been an alarming increase in expulsion of young children with emotion and behavior difficulties from early childhood settings. For example, the presence of ADHD and/or ODD greatly increases the risk for expulsion from preschool settings. In fact, rates of suspension and expulsion for preschoolers with disruptive behavior disorders are significantly higher than for school-age students with similar disorders (e.g., Posner et al., 2007). For example, in Pennsylvania, 3.54 per 1,000 children were expelled from pre-K settings in 2003–2004, more than 3 times the rate of expulsion for K–12 students (Gilliam, 2005). National data indicate that 75% of suspended or expelled preschoolers have a disability; preschoolers with ADHD comprise 53% of preschool suspensions or expulsions (Novoa & Malik, 2018). Furthermore, expulsion rates are highest in early childhood settings that have no access to behavioral professionals or behavioral consultation (i.e., where teachers do not have support in classroom management and behavioral intervention; Gilliam, 2005).

Emotion and behavior difficulties exhibited by young children may be associated with longer-term behavior, academic, and social difficulties that persist across school years. As described previously, of particular concern is the risk for preschoolers with behavior and self-regulation skills to enter elementary school lagging behind their peers in academic and social skills. For example, DuPaul, Morgan, Farkas, Hillemeier, and Maczuga (2016) analyzed data from a nationally representative U.S. cohort in the Early Childhood Longitudinal Study, Kindergarten Class of 1998–1999 for 590 children (72.7% male) whose parents reported a formal diagnosis of ADHD. Children's math, reading, and interpersonal skills were assessed at five time points between kindergarten and fifth grade. Growth mixture model analyses identified four latent trajectory classes for reading, eight classes for math, and four classes for social skills. These findings indicate that children with ADHD display substantial heterogeneity in reading, math, and social skill trajectories, with some groups (e.g., those with most frequent symptomatic behaviors at school entry) especially likely to display relatively severe levels of academic and social impairment over time. Furthermore, children's functioning status at kindergarten entry was highly correlated with their functioning in fifth grade, strongly supporting the need for screening and intervention prior to school entry.

Unfortunately, early childhood educators typically receive minimal preparation for working with young children with emotion and behavior difficulties. Preschool teachers often have very little knowledge of mental health disorders because information regarding psychopathology is not typically included in pre- or in-service training programs. Early childhood educators also receive little training and support in use of effective behavioral strategies and have limited preparation in structuring classroom environment and expectations to promote desired behavior. As a result, teachers often use ineffective practices (e.g., reprimands) to manage behavior that are reactive and punitive (Stormont, Lewis, Beckner, & Johnson, 2008). In contrast, positive behavior support strategies that proactively elicit and reinforce desired child behaviors have been found effective, particularly in the context of an MTSS (Sandomierski, Kincaid, & Algozzine, 2007).

Teacher training in positive behavior support strategies can have positive impacts on preschool classrooms and facilitate successful transition into kindergarten (Curby et al., 2018; see also Chapter 10, this volume). Hemmeter, Snyder, Fox, and Algina (2016) examined the effects of professional development workshops to support teacher implementation of positive support practices. Practices in these workshops included building positive relationships with children, families, and colleagues, designing supportive and engaging environments, teaching social and emotional skills, and developing individualized interventions for children with the most challenging behavior (Hemmeter, Ostrosky, & Fox, 2006). In a randomized controlled trial, preschool teachers who received the workshops significantly improved their implementation of practices relative to control teachers. Additionally, the social–emotional and behavior management strategies taught in the sessions improved child behavior. Postintervention, children whose teachers received training were rated as exhibiting fewer challenging behaviors and engaging in more positive social interactions. These results support the use of positive behavior support strategies by early childhood educators.

MULTITIERED SYSTEMS OF SUPPORT

Tiered intervention models, such as MTSS, are theoretical frameworks of behavior management. In this section, we provide an overview of MTSS models in the context of early education settings. We specifically discuss delivery of positive behavior support strategies as central to MTSS.

What Is a Tiered Model?

An umbrella term, MTSS encompasses response to intervention and school-wide positive behavior intervention and support (Sandomierski et al., 2007). An MTSS model supports students by systematically delivering a range of interventions based on demonstrated levels of need. But most typically, MTSS models involve consistent monitoring or evaluation of student or child needs and increasingly intensive responses or interventions to address these needs. The goal of MTSS is to support children in a systematic fashion. In such a model, all children receive basic levels of support, and some strategies are used universally. For the smaller number of children who need additional intervention, basic individualized strategies are employed. And finally, for the remaining children whose behavior is not improved by such measures, more intensive or restrictive interventions are implemented. Therefore, MTSS is responsive to individual needs while universally providing preventative strategies (Sandomierski et al., 2007).

MTSS models are most commonly used for K–12 students. However, simple adaptations can render MTSS appropriate for early childhood settings. A typical K–12 MTSS model can be visualized as a pyramid. As displayed in Figure 9.1, strategies can be preventative and address all children or specific and target a select group of children with persistent challenges. Tier 1, at the bottom of the pyramid, represents universal supports to address the needs of most children and includes training for school staff, establishing universal school expectations, and providing primary prevention to all students (e.g., school-wide reward or ticket system). In theory, Tier 1 fully meets the needs of about 80% of the student population (Sandomierski et al., 2007). Ideally, the emphasis at this tier is placed on building relationships among faculty, staff, and

FIGURE 9.1. A Model for Promoting Young Children's Social Competence and Addressing Challenging Behavior

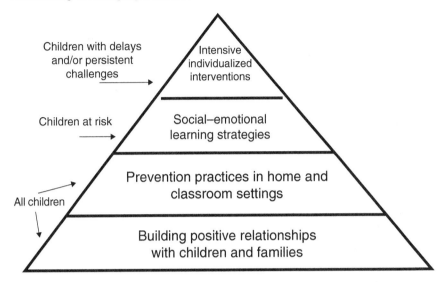

From "Prevention and Intervention for the Challenging Behaviors of Toddlers and Preschoolers," by D. Powell, G. Dunlap, and L. Fox, 2006, *Infants & Young Children*, *19*, p. 27. Copyright 2006 by Wolters Kluwer. Reprinted with permission.

students while also empowering children to seek help for their problems and support them through the process (L. McArthur, personal communication, May 4, 2018).

Tier 2 centers around limited secondary interventions for students of medium behavioral risk. Theoretically, this would address the needs of about 15% of the student population. Tier 2 serves (a) children who are identified as demonstrating behavioral need more significant than can be addressed by a Tier 1 intervention and (b) children who make positive progress and are transitioned out of intensive Tier 3 behavioral interventions (note that the composition of this, or any, tier is not static). Tier 3 or tertiary intervention is provided to students requiring the most targeted, intensive supports (approximately 5%).

Students in Tier 3 may exhibit severe concerns, such as social alienation, aggression, or other risk factors of violence. For these children, professionals should be careful to select evidence-based intervention curricula that are flexible and customizable to the existing early childhood setting culture. A hallmark of MTSS and other tiered models is the use of data-based decision making to move children between levels of support (Benner, Kutash, Nelson, & Fisher, 2013). This can include universal screening for behavioral risk and progress monitoring or tallying of the occurrences of targeted behaviors (frequency count). In early childhood, MTSS targeted at behavior management often manifests as classwide (Tier 1), small-group (Tier 2), and individual child (Tier 3) interventions.

Multitiered Systems of Support and Positive Behavior Support

Behavioral problems in the classroom are a common obstacle in early childhood education settings, and they pose challenges for many children, parents, teachers, and families. Serious misbehavior makes classroom management difficult for teachers and may hinder children's and their peers' abilities to learn effectively and experience early school success. When interviewed, teachers consistently mention student discipline as one of their primary professional concerns (Ingersoll, 2001). And when misbehavior is particularly disruptive, early childhood educators may face additional professional and logistical concerns such as excessive time spent on classroom management, low standardized test scores, and difficulties delivering effective curriculum and learning opportunities (Monroe & Obidah, 2004). Appropriate classroom behavior and expected student conduct are essential to the creation of a productive learning environment (Monroe & Obidah, 2004). However, reactive consequences to challenging behavior are often not effective in producing durable, positive change.

Because MTSS systematically and proactively supports students, it provides an ideal framework for promoting growth in self-regulation skills and altering challenging child behavior using positive and preventative, rather than punitive, strategies. Using collected data, educators can readily transition students between tiers based on their behavioral needs. For example, an educator may commonly have a classwide point or clip system in place. This system can be conceptualized as a Tier 1 intervention. It is implemented universally and establishes expectations for all students. A student who consistently loses points may be given individual goals based on the class system or a unique clip system that provides prizes or rewards for success. The latter type of intervention falls into Tier 2 in an MTSS model. Finally, students who do not respond to individualization and continue to display challenging behaviors may need more intensive interventions. A functional behavior assessment (FBA) may be conducted to determine the function of the individual child's behavior, or the child may receive one-on-one instruction on coping strategies. Such practices would fall within Tier 3 of an MTSS model.

For the most part, research has demonstrated positive effects of MTSS and behavioral interventions in preschool settings. Several models have been developed to train and support teachers in implementing behavioral strategies in preschool classrooms, including the pyramid model for supporting social emotional competence in infants and young children (Fox, Dunlap, Hemmeter, Joseph, & Strain, 2003); Prevent–Teach–Reinforce for Young Children (PTR-YC; Dunlap, Strain, Lee, Joseph, & Leech, 2018; Dunlap, Wilson, Strain, & Lee, 2013); Behavioral, Emotional, and Social Training: Competent Learners Achieving School Success (BEST in CLASS; Vo, Sutherland, & Conroy, 2012); and Incredible Years (Webster-Stratton & Reid, 2001). The majority of preschool training models are focused on universal Tier 1 strategies to respond to and prevent common behavior difficulties. However, BEST in CLASS is a Tier 2 intervention designed to train teachers of young children (pre-K through second grade) positive behavior management strategies (e.g., supportive relationships, rules, precorrection, opportunities to respond, praise). Empirical studies suggest that BEST in CLASS, which includes direct coaching, helps teachers understand and use effective practices and reduce classroom problem behavior. As another example of a model program, Incredible Years is a set of curricula for teachers, parents, and children that aims to develop social and emotional competence and reduce aggressive or disruptive behaviors in children as young as 2 years old. A Tier 3 intervention, the program highlights positive discipline and proactive teaching strategies (e.g., behavior-specific praise, precorrection). Results from several randomized controlled trials show that young children in classrooms where educators received the Incredible Years curriculum were more on task and exhibited fewer behavior problems overall (Webster-Stratton & Reid, 2001). Similarly, PTR-YC (Dunlap et al., 2018) is a positive behavior support intervention for young children (e.g., pre-K, early child care, early Head Start) exhibiting or at risk for challenging behaviors. Using team goal setting, data collection, and intensive implementation of individualized intervention strategies (e.g., positive attention, clear and predictable schedules, direct teaching of expectations and social skills), PTR-YC has been shown to significantly improve ratings of child behavior and social functioning. Teachers are typically the primary intervention agents in PTR-YC.

FACTORS THAT IMPACT STRATEGY SELECTION

Preschool teacher knowledge of behavior management is related to prosocial behavior in preschool (LeBel & Chafouleas, 2010), and many effective behavior management strategies that prevent challenging behavior and promote self-regulation skills are complementary to an MTSS model. When choosing recommended intervention strategies for students, parents and educators should consider several factors, including child developmental level, environmental and cultural influences, and the specific behavior(s) targeted for change.

Challenging behaviors in children can vary by age and developmental level. For example, tantrums may be more frequent and developmentally appropriate in early childhood than in late childhood, and serious delinquency is rarely a concern for early childhood educators. Thus, it is important for practitioners to choose interventions that are effective for shaping the target behavior and that have been deemed developmentally appropriate for the child's specific age. Strategies and intervention procedures should also be reevaluated as a child matures. Prompts using pictures and visual representations of desired behavior may be suitable for very young children but may need to be adapted as a child's vocabulary, reading skills, and independence develop.

Second, observed behaviors can be influenced by innumerable environmental and cultural factors (e.g., home and family dynamic, language skills). When considering behavior management strategies, educators should consider environmental influences that may impact a child's behavior and an intervention's success, such as the context in which the behavior occurs (e.g., silent seatwork, small-group work, transitions), the child's access to resources, and the child's cultural and linguistic background. For example, embedding a child's interest into play and small-group activities can help increase engagement. However, if a student's family does not have sufficient financial resources, it would not be appropriate to require the student to bring in their own toys, and this strategy would not be effective in creating long-term behavioral change in this context.

Finally, children often display several challenging behaviors at the same time. In these instances, it may be necessary for educators to prioritize the most relevant concerns. For example, a student may fidget, rip up coloring sheets during activities, and throw objects at the teacher. Although fidgeting may perhaps be annoying or distracting to an educator, it is not very severe relative to other behaviors. Similarly, ripping papers can be distracting and can lead other children off task, but it is not a safety concern. Throwing objects, however, is potentially dangerous. Behaviors that endanger either the child or others (e.g., hitting, throwing, biting) should be addressed first. A child may exhibit behaviors that are challenging, but dangerous behaviors should always be prioritized over disruptive or distracting behaviors. Next, key areas of impairment, or keystone behaviors, should be targeted. Barnett, Bauer, Ehrhardt, Lentz, and Stollar (1996) defined *keystone behaviors* as "those that, if changed, are likely to positively impact the largest set of other significant behaviors, perceptions, or problem environments to most efficiently provide long-term resolution of problem situations" (p. 95). Perhaps a child commonly wanders the classroom and loudly plays with toys during circle time, distracting other students from the activity. Improving the frequency of a single behavior—staying in the assigned area—can lead to a reduction in both disruptive behaviors. The child will also spend increasing time in a productive environment (the group circle), so engagement and learning may also improve. Keystone behaviors offer the most significant benefits and, by targeting such behaviors, early childhood educators maximize the opportunity for success in effective behavior change.

POSSIBLE POSITIVE GUIDANCE STRATEGIES

The following is a description of methods for early childhood educators to prevent children's challenging behaviors and promote growth in children's self-regulation skills. Techniques can be directed toward an entire class, a group of students, or an individual child, as per a tiered system of support (see Table 9.1).

Classwide (Tier 1) Strategies and Support

Tier 1 strategies could include the following: (a) establish clear rules and expectations, (b) increase predictability, (c) provide when/then statements, (d) use

TABLE 9.1. Summary of Positive Guidance Strategies in Context of a Multitiered System of Support

Classwide (Tier 1) strategies and support	Small-group (Tier 2) strategies and support	Individual (Tier 3) strategies and support
• Establish clear rules and expectations. • Increase predictability. • Provide when/then statements. • Use brief instructions for activities. • Praise specifically and frequently. • Provide ample opportunities to respond.	• Embed interests into activities. • Improve social interactions.	• Identify antecedents and consequences for challenging behaviors. • Offer preferred activities. • Offer choices. • Adjust activity length and offer breaks. • Provide self-regulation training.

brief instructions for activities, (e) praise specifically and frequently, and (f) provide ample opportunities to respond.

Establish Clear Rules and Expectations

Boundaries and expectations can help children successfully navigate environments and understand what is expected of them, leading to increased compliance with classroom rules (Passini, Pihet, & Favez, 2014). Consider posting rules where children can clearly see them as reminders. Pictures and stories may be particularly useful tools in explaining rules to young children. When disruptive or inappropriate behavior does occur, reference preestablished rules when explaining why or why not the behavior is acceptable. Expectations should be consistently reinforced for all children and should be worded in language that is easy to understand (Kern & Clemens, 2007).

Increase Predictability

Children may exhibit fewer problem behaviors when they can predict upcoming events and activities or are familiar with a consistent schedule or routine (Kern & Clemens, 2007). To help increase predictability, early childhood educators can use cues for change, visual schedules, and when/then statements. Educators may also consider announcing when a transition to a different activity is approaching (e.g., "We'll be putting the toys away and moving on to circle time in 2 minutes"). Cues such as timers and bells can also be used to signal transitions. Such signals can help children learn how to independently follow a schedule.

Provide When/Then Statements

Such statements offer a clear expectation as well as a reward for completion or appropriate behavior. They also articulate an effective command (Matheson & Shriver, 2005). Specifically, a child is praised or rewarded after meeting the stated expectation (e.g., "When you finish cleaning up your toy area, then you can play with blocks").

Use Brief Instructions for Activities

Educators should be encouraged to use short, direct instructions for activities and repeat them as necessary. Instructions should be expressed such that only one idea or desired action is presented or requested at a time (Kern & Clemens, 2007). Using analogies or abstract language may be confusing to some children (e.g., "Be on your best behavior"). Instead, the teacher should tell children exactly what they should do (e.g., "Please sit with your hands in your lap"). Educators may also consider using a combination of verbal, visual, and modeled prompts to communicate instructions. For example, educators may say, "Please line up in front of me" while holding their hands high in the air to draw attention to themselves.

Praise Specifically and Frequently

Praise lets children know they are supported and that the teacher considers their behavior to be appropriate and consistent with classroom rules and guidelines (Kern & Clemens, 2007). Verbal approval should be short, clear, and specific so children are able to tell what exactly they are doing that facilitates praise (e.g., "Great job putting your crayons away, Johnny!"). This will reinforce desired behavior (as compared with nonspecific praise such as "Way to go!"; Chalk & Bizo, 2004). It is recommended that children receive three to five positive statements for every negative or corrective statement (Brown, Payne, Lankewich, & Cornell, 1970; Dunlap et al., 2018). Educators should be encouraged not to give attention to students when they are displaying behaviors that are inconsistent with classroom rules and guidelines.

Provide Ample Opportunities to Respond

Opportunities to respond (OTRs) are teacher behaviors that solicit student responses, such as asking questions, responding to a class cue, or sharing with a partner. The delivery of frequent OTRs should help children remain actively engaged in classroom activities and instruction (Kern & Clemens, 2007). OTRs also afford educators the opportunity to provide corrective feedback and praise, as appropriate.

Small-Group (Tier 2) Strategies and Support

Possible Tier 2 strategies include the following: (a) embed interests into activities and (b) improve social interactions.

Embed Interests Into Activities

Strategically embedding child interests into the learning environment can increase motivation and participation in activities (Ninci, Rispoli, Burke, & Neely, 2018). Simple modifications should be made to activities during which problem behaviors typically occur, such as unstructured playtime. Including the child's interests in activities may increase the child's engagement in mundane or nonpreferred activities (Kern & Clemens, 2007). For example, if a child is continuously disruptive during free time, teachers can ensure that the child's favorite toy is readily available during these times. Such modifications have led to reduced disruption and increased time on task (Clarke et al., 1995).

Improve Social Interactions

Young children may require explicit instruction on positive peer and social interactions (Dunlap et al., 2018). Educators can prompt students to engage in positive interactions and use reinforcement strategies to reward students and incentivize appropriate behavior. Smooth social interactions between young children may reduce problematic or challenging behaviors. For example, PTR-YC supports teachers directly instructing children on how to positively interact with peers (Dunlap et al., 2018). Employing role play to create opportunities to practice social interactions can also be a useful teaching strategy (Craig-Unkefer & Kaiser, 2002).

Individual (Tier 3) Strategies and Support

Possible Tier 3 strategies include the following: (a) identify antecedents and consequences for challenging behaviors, (b) offer preferred activities, (c) offer choices, (d) adjust activity length and offer breaks, and (e) provide self-regulation training.

Identify Antecedents and Consequences for Challenging Behaviors

FBAs can be used to help understand why a child is engaging in a particular challenging behavior by identifying antecedent and consequent events that may be eliciting and/or maintaining the specific behavior (O'Neill, Albin, Storey, Horner, & Sprague, 2015). Interventions based on FBAs target the purpose of the behavior and the factors maintaining it. Common functions of challenging behaviors include attention, avoidance, and escape. A child may exhibit challenging behavior (e.g., yelling, clowning around) to seek attention from teachers or peers. Even negative attention, such as reprimands, can maintain such behavior. Educators should ignore minor student provocations that are not a safety risk so as not to reinforce the student's expectation that inappropriate behavior will lead to desired attention (Gable, Hester, Rock, & Hughes, 2009). Additionally, a child may exhibit challenging behavior (e.g., throwing a tantrum, running away) to avoid or escape doing something they do not want to do (e.g., sit still for circle time activity). In such a case, educators may consider using verbal praise or rewards (e.g., a small prize, activity break) to positively reinforce the child's appropriate participation in the activity (Gable et al., 2009). Additional strategies that target the maintaining function of disruptive behavior in early childhood are described below.

Offer Preferred Activities

Educators should be encouraged to give children the option to engage in something they greatly enjoy. For example, if a child is acting disruptive during free
or unstructured times to gain attention from peers, a highly preferred activity
(e.g., play dough) can be offered during these times. Because the activity is
highly preferred, it may replace the need for attention in some situations.
Preferred activities may also be leveraged during times of transition to motivate
student engagement (Sullivan, Martens, Morley, & Long, 2017). For example,
the teacher could say, "If you put away your toys quickly, then you will have
some time to draw before circle time." Children should be allowed to engage
in the preferred activity only if they are doing so appropriately (e.g., silently).

Offer Choices

Educators can provide children with two or three options to choose from,
instead of just assigning one activity or task. Choice allows children to assert
a preference and is often very effective in reducing problem behavior that is
maintained by escape or avoidance (Kern & Clemens, 2007). For example,
the teacher can say, "You can play with either the blocks or the puzzle. You
may not run around the classroom."

Adjust Activity Length and Offer Breaks

Decreasing the length of an assigned task and providing more frequent breaks
during extended activities has been shown to decrease problem behavior
(Kern & Clemens, 2007). Children who are seeking to avoid or escape activities should be praised for effort and attention to an activity even for very
small amounts of time that they are able to stick to a given task. Activity
length can be increased as a child becomes successful in sustaining attention.
Children may also be taught to problem-solve by advocating for themselves.
Early childhood educators can help children identify when they may need a
break and ask for one appropriately (Kreibich et al., 2015). Children may be
taught to identify and verbally express feelings of frustration (e.g., "What
does it feel like when you can't do something you want to do?"). Physical
break cards can be useful for very young children. A certain number of cards
can be given to a child per day, and teachers should honor these break cards
whenever they are presented appropriately. Rules and expectations for breaks
should be established ahead of time (e.g., length, location, allowed activities;
Cihak & Gama, 2008).

Provide Self-Regulation Training

Intervention programs such as Incredible Years stress the importance of teaching students positive and effective strategies to regulate their own emotions
and behavior. Incredible Years uses vignettes and role-play activities to model
and practice emotional literacy, problem-solving, and anger management skills
(Borden, Schultz, Herman, & Brooks, 2010; Webster-Stratton & Reid, 2001).
Progressive units focus on positive communication, emotion language, perspective taking, and calm and focused persistence through difficult talks as means

to self-regulate and reduce challenging behaviors. Teachers can coach children to use learned strategies in the classroom.

Simple interventions can also help students self-regulate and positively advocate for themselves. Kreibich and colleagues (2015) found that teaching a preschool student with autism to request breaks appropriately during classroom activities dramatically increased engagement and tolerance for delay in reinforcement delivery, without increasing off-task or challenging behaviors. Thus, the child was exposed to more teaching opportunities, engaged appropriately in play, and learned an appropriate self-regulation skill.

ASSESSMENT OF BEHAVIOR CHANGE

Once strategies have been implemented in the context of tiered support, assessment data should be gathered periodically to ascertain whether the intervention is successful, whether intervention modifications are necessary, and whether movement from one tier to another is warranted. Specifically, a data-based decision-making process should be followed wherein treatment goals are identified prior to intervention and then data are gathered following intervention implementation to examine whether goals are met (Gischlar, Hojnoski, & Missall, 2009; Hojnoski, Gischlar, & Missall, 2009). If goals are met, then intervention can continue as originally designed and/or goals could be revised upward to obtain even greater behavior change. If goals are not being met, practitioners can consider revising the existing intervention (e.g., increase frequency, intensity, and/or duration of intervention strategies), adding one or more intervention components, moving the child to a more intensive tier of intervention, or revising goals to be more aligned with feasible outcomes. Practitioners can also evaluate whether interventions are being implemented with sufficient fidelity (e.g., adherence with prescribed strategies) to obtain behavior change.

Several possible assessment methods are available to measure intervention-related behavior change. These include brief behavior ratings from teachers and/or parents, direct observation of children's behavior in early education settings (e.g., classroom, playground), and assessment of children's early literacy and numeracy skills (for specifics regarding assessment methods, see Chapters 1 and 2). In addition, one or more measures can be used to assess intervention fidelity, including direct observation of strategy implementation, self-report checklists of intervention steps completed by teachers or parents, and examination of permanent products related to intervention (e.g., posting of visual schedule or calendar).

One option for assessing intervention outcomes is to collect behavior ratings from teachers and parents. For example, brief direct behavior ratings can be completed on a daily or weekly basis (Chafouleas, 2011). Direct behavior ratings can focus on specific target behaviors wherein teachers can quickly rate the degree to which a behavior is observed over a specific period. The emphasis would be on collecting brief ratings on a regular basis over a sufficient period (e.g., several weeks) to ascertain whether the intervention plan is working. Changes in scores before and after intervention can then be compared to decide whether behavior is improving and the degree to which a priori goals are being met.

In similar fashion, practitioners can conduct direct observations of children's classroom and/or playground behavior on a periodic basis prior to and following intervention. In particular, structured observation of children's on-task and interpersonal behaviors can be helpful in assessing the degree to which treatment targets are being met. Several observation systems are available for this purpose (for a review of early childhood observation methods, see Wood, Hojnoski, Laracy, & Olson, 2016). Ideally, several observations would be completed before and after intervention so that practitioners can document treatment-induced changes in the level (i.e., mean), trend (i.e., slope), and intercept (i.e., difference between last pretreatment data point and first data point in intervention phase).

It also is important to identify whether intervention reduces impairments in development of early literacy, numeracy, and social skills that can be associated with young children's emotion or behavior difficulties. Although these skills, particularly social skills, can be measured via teacher ratings or direct observation, practitioners would ideally assess early reading and math skills using structured standardized measures (e.g., Individual Growth and Development Indicators [IGDIs]; McConnell, Bradfield, Wackerle-Hollman, & Rodriguez, 2012). It is important to note that improvements in early academic and social behavior may take longer to develop than would more immediate changes in behaviors directly targeted by intervention. Thus, skills should be assessed over a longer period to evaluate fully the degree to which the intervention plan addresses impairment associated with emotion and behavior difficulties.

As described previously, if data indicate no improvement or only partial improvement in targeted behavior, then changes to intervention should be considered, selected, implemented, and evaluated in an iterative fashion. Once a plan is found to be effective over the short term, data regarding behavior change as well as early academic and social functioning can be collected every several months to monitor functional trajectories over time. This period between assessments allows for treatment effects to occur and precludes concerns regarding practice effects biasing repeated measurements using the same instrument. Furthermore, it is important to collect data that involve multiple respondents (i.e., parents and teachers) and varied modes of measurement (e.g., rating scales and direct observations) so that the limitations of any one measure or respondent are counterbalanced by the strengths of other measures or respondents. For example, rating scale data may reflect, in part, the biased perceptions of the respondent and can be balanced by direct observations conducted by a neutral observer who presumably does not share similar biases. Finally, ongoing measurement of treatment response should take advantage of existing measures designed to document change over time. For example, brief direct assessment of early reading and math skills, such as the IGDIs, are preferred over standardized, norm-referenced indices (e.g., Woodcock–Johnson IV Tests of Achievement; Schrank, Mather, & McGrew, 2014) because of the relative brevity and use of alternate forms for direct assessment measures.

SUMMARY AND CONCLUSIONS

A substantial percentage of young children display significant emotion and behavior difficulties in early childhood settings. In about 10% to 20% of cases, these difficulties may represent an emotional behavior disorder that is chronic and impairing. Even when behavior difficulties do not represent a diagnosable disorder, challenging behaviors can impair the development of a child's early academic and social skills as well as disrupt the learning experience of typically developing peers. Thus, early childhood educators must receive ongoing support in the use of strategies that are effective in not only reducing the frequency of children's challenging behaviors but also improving early academic and social functioning among those children who are at risk of entering elementary school behind their peers.

In contrast to the typical use of reactive and punitive strategies to address children's challenging behaviors, this chapter emphasized utilization of proactive prevention and intervention approaches that can be delivered in the context of an MTSS. In particular, early childhood educators can use classwide (Tier 1) strategies to encourage engagement and prosocial behaviors among all children along with small-group (Tier 2) or individual (Tier 3) interventions to address challenging behaviors exhibited by one or more children, as necessary. To facilitate accurate intervention decisions, practitioners are encouraged to collect ongoing progress monitoring data that allows assessment of the degree to which specific behavioral goals are reached for those children receiving Tier 2 or 3 interventions. The use of effective prevention and intervention MTSS procedures in early childhood education settings should promote successful entry into elementary school for all children.

REFERENCES

Barnett, D. W., Bauer, A. M., Ehrhardt, K. E., Lentz, F. E., & Stollar, S. A. (1996). Keystone targets for change: Planning for widespread positive consequences. *School Psychology Quarterly, 11*(2), 95–117. http://dx.doi.org/10.1037/h0088923

Benner, G. J., Kutash, K., Nelson, J. R., & Fisher, M. B. (2013). Closing the achievement gap of youth with emotional and behavioral disorders through multi-tiered systems of support. *Education & Treatment of Children, 36*(3), 15–29. http://dx.doi.org/10.1353/etc.2013.0018

Borden, L. A., Schultz, T. R., Herman, K. C., & Brooks, C. M. (2010). The Incredible Years parent training program: Promoting resilience through evidence-based prevention groups. *Group Dynamics: Theory, Research, and Practice, 14,* 230–241. http://dx.doi.org/10.1037/a0020322

Brown, W. E., Payne, L. T., Lankewich, C., & Cornell, L. L. (1970). Praise, criticism, and race. *The Elementary School Journal, 70,* 373–377. http://dx.doi.org/10.1086/460595

Carter, A. S., Wagmiller, R. J., Gray, S. A. O., McCarthy, K. J., Horwitz, S. M., & Briggs-Gowan, M. J. (2010). Prevalence of DSM-IV disorder in a representative, healthy birth cohort at school entry: Sociodemographic risks and social adaptation. *Journal of the American Academy of Child & Adolescent Psychiatry, 49*, 686–698. http://dx.doi.org/10.1097/00004583-201007000-00009

Chafouleas, S. M. (2011). Direct behavior rating: A review of the issues and research in its development. *Education & Treatment of Children, 34*, 575–591. http://dx.doi.org/10.1353/etc.2011.0034

Chalk, K., & Bizo, L. A. (2004). Specific praise improves on-task behaviour and numeracy enjoyment: A study of year four pupils engaged in the numeracy hour. *Educational Psychology in Practice, 20*, 335–351. http://dx.doi.org/10.1080/0266736042000314277

Cihak, D. F., & Gama, R. I. (2008). Noncontingent escape access to self-reinforcement to increase task engagement for students with moderate to severe disabilities. *Education and Training in Developmental Disabilities, 43*, 556–568.

Clarke, S., Dunlap, G., Foster-Johnson, L., Childs, K. E., Wilson, D., White, R., & Vera, A. (1995). Improving the conduct of students with behavioral disorders by incorporating student interests into curricular activities. *Behavioral Disorders, 20*, 221–237. http://dx.doi.org/10.1177/019874299502000402

Craig-Unkefer, L. A., & Kaiser, A. P. (2002). Improving the social communication skills of at-risk preschool children in a play context. *Topics in Early Childhood Special Education, 22*(1), 3–13. http://dx.doi.org/10.1177/027112140202200101

Curby, T. W., Berke, E., Alfonso, V. C., Blake, J. J., DeMarie, D., DuPaul, G. J., . . . Subotnik, R. F. (2018). Transition practices into kindergarten and the barriers teachers encounter. In A. Mashburn, J. LoCasale-Crouch, & K. Pears (Eds.), *Kindergarten transition and readiness: Promoting cognitive, social–emotional, and self-regulatory development* (pp. 249–264). Cham, Switzerland: Springer. http://dx.doi.org/10.1007/978-3-319-90200-5_11

Dunlap, G., Strain, P., Lee, J. K., Joseph, J., & Leech, N. (2018). A randomized controlled evaluation of prevent-teach-reinforce for young children. *Topics in Early Childhood Special Education, 37*, 195–205. http://dx.doi.org/10.1177/0271121417724874

Dunlap, G., Wilson, K., Strain, P., & Lee, J. K. (2013). *Prevent-teach-reinforce for young children: The early childhood model of individualized positive behavior support*. Baltimore, MD: Brookes.

DuPaul, G. J., McGoey, K. E., Eckert, T. L., & VanBrakle, J. (2001). Preschool children with attention-deficit/hyperactivity disorder: Impairments in behavioral, social, and school functioning. *Journal of the American Academy of Child & Adolescent Psychiatry, 40*, 508–515. http://dx.doi.org/10.1097/00004583-200105000-00009

DuPaul, G. J., Morgan, P. L., Farkas, G., Hillemeier, M. M., & Maczuga, S. (2016). Academic and social functioning associated with attention-deficit/hyperactivity disorder: Latent class analyses of trajectories from kindergarten to fifth grade. *Journal of Abnormal Child Psychology, 44*, 1425–1438. http://dx.doi.org/10.1007/s10802-016-0126-z

Egger, H. L., & Angold, A. (2006). Common emotional and behavioral disorders in preschool children: Presentation, nosology, and epidemiology. *Journal of Child Psychology and Psychiatry, 47*, 313–337. http://dx.doi.org/10.1111/j.1469-7610.2006.01618.x

Fox, L., Dunlap, G., Hemmeter, M. L., Joseph, G. E., & Strain, P. S. (2003). The Teaching Pyramid: A model for supporting social competence and preventing challenging behavior in young children. *Young Children, 58*(4), 48–52.

Gable, R. A., Hester, P. H., Rock, M. L., & Hughes, K. G. (2009). Back to basics: Rules, praise, ignoring, and reprimands revisited. *Intervention in School and Clinic, 44*, 195–205. http://dx.doi.org/10.1177/1053451208328831

Gilliam, W. S. (2005, May). *Prekindergarteners left behind: Expulsion rates in state prekindergarten programs* (Foundation for Child Development Policy Brief No. 3). Retrieved from https://medicine.yale.edu/childstudy/zigler/publications/briefs

Gischlar, K. L., Hojnoski, R. L., & Missall, K. N. (2009). Improving child outcomes with data-based decision making: Interpreting and using data. *Young Exceptional Children, 13*(1), 2–18. http://dx.doi.org/10.1177/1096250609346249

Hemmeter, M. L., Ostrosky, M., & Fox, L. (2006). Social and emotional foundations for early learning: A conceptual model for intervention. *School Psychology Review, 35,* 583–601.

Hemmeter, M. L., Snyder, P. A., Fox, L., & Algina, J. (2016). Evaluating the implementation of the Pyramid Model for promoting social-emotional competence in early childhood classrooms. *Topics in Early Childhood Special Education, 36,* 133–146. http://dx.doi.org/10.1177/0271121416653386

Hojnoski, R. L., Gischlar, K. L., & Missall, K. N. (2009). Improving child outcomes with data-based decision making: Collecting data. *Young Exceptional Children, 12*(3), 32–44. http://dx.doi.org/10.1177/1096250609333025

Ingersoll, R. (2001). Teacher turnover, teacher shortages, and the organization of schools. *CPRE Research Reports.* Retrieved from https://repository.upenn.edu/cpre_researchreports/12

Kern, L., & Clemens, N. H. (2007). Antecedent strategies to promote appropriate classroom behavior. *Psychology in the Schools, 44*(1), 65–75. http://dx.doi.org/10.1002/pits.20206

Kreibich, S. R., Chen, M., & Reichle, J. (2015). Teaching a child with autism to request breaks while concurrently increasing task engagement. *Language, Speech, and Hearing Services in Schools, 46,* 256–265. http://dx.doi.org/10.1044/2015_LSHSS-14-0081

Lavigne, J. V., Gibbons, R. D., Christoffel, K. K., Arend, R., Rosenbaum, D., Binns, H., . . . Isaacs, C. (1996). Prevalence rates and correlates of psychiatric disorders among preschool children. *Journal of the American Academy of Child & Adolescent Psychiatry, 35*(2), 204–214. http://dx.doi.org/10.1097/00004583-199602000-00014

Lavigne, J. V., LeBailly, S. A., Hopkins, J., Gouze, K. R., & Binns, H. J. (2009). The prevalence of ADHD, ODD, depression, and anxiety in a community sample of 4-year-olds. *Journal of Clinical Child and Adolescent Psychology, 38,* 315–328. http://dx.doi.org/10.1080/15374410902851382

LeBel, T. J., & Chafouleas, S. M. (2010, June). Promoting prosocial behavior in preschool: A review of effective intervention supports. *School Psychology Forum, 4*(2), 25–38.

Martel, M. M., Gremillion, M. L., & Roberts, B. (2012). Temperament and common disruptive behavior problems in preschool. *Personality and Individual Differences, 53,* 874–879. http://dx.doi.org/10.1016/j.paid.2012.07.011

Matheson, A. S., & Shriver, M. D. (2005). Training teachers to give effective commands: Effects on student compliance and academic behaviors. *School Psychology Review, 34*(2), 202–219.

McConnell, S., Bradfield, T., Wackerle-Hollman, A., & Rodriguez, M. (2012). *Individual Growth and Development Indicators of Early Literacy (IGDIs-EL).* Mendota Heights, MN: Early Learning Labs.

Monroe, C. R., & Obidah, J. E. (2004). The influence of cultural synchronization on a teacher's perceptions of disruption: A case study of an African-American middle school classroom. *Journal of Teacher Education, 55,* 256–268. http://dx.doi.org/10.1177/0022487104263977

Ninci, J., Rispoli, M., Burke, M. D., & Neely, L. C. (2018). Embedding interests of individuals with autism spectrum disorder: A quality review. *Review Journal of Autism and Developmental Disorders, 5*(1), 15–28. http://dx.doi.org/10.1007/s40489-017-0120-6

Novoa, C., & Malik, R. (2018, January). *Suspensions are not support: The disciplining of preschoolers with disabilities.* Washington, DC: Center for American Progress.

O'Neill, R. E., Albin, R. W., Storey, K., Horner, R. H., & Sprague, J. R. (2015). *Functional assessment and program development.* Toronto, Ontario, Canada: Nelson Education.

Passini, C., Pihet, S., & Favez, N. (2014). Assessing specific discipline techniques: A mixed-methods approach. *Journal of Child and Family Studies, 23*, 1389–1402. http://dx.doi.org/10.1007/s10826-013-9796-0

Posner, K., Melvin, G. A., Murray, D. W., Gugga, S. S., Fisher, P., Skrobala, A., . . . Greenhill, L. L. (2007). Clinical presentation of attention-deficit/hyperactivity disorder in preschool children: The preschoolers with Attention-Deficit/Hyperactivity Disorder Treatment Study (PATS). *Journal of Child and Adolescent Psychopharmacology, 17*, 547–562. http://dx.doi.org/10.1089/cap.2007.0075

Powell, D., Dunlap, G., & Fox, L. (2006). Prevention and intervention for the challenging behaviors of toddlers and preschoolers. *Infants & Young Children, 19*(1), 25–35. http://dx.doi.org/10.1097/00001163-200601000-00004

Sandomierski, T., Kincaid, D., & Algozzine, B. (2007). Multi-tiered System of Support (MTSS) & PBIS. *Positive Behavioral Interventions and Support Newsletter, 4*(2), 1–7.

Schrank, F. A., Mather, N., & McGrew, K. S. (2014). *Woodcock-Johnson IV Tests of Achievement.* Rolling Meadows, IL: Riverside.

Stormont, M., Lewis, T. J., Beckner, R., & Johnson, N. W. (2008). *Implementing positive behavior support systems in early childhood and elementary settings.* Thousand Oaks, CA: Corwin Press.

Sullivan, W. E., Martens, B. K., Morley, A. J., & Long, S. J. (2017). Reducing transition latency and transition-related problem behavior in children by altering the motivating operations for task disengagement. *Psychology in the Schools, 54*, 404–420. http://dx.doi.org/10.1002/pits.22008

Vo, A. K., Sutherland, K. S., & Conroy, M. A. (2012). Best in class: A classroom-based model for ameliorating problem behavior in early childhood settings. *Psychology in the Schools, 49*, 402–415. http://dx.doi.org/10.1002/pits.21609

Webster-Stratton, C., & Reid, M. J. (2001). The Incredible Years: Parents, teachers, and children training series. *Residential Treatment for Children & Youth, 18*(3), 31–45. http://dx.doi.org/10.1300/J007v18n03_04

Wichstrøm, L., Berg-Nielsen, T. S., Angold, A., Egger, H. L., Solheim, E., & Sveen, T. H. (2012). Prevalence of psychiatric disorders in preschoolers. *The Journal of Child Psychology and Psychiatry, 53*, 695–705. http://dx.doi.org/10.1111/j.1469-7610.2011.02514.x

Wood, B. K., Hojnoski, R. L., Laracy, S. D., & Olson, C. L. (2016). Comparison of observational methods and their relation to ratings of engagement in young children. *Topics in Early Childhood Special Education, 35*, 211–222. http://dx.doi.org/10.1177/0271121414565911

10

Creating Successful Early Learning Environments

Timothy W. Curby

If a child could enroll in any preschool in America, which one would be best and why? What can a teacher or administrator do to make sure that children gain the most out of their preschool experiences? What should a parent look for when choosing a preschool? Each of these questions approaches the same idea from different perspectives that can be summarized in the question "What constitutes a high-quality, successful learning environment for a preschool child?" The purpose of this chapter is to delineate important elements for teachers and administrators to consider when creating a successful early learning environment. The chapter first focuses on elements that make for a high-quality classroom centered on the interactions that teachers have with children. Then, the focus shifts to elements, such as assessing children, that can help those teacher–student interactions be effective. Finally, the chapter describes policies and procedures, at the center level, that can support children's growth.

INTERACTIONS THAT SUPPORT CHILDREN'S LEARNING

The interactions a child has with the environment—including interactions with teachers, peers, and materials (Downer, Booren, Lima, Luckner, & Pianta, 2010)—can be considered "the primary engines of development" (Bronfenbrenner & Morris, 2006, p. 798). Notably, all interactions are not

http://dx.doi.org/10.1037/0000197-011
Healthy Development in Young Children: Evidence-Based Interventions for Early Education,
V. C. Alfonso and G. J. DuPaul (Editors)

equally efficacious in promoting development. Some interactions challenge children's thinking, whereas others may be too easy or too difficult to cause children to ponder and grow. To maximize learning, the opportunity for high-quality interactions should be provided to support the child just beyond what the child can do independently (Vygotsky, 1978) and give the child the practice needed to master the content. As children engage in tasks that are just beyond what they can do themselves, their own thinking is maximized. With additional instruction and practice, children internalize those supports and are able to accomplish the task (increasingly) on their own.

As an example, consider the case in which a teacher wants to show children the idea of sequencing objects. In this case, a teacher might show how objects can be ordered from smallest to largest. Then the teacher might make the task more challenging by adding more objects or giving them a new object to insert into the sequence—a challenging task for preschoolers who often put the object at the beginning or end of the sequence, regardless of its size. By providing many cues at first that are slowly removed, children can learn how to sequence objects and insert new objects into that sequence (Kidd et al., 2012). Thus, the teacher's role is to support children's learning by guiding the opportunities and providing the supports children need.

The supports children experience in the classroom can take different forms, but the classroom is typically set up such that teachers are directing the activities and providing instruction (Curby, Downer, & Booren, 2014). Trained teachers knowledgeable about child development should be better able to provide the guidance that children need to engage successfully in a task that would otherwise be out of reach (although education levels of the teacher tend to not be strongly related to child outcomes; Early et al., 2006). Teachers are not the only source of support in the classroom. More knowledgeable peers can provide some of the same supports for other children. Furthermore, the available materials or curriculum can be designed in such a way that the supports for learning are provided by the objects or materials themselves. For example, cylinders of different diameters that fit only in corresponding holes in a wood block guide children to the goal of having all the right cylinders in the right holes. Therefore, it is important to consider the different ways in which teachers, peers, and materials can offer the supports children need to stay engaged in a challenging task (Vitiello, Booren, Downer, & Williford, 2012).

Emotional Supports

The emotional tenor of the classroom can prove to be an important determinant of children's experiences in the classroom. Children entering a classroom who are warmly greeted will have a different experience than will children entering a classroom who are brusquely told to hurry up. These emotional climate elements are quite stable throughout the day, regardless of the classroom activity (Chomat-Mooney et al., 2008). These emotionally supportive interactions may not be a part of directly instructing a child about content but are frequently the backdrop for other interactions that are intended to instruct a child. For example, a child might have a calendar lesson while having warm, positive interactions with the teacher. Thus, interactions that influence how children feel can have profound effects on the experiences children have in the classroom.

Markers of a supportive emotional climate are multifaceted. At its core, the emotional supportiveness relates to the prevalent emotions in a classroom. If the majority of emotions present—by the teacher and other children—are positively valanced (e.g., enthusiasm, happiness, anticipation), then children are likely to be experiencing those interactions in a positive emotional context themselves (Morris, Denham, Bassett, & Curby, 2013). Conversely, children who are in an environment marked by negatively valanced emotions (e.g., frustration, anger, sadness) are likely to experience those negative emotions themselves. Although healthy development likely involves experiencing and learning to navigate negative emotions (Morris et al., 2013), frequent or severe negative emotions are likely to hinder or be deleterious to healthy development (Curby & Chavez, 2013). Because teachers often interact with multiple children at the same time, the emotions of the teacher drive more of the emotional tenor of the classroom than do a child's peers (Curby et al., 2014). Materials can evoke emotions from the child (such as frustration at challenges or joy at solving a problem), but they are not a direct part of the emotional environment. Nonetheless, guiding a child to novel or interesting materials and away from too-challenging materials can be an important element in providing good emotional support.

Other facets of emotional support may have less to do with expressed emotions in the classroom but may be related nonetheless to how a child might feel in the environment. Specifically, a teacher can know children as individuals and be sensitive to their individual needs. For example, a teacher might be aware that a child has a small surgery planned and intentionally engage with him in pretend play at the doctor's office. Or a teacher might acknowledge a child feeling scared when a thunderstorm is happening and read a book about weather. These sensitive elements acknowledge the child as an individual and can promote better emotional functioning in the child, therefore helping the child to be ready to learn.

Another element that teachers can provide in their classroom is opportunities for children to make their own decisions. Choice can give a person a sense of autonomy and control and, therefore, can help promote a sense of motivation, efficacy, and fulfillment (Glasser, 1999). When teachers design activities, constraints on the activity should be used to accomplish the educational goals, but, aside from those, children should not be overcontrolled (Pianta, La Paro, & Hamre, 2008). For example, if a teacher has an art activity for children to practice their fine motor skills, the teacher may want the children to practice using the scissors but should not correct children's use of color in the picture. Not only does this allow children some freedom of expression, but it also diminishes the number of negative interactions.

Organizational Supports

Teachers also need to organize and manage the classroom environment to make it a productive, engaging, and healthy environment for children to spend their days. Teachers play a critical role in managing social interactions between children as well as constraining and redirecting disruptive or destructive behavior of individual children. Behavior management concerns can be important because they can be related to the emotions present in the classroom and the extent to which there may be time to provide instruction (Pianta, La Paro, & Hamre, 2008). Furthermore, when children experience higher-quality behavior management, they begin to internalize that behavior management, which helps them to become more self-regulated in the classroom (Rimm-Kaufman, Curby, Grimm, Nathanson, & Brock, 2009).

The best behavior management is somewhat invisible in the classroom (see Chapter 9, this volume). This is, in part, due to it already having happened. Teachers who manage behavior well may spend more of the beginning of the year on behavior management (Emmer, Evertson, & Anderson, 1980; Wong & Wong, 2004). Fundamentally, these are lessons in how the classroom is organized and often are focused on classroom procedures. Teachers may spend time telling children how they want children to be arranged during circle time, how children are dismissed to centers, what to do if they need to go to the bathroom, and what to do if one child wants to do an activity that someone else is doing. Later in the year, the teacher may be able to spend less time managing behavior because clear expectations have been set that children are able to follow. In other words, a well-behaved classroom may suggest that the teacher has spent time in the past creating procedures and enforcing expectations that have resulted in the well-managed behavior being seen at that time (Pianta, La Paro, & Hamre, 2008).

The teacher can also make behavior management more invisible by anticipating problems before they happen and managing or addressing a problem before it comes to fruition (Brophy, 1983). For example, a teacher might have only two computer workstations for a popular activity. The teacher may anticipate this problem and have a procedure to manage it, such as setting a fixed amount of time a child can engage in the activity when other children are waiting. This speaks to one challenging element of behavior management: It often involves managing disputes between children that inherently have emotions involved. When children both want to do the same activity, one child might feel frustrated with having to wait and jealous of his peer, and the other child might feel excited about the activity and threatened by the other child waiting to do it. The teacher has to step into this emotionally fraught situation to help resolve it. Young children often do not have the skills to navigate these emotions and tend to privilege their own point of view, making a resolution elusive. Especially at first, they need a teacher to teach them the social and emotional skills to work through the problem calmly—they will often not be able to work out an acceptable solution without the assistance of an adult (at that time or in the past). If, however, the teacher has taught them some strategies to calm down—for example, go to a peace corner with the other child, express their feelings, listen, and compromise—the children may be able to work through their problem. This demonstrates why kindergarten teachers prioritize social and emotional skills in kindergarten readiness (Curby et al., 2017).

Behavior management can also be invisible by not noticeably taking away instructional time, even when an unanticipated problem comes up (Brophy, 1983). In other words, behavior management should efficiently address problems so that they do not interfere with instructional activities. Part of this means that the teacher needs to be aware of when problems are starting and mitigate them before emotions elevate. Additionally, the teacher can have taught children problem-solving procedures for when children are having a problem instead of handling every dispute in an *ad hoc* fashion. For example, in the peace corner example stated previously, the teacher has taught the children to go there when there is a disagreement, which helps them focus on solving the problem, and involve teachers only when those efforts are unsuccessful. This can result in less time spent by the teacher and the children in managing problems. Thus, part of creating a successful early learning environment is setting expectations and putting procedures in place (Emmer et al., 1980) that help children navigate conflict, so that the environment is more positive and more time can be focused on instructional activities.

Another element of organizational supports involves having a variety of modalities and materials that can increase children's interest in an activity and help facilitate their engagement. Providing activities that accomplish the teachers' instructional purposes while still giving children choice can be an important element in promoting engagement (Vitiello et al., 2012). However, free-choice activities may not be the most effective at promoting thought processes and thus may need to be balanced with large-group activities (Cabell, DeCoster, LoCasale-Crouch, Hamre, & Pianta, 2013). For example, free-choice activities that promote engagement may include a sand and water table, books, a computer station, and a center focused on sound. Engagement is critical because children must be engaged in order to learn. The materials themselves and the ways in which a teacher facilitates the use of those materials can have a profound influence on the ways in which children engage with the classroom. Maximizing the extent to which children engage in an activity can optimize how much children can learn from that activity. Relatedly, these supports can make it so there is nearly always something for children to do in the classroom. Children spend a surprising amount of time unoccupied in preschool (Early et al., 2010), and by simply always having something to do, children will learn more.

People learn best when information relevant to their lives is presented multimodally (Moreno & Mayer, 2007). Having activities for children that are presented through multiple means allows them to experience and process the material through different channels, enhancing their engagement and increasing the likelihood of them learning from the activity (e.g., Guichon &

McLornan, 2008; Morgan, 2013). For example, if a teacher wanted children to learn about erosion, a lesson might involve reading a book, showing a video, discussing what they've seen on the playground, and having them use a sand and water table. Part of the teacher's role in facilitating children's engagement happens when designing the lesson to have multiple elements, but teachers can also play a critical role during a lesson. Teachers can ask questions, prompt a child to participate, provide more information, or notice that attention is waning and provide a new element to the activity. The teacher might also pair children up to introduce a social element to the task and give children the opportunity to talk through the activity with a partner. The goal during instruction is to maximize each child's engagement and time on task.

Instructional Supports

When we think about schools and classrooms, we often think of classroom instruction—the teaching of content areas—as the primary activity. However, as can be seen in the discussion of emotional and organizational supports, the early childhood classroom must be attuned to children's emotional and organizational needs to be able to have the opportunity to provide instructional supports. Therefore, when instructional time is being provided, it needs to be high quality.

High-quality instruction teaches children new things and gives them a chance to practice their knowledge (Willingham, 2009). It challenges misconceptions while also building off of prior knowledge. It provides children with assistance but also helps them to do things on their own. With these competing demands, providing high-quality instructional support is challenging.

At its most basic level, instruction should present challenging, developmentally appropriate material while also making the material accessible and providing assistance as necessary to children so that they can do the task (Sweller, van Merriënboer, & Paas, 1998). If too great a challenge is presented, children may not be able to comprehend the idea and may give up, which prevents them from learning from the activity. If this keeps happening over a sustained period, children may learn to give up when presented with a challenge (Seligman, 1972). This is compounded by the fact that teachers in early childhood tend to have low self-efficacy for teaching some subjects such as math (Gerde, Pierce, Lee, & Van Egeren, 2018). However, at the other end of the continuum, another problem can develop. If children are presented with material that is too easy, they can become bored. This can result in several problems such as a child becoming disruptive or developing a negative attitude about school and learning. Furthermore, a teacher might offer too much support for an activity. Learning happens only when a child comes to a new understanding of something. Supports should be provided that children can learn themselves. In a way that seems oxymoronic, the teacher needs to provide the assistance so that children can do the task for themselves. By way of analogy, a preschool child cannot shoot a basketball into a hoop at its normal height. The teacher's role is to lower the hoop, not shoot for the child. In the classroom, teachers need to have a sense of what children can do on their own. Unless the goal is to provide practice, the teacher should then target activities just beyond that level. Time for consolidating learning through practice can also be important for skill mastery.

Two elements complicate this task for teachers. First, children are different from one another. For example, one child may have some difficulties with letter–sound correspondence but not sorting, whereas another child can have the opposite challenge. Teachers have to be attuned to these differences and yet still provide activities for all children in the class. Moreover, even two children with similar understandings may respond to different kinds of assistance. One child may show understanding after a demonstration of what to do, whereas another child may also need direct assistance at each step, and another child may need a different explanation. Thus, good instruction can take many forms but recognizes these differences between children in terms of their abilities in a given area and offers a variety of supports for children.

Another complicating factor for teachers in offering high-quality instruction is that children change and develop. Thus, over time, instruction needs to be dynamic. A child who is struggling one month may be ready for extra challenges the next. Teachers therefore must not have a static view of how children are performing in school but must always be willing to reevaluate what children are ready for. In fact, when children view intelligence as changeable, it tends to change (Blackwell, Trzesniewski, & Dweck, 2007). Thus, teachers should be open to the idea that children can learn and improve their skills. Regular monitoring of children's knowledge and skills can help teachers understand what material some children are still struggling to understand.

Although good instruction challenges children and supports them, there is also a role for practice so that children can master a concept (Willingham, 2009). Once children learn something new, they often need to engage with the idea several more times to come to a solid understanding. Thus, once something new is learned, children should be given the chance to try it again with less support until they get to the point where no support is needed. Even then, they may need additional practice in transferring the concept to different situations or in different contexts (McKeough, Lupart, & Marini, 1995). For example, a child may be able to say what day of the week the 5th of March is when looking at the March calendar but may need practice to say what day of the week the 5th of April is or what day of the week the 5th of March is the following year. It is now recognized that applying the same knowledge to different contexts and situations is more challenging than first realized (Gick & Holyoak, 1980; Marcus, Haden, & Uttal, 2018) and that transferring knowledge from one area to another often needs to be facilitated (Nokes-Malach & Richey, 2015).

Although teachers may be tempted to target instruction based on learning styles, an abundance of data indicates this should not be done (Pashler, McDaniel, Rohrer, & Bjork, 2009). Rather, a much more effective approach is to target instruction based on what children already know (Willingham, 2009). Prior knowledge not only is a prime determinant of what children will find engaging but is central to what they are able to comprehend and, therefore, learn. For example, children who are struggling with letter–sound correspondence are likely going to struggle with word decoding (Ehri, 1995). The more attuned the teacher is to these points of knowledge, the better the teacher is able to target instruction to benefit the child. Being aware of what a student already knows also creates the opportunity for greater differentiation, so that children are receiving the instruction that will benefit them the most based on their current knowledge (C. A. Tomlinson, 2003). Furthermore, prior knowledge can inform children's interests. For example, children who live in rural areas may not have the background knowledge to understand what a subway is or how to call an Uber. To the extent that stories and instruction rely on topics outside of children's lived experience, careful attention needs to be given to the necessary precursor knowledge to make the topic interesting to children.

Good instruction can also recognize that learning is inherently social. Children are frequently interacting with one another or a teacher. This can create behavior management challenges, but it can also be leveraged to help children learn. As noted previously, children need to be engaged in order to learn. Social interactions can be engaging, and thus having children work with a buddy can have more appeal than completing the same task alone. Furthermore, children can help one another. Peers can even be incorporated into classroom instruction. This can take the form of more-knowledgeable peers being used to instruct less-knowledgeable peers. For example, a teacher shows one child how to cut out and assemble pieces in an art center, who can then show the next child how to do it.

Interestingly, high-quality classroom materials can also provide instructional support to children. This might be more easily seen in a computer program that offers children assistance if they select a wrong answer, but it can happen in the way that some materials for some tasks are designed. For example, in Montessori education a common set of materials is a set of 10 nested cubes that come in 1 cm increments (The Pink Tower). This tower helps children not only with motor skills but also with understanding the spatial relations of objects in the metric system (Lillard, 2008). The example provided previously of cylinders of different diameters is also an example of this idea. Thus, the materials themselves, in some circumstances, can offer assistance and feedback to a child.

Feedback is another important element of high-quality instruction. If children are making a tower and it falls over, that is one type of feedback to the children about what is necessary for a tower to be stable. Teachers can also provide feedback. Teachers vary in the quality of feedback they give to children (Curby & Chavez, 2013). High-quality feedback is timely, helpful, and targeted (Pianta, La Paro, & Hamre, 2008). This feedback is specific and focused on effort (Mueller & Dweck, 1998). Low-quality feedback is often perfunctory (e.g., "Good job") or focuses only on the final product (e.g., "Nice tower").

Low-quality feedback does little to further children's understanding or persistence (Pianta, La Paro, & Hamre, 2008). Higher-quality feedback might be "I notice that towers can be taller when there are bigger blocks on the bottom." Or a teacher might simply say, "I like how hard you are working on the tower." This praising of effort, not results, has been related to greater persistence and results on academic tasks (Mueller & Dweck, 1998). In this way, the teacher's feedback can directly help the child learn by focusing on relevant elements of the task and help the child persist in the task, which will also help with learning.

ELEMENTS THAT ENHANCE CLASSROOM SUPPORTS

Although high-quality interactions can promote learning, they are not the only points to consider when creating successful early learning environments. The extent to which the interactions children have with their environment will be modified by other characteristics including the consistency of emotional support, time spent engaged, the relationships between teachers and children, and the quality of materials and physical environment.

A small but growing literature investigates the extent to which consistency in classroom emotional support is an important predictor of children's academic and social outcomes (Brock, Curby, & Cannell-Cordier, 2018; Curby, Brock, & Hamre, 2013). *Consistency* refers to the idea that some teachers might offer an emotional climate that is stable over the course of a day, whereas others might be quite variable in their emotional climate. Importantly, two teachers could have the same average emotional climate but be quite different in how consistent they are over the course of a morning. Work in this area has shown that inconsistency in the teachers' emotional support over the course of a day results in poorer outcomes for children. Children who experience consistent, supportive interactions feel less stressed and may be better able to attend to classroom activities (Hatfield & Williford, 2017).

Consistent emotional support can also promote better relationships with teachers (Brock & Curby, 2014). Over the course of time, the interactions that teachers and children have cumulatively constitute a relationship (Stillerova, Tavassolie, Curby, & Brock, 2017). This teacher–child relationship can function in ways similar to an attachment relationship between parent and child (Pianta, 1999). Attachments are important because they promote healthy views of relationships in general and prompt exploration by the child of the environment (Karen, 1998). Teacher–child relationships in early childhood often have been described in terms of their conflict, closeness, and dependence (cf. Koomen & Jellesma, 2015; Pianta, 2001). Conflictual relationships are ones in which the teacher and student are often at odds with one another and have more negative interactions. Close relationships are marked by their warmth and support. In dependent relationships, children often are perceived as clingy and needy, unable or unwilling to engage in the environment without adult support. Children who have relationships that are closer, less conflictual, and less dependent tend to have better academic and social outcomes (Birch & Ladd, 1997; Hamre & Pianta, 2001). Fostering relationships between teachers and children—even through simply spending some individual time with each child—is good teaching practice in early childhood (Sabol & Pianta, 2012).

Assessments can play a helpful role in providing instruction to children (American Psychological Association, Coalition for Psychology in Schools and Education, 2015). In the early childhood context, assessments are usually informal, although in some programs they are mandated and formal (see Chapter 2, this volume). An informal assessment may be as simple as a teacher determining which letters each child already knows. Formal assessments, often tied to a curriculum, can be more comprehensive about the current knowledgebase of a student. Assessments can be helpful to teachers. Before instruction, they help target the instruction based on prior knowledge; after instruction, assessments help identify areas of understanding.

Children tend to be in preschool environments with children from the same local area. Thus, early childhood environments usually reflect the area around them with regard to child attributes such as race/ethnicity. Furthermore, some preschools are expensive, whereas others are available for families with demonstrated financial need, and thus children tend to go to school with children from a similar socioeconomic status. For these and other reasons, classrooms tend to be somewhat homogenous on many child characteristics. However, this is less true in some areas and with some characteristics. In many areas, preschools may reflect a wide diversity for the children that is not seen in their home lives. Children may go to school with children who differ in culture, national origin, and religion. As such, the preschool environment needs to be attuned to some of the differences between children, be sensitive to the needs of their various populations, help children appreciate the diversity in the classroom, and fundamentally be appropriate to the cultures represented in the school (Copple & Bredekamp, 2009). Generally, this is accomplished by helping to broaden children's perspectives to include different ones than their own—a good practice in any preschool. A sensitive teacher can recognize that some challenges in the classroom (e.g., arguments between children) might be due to children having different expectations based on their culture or family of origin (Isik-Ercan, 2017). Helping children discuss their own points of view can help others recognize that there are different perspectives.

Although teachers will be quick to recognize if children are nonnative English speakers (or English learners), they may not know what resources to put in place for those children or their parents. English learners in early childhood often evidence achievement gaps with their non–English learner peers (Garcia & Frede, 2010) and thus can be in need of extra attention. Children typically can communicate socially in English in less than 2 years (Lake & Pappamihiel, 2003), but the knowledge required to learn academic content can take more years. This is perhaps best illustrated using reading research. Although based on reading comprehension with older students, evidence suggests that people learning another language need to know 95% to 98% of the vocabulary to comprehend a text (Schmitt, Jiang, & Grabe, 2011). As English learner students have the dual task of learning English and learning content, it is not surprising that content-area knowledge lags because children may not be able to comprehend what is being talked about in class. This is where the notion of having at least one teacher who is able to communicate with the English learner children in their native language comes in. The general idea is that English learner children can continue to learn English but also develop the content-area knowledge—and even their native language—through interactions with the teacher who speaks their native language.

POLICIES AND PROCEDURES THAT SUPPORT CHILDREN

Early childhood learning environments can have a variety of policies and procedures that may influence the experience of children and families. These policies and procedures are often at the discretion of the center director and therefore are likely to influence many classrooms at the same time. Therefore, important consideration should be given to these factors because they affect many children and families.

Consistent Caregivers

Accrediting agencies delineate teacher-to-student ratios that define how many adults must be in the room when children are present. For example, the National Association for the Education of Young Children (2013) stated that classrooms should have two teachers for classes of 16 to 20 48- to 60-month-olds. To maintain the ratio, centers often move teachers and children into different classrooms at different parts of the day. Because many centers have long hours that allow children to be dropped off quite early and picked up late, the number of children at a center at any given time can flux over the course of a day. Many centers manage this by having teachers and children changing rooms throughout the day. For example, two classes might be combined until 8:30 a.m., when they split after enough children have arrived, and then they might recombine at 4:00 p.m. when a number of children have left. Furthermore, staffing these arrangements might mean that two early morning teachers teach the combined classes and then be joined by two daytime teachers when the classes split. Depending on how late the center is open, some of these teachers may be replaced by evening teachers. From a child's perspective, this situation can result in great instability in their caregiving arrangements. This instability may have some important implications. Consistent caregiving is a hallmark of a secure attachment relationship (Karen, 1998). Thus, to the extent that a center is able to, it is important to provide stability regarding the adults with whom children interact. Beyond that, it can be important for children to experience day-to-day stability (An, 2019). Thus, even if a child has to move from one teacher to another as more children show up for or leave from schools, it would be helpful to have the same adults present so that the child is experiencing the same adults over the course of the day, from day to day.

School Transitions

Part of the responsibility for successful early learning environments is ensuring that the children have success when they leave the program. Transitions can be a time of stress and vulnerability for children and their families. Thus, the transition practices that centers provide for children as they prepare to move classrooms are worthy of consideration (Curby et al., 2018). Transition practices are special procedures that are specifically focused on helping children be prepared to move from one environment to another. Transition practices are often seen as the responsibility of the receiving school, but many practices can be a part of the early childhood environment to help children prepare for changes. Practices that coordinate the transfer of children from one environment are particularly good. For example, centers that arrange for a visit in the spring to a kindergarten classroom can help children know what it will be like by seeing the environment and meeting kindergarten teachers (LoCasale-Crouch, Mashburn, Downer, & Pianta, 2008). This practice can be supported by activities that also give parents a chance to talk to teachers, see the environment, and ask questions, such as a parent night. Furthermore, for children who need special supports, teacher–teacher conversations can ensure continuity of care. Generally, when preschools engaged in more transition practices for children moving up to kindergarten, the children were seen as more ready for kindergarten than were children from classrooms that provided fewer transition activities (LoCasale-Crouch et al., 2008).

Parental Access and Involvement

Successful learning environments provide several ways for parents to be involved (or at least informed of what is happening) in the classroom. Parental involvement starts with making sure that parents know they can visit the classroom. Of course, this visit should not be used to talk to the teachers, but parents who want to visit should be able to do so. Parent involvement can also be solicited for regular or special requests, such as through book readings. This may allow the teacher to have more focused time with particular children. Offerings for parent involvement need to be sensitive to parents. Parents who may not be able to come into school during operating hours often are happy to help out with preparations for activities, such as cutting out shapes for an art project. Many parents who cannot regularly come in may be interested in taking a day off for a special activity (e.g., a field day, a field trip). Offering parents a variety of ways to be involved that are sensitive to their own needs can facilitate parent investment in the school and their child's learning.

Curricula

Every center faces choices about the curricula they are going to use. Some centers are accredited based on an entire curricular approach (e.g., Montessori) and, in that way, do not have as many curricular decisions to make. Successful early childhood environments will choose curricula that are evidence-based— meaning they have been scientifically compared with alternatives and found to promote learning of the content area. Evidence-based curricula can be found using the What Works Clearinghouse (https://ies.ed.gov/ncee/wwc), among others.

Discussing specific curricula is beyond the scope of this chapter, but it is worth considering the content areas that should be covered. Some have argued that children's developmental trajectories stabilize in early elementary school, making the early years of learning particularly important (Alexander, Entwisle, Blyth, & McAdoo, 1988; Caro, 2009). Thus, curricular decisions that allow for children to have a good base of knowledge to move forward into that content area and branch out into other content areas are important to consider.

Language and literacy instruction tend to be the dominant focus in early childhood classrooms (Early et al., 2010). Letter identification, letter–sound correspondence, and early word reading are all commonly taught skills meant to prepare children for kindergarten (see Chapter 4, this volume). Reading is considered a foundational skill in its own right and also eventually becomes foundational in other areas as well when children switch from learning to read to reading to learn.

Early childhood also is an important time for developing early math skills, such as number recognition and one-to-one correspondence (see Chapter 5, this volume). Math seems to be an important skill set to develop because early math skills are the best predictor of later academics; they are even a better predictor of later reading than earlier reading (Duncan et al., 2007). Children spend about half the amount of time doing math activities as they do language and literacy activities (Early et al., 2010).

Science is another important area to begin developing in early childhood. Content-area knowledge (e.g., life sciences) as well as process skills (e.g., observing, describing) have been identified as target areas for preschool science instruction (Greenfield et al., 2009). In particular, science instruction during early childhood may help provide higher-quality instruction (Whittaker, Kinzie, Williford, & DeCoster, 2016) and narrow the achievement gap between children from high- and low-income backgrounds (Bustamante, White, & Greenfield, 2017). However, having high-quality science instruction in pre-school faces several hurdles. There are relatively fewer evidence-based science curricula, teachers tend to be less comfortable teaching science than other subjects, and schedules and classroom materials may not provide as much space for science (Greenfield et al., 2009). Nonetheless, given the ability of science instruction to promote higher order cognition, science instruction should be incorporated into early childhood curricula.

Another common focus during early childhood is in promoting children's social–emotional skills. In fact, all 50 states have learning standards for social–emotional skills in preschool (Dusenbury et al., 2015). This attention is warranted given the positive associations between social–emotional learning and children's academic outcomes (Curby, Brown, Bassett, & Denham, 2015; Weissberg & Cascarino, 2013), as well as kindergarten teachers' preference for social–emotional skills as key determinants of kindergarten readiness (Curby et al., 2018). As with academics, evidence-based curricula are available (Collaborative for Academic, Social, and Emotional Learning, 2013) for preschools. An emerging body of literature focuses on components of emotion teaching that are not bound to a particular curriculum (Zinsser, Denham, & Curby, 2018).

Last, promoting physical development should be considered part of the curriculum (H. B. Tomlinson & Hyson, 2009). Recommendations for preschoolers by the National Association for Sport and Physical Education (2009) indicate that physical activity should be incorporated into their day in structured (at least 60 minutes) and unstructured (at least 60 minutes) ways. In light of the large amount of time many children in preschool spend at school, clearly a majority of the physical activity should take place during the school day. Motor development—particularly fine motor development—can even be important for developing academics (Carlson, 2013). Thus, in the pursuit of early academic skill preparation, children should be given frequent opportunities to move and play.

Nap Time

A common feature of early childhood programs is nap time. Some young children need a nap, or at least a time of rest, commonly after lunch (Staton, Smith, & Thorpe, 2015). Programs are sensitive to these developmental needs and offer children the opportunity to take a nap. However, the need for a nap is not universal, particularly in the pre-K year, and some programs make nap time mandatory, with no other activity allowed. Some children simply do not need a nap or may need a short nap. This can become a problem when centers have rigid policies about what children must do during nap time (e.g., children cannot look at books) and when the nap times are particularly long. For example, in one study, preschool classrooms on average were observed to have about an hour of nap time, but some had a nap time that lasted 2 hours and 25 minutes (Staton, Smith, Hurst, Pattinson, & Thorpe, 2017). This same study found that less than one third of 4- and 5-year-olds actually napped during nap time. When combined with the notion that mandatory napping, particularly over 1 hour, is linked to nighttime sleep disruptions (Staton, Smith,

Pattinson, & Thorpe, 2015), centers should consider having nap/rest time that is sensitive to children who need naps as well as those who do not need naps (Staton, Smith, & Thorpe, 2015).

Avoiding Expulsion

There is an epidemic of preschooler expulsion in the United States. Preschool children are expelled at rates that dramatically exceed the rates in kindergarten through Grade 12 (Gilliam & Shahar, 2006). These expulsions, by their nature, are extreme. Children who are expelled in their educational careers have long-term outcomes that are worse than those of children who are not expelled (Hwang, 2018; Zinsser & Wanless, in press). Furthermore, families may have difficulty finding another center to take their child, particularly if they were in a funded preschool. Policies and procedures can assist centers in reducing the number of expulsions. Teachers who use utilize more social–emotional supports have fewer expulsions (Zinsser, Zulauf, Das, & Silver, 2019). These supports include components such as being able to consult with a mental health professional about a child or having an in-class behavioral aide. But teachers who are more stressed have more child expulsions. Thus, a center can offer more supports for teachers with respect to their training and personnel supports to mitigate the challenges teachers experience in the classroom. In doing so, centers not only can fight against teacher stress and burnout (Zinsser, Bailey, Curby, Denham, & Bassett, 2013) but also can promote adaptive behaviors in children and decrease rates of expulsion.

Professional Development

Most professional development activities in which teachers participate are not actually effective in changing teacher practice. Effective professional development has several features. As outlined in Desimone (2011), these aspects include professional development that is content focused, active, coherent, sustained, and collective. Other research in early childhood has indicated that coaching may also play an important role in helping to change teacher practice (Neuman & Cunningham, 2009), particularly when focusing on enhancing the quality of teacher–child interactions (Pianta, Mashburn, Downer, Hamre, & Justice, 2008).

One challenge is having professional development that is sustained for enough time to cause change (Garet, Porter, Desimone, Birman, & Yoon, 2001). One-time professional development confined to particular training days is typically not effective in changing teacher practice. Thus, whether it be professional development around improving teacher–child interactions or relationships, curricula, or behavior problems, centers should focus on what they deem to be most important and sustain professional development in that area until the desired changes are seen.

CONCLUSION

Early childhood education is a key time to help children develop knowledge and skills that will establish a positive trajectory through school. There are a variety of factors to focus on to optimize children's learning in the classroom. First and foremost, the way that teachers interact with children is a prime indicator of children's experience in the classroom. In particular, teachers can work to support students emotionally, organizationally, and instructionally. Consideration should also be given to how teachers structure interactions with peers and objects.

Beyond these interactions that children directly experience, teachers can facilitate learning in the classroom in other ways. Children learn best when there is consistency in the emotional environment over the course of the day, which seemingly puts them at ease to engage with classroom materials and maximize learning. Assessments can also be helpful because they allow a teacher to target instruction based on individual learning needs so that each child is being provided challenging instruction as well as practice for newly learned skills. Helping children understand that other children have experiences and needs and sensitively addressing those differences can help all children feel a part of their classroom. This notion can be seen with children or parents who are nonnative English speakers. English learners can best be supported when a teacher who speaks their native language is in the classroom.

Center policies can also affect children greatly because of how they shape children's classroom experiences. Centers should consider how they are providing consistency in the caregivers in the classroom, over the course of a single day as well as from day to day. Consistency in the caregivers will help provide an atmosphere conducive to fostering positive teacher–child relationships. Centers can also help prepare children for grade transitions or the transition to kindergarten. Although some transition practices need to be done by the receiving school, centers can help children understand what the next year is going to be like. Centers can also help parents have access to and involvement in their child's classroom through policies that promote communication and opportunities for parent involvement. Curricular decisions are also mostly the purview of the center. Centers should consider how they help children learn not only early literacy skills but also math, science, and social–emotional skills, as well as provide opportunities for physical activity. Centers also need to make sure that children have an opportunity to rest. Some children may need to actually nap, but many children do not need to nap, so allowing for quiet activities such as reading may be appropriate. Centers can also support teachers who are having trouble managing children's behavior to avoid school expulsion. Training teachers on any number of center priorities is done through professional development. However, to be effective, professional development activities need to be focused and sustained.

REFERENCES

Alexander, K. L., Entwisle, D. R., Blyth, D. A., & McAdoo, H. P. (1988). Achievement in the first 2 years of school: Patterns and processes. *Monographs of the Society for Research in Child Development, 53*(2), 1–157. http://dx.doi.org/10.2307/1166081

American Psychological Association, Coalition for Psychology in Schools and Education. (2015). *Top 20 principles from psychology for preK–12 teaching and learning.* Retrieved from http://www.apa.org/ed/schools/cpse/top-twenty-principles.pdf

An, X. (2019). *Can the consistency of emotional support from teachers predict child outcomes?* (Unpublished doctoral dissertation). George Mason University, Fairfax, VA.

Birch, S. H., & Ladd, G. W. (1997). The teacher–child relationship and children's early school adjustment. *Journal of School Psychology, 35*, 61–79. http://dx.doi.org/10.1016/S0022-4405(96)00029-5

Blackwell, L. S., Trzesniewski, K. H., & Dweck, C. S. (2007). Implicit theories of intelligence predict achievement across an adolescent transition: A longitudinal study and an intervention. *Child Development, 78*, 246–263. http://dx.doi.org/10.1111/j.1467-8624.2007.00995.x

Brock, L. L., & Curby, T. W. (2014). Emotional support consistency and teacher–child relationships forecast social competence and problem behaviors in pre-kindergarten and kindergarten. *Early Education and Development, 25*, 661–680. http://dx.doi.org/10.1080/10409289.2014.866020

Brock, L. L., Curby, T. W., & Cannell-Cordier, A. L. (2018). Consistency in children's classroom experiences and implications for early childhood development. In A. Mashburn, J. LoCasale-Crouch, & K. Pears' (Eds.), *Kindergarten transition and readiness: Promoting cognitive, social–emotional, and self-regulatory development* (pp. 59–83). Cham, Switzerland: Springer. http://dx.doi.org/10.1007/978-3-319-90200-5_3

Bronfenbrenner, U., & Morris, P. A. (2006). The bioecological model of human development. In R. M. Lerner (Ed.), *Handbook of child psychology: Vol. 1. Theoretical models of human development* (5th ed., pp. 793–828). New York, NY: Wiley.

Brophy, J. (1983). Classroom organization and management. *The Elementary School Journal, 83*, 264–285. http://dx.doi.org/10.1086/461318

Bustamante, A., White, L. J., & Greenfield, D. B. (2017). Approaches to learning and school readiness in Head Start: Applications to preschool science. *Learning and Individual Differences, 56*, 112–118. http://dx.doi.org/10.1016/j.lindif.2016.10.012

Cabell, S. Q., DeCoster, J., LoCasale-Crouch, J., Hamre, B. K., & Pianta, R. C. (2013). Variation in the effectiveness of instructional interactions across preschool classroom settings and learning activities. *Early Childhood Research Quarterly, 28*, 820–830. http://dx.doi.org/10.1016/j.ecresq.2013.07.007

Carlson, A. G. (2013). *Kindergarten fine motor skills and executive function: Two nonacademic predictors of academic achievement* (Unpublished doctoral dissertation). George Mason University, Fairfax, VA.

Caro, D. H. (2009). Socio-economic status and academic achievement trajectories from childhood to adolescence. *Canadian Journal of Education, 32*, 558–590.

Chomat-Mooney, L. I., Pianta, R. C., Hamre, B. K., Mashburn, A., Luckner, A. E., Grimm, K. J., & Downer, J. (2008). *A practical guide for conducting classroom observations: A summary of issues and evidence for researchers* (Report to The W. T. Grant Foundation). Charlottesville: University of Virginia.

Collaborative for Academic, Social, and Emotional Learning. (2013). *2013 CASEL guide: Effective social and emotional learning programs—Preschool and elementary school edition.* Chicago, IL: Author.

Copple, C., & Bredekamp, S. (2009). *Developmentally appropriate practice in early childhood programs serving children from birth through age 8.* Washington, DC: National Association for the Education of Young Children.

Curby, T. W., Berke, E., Alfonso, V. C., Blake, J. J., DeMarie, D., DuPaul, G. J., . . . Subotnik, R. F. (2017). Kindergarten teacher perceptions of kindergarten readiness: The importance of social–emotional skills. *Perspectives on Early Childhood Psychology and Education, 2,* 115–137.

Curby, T. W., Berke, E., Alfonso, V. C., Blake, J. J., DeMarie, D., DuPaul, G. J., . . . Subotnik, R. F. (2018). Transition practices into kindergarten and the barriers teachers encounter. In A. Mashburn, J. LoCasale-Crouch, & K. Pears (Eds.), *Kindergarten transition and readiness: Promoting cognitive, social–emotional, and self-regulatory development* (pp. 249–264). Cham, Switzerland: Springer. http://dx.doi.org/10.1007/978-3-319-90200-5_11

Curby, T. W., Brock, L., & Hamre, B. (2013). Teachers' emotional support consistency predicts children's achievement gains and social skills. *Early Education and Development, 24,* 292–309. http://dx.doi.org/10.1080/10409289.2012.665760

Curby, T. W., Brown, C. A., Bassett, H. H., & Denham, S. A. (2015). Associations between preschoolers' social–emotional competence and preliteracy skills. *Infant and Child Development, 24,* 549–570. http://dx.doi.org/10.1002/icd.1899

Curby, T. W., & Chavez, C. (2013). Examining CLASS dimensions as predictors of pre-K children's development of language, literacy, and mathematics. *NHSA Dialog: A Research to Practice Journal, 16*(2), 1–17.

Curby, T. W., Downer, J. T., & Booren, L. (2014). Behavioral exchanges between teachers and children over the course of a typical preschool day: Testing bi-directional associations. *Early Childhood Research Quarterly, 29,* 193–204. http://dx.doi.org/10.1016/j.ecresq.2014.01.002

Desimone, L. M. (2011). A primer on effective professional development. *Phi Delta Kappan, 92*(6), 68–71. http://dx.doi.org/10.1177/003172171109200616

Downer, J. T., Booren, L. M., Lima, O. K., Luckner, A. E., & Pianta, R. C. (2010). The Individualized Classroom Assessment Scoring System (inCLASS): Preliminary reliability and validity of a system for observing preschoolers' competence in classroom interactions. *Early Childhood Research Quarterly, 25,* 1–16. http://dx.doi.org/10.1016/j.ecresq.2009.08.004

Duncan, G. J., Dowsett, C. J., Claessens, A., Magnuson, K., Huston, A. C., Klebanov, P., . . . Japel, C. (2007). School readiness and later achievement. *Developmental Psychology, 43,* 1428–1446. http://dx.doi.org/10.1037/0012-1649.43.6.1428

Dusenbury, L. A., Newman, J. Z., Weissberg, R. P., Goren, P., Domitrovich, C. E., & Mart, A. K. (2015). The case for preschool through high school state learning standards for SEL. In J. A. Durlak, C. E. Demitrovich, R. P. Weissberg, & T. P. Gullotta (Eds.), *Handbook of social and emotional learning: Research and practice* (pp. 532–548). New York, NY: Guilford Press.

Early, D. M., Bryant, D. M., Pianta, R. C., Clifford, R. M., Burchinal, M. R., Ritchie, S., . . . Barbarin, O. (2006). Are teachers' education, major, and credentials related to classroom quality and children's academic gains in pre-kindergarten? *Early Childhood Research Quarterly, 21,* 174–195. http://dx.doi.org/10.1016/j.ecresq.2006.04.004

Early, D. M., Iruka, I. U., Ritchie, S., Barbarin, O. A., Winn, D. C., Crawford, G. M., . . . Pianta, R. C. (2010). How do pre-kindergarteners spend their time? Gender, ethnicity, and income as predictors of experiences in pre-kindergarten classrooms. *Early Childhood Research Quarterly, 25,* 177–193. http://dx.doi.org/10.1016/j.ecresq.2009.10.003

Ehri, L. C. (1995). Phases of development in learning to read words by sight. *Journal of Research in Reading, 18,* 116–125. http://dx.doi.org/10.1111/j.1467-9817.1995.tb00077.x

Emmer, E., Evertson, C., & Anderson, L. (1980). Effective management at the beginning of the school year. *The Elementary School Journal, 80,* 219–231. http://dx.doi.org/10.1086/461192

Garcia, E., & Frede, E. (2010). *Young English language learners: Current research and emerging directions for practice and policy.* New York, NY: Teachers College Press.

Garet, M. S., Porter, A. C., Desimone, L., Birman, B. F., & Yoon, K. S. (2001). What makes professional development effective? Results from a national sample of teachers. *American Educational Research Journal, 38*, 915–945. http://dx.doi.org/10.3102/00028312038004915

Gerde, H. K., Pierce, S. J., Lee, K., & Van Egeren, L. A. (2018). Early childhood educators' self-efficacy in science, math, and literacy instruction and science practice in the classroom. *Early Education and Development, 29*, 70–90. http://dx.doi.org/10.1080/10409289.2017.1360127

Gick, M. L., & Holyoak, K. J. (1980). Analogical problem solving. *Cognitive Psychology, 12*, 306–355. http://dx.doi.org/10.1016/0010-0285(80)90013-4

Gilliam, W. S., & Shahar, G. (2006). Preschool and child care expulsion and suspension rates and predictors in one state. *Infants and Young Children, 19*, 228–245. http://dx.doi.org/10.1097/00001163-200607000-00007

Glasser, W. (1999). *Choice theory: A new psychology of personal freedom*. New York, NY: HarperPerennial.

Greenfield, D. B., Jirout, J., Dominguez, X., Greenberg, A., Maier, M., & Fuccillo, J. (2009). Science in the preschool classroom: A programmatic research agenda to improve science readiness. *Early Education and Development, 20*, 238–264. http://dx.doi.org/10.1080/10409280802595441

Guichon, N., & McLornan, S. (2008). The effects of multimodality on L2 learners: Implications for CALL resource design. *System, 36*, 85–93. http://dx.doi.org/10.1016/j.system.2007.11.005

Hamre, B. K., & Pianta, R. C. (2001). Early teacher–child relationships and the trajectory of children's school outcomes through eighth grade. *Child Development, 72*, 625–638. http://dx.doi.org/10.1111/1467-8624.00301

Hatfield, B. E., & Williford, A. P. (2017). Cortisol patterns for young children displaying disruptive behavior: Links to a teacher–child, relationship-focused intervention. *Prevention Science, 18*, 40–49. http://dx.doi.org/10.1007/s11121-016-0693-9

Hwang, N. (2018). Suspensions and achievement: Varying links by type, frequency, and subgroup. *Educational Researcher, 47*, 363–374. http://dx.doi.org/10.3102/0013189X18779579

Isik-Ercan, Z. (2017). Culturally appropriate positive guidance with young children. *Young Children, 72*(1), 15–21. Retrieved from https://www.naeyc.org/resources/pubs/yc/mar2017/culturally-appropriate-positive-guidance

Karen, R. (1998). *Becoming attached: First relationships and how they shape our capacity to love*. New York, NY: Oxford University Press.

Kidd, J. K., Curby, T. W., Boyer, C. E., Gadzichowski, K. M., Gallington, D. A., Machado, J. A., & Pasnak, R. (2012). Benefits of an intervention focused on oddity and seriation. *Early Education and Development, 23*, 900–918. http://dx.doi.org/10.1080/10409289.2011.621877

Koomen, H. M. Y., & Jellesma, F. C. (2015). Can closeness, conflict, and dependency be used to characterize students' perceptions of the affective relationship with their teacher? Testing a new child measure in middle childhood. *British Journal of Educational Psychology, 85*, 479–497. http://dx.doi.org/10.1111/bjep.12094

Lake, V., & Pappamihiel, N. E. (2003). Effective practices and principles to support English language learners in the early childhood classroom. *Childhood Education, 70*, 200–203.

Lillard, A. (2008). How important are Montessori materials? *Montessori Life, 8*, 20–25.

LoCasale-Crouch, J., Mashburn, A. J., Downer, J. T., & Pianta, R. C. (2008). Pre-kindergarten teachers use of transition practices and children's adjustment to kindergarten. *Early Childhood Research Quarterly, 23*, 124–139. http://dx.doi.org/10.1016/j.ecresq.2007.06.001

Marcus, M., Haden, C. A., & Uttal, D. H. (2018). Promoting children's learning and transfer across informal science, technology, engineering, and mathematics learning experiences. *Journal of Experimental Child Psychology, 175,* 80–95. http://dx.doi.org/ 10.1016/j.jecp.2018.06.003

McKeough, A., Lupart, J. L., & Marini, A. (1995). *Teaching for transfer: Fostering generalization in learning.* New York, NY: Routledge.

Moreno, R., & Mayer, R. (2007). Interactive multimodal learning environments. *Educational Psychology Review, 19,* 309–326. http://dx.doi.org/10.1007/s10648-007-9047-2

Morgan, H. (2013). Multimodal children's e-books help young learners in reading. *Early Childhood Education Journal, 41,* 477–483. http://dx.doi.org/10.1007/s10643-013-0575-8

Morris, C. A. S., Denham, S. A., Bassett, H. H., & Curby, T. W. (2013). Relations among teachers' emotion socialization beliefs and practices, and preschoolers' emotional competence. *Early Education and Development, 24,* 979–999. http://dx.doi.org/10.1080/10409289.2013.825186

Mueller, C. M., & Dweck, C. S. (1998). Praise for intelligence can undermine children's motivation and performance. *Journal of Personality and Social Psychology, 75,* 33–52. http://dx.doi.org/10.1037/0022-3514.75.1.33

National Association for the Education of Young Children. (2013). *Teacher–child ratios within group size (assessed in Criterion 10.B.12).* Retrieved from https://idahostars.org/portals/61/Docs/Providers/STQ/TeacherChildRatioChart.pdf

National Association for Sport and Physical Education. (2009). *Active start: A statement of physical activity guidelines for children from birth to age 5.* Reston, VA: Author.

Neuman, S. B., & Cunningham, L. (2009). The impact of professional development and coaching on early language and literacy instructional practices. *American Educational Research Journal, 46,* 532–566. http://dx.doi.org/10.3102/0002831208328088

Nokes-Malach, T. J., & Richey, J. E. (2015). Knowledge transfer. In R. A. Scott, S. M. Kosslyn, & M. Buchmann (Eds.), *Emerging trends in the social and behavioral sciences.* http://dx.doi.org/10.1002/9781118900772.etrds0197

Pashler, H., McDaniel, M., Rohrer, D., & Bjork, R. A. (2009). Learning styles: concepts and evidence. *Psychological Science in the Public Interest, 9*(3), 105–119. http://dx.doi.org/ 10.1111/j.1539-6053.2009.01038.x

Pianta, R. C. (1999). *Enhancing relationships between children and teachers.* Washington, DC: American Psychological Association. http://dx.doi.org/10.1037/10314-000

Pianta, R. C. (2001). *Student–teacher relationship scale: Professional manual.* Lutz, FL: Psychological Assessment Resources.

Pianta, R. C., La Paro, K. M., & Hamre, B. K. (2008). *Classroom Assessment Scoring System (CLASS) Manual, Pre-k.* Baltimore, MD: Brookes.

Pianta, R. C., Mashburn, A. J., Downer, J. T., Hamre, B. K., & Justice, L. (2008). Effects of web-mediated professional development resources on teacher–child interactions in pre-kindergarten classrooms. *Early Childhood Research Quarterly, 23,* 431–451. http://dx.doi.org/10.1016/j.ecresq.2008.02.001

Rimm-Kaufman, S. E., Curby, T. W., Grimm, K. J., Nathanson, L., & Brock, L. L. (2009). The contribution of children's self-regulation and classroom quality to children's adaptive behaviors in the kindergarten classroom. *Developmental Psychology, 45,* 958–972. http://dx.doi.org/10.1037/a0015861

Sabol, T. J., & Pianta, R. C. (2012). Recent trends in research on teacher–child relationships. *Attachment & Human Development, 14,* 213–231. http://dx.doi.org/10.1080/14616734.2012.672262

Schmitt, N., Jiang, X., & Grabe, W. (2011). The percentage of words known in a text and reading comprehension. *Modern Language Journal, 95,* 26–43.

Seligman, M. E. P. (1972). Learned helplessness. *Annual Review of Medicine, 23,* 407–412. http://dx.doi.org/10.1146/annurev.me.23.020172.002203

Staton, S. L., Smith, S. S., Hurst, C., Pattinson, C. L., & Thorpe, K. J. (2017). Mandatory nap times and group napping patterns in child care: An observational study.

Behavioral Sleep Medicine, 15, 129–143. http://dx.doi.org/10.1080/15402002.2015. 1120199

Staton, S. L., Smith, S. S., Pattinson, C. L., & Thorpe, K. J. (2015). Mandatory naptimes in child care and children's nighttime sleep. *Journal of Developmental and Behavioral Pediatrics, 36*, 235–242. http://dx.doi.org/10.1097/DBP.0000000000000157

Staton, S. L., Smith, S. S., & Thorpe, K. J. (2015). "Do I really need a nap?": The role of sleep science in informing sleep practices in early childhood education and care settings. *Translational Issues in Psychological Science, 1*, 32–44. http://dx.doi.org/10.1037/tps0000011

Stillerova, L., Tavassolie, T., Curby, T. W., & Brock, L. L. (2017, August). *How negative climate in first grade classrooms affects student-teacher relationships.* Poster presented at the American Psychological Association Annual Convention, Washington, DC.

Sweller, J., van Merriënboer, J. J. G., & Paas, F. P. W. C. (1998). Cognitive architecture and instructional design. *Educational Psychology Review, 10*, 251–296. http://dx.doi.org/10.1023/A:1022193728205

Tomlinson, C. A. (2003). Differentiation of instruction in the early grades (ERIC Document Reproduction Service No. ED443572). Washington, DC: ERIC Clearinghouse on Teaching and Teacher Education. Retrieved from https://eric.ed.gov/?id=ED443572

Tomlinson, H. B., & Hyson, M. (2009). Developmentally appropriate practice in the preschool years. In C. Copple & S. Bredekamp (Eds.), *Developmentally appropriate practice in early childhood programs service children from birth through age 8* (pp. 187–216). Washington, DC: National Association for the Education of Young Children.

Vitiello, V. E., Booren, L. M., Downer, J. T., & Williford, A. (2012). Variation in children's classroom engagement throughout a day in preschool: Relations to classroom and child factors. *Early Childhood Research Quarterly, 27*, 210–220. http://dx.doi.org/10.1016/j.ecresq.2011.08.005

Vygotsky, L. S. (1978). *Mind in society: The development of higher psychological processes.* Cambridge, MA: Harvard University Press.

Weissberg, R. P., & Cascarino, J. (2013). Academic learning + social–emotional learning = national priority. *Phi Delta Kappan, 95*(2), 8–13. http://dx.doi.org/10.1177/003172171309500203

Whittaker, J. V., Kinzie, M. B., Williford, A., & DeCoster, J. (2016). Effects of MyTeachingPartner–Math/Science on teacher–child interactions in prekindergarten classrooms. *Early Education and Development, 27*, 110–127. http://dx.doi.org/10.1080/10409289.2015.1047711

Willingham, D. T. (2009). *Why don't students like school?* San Francisco, CA: Jossey-Bass.

Wong, H. K., & Wong, R. T. (2004). *The first days of school: How to be an effective teacher.* Mountain View, CA: Harry K. Wong.

Zinsser, K., Bailey, C., Curby, T. W., Denham, S., & Bassett, H. (2013). Exploring the predictable classroom: Preschool teacher stress, emotional supportiveness, and students' social–emotional behavior in private and Head Start centers. *NHSA Dialog: A Research to Practice Journal, 16*(2), 90–108.

Zinsser, K. M., Denham, S. A., & Curby, T. W. (2018). Being a social–emotional teacher: The heart of good guidance. *Young Children, 73*(4), 77–83.

Zinsser, K. M., & Wanless, S. (in press). Racial disproportionality in the school-to-prison pipeline. In M. Stevenson, B. L. Bottoms, & K. C. Burke (Eds.), *The legacy of race for children: Psychology, public policy, and law.* Oxford, England: Oxford University Press.

Zinsser, K. M., Zulauf, C. A., Das, V. N., & Silver, H. C. (2019). Utilizing social–emotional learning supports to address teacher stress and preschool expulsion. *Journal of Applied Developmental Psychology, 61*, 33–42. http://dx.doi.org/10.1016/j.appdev.2017.11.006

11

Creativity and Creative Potential in Early Childhood Education

Pablo P. L. Tinio, Jennifer Katz-Buonincontro, and Baptiste Barbot

"We're gonna have a contest," the teacher announced as the kids filed into the classroom after playing outside. "The one who builds the tallest tower gets to pick the book for today's reading circle." Piles of blocks of various sizes, shapes, and colors were already set around the classroom waiting to be thoughtfully arranged into structures by a dozen excited 4- and 5-year-olds. "Ready, set, go!" The work of building proceeded quickly and efficiently, and, in only a few minutes, the foundations were laid and towers were built. There were thin towers and there were thick towers. Most were stable and a few were barely standing. But they all had one very visible characteristic in common: They were roughly the same height. This is not surprising, in hindsight. Wanting to be fair, the teacher gave everyone about the same number of blocks. Realizing what had happened, the teacher announced, "You all built amazing towers, but you really made it hard for me to see which is the tallest one! Let's make this easier. I give you permission to use something else in the room to create your tallest tower. But you can use only one thing," as he held up one finger in front of him to really emphasize *one*. "Go!" It took about a minute of wandering and looking around before one child took one of the boxes that was used to hold the blocks and brought it back to her tower, which she knocked down with great intent. She proceeded to rebuild her tower—on the box this time. Seeing the strategy's potential, the others followed until all of the remaining boxes were all claimed, leaving a

http://dx.doi.org/10.1037/0000197-012
Healthy Development in Young Children: Evidence-Based Interventions for Early Education,
V. C. Alfonso and G. J. DuPaul (Editors)

few children with no boxes to use but with the challenge of finding some other one thing that could actually be better. One child grabbed a stepping stool. Another a small chair. The last empty-handed child took several armfuls of blocks to a table, on which the tallest tower was built.

In the active, buzzing daily life of a classroom, expressions of creativity are ever present. They are expressed by teachers and children during lessons and playtime, in the classroom and on the playground, and during social interactions among children and adults. Our teacher above planned a learning activity that required children to plan ahead ("How should I get started?" "What should my tower look like?"), carry out their plans, and, if needed, adapt them ("The bottom needs to be bigger or else it topples over") and problem-solve ("I'm out of blocks—what should I do next?"). Importantly, especially for young children, the activity was engaging and fun, but it also allowed the children to express their creativity.

In this chapter, we discuss creativity as expressed in early educational contexts. We describe the formal conceptualizations and definitions of creativity and how educators, parents, and scholars think about creativity. We also examine the key factors that influence the expression (or nonexpression) of creative behaviors. Finally, we provide some guidelines for how these behaviors could be promoted in children, and we discuss the importance of considering creativity as a long-term, even lifelong, process that can be nurtured (Barbot, Besançon, & Lubart, 2015; Tinio & Barbot, 2016). Along the way, we revisit our classroom of tower-builders as a way to illustrate and imagine how creativity transpires in the buzzing life of a classroom.

COMMON MISCONCEPTIONS ABOUT CREATIVITY IN EDUCATION

It is rarely said, if ever, that creativity is not a good thing, especially when talking about young children. It is not often said that we wish that our children were less creative—of course barring those moments when they outsmarted us, in words or actions, and triumphed over our better judgment. Creativity is largely considered to be a good thing. It is valued. We want our children to be creative, just as much as we want the teachers who teach and care for them to be creative themselves—when developing lessons and delivering them, in thinking about problems that arise in the classroom and finding solutions for solving them, and in how they nurture creativity and curiosity in children through engaging and motivating them. Creativity is something that we would like to see expressed, especially in learning and teaching (Cropley, 2003).

Interestingly, within the context of young children's education, the topic of creativity holds a special status that distinguishes it in many ways from other education-related topics. For example, as educators, we assume that specific subjects, such as math, social studies, geography, and reading, can be taught. On the basis of our experiences working with children as well as our own upbringing, we also assume that children can be taught how to behave appropriately in class—to sit quietly during a lesson, to raise their hands when they want to speak, to wash their hands after a trip to the bathroom, and to chew with their mouths closed during lunch. We can also teach them to speak politely with others, make eye contact when being scolded (or look away depending on cultural norms), and share with others. Creativity, in contrast, is seen and treated quite differently and is generally not considered as something that can be taught (Tinio & Tinio, 2018). This is one of the great misconceptions about creativity, which is often deeply rooted in people's personal beliefs, which are themselves rooted in their personal experiences. The three main misconceptions about creativity that affect how it is dealt with in educational settings are reflected in the following three questions: Who should be considered creative? How is creativity expressed? Can creativity be effectively and consistently taught and learned?

Who Is Creative?

The individuals who are readily thought of as creative are those who have demonstrated high-level performance, even genius: da Vinci, Matisse, and Picasso in the visual arts; Mozart, Schubert, and Lennon and McCartney in music; and Edison, Graham Bell, Tesla, and Jobs in technology. There are also Hemingway, Tolstoy, and Shakespeare in literature. Even in education, we have Montessori, Bloom, and Piaget. These individuals achieved the pinnacle of their respective fields and, importantly for the present discussion, through their creative endeavors, they made important discoveries in theory or practice and significantly impacted the direction of their respective fields; they were the state-of-the-art creative minds during their time. The problem with this eminence view of creativity (e.g., Simonton, 1999) is that thinking of creative behavior as available to only a few largely eminent individuals disregards the majority of the population who are creative in their own ways—as children and teachers, as writers and performers, and as musicians and artists (Tinio & Tinio, 2018). Since the 1950s, it has been established that individual differences in creativity exist and that any individual has the potential to be creative to some extent. For each individual, creativity could be expressed in different ways, at different points in a lifetime, and in different contexts (e.g., Barbot, Besançon, & Lubart, 2011).

How Is Creativity Expressed?

Answers to the question of how creativity is expressed often emphasize high-level performance and achievements, as well as groundbreaking innovations and often paradigm-shifting discoveries (Kuhn, 1962). These expressions of creativity may be seen as the products of what are commonly considered "aha" moments, which are moments of insight and discovery that seem to come out of nowhere. At times, such moments may be said to stem from divine intervention or inspiration from a muse (Tinio & Tinio, 2018). Viewed in this way, creativity becomes tinged with mystery, as something that happens without our control—that creativity cannot be readily summoned through work, skill, or will. In other words, it is viewed as being largely beyond the scope of normal human behavior.

This view of creative expression, however, becomes questionable when creativity is conceptualized more broadly, as involving a wide range of expressions: from eminent creators with their high-level achievements to the general population who, day in and day out, draw on their own creativity to successfully manage everyday issues, solve various problems at home and at work, and express themselves creatively when performing, writing poetry, playing music, and making art. A pure eminence approach to creativity leads to a neglect of the many instances of creative behavior in the classroom. In fact, early educational researchers such as Dewey (1934) suggested that creative expression is evident across a variety of fields such as science, art, and technology and is thus important for education. As the tower-building vignette shows, on the surface, the work of children and teachers could seem unimpressive. Creative behaviors may not be readily visible, as is the case of the child's use of a box on which to build her tower. But this behavior is creative when seen in the context of this specific classroom, this child's daily behavior, and the particular task of building the tallest tower. As is discussed below, the scope and context of creative behavior matter.

Can Creativity Be Taught?

Thinking of creativity as being largely within reach of a few and as something beyond deliberate control has negative repercussions for how it is addressed in practical settings. In the context of education, the teaching or direct facilitation of creative behavior is limited even in situations in which children are assigned a task that has an open-ended element, such as a science or art project or a story-writing assignment—tasks that are optimal for facilitating creative behavior. In these situations, creative outcomes may happen to some degree, and when they do, they are treated differently from other outcomes, such as appropriate use of science concepts, good writing, or a well-crafted response to a question. The addition of a creative element is typically awarded a few extra points, perhaps extra credit, but no more (and typically less) than other, expected elements of an assignment.

This approach to creativity is not surprising given that most teachers are not explicitly taught how to facilitate and teach creativity (Besançon, Lubart, & Barbot, 2013). An exception to this is teachers who work with gifted and talented children. Many states require teachers of gifted and talented programs to receive formal training on the subject of creativity. The majority of educators do not receive such training because creativity and creative expression are not attributes that are expected of most children, a situation that again has its source in the misconceptions regarding creativity.

THE SCIENCE OF CREATIVITY

The psychology of creativity, as a scientific field, has a very long history (e.g., Binet, 1900; Guilford, 1950), and a vast amount of knowledge helps to explain the emergence of the previously mentioned misconceptions. However, much of this knowledge has not yet trickled into mainstream educational settings. There are, of course, exceptions, and we see creativity being given more emphasis in progressive charter and private schools as well as in gifted and talented programs. The variation in how much creativity is included in school curricula is related to policy issues, which are beyond the scope of this chapter. Instead, we describe how creativity is conceptualized and defined by drawing on scientific research. The aim here is to address the misconceptions about creativity and subsequently to provide guidelines for how creativity could be fostered in early education settings.

The Concept of Creativity

Of the many definitions of creativity, the most commonly accepted one is that creativity involves the production of something that is novel and useful or of value to a given domain or situation (Runco & Jaeger, 2012). What is created could be a physical object such as a painting, diorama, or LEGO structure; an idea such as a model or theory; a process such as a scientific experiment or design of a robot; or something more rudimentary, such as a song or rhyme for teaching children the alphabet or a made-up story created by a child. The key elements of this definition are novelty and usefulness. Novelty could involve not just a completely new creation but an improvement of an existing object, idea, or process as well as a new way of combining or reinterpreting any of these products. As more formally discussed below, the extent of novelty could range from historically groundbreaking and at a level of eminence and genius to a degree that is barely perceptible by most people.

Usefulness is perhaps the more controversial aspect of creativity because it must be evaluated within a particular context. For example, a new way to structure and deliver a lesson on common nouns and verbs might be considered extremely useful and valuable to a school, yet outside of this context, it likely may not be perceived as such. This issue of context becomes apparent with what is known as everyday creativity, in which the creators and the creations are situated at a local level. This stands in contrast to situations in which a large percentage of the population is directly affected by the creation of a particular product. One example is Thomas Edison's invention of the electric light bulb (Simonton, 2015). Another is the Post-it note, a less life-changing invention but still globally widespread in use. In education, Howard Gardner's theory of multiple intelligences (Gardner, 1983) is taught in every teacher education program and has been featured in school curricula the world over. In stark contrast to these big creativity examples is a child who invents a new game that all of the other children in the classroom play for the rest of the school year. Here, entertainment counts as utility and value. Context is key.

The Four-C Model of Creativity

The consideration of the context in which creativity is expressed is essential because it enables us to take into account the full range of creative behaviors, from those that are widely recognized to those that are localized within an individual or a small group of people. Kaufman and Beghetto (2009) proposed the four-C model of creativity, which not only characterizes these two extremes but also captures expressions of creativity that fall somewhere in between. Importantly, this model helps us to address the previously discussed misconceptions related to the questions of who is creative and how creativity is expressed. The four-C model comprises four categories of creativity: Big-C, Pro-c, little-c, and mini-c.

Big-C Creativity

According to Kaufman and Beghetto (2009), Big-C creativity refers to eminent creativity, the type that is widely talked and written about and that is known to many people. It is the type of creativity that is often discussed in case studies of historically famous creators. The works by recipients of momentous awards such as the Pulitzer Prize, Nobel Prize, and Fields Medal fall under this category. Individuals who exhibit Big-C creativity are rare, as is the level of creativity that they exhibit. For most people and in most settings, Big-C creativity may be aspirational and inspirational, yet its real-world applicability is limited. In fact, Kaufman and Beghetto recognized this, stating that "most theoretical conceptions of Big-C nearly require a posthumous evaluation. As a result, the concept of Big-C is less helpful in real-world, practical situations" (p. 4).

Pro-c Creativity

Pro-c is realistically the highest level of creativity that most people are able to achieve. It refers to creativity that is expressed mainly by an individual who has routinely engaged in a given creative pursuit and, because of this, has achieved a high level of expertise and experience. Main factors that lead to Pro-c creativity include a high level of motivation and long-term and focused training in a particular skill or mental ability as well as the presence of various personal, financial, social, and other relevant resources. Pro-c creatives probably never reach eminence in their lifetime, although they may be quite known within their respective areas or fields. As an example, in the field of psychology, Big-C achievers include William James, Jean Piaget, B. F. Skinner, and Sigmund Freud, each of whom is a famous historical figure known to have made a significant and creative contribution to the field of psychology (and beyond). One only needs to flip through an introduction to psychology or education textbook to see the extent of their influence. Pro-c achievers would include psychologists who have made significant creative intellectual contributions known mostly to peers in their respective fields. Examples include improving on an existing research method, creating a new approach for measuring people's emotional responses to traumatic situations, or developing a new therapy for helping children cope with debilitating performance anxiety. Each of these is a definite creative achievement, and each of these creators is at or near the pinnacle of outstanding achievement within his or her respective field.

Little-c Creativity

A third category of creativity is little-c creativity, which refers to creativity expressed in day-to-day situations. Examples of people engaging in little-c creativity include a school counselor who develops a new after-school program that effectively supports the socioemotional development of the children in her school; a middle-school child who wins a science, technology, engineering, and mathematics (STEM) competition for developing an innovative method for using hydroponics (growing plants without soil); and a university professor who creates an arts-based curriculum that enables elementary students to learn college-level biochemistry concepts. In each of these examples, the creative achievement is novel and of value to the creator and to others, such as students and teachers. The achievement is also easily recognizable by the creator and others. However, unlike with Pro-c, the impact and recognition of such achievement typically do not extend beyond the local context of the creator.

Mini-c Creativity

With regard to creativity in learning and teaching, little-c and mini-c creativity— the final two types of creativity in Kaufman and Beghetto's (2009) four-C model—are the two most relevant types of creativity. Mini-c refers to creativity that is personally meaningful and/or that is related to personal development. Mini-c creativity includes a preschooler who learns that when stacking blocks, it is better to put the bigger pieces at the bottom. Finding out about this principle may not represent an eminent contribution to humankind, but it may represent a significant leap for the child who discovered it. Another example is a child who comes to understand (after a week of struggling) the difference between odd and even numbers. According to Kaufman and Beghetto, mini-c creativity is closely tied to learning and development. Of the four types of creativity, it is the most internal and therefore easily overlooked by the actual creator and by others.

The usefulness of the four-C model (Kaufman & Beghetto, 2009) lies in its ability to account for a wide range of creative behaviors from eminent creativity and levels characteristic of being at the top of one's profession or area of expertise to creativity that is expressed in day-to-day situations and that is considered creative within the life of an individual. The model has a developmental trajectory in that mini-c and little-c creativity, in the right circumstances and given the right resources, could progress to Pro-c and, in the rarest instances, to Big-C.

Within the classroom setting, Big-C and, to an extent, Pro-c could be considered as largely aspirational. Emphasis should be placed on recognizing, supporting, and, when possible, promoting expressions of little-c and mini-c creativity. Such an approach helps to avoid the common bias of associating creativity with the work of a few famous people, a bias that has led to misconceptions about who is creative and how creativity is expressed in everyday settings. For educators, focusing on little-c and mini-c is more directly relevant to the work that they are doing to help children learn, mature, and become positive and productive members of society. For a child, knowing that others around her support and recognize her creativity is more motivating than hearing about a famous creative person and being told that she should try to be like or do like that person. A focus on the more common, everyday expressions of creativity also helps to develop a culture of appreciation of such creative expressions within a classroom community. This culture of appreciation involves openness to the ideas of others even when those ideas are very different from or run counter to one's own ideas. It also shows that it is acceptable for an idea to be useful or new to one person, even though it may not be to another.

The Four Ps of Creativity and Factors Affecting Creativity

We learned from the previous section that shifting focus from eminent creativity to creativity that is typical of everyday settings is more conducive to promoting a culture of openness that encourages creative behaviors within educational settings. It is also important to take into account the critical factors that promote or inhibit creativity. In knowing these factors, educators are in a position to create classroom contexts that encourage rather than inhibit creative behaviors in children. In our discussion of such factors, we use Rhodes's (1961) four Ps of creativity as an organizing framework: product, process, person, and press (or place).

Product

Product, which refers to any outcome of a creative process, could involve ideas such as a new mnemonic method that a child comes up with to help her remember new vocabulary words. Product can also be a physical creation such as a creatively designed collage that is entered in an art contest or a new rendition of a classic children's song that a child performs in a kindergarten music show. Of course, some creative outcomes are a combination of ideas and physical products as exemplified by the children in our opening vignette who were building the tallest tower. The towers were the physical products, and the ideas included the use of boxes, chairs, and desks. Because of the variety of potential creative products that children can produce, it is important to recognize not only things that are made but also ideas and new thinking that may be more difficult to notice yet are just as novel and valuable as a tangible product.

Process

As we continue with the tower-building example, process involves the aspects of the children's cognitions that led to their final creations. These cognitions include *problem identification* or recognizing that there is actually a problem that requires a solution (e.g., I must try to build the tallest tower in class); *problem construction* or mentally representing the problem or set of problems (e.g., I have this many blocks that I need to somehow stack into a tower); *idea generation* or coming up with different possible ways to solve a problem (e.g., I can rebuild my tower on the floor or build on something else to make it taller); *idea evaluation* or determining the relative advantages and disadvantages of each possible solution to the problem (e.g., Rebuilding the tower on the floor probably won't make a big difference, but doing it on the table will, although it might be breaking the rules); and *idea selection* or choosing the best solution out of all the alternatives (e.g., Building on the table will probably let me build the tallest tower, and it should be allowed because the teacher said we could use one thing in the room; Mumford, Mobley, Reiter-Palmon, Uhlman, & Doares, 1991; Reiter-Palmon, 2018).

These processes, which are often implicit, could be made salient in situations where creativity is encouraged. This sort of cognitive scaffolding is particularly useful for younger children, who may struggle to understand what is being asked of them and that there could be several possible solutions. For example, teachers could suggest that children restate in their own words a question or problem that they are being asked to solve. They could be encouraged to come up with as many unique and different answers or solutions as possible before starting their work. Teachers might also instruct children that once they have come up with a few ideas, they should revisit the initial question or problem to ensure that their ideas actually address the question or problem. One very straightforward strategy that could help to scaffold creative behavior is to tell children to be creative in situations when creativity could be helpful. The be-creative effect has been shown to be effective in helping people come up with more creative solutions to problems requiring creativity (Christensen, Guilford, & Wilson, 1957; Nusbaum, Silvia, & Beaty, 2014).

Person

The creative person is the next *P* in Rhodes's (1961) conceptualization of creativity. Included in this category are all person-level factors that could support or hinder the expression of creativity. A well-researched person-level factor is motivation (Kaufman & Beghetto, 2009), which could be categorized into two types: extrinsic and intrinsic. Extrinsic motivation is due to external factors that motivate behavior, such as a child striving to do well in school in order to please and receive praise from his parents. Praise, grades, attention, and a new toy are all possible extrinsic motivators. Intrinsic motivation is internal and self-generated, and it provides impetus for action without the need for external reward or validation. A child may become an early reader and have a large vocabulary not because of her desire to please her parents but because she simply loves to look at and read books. This child truly enjoys learning new and increasingly sophisticated words that she can then put to use when reading increasingly more advanced texts. Whereas extrinsic motivation is often associated with lower creative performance, intrinsic motivation is associated with higher creative performance (Amabile, 1985; Greer & Levine, 1991; Prabhu, Sutton, & Sauser, 2008).

Interest is related to intrinsic motivation. The higher one's interest is in a subject or domain, the more likely one will be intrinsically motivated to engage with—and the more potential there is for creativity to be expressed in—a particular subject or domain (Barbot & Tinio, 2015). Teachers could leverage children's interests by giving them more opportunities to choose the topics that they would like to learn about. In doing so, they are increasing the likelihood that children's work will be creative. Not all tasks and activities will lend themselves to such a choice approach. However, teachers could identify aspects of the curriculum or daily routine in which the approach could be implemented.

Another important person-level factor is creative metacognition or the ability to think about one's own creative abilities and knowing when it is and is not appropriate to be creative (Kaufman & Beghetto, 2009). This latter point is critical for teachers to keep in mind because in some situations, creativity could actually be disadvantageous. Such is the case when a situation demands rote learning or when one solution to a problem is being sought. Contrast these against situations that require creativity to solve ambiguous, ill-defined, and multidimensional problems that may require several unique solutions that could subsequently be evaluated for their ability to address the problem. Creativity would not be helpful when children are simply memorizing the vowels. It could, however, be very useful when they are trying to come up with different words in which the vowels are used.

Press

Also known as place or environment, *press* refers to the context in which creativity is expressed as well as the characteristics of such context that could support or hinder creativity. An important factor is a child's home life. This environment could support creative endeavors and provide resources the child needs to pursue activities in which he or she is interested. A child who is interested in robots might have resources that would allow her to enroll in a special early childhood summer program for learning about robots. Her parents might also purchase books about robots as well as a robot-building kit designed specifically for young children. A few years later, this same child might attend a school that emphasizes innovation in STEM and offers robotics-related programs and activities. Contrast the experience of this child with another who also becomes interested in the same topic but does not have the support and resources at home or at school. This child's environment would not support his creative accomplishments in robotics and, worse, could stifle the child's interest in the subject altogether.

Press could also refer to broader contexts beyond the home and school. Csikszentmihalyi's (1999) systems model of creativity places emphasis on the influence of culture, society, and a particular field of study on a person's creativity and creative achievements. Specifically, social systems support, recognize, and evaluate the work of individuals for their novelty and usefulness. An important aspect of social systems is the gatekeepers of a field who can sanction a creative product and its creator. Such support could serve as an acknowledgment that the product in question as well as its creator is indeed creative and worthy of acceptance. Gatekeepers are important not only because they have the ability to endorse but also because they have the power to critique, obstruct, and censure creative products, deeming them inconsequential or not novel and useful.

In academic fields, gatekeepers could consist of journal editors, senior members of impactful organizations, and directors of prominent research labs. In early childhood and primary education settings, caregivers, teachers, and school administrators may be considered the gatekeepers who can support or stifle the creative work of children. These individuals could model certain behaviors such as openness to new or emerging ideas, risk taking and experimentation, and acceptance of bold and even unusual creations. They could also promote a climate in which children collaborate with each other and are able to consider the suggestions and constructive criticism of others for the purpose of improving their work.

An environment that is supportive of creativity is one that shows tolerance for occasional disruption—of classroom routine, lessons and curricula, and even social harmony. Children who are highly creative are often considered unusual, disruptive, and unruly. The common classroom response to this type of behavior is punishment and smothering of the behaviors that are different. Although there is no room for unethical, delinquent, and harmful behavior in any classroom, some level of occasional disruption should be tolerated, particularly in situations when children are experimenting, taking risks, pushing their intellectual boundaries, or trying new and different approaches. One of the challenges of being an educator is to achieve a balance between effective classroom management and tolerance for, and acceptance of, some level of disruption.

CREATIVE POTENTIAL: SEEING CREATIVITY AS A LONG-TERM PROCESS

A concept that helps to integrate the different topics that we have discussed is *creative potential*, defined as the latent capacity to produce novel and useful work (Barbot, Besançon, & Lubart, 2015). Creative potential results from a combination of factors associated with each of the four Ps, as described previously. For example, creative potential is influenced by the resources a person has, including personality characteristics, motivation and interest in a subject, and other resources that could be used to support creative pursuits (e.g., Barbot, 2018).

In educational contexts, it may be more useful to focus on children's creative potential instead of individual instances of creative achievement because the former has a developmental component. The amount of long-term commitment to and the knowledge a person has about a particular subject is critical to how creative one can be in that subject. Research has shown that it takes approximately 10–years or 10,000–hours of deliberate and focused practice for a person to develop expertise in an area (e.g., Ericsson, Krampe, & Tesch-Römer, 1993; Macnamara, Hambrick, & Oswald, 2014). Expertise serves as the foundation for creative work as it is one of the main factors that facilitate the expression of a person's creative potential (Tinio & Barbot, 2016). The long-term and perhaps lifelong acquisition of expertise points to the developmental nature of creativity, which according to Kaufman and Beghetto's (2009) model, has the possibility of progressing from mini-c and little-c to Pro-c and, in the most favorable circumstances, to Big-C creativity.

Take, for instance, a young child who comes from a long line of artists. Her parents are accomplished professional painters who frequently exhibit works in prominent art galleries and museums. From the very beginning, this child is immersed in a world full of art. Her home is a bustling art studio with art materials on every surface and in every corner. On a daily basis, she observes her parents use these materials to create artworks of various types, and when she is old enough to be able to hold a pencil or a brush, they begin to teach her how to sketch, paint, sculpt, and perform other art techniques. On weekends, the family visits museums, galleries, and performance art shows, and evenings might be spent with her parents' close circle of friends who are themselves artists. Throughout this child's life, she will experience countless moments of mini-c (learning a new technique for creating shadows in a drawing or for combining pigments to create a unique color of paint) and little-c (the first realistic portrait she creates or winning a school art contest) creativity. Because she has been immersed in a life of art and over the years has received a type of informal apprenticeship from her parents, she will grow up having the necessary skills, knowledge of the art world, and guidance needed to be able to succeed as an artist. Her creative potential to experience Pro-c creativity has great likelihood of being fulfilled, and if her creative accomplishments are consistent, if her motivation and interest in art persist through her adult life, and if the art market and gatekeepers of the art world are receptive to her creative work, she has the foundation to achieve Big-C creativity.

Teachers and caregivers have an important role in facilitating the fulfillment of a child's creative potential. To maximize the chance of success, Tinio and Barbot (2016) suggested that creative potential develops over a long time, perhaps even over a lifetime; that personal resources—such as money, effort, and time—must be invested; and that focused and deliberate effort must be made not only to develop expertise but also to acquire knowledge about the domain of interest, such as who the gatekeepers are and what their expectations are as well as what creative products are valued in the domain. Many of these steps require the support of teachers and caregivers, especially during the early years of a child's life.

CREATIVE MIND-SETS

Second to parents, educators play an extremely powerful role in affecting children's creativity. That is why it is also important to understand educators' beliefs about teaching for creativity and whether they hold fixed or growth creative mind-sets. Related to creative potential, creative mind-set research examines people's beliefs about the ability to be creative (Dweck, 1999, 2006; Hass, Katz-Buonincontro, & Reiter-Palmon, 2016). Not everyone believes that he or she can develop his or her own creativity or help develop the creativity of others. If a teacher thinks that children are born creative or uncreative, then he or she holds a *fixed creative mind-set*. However, if a teacher believes that children can develop their creativity to an unlimited extent, then he or she holds a *growth creative mind-set*. Which teacher would we entrust our children's education to? Likely, most people would prefer the teacher with a growth creative mind-set.

We are just beginning to understand how these types of creative mind-sets shape teaching for creativity. For example, children tend to rate themselves as having a high growth creative mind-set in class (Katz-Buonincontro, Hass, & Friedman, 2017). However, when talking about their beliefs, children downplay their abilities to perform creatively in class and therefore cannot envision their long-term creative potential. One reason that children downplay their creativity is that they compare themselves with eminent, Big-C individuals. This can result in a creativity backlash or feeling overwhelmed when comparing one's own creativity to that of high-performing individuals. Therefore, it is important for children to develop realistic goals, including building technical competence and expertise as a foundation for creativity, and to resist social comparison of their creative productions with older, more experienced people.

CREATIVE MORTIFICATION

Thus far, we have focused on the many ways in which we could facilitate creative behavior and achievements of children. Regrettably, the educational settings of today present many factors that actually suppress creative behavior and achievements. These include rigorous curricula, teachers under immense pressure to ensure that children attain specific early literacy and numeracy skills, and decreasing emphasis on play, music, and art—activities that are most conducive to eliciting ambiguous, open-ended, and creative thinking and problem solving. In intellectually constrained contexts such as these, there is less openness to take risks, experiment, make mistakes, and tolerate behaviors that might be deemed mildly disruptive of routines. These are exactly the types of behaviors that children need to be able to express themselves creatively and push themselves intellectually.

When the negative effects of adverse factors become pervasive and over-whelming, the result can be what Beghetto (2014) termed *creative mortifica-tion*, which refers to

> the loss of one's willingness to pursue a particular creative aspiration following a negative performance outcome. Central to the experience of creative mortifi-cation is a crushing of the creative spirit. What dies in such moments is not one's creativity, but one's will to create. (p. 266)

Beghetto (2013) identified specific factors that could lead to creative mortifi-cation. The first factor is not taking intellectual risks for fear of making mis-takes and failing as well as being the subject of criticism by others. The second is experiencing self-conscious emotions such as guilt, shame, and embarrass-ment. These emotions could result from a bad performance, outright failure, and negative feedback from others. For example, being shamed and embar-rassed by others, especially publicly, for doing something new and different could cause a child to lose motivation and interest in what he is doing and eventually dissuade him from performing the behavior altogether. The third factor that could lead to creative mortification is related to Dweck's (1999, 2006) distinction of fixed and growth mind-sets. In essence, believing that one cannot improve through effort or practice is more likely to lead to creative mortification.

CONCLUSION

Educators and caregivers are in a great position to make a positive impact on children's creative lives. Creativity, like typical school subjects, involves a set of skills that can be taught. The fulfillment of creative potential can also be facil-itated. Being mindful of the common misconceptions about creativity (Tinio & Tinio, 2018), of the factors that could lead to creative mortification (Beghetto, 2014), and of the different ways in which creativity is expressed (Kaufman & Beghetto, 2009) is a good first step for educators who aspire to create a class-room context that supports rather than inhibits creativity. Furthermore, it is important to establish an environment that encourages risk taking, making mistakes, and experimenting (such as in our vignette) and that promotes con-structive criticism instead of negative feedback and shaming. Educators could also take steps to teach and model ways of thinking that are more consistent with a growth as opposed to a fixed mind-set. One approach for doing this is to focus on effort during successes and failures. One can emphasize the amount of effort and use of effective strategies when a child performs well and succeeds in a task and emphasize lack of effort and use of ineffective strategies when a child fails or does not perform well. It is also important to see creativity as a long-term process, as being related to fulfilling one's creative potential incre-mentally, instead of focusing on one-time creative achievements. To help our children reach their highest creative potential, we must first recognize that creative growth is possible and that it requires dedication of time and resources as well as the positive support of teachers.

REFERENCES

Amabile, T. M. (1985). Motivation and creativity: Effects of motivational orientation in creative writers. *Journal of Personality and Social Psychology, 48*, 393–399. http://dx.doi.org/10.1037/0022-3514.48.2.393

Barbot, B. (2018). "Generic" creativity as a predictor or outcome of identity development? *Creativity: Theories – Research – Applications, 5*, 159–164. http://dx.doi.org/10.1515/ctra-2018-0013

Barbot, B., Besançon, M., & Lubart, T. (2015). Creative potential in educational settings: Its nature, measure, and nurture. *Education 3–13, 43*, 371–381.

Barbot, B., Besançon, M., & Lubart, T. I. (2011). Assessing creativity in the classroom. *The Open Education Journal, 4*, 58–66. http://dx.doi.org/10.2174/1874920801104010058

Barbot, B., & Tinio, P. P. L. (2015). Where is the "g" in creativity? A specialization-differentiation hypothesis. *Frontiers in Human Neuroscience, 8*, 1041. http://dx.doi.org/10.3389/fnhum.2014.01041

Beghetto, R. A. (2013). *Killing ideas softly? The promise and perils of creativity in the classroom.* Charlotte, NC: Information Age.

Beghetto, R. A. (2014). Creative mortification: An initial exploration. *Psychology of Aesthetics, Creativity, and the Arts, 8*, 266–276. http://dx.doi.org/10.1037/a0036618

Besançon, M., Lubart, T., & Barbot, B. (2013). Creative giftedness and educational opportunities. *Educational and Child Psychology, 30*(2), 79–88.

Binet, A. (1900). Un nouvel appareil pour la mesure de la suggestibilité [A new device for the measurement of suggestibility]. *L'Année Psychologique, 7*, 524–536. http://dx.doi.org/10.3406/psy.1900.3229

Christensen, P. R., Guilford, J. P., & Wilson, R. C. (1957). Relations of creative responses to working time and instructions. *Journal of Experimental Psychology, 53*(2), 82–88.

Cropley, A. J. (2003). *Creativity in education and learning: A guide for teachers and educators.* Sterling, VA: Kogan Page.

Csikszentmihalyi, M. (1999). Implications of a systems perspective for the study of creativity. In R. J. Sternberg (Ed.), *Handbook of creativity* (pp. 313–335). Cambridge, England: Cambridge University Press.

Dewey, J. (1934). *Art as experience.* New York, NY: Perigee Books.

Dweck, C. S. (1999). *Self-theories: Their role in motivation, personality, and development.* Philadelphia, PA: Psychology Press/Taylor & Francis.

Dweck, C. S. (2006). *Mindset: The new psychology of success.* New York, NY: Random House.

Ericsson, K. A., Krampe, R. T., & Tesch-Römer, C. (1993). The role of deliberate practice in the acquisition of expert performance. *Psychological Review, 100*, 363–406. http://dx.doi.org/10.1037/0033-295X.100.3.363

Gardner, H. (1983). *Frames of mind: The theory of multiple intelligences.* New York, NY: Basic Books.

Greer, M., & Levine, E. (1991). Enhancing creative performance in college students. *The Journal of Creative Behavior, 25*, 250–255. http://dx.doi.org/10.1002/j.2162-6057.1991.tb01377.x

Guilford, J. P. (1950). Creativity. *American Psychologist, 5*, 444–454.

Hass, R., Katz-Buonincontro, J., & Reiter-Palmon, R. (2016). Disentangling creative mindsets from creative self-efficacy and creative identity: Do people hold fixed and growth theories of creativity? *Psychology of Aesthetics, Creativity, and the Arts, 10*, 436–446. http://dx.doi.org/10.1037/aca0000081

Katz-Buonincontro, J., Hass, R., & Friedman, G. (2017). "Engineering" student creativity in a probability & statistics course: Investigating perceived versus actual creativity. *Psychology of Aesthetics, Creativity, and the Arts, 11*, 295–308. http://dx.doi.org/10.1037/aca0000118

Kaufman, J. C., & Beghetto, R. A. (2009). Beyond big and little: The four C model of creativity. *Review of General Psychology, 13*(1), 1–12. http://dx.doi.org/10.1037/a0013688

Kuhn, T. S. (1962). *The structure of scientific revolutions.* Chicago, IL: University of Chicago Press.

Macnamara, B. N., Hambrick, D. Z., & Oswald, F. L. (2014). Deliberate practice and performance in music, games, sports, education, and professions: A meta-analysis. *Psychological Science, 25,* 1608–1618. http://dx.doi.org/10.1177/0956797614535810

Mumford, M. D., Mobley, M. I., Reiter-Palmon, R., Uhlman, C. E., & Doares, L. M. (1991). Process analytic models of creative capacities. *Creativity Research Journal, 4,* 91–122. http://dx.doi.org/10.1080/10400419109534380

Nusbaum, E. C., Silvia, P. J., & Beaty, R. E. (2014). Ready, set, create: What instructing people to "be creative" reveals about the meaning and mechanisms of divergent thinking. *Psychology of Aesthetics, Creativity, and the Arts, 8,* 423–432.

Prabhu, V., Sutton, C., & Sauser, W. (2008). Creativity and certain personality traits: Understanding the mediating effect of intrinsic motivation. *Creativity Research Journal, 20,* 53–66. http://dx.doi.org/10.1080/10400410701841955

Reiter-Palmon, R. (2018). Creative cognition at the individual and team levels: What happens before and after idea generation. In R. J. Sternberg & J. C. Kaufman (Eds.), *The nature of human creativity* (pp. 184–208). New York, NY: Cambridge University Press. http://dx.doi.org/10.1017/9781108185936.015

Rhodes, M. (1961). An analysis of creativity. *Phi Delta Kappan, 42,* 305–310.

Runco, M. A., & Jaeger, G. J. (2012). The standard definition of creativity. *Creativity Research Journal, 24*(1), 92–96. http://dx.doi.org/10.1080/10400419.2012.650092

Simonton, D. K. (1999). Creativity from a historiometric perspective. In R. J. Sternberg (Ed.), *Handbook of creativity* (pp. 116–133). New York, NY: Cambridge University Press.

Simonton, D. K. (2015). Thomas Edison's creative career: The multilayered trajectory of trials, errors, failures, and triumphs. *Psychology of Aesthetics, Creativity, and the Arts, 9*(1), 2–14. http://dx.doi.org/10.1037/a0037722

Tinio, P. P. L., & Barbot, B. (2016). Purposeful fulfillment of creative potential. In R. A. Beghetto & B. Sriraman (Eds.), *Creative contradictions in education: Cross disciplinary paradoxes and perspectives* (pp. 115–128). New York, NY: Springer.

Tinio, P. P. L., & Tinio, S. A. (2018). Beyond the genius and the muse: Creativity in learning and teaching. In D. Schwarzer & J. Grinberg (Eds.), *Understanding glocal contexts in education: What every novice teacher needs to know* (pp. 212–221). Dubuque, IA: Kendall-Hunt.

IV

SPECIAL POPULATIONS

12

Promoting Social Competence in Young Children With Disabilities

Tina L. Stanton-Chapman and Eric L. Schmidt

This chapter discusses social competence, including what it means and how professionals can facilitate its development, especially in preschoolers with disabilities. Social competence is important for two reasons. First, young children are social beings in a social world (Bailey & Wolery, 1992). Their social behaviors, including how they initiate and respond to other adults and children, influence how these individuals initiate and respond to other young children. Second, play skills, social pragmatic skills, and emotional regulation skills are critical to how young children are perceived, the enjoyment others derive from them, the potential friendships that develop, and how they are included in their school, church, and neighborhood (Bailey & Wolery, 1992; Hoffmann & Russ, 2012). For these reasons, promoting social competence in children who lack the needed skills is critical in the early childhood years.

SOCIAL COMPETENCE

As previously mentioned, social competence is a primary component of healthy social and emotional development. This section defines social competence and discusses (a) the impact of developmental disabilities on social competence, (b) the importance of the environmental context and individuals for social competence, and (c) the skills necessary for the development of socially competent play skills.

http://dx.doi.org/10.1037/0000197-013
Healthy Development in Young Children: Evidence-Based Interventions for Early Education,
V. C. Alfonso and G. J. DuPaul (Editors)

Definition of Social Competence

A socially competent preschooler is a child who has the knowledge, skills, and behaviors to fulfill his or her needs and meet his or her expectations in social interactions (Blair et al., 2015; Goldstein & Morgan, 2002). Social competence includes (a) social behavior and play skills, (b) social communication or pragmatic skills, and (c) emotional regulation skills. Children who have proficient skills in all three areas are socially competent.

Impact of Developmental Disabilities on Social Competence

The preschool years are a time of rapid social competence when children must acquire skills related to (a) play, (b) interacting with peers, (c) responding to increasing social demands, and (d) regulating their emotions. The presence of developmental disabilities appears to have a substantial impact on children's social competence. Prior research identifies several difficulties displayed by preschool children with various developmental delays and disabilities. These difficulties include initiating social interactions and play with peers, engaging in more solitary play than peer play, and problems responding to peers and maintaining reciprocal interactions (Stanton-Chapman & Brown, 2015). Hartup (1988) noted the consequences of a lack of appropriate and effective social skills: "the single best childhood predictor of adult adaptations is not school grades, and not classroom behavior, but rather, the adequacy with which the child gets along with other children" (p. 1). The severity and onset of the developmental disability also play a considerable role in children's overall social competence abilities (Yagmurlu & Yavuz, 2015).

Children who have two or more disabilities, a condition known as comorbidity, tend to have more exacerbated social competence difficulties. For example, children with an intellectual disability and a behavior disorder are more likely to have compromised play skills and increased problem behavior and display poor peer relationships because the dual disability impairs the child's ability to interpret social situations and develop strategies for responding to them (Leffert, Siperstein, & Widaman, 2010). Comorbidity also influences a child's ability to catch up socially with typically developing peers. In fact, the majority of children with two disabilities are not able to catch up to typical peers as readily as can children with only one disability (Bennett et al., 2014).

Importance of the Environmental Context and Individuals for Social Competence

Social competence is directly related to the context or situation and the individuals who are present for the social interaction (Fiske, Gilbert, & Lindzey, 2010). Social competence skills that are effective and appropriate in one situation may not be effective and appropriate in another situation. For example, how preschoolers socially interact in the home setting may vary from how they socially interact at school. In the classroom setting, the preschooler must utilize certain social competence skills (e.g., patiently wait your turn, raise your hand to talk) to be successful. Similarly, social competence skills that are effective with one individual may not be effective and appropriate with another individual. The social competence skills needed by a preschooler to negotiate who is going to assume a particular role during play (e.g., mother, father, or baby) with a same-age peer may be quite different from the social competence skills needed if the play partner is an adolescent sibling or a caregiver. In this example, a preschooler may argue with a peer over the same role, whereas the adolescent sibling or caregiver will assume whatever role is given to them by the young child.

The implications of the environmental context and the variance of the individuals present during such social interactions are immense. First, it is clear that multiple direct observations are needed to have a clear understanding of a child's true social competence abilities. The results of these observations will better reveal the contexts and individuals through which the child can or cannot apply the needed social competence skills (for additional details regarding assessment, see Chapters 1–2, this volume). Second, once the contexts and individuals for the application of inappropriate social competence skills are identified, interventions must then be designed and delivered with those contexts and individuals in mind. Finally, social competence interventions must include a generalization component. Because effective and appropriate social competence skills vary in context and by individual, children must be taught to discriminate when and under what condition certain behaviors occur (Bailey & Wolery, 1992; Hoffmann & Russ, 2012). Thus, social competence intervention must involve teaching social competence skills and teaching effective and appropriate responses to peers and adults. For example, a child with a language disability can be taught how to initiate play with a peer by using the phrase "Can I play?" However, the same child must also be taught how to respond to a peer if the peer's response is "Yes, you can play" versus "No, you cannot play." Thus, social competence interventions must include multiple levels of skill building.

Skills Necessary for the Development of Social Competence

Each day, preschool children are required to negotiate a wide range of challenging social situations. Successful management of these social situations requires a sophisticated repertoire of social skills and an interpersonal problem-solving capacity (Spence, 2003).

Play Skills

Children's successful participation in pretend and physical play is largely due to their use of sophisticated play skills. Pretend play provides children with opportunities to practice their developing perspective-taking abilities, including the ability to identify and understand another person's emotions (Lindsey & Colwell, 2013). Pretend play allows children to act out a series of complex narrative sequences with peers. For example, children who declare that they are a doctor and then enact behavior with peers indicative of taking care of patients and making them feel better are using complex pretend play skills to engage in pretend play. Similarly, children who engage in physical play must be skilled at signaling their own emotions and at detecting the emotions of their play partner (Pellegrini, 1988). Together, pretend and physical play require fundamental skills such as (a) the regulation of negative emotions and inhibition of inappropriate behaviors, (b) the ability to remain engaged and sustain attention to the task, and (c) adequate language skills (Hebert-Myers, Guttentag, Swank, Smith, & Landry, 2006). Children who are unsuccessful at pretend and physical play tend to display high levels of negative emotionality and impulsive behavior (Hubbard & Dearing, 2004). Oftentimes, it is children with disabilities who fall into this category and require intervention to build their play skills.

Social Pragmatic Skills

Communication skills are important to the development of social play in preschoolers. Preschoolers who have good communication skills tend to be successful in peer-to-peer interactions and have learned how to use language across diverse situations and for a variety of reasons (Stanton-Chapman, Walker, & Jamison, 2014). These skills, known as *social pragmatic skills* (Phelps-Terasaki & Phelps-Gunn, 1992), include a wide range of verbal and nonverbal responses (Spence, 2003) such as initiating and maintaining a conversation, turn-taking, semantic (i.e., meaning in language) and syntactic (i.e., the way words are arranged) cohesion (Kaczmarek, 2002), making eye contact, body posture, maintaining social distance, physically approaching peers, and engaging peers in play (Spence, 2003). Social pragmatic skill development in typically developing children is often intentional and develops through daily interactions with adults and peers (Stanton-Chapman et al., 2014). Children with disabilities, however, may have major or slight social skills deficits that may inhibit the development of social pragmatic skills (Stanton-Chapman & Snell, 2011). Children who have limited or no social pragmatic skills may have compromised peer interactions. Specifically, children with social pragmatic impairments tend to misinterpret social cues, make inappropriate or off-topic comments during conversations, have difficulty making and maintaining friends, and have trouble understanding that peers have rejected them during play (Laws, Bates, Feuerstein, Mason-Apps, & White, 2012). Once a child has established a reputation among peers as someone with whom joint play is unsuccessful, unpleasant, or dissatisfying, this reputation may influence the way peers perceive the child as a potential play partner in the future (Stanton-Chapman et al., 2014). Early intervention can be a powerful tool to prevent these serious social competence consequences later in a child's life.

Emotional Regulation Skills

Socialization in young children begins with early infant–caregiver interactions. Caregivers who respond to their infant's distress by providing comfort and safety not only soothe their child but bring the child to a state of rewarding calm (Russell, Lee, Spieker, & Oxford, 2016). Caregivers, in a sense, coregulate emotions with their infants until infants develop the capacity to regulate their emotions independently (Kopp, 1989). During the preschool years, children continue to rely on caregiver guidance to regulate emotions, but they are increasingly able to incorporate what they have learned into growing self-regulatory efforts (Carlson, 2005). Preschoolers' growing ability to manage their emotional reactions is associated with positive social competence and quality peer-to-peer relationships (Caiozzo, Yule, & Grych, 2018). This ability to self-regulate one's emotions is known as *emotional regulation*. Emotional regulation is defined as the process of monitoring and modulating emotional reactions to accomplish goals (Eisenberg & Spinrad, 2004). Successful emotional regulation in children means that children are able to (a) recognize their own emotional states at age-appropriate levels, (b) access learned strategies to self-soothe or relax when experiencing a negative emotion or strong levels of arousal, and (c) maintain progress in current activities when exposed to potentially interfering emotions (Berkovits, Eisenhower, & Blacher, 2017). Children with disabilities often lack the ability to self-regulate their emotions. For example, children with autism have been found to have poorer emotion regulation than do typically developing children (Berkovits et al., 2017). Poor emotion regulation tends to lead to negative peer-to-peer relationships and higher externalizing and internalizing problem behavior. Early intervention targeting children's emotional knowledge, self-regulation, and social competence should start in the infant and toddler years to prevent a negative developmental trajectory.

Involvement of Language, Motor Skills, and Cognitive Skills in Social Competence

Although social competence primarily involves the social domains, it also requires the contributions of language, motor, and cognitive domains. Peer play requires gross and fine motor skills. Children must be able to move from place to place and manipulate objects with their hands. Peer interactions require language and cognition. Children must have language skills to express their message to peers. In return, they must use their cognitive skills to process and comprehend a peer's message to respond appropriately. Deficits in any of these domains will greatly affect young children's abilities to engage in peer play. Additionally, the demands and expectations of the social environment change as children become older. More advanced and sophisticated social responses will be required. Earlier deficits in cognitive, language, and motor domains could further complicate a child's social competence abilities if early intervention is not implemented at a young age.

PLAY STAGES AND PLAY SKILLS

Parten's (1932) research on the stages of social play in young children has stood for decades as the definitive study on this topic. She suggested, for children 2 years of age and older, that social play emerges through a hierarchical sequence (see Table 12.1). Each of these play categories requires a more

TABLE 12.1. Play Stages Utilized by Children With and Without Disabilities

Play stage	Description of play stage	Age of a typical child	Age of a child with a disability	Inclusion considerations
Unoccupied play	The child is not playing but occupies himself/herself with watching anything that happens to be of momentary interest.	Can occur at any age	Can occur at any age	Children with autism spectrum disorder tend to use this play frequently.
Solitary play	The child plays alone and independently with toys that are different from those used by children within speaking distance and makes no effort to get close to other children. He or she pursues his/her own activity without reference to what others are doing.	Most common in children under 3 years but can occur at any age	Most common in children with disabilities under 4 years.	Children with disabilities tend to use this play style frequently. It is easier for them to play on their own rather than with others because their language and play skills are typically less advanced than are those of their same-age peers.
Onlooker play	The child spends most of his or her time watching other children play. He or she often talks to children whom he or she is observing, asks questions, or gives suggestions but does not overtly enter into the play himself/herself.	Most common in children who are 2–3 years	Usually appears around 2.5–3 years	Children with disabilities tend to use this play style frequently. It is easier for them to play on their own rather than with others because their language and play skills are typically less advanced than are those of their same-age peers.

Play type	Description	Most common	Appearance	Children with disabilities
Parallel play	The child plays independently, but the activity he or she chooses naturally brings him or her among other children. He or she plays with toys that are like those that children around him or her are using, but he or she plays with the toys as he or she sees fit and doesn't try to influence or modify the activity of other children near him or her.	Most common in children who are 2.5–5 years	Usually appears around 3–3.5 years. Some children with disabilities do not go beyond this play stage.	Children with disabilities tend to use this play style frequently. It is easier for them to play on their own rather than with others because their language and play skills are typically less advanced than are those of their same-age peers.
Associative play	The child plays with other children. The conversation concerns the common activity. There is borrowing and loaning of play materials. All the members engage in similar if not identical activity. There is no division of labor and no organization of the activity.	Most common in children who are 3–5 years	May not appear until 5 years or later in children with disabilities. Some children with disabilities will not reach this level of play.	Children with significant disabilities may not reach this play style. Children with milder disabilities may need adult assistance to interact with other children.
Cooperative play	The child plays in a group that is organized for the purpose of making some material product, striving to attain some competitive goal, or dramatizing situations of adult life (e.g., house roles). There is a marked sense of belonging or not belonging to the group. The control of the group situation is in the hands of one or two of the members who direct the activity of others.	Most common in children who are 4.5 years and older. Most children are at least 5 years before this appears in their play.	May not appear until 6 years or later. Some children with disabilities will not reach this level of play.	Children with significant disabilities may not reach this play style. Children with milder disabilities may need adult assistance to interact with other children.

Note. Adapted from "Social Participation Among Pre-School Children," by M. B. Parten, 1932, *Journal of Abnormal and Social Psychology, 27*, p. 143. Copyright 1932 by the American Psychological Association.

advanced level of play than the previous category does. For example, in unoccupied play, children are not playing with toys or peers. Instead, they occupy themselves with observing anything that happens to be of momentary interest. The next stage in the hierarchy is solitary play. In this stage, children play alone and independently with toys that are different from those used by children within speaking distance. The main similarity between these two stages is that children are not interacting with peers. The main difference between the two stages is the use of toys in solitary play but not in unoccupied play.

More advanced social interactions are also required within each stage of the hierarchy. For example, in parallel play, children play independently, but the selected activity brings them within speaking distance of peers. They play with toys similar to those of their peers, but no attempt is made to modify the activities of the children near them. With cooperative play, however, children play in a group that is organized for the purpose of making a product, dramatizing adult roles (e.g., playing house), or playing formal games. The main similarity between the two stages is the proximity to peers. The main differences between the two stages are the social interaction between children and overall purpose of the play.

Although the play categories describe the sequence of social play development across the 2- through 5-year age span, children can move back and forth across categories once they have achieved the needed skill set for a given category. For example, a child may play cooperatively with two peers in the dramatic area of the classroom for a short period and then move to the art area of the classroom to participate in solitary play with play dough. It is also typical for children to participate in solitary or parallel play when novel toys and materials are introduced. Once children play with the novel items and discover what the items can do, they will naturally move into the associative and cooperative play categories and use the toys and materials with peers. However, over the course of the preschool years, the percentage of time spent in each play category should shift toward greater percentages spent in the associative and cooperative play categories.

Children With Disabilities and the Play Stages

Children with disabilities tend to lack the needed skills to play with toys appropriately or to participate in play opportunities with peers. This skill-set deficit may affect the child's overall ability to develop friendships and to have positive social interactions with peers (Fallon & MacCobb, 2013).

Several descriptive studies have investigated the effects of specific disabilities on the play skills of children. For example, children with specific language impairments tend to wait and hover over a group of peers playing rather than using a verbal statement to gain entry to peer play (Beilinson & Olswang, 2003). Children with autism tend to engage in more lower level play styles rather than play styles more appropriate to their chronological age (Holmes & Willoughby, 2005). Children with learning disabilities and Down syndrome

tend to prefer observing peers as they play instead of playing alone or requesting access to peer play (Diamond, 2002; Fallon & MacCobb, 2013). Children
with sensory disabilities such as visual impairments and hearing impairments
tend to be more isolated from peer interactions, have more frequent interactions with adults than with peers, and engage in more solitary play than do
their typical peers because their lack of sight or hearing impacts their ability to
recognize and interpret social cues and many nonverbal behaviors (Diamond,
2002). Children with physical disabilities such as spina bifida and cerebral palsy
tend to play alone and have less interactions with peers because their disability
limits the type and extent of their physical disabilities, their contact with peers,
and school attendance (Pinquart & Teubert, 2012). Table 12.1 outlines the play
stages typically used by children with disabilities. It is important to remember
that this table is designed to describe the development of social play. Many
individuals, for this reason, may devalue solitary or parallel play as these stages
do not include peer play. However, such play may be critical for young children with disabilities because it is more advanced than the stage they were
previously doing, occupies their time, and provides them with opportunities
to manipulate toys.

Assessment of Children's Play

The assessment of children's play is a complicated process for several reasons.
First, children's play must occur naturally rather than in a contrived context.
Naturalistic direct observation must occur at times when the children in question are playing (Yoder, Lloyd, & Symons, 2018). Second, the toys and peers
available for play will affect the conclusions drawn from the direct observation. For example, if Child A is ignored by peers during a direct observation,
the observer may conclude that Child A does not possess the needed skills for
social play with peers. However, if Child A is observed playing cooperatively
with a peer, the observer may conclude that the child does possess the needed
skills for social play with peers. Multiple observations across multiple peers
with a variety of toys provides a more accurate picture of Child A's play abilities. Third, the structure adults provide or do not provide during a target child's
peer play may influence observation results. For example, if a teacher prompts
Child A to respond to a peer's bid to play together, the teacher will assist Child A
in having more positive peer play during a direct observation than would
Child A when not prompted by a teacher. Finally, the form of direct observation used by an observer may influence the extent to which the results will be
useful in intervention. An observer who uses a frequency count observational
system will have different results than would an observer who uses a running
record observational system. A frequency count observation provides the total
number of target behaviors in question, whereas a running record provides a
more thorough description of the target behavior (e.g., a detailed narrative).
Additionally, a variety of observation techniques (e.g., time samples, duration,
running records) across sessions will provide a more comprehensive picture

of a child's play skills. For these reasons, professionals must carefully plan the assessment activities based on the type of information needed.

Interventions for Promoting Positive Play

Once assessment information on a target child's play skills is collected and analyzed, intervention goals are developed, with four considerations. First, intervention goals may focus on teaching a new play skill (e.g., teaching children how to ask a peer if they can join in on play when outside on the playground because they are able to demonstrate the skill in the preschool classroom). Second, play skill interventions require careful planning because play skills are challenging to teach. The play skills of other children and the environmental setting will influence the success or failure of an intervention program. For example, if a target child's intervention goal is to respond verbally to a peer's request to join in on play, then it is necessary to recruit several peers who are able to verbally request to join in on the play. If there are no peers who possess this skill set, then new intervention goals must be selected. Third, an observational system to assess the success or failure of an intervention program must be developed. The observational system should match the goals of the intervention program. If the goal of an intervention program is to increase the amount of time a target child spends in cooperative play, then an observational system involving duration should be developed. Finally, an intervention program should consider the target child's skills in other domains. For example, if a child is nonverbal, an intervention program requiring a child to deliver a four-word response would be developmentally inappropriate. A more realistic intervention goal may be a one-word response or moving closer to a peer (i.e., peer proximity).

Guidelines for Implementing Interventions for Positive Play

Using play interventions with young children offers numerous benefits. However, there are suggested guidelines to consider when developing play interventions, including the selection of toys and the use of child-directed play.

Selection of Intervention Toys

When selecting toys for positive play interventions, make sure that the selected toys are developmentally appropriate for the target child's age and gender. Although children may choose to play with a variety of toys, it is important to recognize that boys and girls have preferences, and these preferences may have an impact on the success of an intervention program (Kelly-Vance & Ryalls, 2002). By 2 years of age, boys and girls tend to prefer to play with toys that are stereotypically consistent with their gender (O'Brien & Huston, 1985). Specifically, Cherney, Kelly-Vance, Gill Glover, Ruane, and Oliver Ryalls (2003) found that boys tend to play with predominantly male-stereotyped toys such as cars and trains whereas girls play with more gender-neutral toys such as cash registers and puzzles. This is why it is important to select a variety of toys that are gender appropriate when developing play interventions.

Some toys and materials appear to elicit more solitary play behavior, whereas other toys and materials appear to produce more associative and/or cooperative play in peers (Hendrickson, Tremblay, Strain, & Shores, 1981). For example, in a review of literature, Odom and Strain (1984) identified a list of toys and materials that appear to have high or low social value (see Table 12.2). Therefore, it is important to select toys and materials that lend themselves to more social play when designing play intervention programs.

Child-Directed Play

One technique for building play skills in children is the use of child-directed play. In child-directed play, children lead the play in any manner that they wish, provided the play is not harmful or destructive (Gmitrová & Gmitrov, 2003). Play interventions that utilize child-directed play (a) enhance the target child's sense of self-direction and self-confidence, (b) increase opportunities for positive peer interactions, and (c) enhance the possibility of friendship building between the target child and peers. The adult's role during child-directed play is to follow the children's lead during their play; support the target children, as needed, while they play; and praise appropriate behavior occasionally. When target children participate in child-directed play in play interventions, they receive a greater sense of purpose and feel in greater direct control over their play as they are making choices.

TABLE 12.2. Toys and Materials With High and Low Social Value

Toys and materials	High social value	Low social value
Balls	X	X
Blocks	X	
Books	X	X
Cars/trains/trucks	X	
Crayons/markers		X
Dolls	X	X
Dress-up clothes	X	
House area	X	
Kitchen play materials	X	
Paint/paint easel		X
Pegs/pegboards		X
Paper/paper materials (e.g., scissors)		X
Puppets	X	
Puzzles		X
Sand	X	
Shape templates		X
Toy animals		X

Note. From "Classroom-Based Social Skills Instruction for Severely Handicapped Preschool Children," by S. L. Odom and P. S. Strain, 1984, *Topics in Early Childhood Special Education, 4,* p. 102. Copyright 1984 by Sage. Adapted with permission.

PEER INTERACTIONS AND RELATIONSHIPS: SOCIAL PRAGMATIC SKILLS

Language is the foundation for children's social interactions. Children use language to acquire information, make requests, and convey their thoughts and feelings. The term *social pragmatics* is typically used to refer to the ways in which speakers and listeners use language during social interactions (Abbeduto & Short-Meyerson, 2002). The first 3 years of a child's social life are typically characterized by interactions with caregivers. A child's early interactions with caregivers are critical for several reasons (Goldstein & Morgan, 2002). First, caregiver and child relationships may influence children's overall development. The child and caregiver influence one another, and subsequent interactions are based on their history of previous interactions (Sameroff & Fiese, 1990). Second, secure attachment between caregivers and children appears to be related to other positive social outcomes. According to Ainsworth (1973), *attachment* is defined as "an affectional tie that one person forms to another specific person or persons, binding them together in space and enduring over time" (p. 1). The overall quality of the caregiver–child attachment appears to be related to the sensitivity and responsivity of the caregiver to the child's signals and cues (Marvin, Cooper, Hoffman, & Powell, 2002). These early attachment relationships have a large impact on personality development (Wright, Hill, Sharp, & Pickles, 2018). For example, a child who has a caregiver who quickly responds to his or her distress signals tends to have an enthusiastic personality. Third, children with a disability may send mixed signals to their caregiver, which consequently affects their ability to participate in positive social interactions with caregivers. For example, children with autism may continue crying when a caregiver attempts to soothe them. This behavior, if frequent, may frustrate caregivers and lead them to delay responding to their child's crying. If this occurs, children with a disability may have a compromised attachment to their caregiver, which creates a poor trajectory for social relationships with peers.

Description of Child-to-Peer Interactions

After the age of 3 years, children become more interested in their peers. Their ability to interact appropriately and effectively with peers influences how peers perceive them, determines how they will or will not be accepted in peer social groups, and affects the extent to which they are fully included in the general education classroom (Han, 2012). In other words, positive child-to-peer interactions are central to a child's adjustment and long-term outcomes (Stanton-Chapman, 2015).

Repeated and sustained contact with peers does not necessarily result in the acquisition and use of appropriate and effective social skills (Roffey, 2011). This is especially true for children with disabilities, who may be entering the peer relationship stage with compromised attachment relationships with caregivers. Careful assessment and intervention planning may be needed to assist children with disabilities to interact with their peers.

Importance of Child-to-Peer Interactions

Child-to-peer interactions are a "direct exchange of words, gestures, toys, or materials between two or more children" (Odom & Brown, 1993, p. 41). A critical component in child-to-peer interactions is the reciprocal exchange between two or more children (Conroy & Brown, 2002).

Child-to-peer interactions are typically characterized as forms and functions. Social pragmatic forms may range from simple (e.g., smiling) to highly complex (e.g., conversation). Examples of forms used by young children during social interactions with peers include vocalizations, peer proximity, touching a peer, giving toys or materials to peers, and requesting toys or materials from peers (Stanton-Chapman & Brown, 2015). Social pragmatic functions are essentially the overall goal of the social interaction. Examples of functions used by young children include obtaining a peer's attention, initiating interactions, responding to a peer's initiations, maintaining an interaction, and ending an interaction (Stanton-Chapman & Brown, 2015).

Successful child-to-peer interactions tend to move through a sequence of four stages: initiations, responses, maintaining interactions, and terminating interactions (Strain, Shores, & Timm, 1977). Children who are socially competent can effectively and appropriately use forms and functions in their social interactions with peers. It is the overall context and setting that determines what forms and functions are the most appropriate.

Assessment of Child-to-Peer Interactions

Before a social pragmatic intervention can be developed for a child, an assessment of the child's social pragmatic skills must be conducted. Direct observation of a target child interacting in natural and familiar environments during typical activities is the most effective assessment technique for child-to-peer interactions (Stivers, 2015). Direct observations should begin with the identification of several routines, activities, and peers in order to examine a child's social pragmatic competencies. The observations should occur over several days and be scheduled at different times and locations during the day (Conroy & Brown, 2002). Multiple peers should also be used for observations because the peers' social pragmatic skills will have an effect on the target child's social pragmatic results.

The physical and social environments should be carefully assessed because they could influence a child's social pragmatic skills. Prior research suggests that familiarity of the peers (Doyle, Connolly, & Rivest, 1980), whether the peers are of the same age and gender (Hartup, 1983), the size of the peer group (Asher & Erickson, 1979), and the pairing of young children with developmental disabilities with socially competent peers (Guralnick & Paul-Brown, 1984) are likely to increase child-to-peer interactions. The classroom schedule also has a direct impact on children's peer interactions. Free play or center time, cleanup (Odom, Peterson, McConnell, & Ostrosky, 1990), and snack (Kohl & Beckman, 1984) are likely to increase child-to-peer interactions. The type of toys and materials available during these scheduled activities may influence how children interact with one another.

Interventions for Promoting Positive Child-to-Peer Interactions

Several social pragmatic interventions have been developed to assist target children with peer interactions, including (a) inclusion with socially responsive peers (Odom & Munson, 1996), (b) arrangement of developmentally appropriate and engaging environments (Bredekamp & Copple, 1997), (c) use of incidental teaching strategies (McGee, Almeida, Sulzer-Azaroff, & Feldman, 1992), and (d) implementation of coaching interventions (English, Goldstein, Shafer, & Kaczmarek, 1997).

Inclusion of children with socially responsive peers (Odom & Munson, 1996) is a classroom-wide intervention strategy where children with disabilities are given access to peers without disabilities. Inclusion provides children with disabilities multiple opportunities to interact with several peers who have sophisticated social pragmatic skills. Teachers encourage children with and without disabilities to interact by providing direct (e.g., heterogeneous play groups) and indirect (e.g., positive stories about children with disabilities that are read to the class) opportunities.

Arrangement of developmentally appropriate and engaging environments (Bredekamp & Copple, 1997) is another classroom-wide intervention strategy. With this intervention approach, children with disabilities are included in the general education classroom. The teacher differentiates instruction to meet the needs of all students in the classroom. Social pragmatic skills increase when children with disabilities are grouped with children without disabilities. Children without disabilities are essentially appropriate role models to their peers with disabilities.

Incidental teaching of social pragmatic skills (McGee et al., 1992) involves teachers providing individualized instruction of social pragmatic skills to children with disabilities. Instruction is provided when it is needed, during everyday situations. When children with disabilities are interacting with peers, teachers may prompt certain responses or model appropriate statements when the peer interaction appears to be breaking down. By providing the needed support to children with disabilities, teachers are increasing the likelihood that child-to-peer interaction is more successful.

Coaching interventions (English et al., 1997) involve intensive direct instruction of specific social pragmatic skills. Teachers provide step-by-step instruction on how to perform a specific social pragmatic skill. Peers without disabilities are systematically trained by teachers to employ tactics (e.g., eye contact, using a child's name, proximity) to support the target children with disabilities during play.

Guidelines for Implementing Interventions
for Positive Child-to-Peer Interactions

When implementing interventions for positive child-to-peer interventions, educators should follow several guidelines. First, the child with a disability must display the target behavior at some level. For example, if the purpose of a given intervention is to teach a child with a disability how to respond to a peer's verbal invitation to play, then the target child, at a minimum, must be aware of the peer's existence, must have a desire to interact with a peer, and must have the ability to respond verbally. If the child with a disability is missing any of these requirements, then it does not make sense to teach the child how to respond to a peer because the child is not ready to learn this skill. Second, powerful reinforcers must be identified. With some children, teacher attention is not a reinforcer, and thus its use is not likely to increase child-to-peer interactions. Third, reinforcers must be delivered immediately for them to be effective. If teacher praise is used as a reinforcer to reward a target child for using a social pragmatic skill during a peer interaction, it has the potential to interrupt the child-to-peer interaction. One solution is to use tokens such as poker chips that can be exchanged for prizes (e.g., stickers, candy, small toy) at the end of the day. Finally, it is critical to fade out teacher reinforcers once the target child has consistently demonstrated a social pragmatic skill over a given period.

EMOTIONAL REGULATION SKILLS

A child's ability to manage his or her emotions and behavior, in accordance with the demands of the environmental context, has received much attention in recent years. Emotional regulation skills are the skills that help a child resist highly emotional reactions to upsetting situations, to remain calm despite situations that may cause frustration, and to handle disappointment without an outburst. Difficulties in emotional regulation skills manifest in different ways depending on the child. Interventions targeting emotional regulation skills must match the child's temperament and learned behavior.

Description of Emotional Regulation Skills

The ability to regulate one's emotions is considered core to mental health and overall well-being. Individuals carry a toolbox of strategies to regulate their emotions (Nuske et al., 2017). Emotional regulation is the process through which individuals manipulate which, how, and when emotions are experienced and expressed (Gross, 1998). Preschool children with typical emotional regulation development can successfully attend to the socially significant aspects of their environment (Anzalone & Williamson, 2000). When young children do this, they are more equipped to maintain social interactions with adults and peers, communicate effectively, and adapt to changes in their surroundings (Goldsmith & Kelley, 2018). Appropriate emotional regulation skills have been shown to predict school success (Graziano, Reavis, Keane, & Calkins, 2007), including math and literacy achievement throughout the school years and college completion (McClelland, Acock, Piccinin, Rhea, & Stallings, 2013).

Importance of Emotional Regulation Skills

Children with disabilities, including behavioral difficulties, are at risk for poor kindergarten transitions, which may place children on long-term negative academic and social trajectories (Pears, Kim, Healey, Yoerger, & Fisher, 2015). This poor, long-term trajectory is typically due to children not being able to regulate their emotions. In a study examining parent scaffolding predicting social skills in children with and without disabilities, children with disabilities were not able to regulate their emotions successfully and had fewer social skills than did their typical peers (Baker, Fenning, Crnic, Baker, & Blacher, 2007).

The importance of emotional regulation skills in children with disabilities suggests a critical intervention point to improve school adjustment (Pears et al., 2015). Interventions targeting children who lack emotional regulation skills should address areas of great need. Children with attention-deficit/hyperactivity disorder, for example, are unable to match emotional faces portraying the same emotion (Da Fonseca, Seguier, Santos, Poinso, & Deruelle, 2009), cannot recognize emotions based on contextual cues given to them (Yuill & Lyon, 2007), and have a limited emotion vocabulary and are less able to verbalize understanding of their own and others' emotions (Kats-Gold & Priel, 2009). Children with autism spectrum disorder have difficulty recognizing their emotions and the emotions of others (Mazefsky, Pelphrey, & Dahl, 2012). Additionally, they have difficulties deploying adequate emotion coping strategies and show more venting, tantrumming, and avoidance strategies (Zantinge, van Rijn, Stockmann, & Swaab, 2017). It is the adult's responsibility to try to recognize what children are trying to communicate and assist them in learning socially acceptable ways to communicate thoughts and needs.

Assessment of Emotional Regulation Skills

Specific measures of emotional regulation skills such as the Emotion Recognition Questionnaire (Ribordy, Camras, Stefani, & Spaccarelli, 1988) tend to be geared for children ages 5 years and up. For preschoolers, the best method for assessing children's emotional regulation skills is direct observation. Because many preschoolers with disabilities struggle with emotion identification and regulation, it may be challenging to ascertain the purpose of a child's tantrumming, venting, or avoidant behavior. A functional behavior assessment may assist professionals in understanding the conditions that predict when problem behaviors will occur and the consequences that seem to motivate or maintain the behavior problems (Janney & Snell, 2006).

The underlying purpose of a functional behavior assessment is to gather information about the antecedents, behaviors, and consequences (ABCs) of problem behavior. This information is then analyzed to determine the functional relationship between the three sources of data. A simple ABC form (see Figure 12.1) may be used to record this information.

Antecedents are the conditions that precede a behavior (Janney & Snell, 2006). When conducting a direct observation, the observer focuses on the antecedent events that seem to predict when the problem behavior will occur. These antecedents are typically known as triggers and may include specific people, particular locations, statements made by others (e.g., "No, you can't have that," "It is time to clean up"), and specific tasks (e.g., transitions between activities). The observer, when identifying antecedents, should also record the people who are present in close proximity to the target children, the time, the context, and the location of the problem behavior. An example of an antecedent behavior is a teacher announcing that it is time to clean up because center time is over.

Setting events are also important to consider as antecedent data. Setting events are factors that are more distant in time or place from the problem behavior but seem to alter the likelihood that certain categories of antecedent events will result in problem behavior (Janney & Snell, 2006). Categories of setting events include biological (e.g., sleep deprivation, not taking needed

FIGURE 12.1. ABC Form Example

Name: ________________ **Setting:** ____________ **Behavior(s):** ______________________________

Date and Time	Antecedent What happened before?	Behavior What did the child do?	Consequence What happened after?	Perceived Function Comments

From *Social Relationships and Peer Support* (2nd ed., p. 172), by R. Janney and M. E. Snell, 2006, Baltimore, MD: Paul H. Brookes Publishing Co., Inc. Copyright 2006 by Paul H. Brookes. Adapted with permission.

medication), social (e.g., crowding, argument with parents), and physical (e.g., room temperature, pain).

The next step in the direct observation is a description of the problem behavior. Along with a description of the problem behavior, the observer should record the frequency or duration of the behavior. Finally, the observer should record the consequences for each instance of the problem behavior. This information includes writing down what actually happened following the behavior (e.g., what adults or peers said and did to the target student even if it was planned ignoring; Janney & Snell, 2006). The observer should also make an educated guess regarding the function the problem behavior has for the student. Four possible functions include (a) escaping from or avoiding a situation that may be too difficult, demanding, disliked, or boring; (b) obtaining attention, assistance, or comfort from others; (c) obtaining access to a desired object; or (d) experiencing sensory reinforcement by repetitive movements (e.g., arm flapping, rocking). The data obtained from the ABC form allows the practitioner to predict when the problem behavior will occur and to make an educated guess about what function the behavior serves for the child and how it is being maintained (Horner & Carr, 1997).

Interventions for Promoting Emotional Regulation Skills

The direct observation conducted for the functional behavior assessment will help determine which skills should be targeted to replace the problem behavior and to teach replacement skills for achieving the same functional outcomes. Examples of replacement skills include teaching the child how to request a break, how to ask for help, or how to raise a hand to answer a question.

Problematic emotional behavior as expressed in tantrums, irritability, aggression, self-injury, anxiety, and impulsivity is common in children with autism spectrum disorder and/or behavior disorders (Zantinge et al., 2017). As previously mentioned, these emotional problems could be the consequence of compromised expression of emotion. In typical development, adequately coping with emotions can be helpful for decision making, motivation, and communication (Izard, 2013). Emotions can be problematic when the timing is off, when emotional responses are directed toward irrelevant situations, or when the emotional intensity levels are not adapted to the situation (Zantinge et al., 2017).

Emotional regulation intervention research is emerging. Many suggestions have been offered for ways in which teachers can support young children's emotional regulation development. One strategy includes reading books that focus on emotions and friendship building (Kemple, 2004). Other strategies include clipart representing different emotions, social stories, the emotions thermometer, and zones of regulation (Center on the Social and Emotional Foundations for Early Learning, 2013) and mindfulness training (Healthy Minds Innovations, Inc., 2017). However, there is limited evidence for the effectiveness of these strategies in promoting emotional regulation development, particularly among young children with disabilities.

Guidelines for Implementing Interventions
for Emotional Regulation Skills

When designing emotional regulation interventions, educators should follow several guidelines. First, it is important for children to learn the connections between emotions and behaviors. Discussing emotions in isolation can be confusing for children. Children with disabilities may not know how to answer the question "How do you feel?" but they may be able to answer the question "How do you feel when a friend takes a toy from you?" Teaching the connections between emotions and behaviors makes an abstract concept more concrete for children with disabilities who find abstract concepts confusing. Second, children with disabilities may benefit from an emotion check-in when they enter the classroom first thing in the morning. Some children may carry an emotional reaction to a setting antecedent event (e.g., argument at home or on the school bus, didn't get enough sleep) into the classroom. By having an emotion check-in when children enter the classroom, teachers can have a sense of who is having a bad morning and do what they can to prevent triggers known to cause problem behavior in certain students. Third, teachers can use emotional regulation checks throughout the day for the needed students. Systems such as the emotions thermometer or the zones of regulation can assist children with disabilities in catching negative emotions before they become a problem. Finally, an area of the classroom should be designated as a calm-down spot. Children with disabilities or any child who has emotional regulation difficulties can be taught to go to this area whenever they feel upset, angry, or frustrated. The calm-down area should have soft pillows, stuffed animals, headphones to listen to calming music, stress-relief objects such as fidget spinners and stress balls, and an emotion clipart poster depicting various feelings.

CONCLUSION

Promoting social competence in young children with disabilities is a complex task, but ample research is available to guide professionals, especially in the areas of play skills and social pragmatic skills. In this chapter, we discussed play skills, social pragmatic skills, and emotional regulation skills and how all are related to social competence. In addition, we identified assessment strategies in all three areas. When intervention is warranted, several intervention strategies can assist in improving social competence skills in children with disabilities. These interventions have been found to be successful in the research literature.

REFERENCES

Abbeduto, L., & Short-Meyerson, K. (2002). Linguistic influences on social interaction. In H. Goldstein, L. A. Kaczmarek, & K. M. English (Eds.), *Communication and language intervention series: Vol. 10. Promoting social communication: Children with developmental disabilities from birth to adolescence* (pp. 27–54). Baltimore, MD: Paul H. Brookes.

Ainsworth, M. D. S. (1973). The development of infant–mother attachment. In B. Caldwell & H. Ricciuti (Eds.), *Review of child development research* (pp. 1–94). Chicago, IL: University of Chicago Press.

Anzalone, M., & Williamson, G. (2000). Sensory processing and motor performance in autism spectrum disorders. In A. M. Wetherby & B. M. Prizant (Eds.), *Autism spectrum disorders: A transactional developmental perspective* (pp. 142–166). Baltimore, MD: Paul H. Brookes.

Asher, K. N., & Erickson, M. T. (1979). Effects of varying child-teacher ratio and group size on day care children's and teachers' behavior. *American Journal of Orthopsychiatry, 49*, 518–521. http://dx.doi.org/10.1111/j.1939-0025.1979.tb02637.x

Bailey, D. B., & Wolery, M. (1992). *Teaching infants and preschoolers with disabilities* (2nd ed.). Englewood Cliffs, NJ: Merrill.

Baker, J. K., Fenning, R. M., Crnic, K. A., Baker, B. L., & Blacher, J. (2007). Prediction of social skills in 6-year-old children with and without developmental delays: Contributions of early regulation and maternal scaffolding. *American Journal on Mental Retardation, 112*, 375–391. http://dx.doi.org/10.1352/0895-8017(2007)112[0375:POSSIY]2.0.CO;2

Beilinson, J. S., & Olswang, L. B. (2003). Facilitating peer-group entry in kindergartners with impairments in social communication. *Language, Speech, and Hearing Services in Schools, 34*, 154–166. http://dx.doi.org/10.1044/0161-1461(2003/013)

Bennett, T. A., Szatmari, P., Georgiades, K., Hanna, S., Janus, M., Georgiades, S., . . . & The Pathways in ASD Study Team. (2014). Language impairment and early social competence in preschoolers with autism spectrum disorders: A comparison of DSM-5 profiles. *Journal of Autism and Developmental Disorders, 44*, 2797–2808. http://dx.doi.org/10.1007/s10803-014-2138-2

Berkovits, L., Eisenhower, A., & Blacher, J. (2017). Emotion regulation in young children with autism spectrum disorders. *Journal of Autism and Developmental Disorders, 47*, 68–79. http://dx.doi.org/10.1007/s10803-016-2922-2

Blair, B. L., Perry, N. B., O'Brien, M., Calkins, S. D., Keane, S. P., & Shanahan, L. (2015). Identifying developmental cascades among differentiated dimensions of social competence and emotion regulation. *Developmental Psychology, 51*, 1062–1073. http://dx.doi.org/10.1037/a0039472

Bredekamp, S., & Copple, C. (Eds.). (1997). *Developmentally appropriate practice in early childhood programs*. Washington, DC: National Association for the Education of Young Children.

Caiozzo, C. N., Yule, K., & Grych, J. (2018). Caregiver behaviors associated with emotion regulation in high-risk preschoolers. *Journal of Family Psychology, 32*, 565–574. http://dx.doi.org/10.1037/fam0000425

Carlson, S. M. (2005). Developmentally sensitive measures of executive function in preschool children. *Developmental Neuropsychology, 28*, 595–616. http://dx.doi.org/10.1207/s15326942dn2802_3

Center on the Social and Emotional Foundations for Early Learning. (2013). Training modules for preschool. Retrieved from http://csefel.vanderbilt.edu/resources/training_preschool.html

Cherney, I. C., Kelly-Vance, L., Gill Glover, K., Ruane, A., & Oliver Ryalls, B. (2003). The effects of stereotyped toys and gender on play assessment in children aged 18–47 months. *Educational Psychology, 23*, 95–106. http://dx.doi.org/10.1080/01443410303222

Conroy, M. A., & Brown, W. H. (2002). Preschool children: Putting research into practice. In H. Goldstein, L. A. Kaczmarek, & K. M. English (Eds.), *Communication and language intervention series: Vol. 10. Promoting social communication: Children with developmental disabilities from birth to adolescence* (pp. 211–231). Baltimore, MD: Paul H. Brookes.

Da Fonseca, D., Seguier, V., Santos, A., Poinso, F., & Deruelle, C. (2009). Emotion understanding in children with ADHD. *Child Psychiatry and Human Development, 40,* 111–121. http://dx.doi.org/10.1007/s10578-008-0114-9

Diamond, K. E. (2002). The development of social competence in children with disabilities. In P. K. Smith & C. H. Hart (Eds.), *Blackwell Handbook of Childhood Social Development* (pp. 571–587). Oxford, England: Blackwell.

Doyle, A. A., Connolly, J., & Rivest, L. (1980). The effects of playmate familiarity on the social interactions of young children. *Child Development, 51,* 217–223. http://dx.doi.org/10.2307/1129609

Eisenberg, N., & Spinrad, T. L. (2004). Emotion-related regulation: Sharpening the definition. *Child Development, 75,* 334–339. http://dx.doi.org/10.1111/j.1467-8624.2004.00674.x

English, K., Goldstein, H., Shafer, K., & Kaczmarek, L. (1997). Promoting interactions among preschoolers with and without disabilities: Effects of a buddy skills training program. *Exceptional Children, 63,* 229–243. http://dx.doi.org/10.1177/001440299706300206

Fallon, J., & MacCobb, S. (2013). Free play time of children with learning disabilities in a non-inclusive preschool setting: An analysis of play and non-play behaviors. *British Journal of Learning Disabilities, 41,* 212–219. http://dx.doi.org/10.1111/bld.12052

Fiske, S. T., Gilbert, D. T., & Lindzey, G. (Eds.) (2010). *Handbook of social psychology* (5th ed.). New York, NY: Wiley. http://dx.doi.org/10.1002/9780470561119

Gmitrová, V., & Gmitrov, J. (2003). The impact of teacher-directed and child-directed pretend play on cognitive competence in kindergarten children. *Early Childhood Education Journal, 30,* 241–246. http://dx.doi.org/10.1023/A:1023339724780

Goldsmith, S. F., & Kelley, E. (2018). Associations between emotion regulation and social impairment in children and adolescents with autism spectrum disorder. *Journal of Autism and Developmental Disorders, 48,* 2164–2173. http://dx.doi.org/10.1007/s10803-018-3483-3

Goldstein, H., & Morgan, L. (2002). Social interaction and models of friendship development. In H. Goldstein, L. A. Kaczmarek, & K. M. English (Eds.), *Communication and language intervention series: Vol. 10. Promoting social communication: Children with developmental disabilities from birth to adolescence* (pp. 5–25). Baltimore, MD: Paul H. Brookes.

Graziano, P. A., Reavis, R. D., Keane, S. P., & Calkins, S. D. (2007). The role of emotion regulation and children's early academic success. *Journal of School Psychology, 45*(1), 3–19.

Gross, J. J. (1998). The emerging field of emotion regulation: An integrative review. *Review of General Psychology, 2,* 271–299. http://dx.doi.org/10.1037/1089-2680.2.3.271

Guralnick, M. J., & Paul-Brown, D. P. (1984). Communicative adjustments during behavior request episodes among children at different developmental levels. *Child Development, 55,* 911–919. http://dx.doi.org/10.2307/1130142

Han, H. S. (2012). Professional development that works: Shifting preschool teachers' beliefs and use of instructional strategies to promote children's social competence. *Journal of Early Childhood Teacher Education, 33,* 251–268. http://dx.doi.org/10.1080/10901027.2012.705804

Hartup, W. W. (1983). Peer relations. In P. H. Mussen & E. M. Hetherington (Eds.), *Carmichael's manual of child psychology* (Vol. 4, pp. 103–196). New York, NY: John Wiley & Sons.

Hartup, W. W. (1988). *Early peer relations: Developmental significance and prognostic implications* [Monograph]. Retrieved from https://eric.ed.gov/?id=ED297885

Healthy Minds Innovations, Inc. (2017). *A mindfulness-based kindness curriculum for preschoolers.* Retrieved from http://www.mindfulmomentsinedu.com/uploads/1/8/8/1/18811022/kindnesscurriculum.pdf

Hebert-Myers, H., Guttentag, C. L., Swank, P. R., Smith, K. E., & Landry, S. H. (2006). The importance of language, social, and behavioral skills across early and later childhood as predictors of social competence with peers. *Applied Developmental Science, 10*(4), 174–187. http://dx.doi.org/10.1207/s1532480xads1004_2

Hendrickson, J. M., Tremblay, A., Strain, P. S., & Shores, R. E. (1981). Relationship between toy and material use and the occurrence of social interactive behaviors by normally developing preschool children. *Psychology in the Schools, 18*, 500–504. http://dx.doi.org/10.1002/1520-6807(198110)18:4<500::AID-PITS2310180423>3.0.CO;2-N

Hoffmann, J., & Russ, S. (2012). Pretend play, creativity, and emotion regulation in children. *Psychology of Aesthetics, Creativity, and the Arts, 6*(2), 175–184. http://dx.doi.org/10.1037/a0026299

Holmes, E., & Willoughby, T. (2005). Play behavior of children with autism spectrum disorders. *Journal of Intellectual & Developmental Disability, 30*(3), 156–164. http://dx.doi.org/10.1080/13668250500204034

Horner, R. H., & Carr, E. G. (1997). Behavioral support for students with severe disabilities: Functional assessment and comprehensive intervention. *The Journal of Special Education, 31*, 84–104. http://dx.doi.org/10.1177/002246699703100108

Hubbard, J. A., & Dearing, K. F. (2004). Children's understanding and regulation of emotion in the context of their peer relations. In J. B. Kupermidt & K. A. Dodge (Eds.), *Children's peer relations: From development to intervention* (pp. 81–99). Washington, DC: American Psychological Association. http://dx.doi.org/10.1037/10653-005

Izard, C. E. (2013). *Human emotions.* Berlin, Germany: Springer.

Janney, R., & Snell, M. E. (2006). *Social relationships & peer support* (2nd ed.). Baltimore, MD: Paul H. Brookes.

Kaczmarek, L. A. (2002). Assessment of social-communicative competence: An interdisciplinary model. In H. Goldstein, L. A. Kaczmarek, & K. M. English (Eds.), *Communication and language intervention series: Vol. 10. Promoting social communication: Children with developmental disabilities from birth to adolescence* (pp. 55–115). Baltimore, MD: Paul H. Brookes.

Kats-Gold, I., & Priel, B. (2009). Emotion, understanding, and social skills among boys at-risk for attention deficit hyperactivity disorder. *Psychology in the Schools, 46*, 658–678. http://dx.doi.org/10.1002/pits.20406

Kelly-Vance, L., & Ryalls, B. O. (2002). Best practices in play assessment and intervention. In A. Thomas & J. Grimes (Eds.), *Best practices in school psychology* (4th ed., Vol. 2, pp. 549–559). Bethesda, MD: National Association of School Psychologists.

Kemple, K. M. (2004). *Let's be friends: Peer competence and social inclusion in early childhood programs.* New York, NY: Teachers College Press.

Kohl, F. L., & Beckman, P. J. (1984). A comparison of handicapped and nonhandicapped preschoolers' interactions across classroom activities. *Journal of the Division for Early Childhood, 8*, 49–56. http://dx.doi.org/10.1177/105381518400800106

Kopp, C. B. (1989). Regulation of distress and negative emotions: A developmental view. *Developmental Psychology, 25*, 343–354. http://dx.doi.org/10.1037/0012-1649.25.3.343

Laws, G., Bates, G., Feuerstein, M., Mason-Apps, E., & White, C. (2012). Peer acceptance of children with language and communication impairments in a mainstream primary school: Associations with type of language difficulty, problem behaviours, and a change in placement organization. *Child Language Teaching and Therapy, 28*(1), 73–86. http://dx.doi.org/10.1177/0265659011419234

Leffert, J. S., Siperstein, G. N., & Widaman, K. F. (2010). Social perception in children with intellectual disabilities: The interpretation of benign and hostile intentions. *Journal of Intellectual Disability Research, 54*, 168–180. http://dx.doi.org/10.1111/j.1365-2788.2009.01240.x

Lindsey, E. W., & Colwell, M. J. (2013). Pretend and physical play: Links to preschoolers' affective social competence. *Merrill-Palmer Quarterly, 59*, 330–360. http://dx.doi.org/10.1353/mpq.2013.0015

Marvin, R., Cooper, G., Hoffman, K., & Powell, B. (2002). The Circle of Security project: Attachment-based intervention with caregiver-pre-school child dyads. *Attachment & Human Development*, *4*(1), 107–124. http://dx.doi.org/10.1080/14616730252982491

Mazefsky, C. A., Pelphrey, K. A., & Dahl, R. E. (2012). The need for a broader approach to emotion regulation research in autism. *Child Development Perspectives*, *6*(1), 92–97. http://dx.doi.org/10.1111/j.1750-8606.2011.00229.x

McClelland, M. M., Acock, A. C., Piccinin, A., Rhea, S. A., & Stallings, M. C. (2013). Relations between preschool attention span persistence and age 25 educational outcomes. *Early Childhood Research Quarterly*, *28*, 314–324. http://dx.doi.org/10.1016/j.ecresq.2012.07.008

McGee, G. G., Almeida, M. C., Sulzer-Azaroff, B., & Feldman, R. S. (1992). Promoting reciprocal interactions via peer incidental teaching. *Journal of Applied Behavior Analysis*, *25*, 117–126. http://dx.doi.org/10.1901/jaba.1992.25-117

Nuske, H. J., Hedley, D., Woollacott, A., Thomson, P., Macari, S., & Dissanayake, C. (2017). Developmental delays in emotion regulation strategies in preschoolers with autism. *Autism Research*, *10*, 1808–1822. http://dx.doi.org/10.1002/aur.1827

O'Brien, M. O., & Huston, A. C. (1985). Development of sex-typed play behavior in toddlers. *Developmental Psychology*, *21*, 866–871. http://dx.doi.org/10.1037/0012-1649.21.5.866

Odom, S. L., & Brown, W. H. (1993). Social interaction skills interventions for young children with disabilities in integrated settings. In C. A. Peck, S. L. Odom, & D. D. Bricker (Eds.), *Integrating young children with disabilities in community programs: Ecological perspectives on research and implementation* (pp. 39–64). Baltimore, MD: Paul H. Brookes.

Odom, S. L., & Munson, L. (1996). Assessing social performance. In M. McLean, D. B. Bailey, & M. Wolery (Eds.), *Assessing infants and preschoolers with special needs* (pp. 398–434). Columbus, OH: Charles E. Merrill.

Odom, S. L., Peterson, C., McConnell, S., & Ostrosky, M. (1990). Ecobehavioral analysis of early education/special education settings and peer social interaction. *Education and Treatment of Children*, *13*, 316–330.

Odom, S. L., & Strain, P. S. (1984). Classroom-based social skills instruction for severely handicapped preschool children. *Topics in Early Childhood Special Education*, *4*(3), 97–116. http://dx.doi.org/10.1177/027112148400400307

Parten, M. B. (1932). Social participation among pre-school children. *Journal of Abnormal and Social Psychology*, *27*, 243–269. http://dx.doi.org/10.1037/h0074524

Pears, K. C., Kim, H. K., Healey, C. V., Yoerger, K., & Fisher, P. A. (2015). Improving child self-regulation and parenting in families of pre-kindergarten children with developmental disabilities and behavioral difficulties. *Prevention Science*, *16*, 222–232. http://dx.doi.org/10.1007/s11121-014-0482-2

Pellegrini, A. D. (1988). Elementary school children's rough and tumble play and social competence. *Developmental Psychology*, *24*, 802–806. http://dx.doi.org/10.1037/0012-1649.24.6.802

Phelps-Terasaki, D., & Phelps-Gunn, T. (1992). *Test of pragmatic language*. Austin, TX: Pro-Ed.

Pinquart, M., & Teubert, D. (2012). Academic, physical, and social functioning of children and adolescents with chronic physical illness: A meta-analysis. *Journal of Pediatric Psychology*, *37*, 376–389. http://dx.doi.org/10.1093/jpepsy/jsr106

Ribordy, S. C., Camras, L. A., Stefani, R., & Spaccarelli, S. (1988). Vignettes for emotion recognition research and affective therapy with children. *Journal of Clinical Child Psychology*, *17*, 322–325. http://dx.doi.org/10.1207/s15374424jccp1704_4

Roffey, S. (2011). Developing positive relationships in schools. In S. Roffey (Ed.), *Positive relationships: Evidence-based practice across the world* (pp. 36–55). New York, NY: Springer.

Russell, B. S., Lee, J. O., Spieker, S., & Oxford, M. L. (2016). Parenting and preschool self-regulation as predictors of social emotional competence in 1st grade. *Journal of Research in Childhood Education, 30*(2), 153–169. http://dx.doi.org/10.1080/02568543.2016.1143414

Sameroff, A. J., & Fiese, B. H. (1990). Transactional regulation and early intervention. In S. J. Meisels & J. P. Shonkoff (Eds.), *Handbook of early childhood intervention* (pp. 119–149). New York, NY: Cambridge University Press.

Spence, S. H. (2003). Social skills training with children and young people: Theory, evidence, and practice. *Child and Adolescent Mental Health, 8*(2), 84–96. http://dx.doi.org/10.1111/1475-3588.00051

Stanton-Chapman, T. L. (2015). Promoting positive peer interactions in the preschool classroom: The role and the responsibility of the teacher in supporting children's sociodramatic play. *Early Childhood Education Journal, 43*(2), 99–107. http://dx.doi.org/10.1007/s10643-014-0635-8

Stanton-Chapman, T. L., & Brown, T. S. (2015). A strategy to increase the social interactions of 3-year-old children with disabilities in an inclusive classroom. *Topics in Early Childhood Special Education, 35*(1), 1–11. http://dx.doi.org/10.1177/0271121414554210

Stanton-Chapman, T. L., & Snell, M. E. (2011). Promoting turn-taking skills in preschool children with disabilities: The effects of a peer-based social communication intervention. *Early Childhood Research Quarterly, 26*, 303–319. http://dx.doi.org/10.1016/j.ecresq.2010.11.002

Stanton-Chapman, T. L., Walker, V., & Jamison, K. R. (2014). Building social competence in preschool: The effects of a social skill intervention targeting children enrolled in Head Start. *Journal of Early Childhood Teacher Education, 35*, 185–200. http://dx.doi.org/10.1080/10901027.2013.874385

Stivers, T. (2015). Coding social interaction: A heretical approach in conversation analysis? *Research on Language and Social Interaction, 48*(1), 1–19. http://dx.doi.org/10.1080/08351813.2015.993837

Strain, P. S., Shores, R. E., & Timm, M. A. (1977). Effects of peer social initiations on the behavior of withdrawn preschool children. *Journal of Applied Behavior Analysis, 10*, 289–298. http://dx.doi.org/10.1901/jaba.1977.10-289

Wright, N., Hill, J., Sharp, H., & Pickles, A. (2018). Maternal sensitivity to distress, attachment and the development of callous-unemotional traits in young children. *Journal of Child Psychology and Psychiatry, 59*, 790–800. http://dx.doi.org/10.1111/jcpp.12867

Yagmurlu, B., & Yavuz, H. M. (2015). Social competence and temperament in children with chronic orthopaedic disability. *International Journal of Disability, Development and Education, 62*(1), 83–98. http://dx.doi.org/10.1080/1034912X.2014.984590

Yoder, P. J., Lloyd, B. P., & Symons, F. J. (2018). *Observational measurement of behavior* (2nd ed.). Baltimore, MD: Paul H. Brookes.

Yuill, N., & Lyon, J. (2007). Selective difficulty in recognising facial expressions of emotion in boys with ADHD. General performance impairments or specific problems in social cognition? *European Child & Adolescent Psychiatry, 16*, 398–404. http://dx.doi.org/10.1007/s00787-007-0612-5

Zantinge, G., van Rijn, S., Stockmann, L., & Swaab, H. (2017). Physiological arousal and emotion regulation strategies in young children with autism spectrum disorders. *Journal of Autism and Developmental Disorders, 47*, 2648–2657. http://dx.doi.org/10.1007/s10803-017-3181-6

13

Working With Young Children Who Are Culturally and Linguistically Diverse

Amber Radzicki, Tammy L. Hughes, Ashley Schoenenberger, Marissa Park, and Yadira Sánchez

The population of culturally and linguistically diverse children and families in the United States is growing; therefore, there is an ever-growing need for educators to adapt instruction to the learning needs of each student. In 2018, 15.3% of students enrolled in school identified as African American, 27.5% as Hispanic, 5.6% as Asian/Pacific Islander, and 3.1% as two or more races (National Center for Education Statistics, 2018). Furthermore, 9.5% of students enrolled in public school in the United States in 2015 were described as English learners (National Center for Education Statistics, 2018), indicating that these children do not communicate fluently or learn effectively in English (Castro-Olivo, Preciado, Le, Marciante, & Garcia, 2018). The United States Census Bureau (Vespa, Armstrong, & Medina, 2018) predicted that by 2060, 17% of the population will be foreign-born. Additionally, the population of children who identify as two or more races is predicted to double from 5.3% to 11.3% by 2060.

Although the U.S. population is growing more diverse, there is a lack of diversity among educators in the United States. As of 2015, 76.6% of teachers are female and 80.1% are Caucasian. Furthermore, 6.7% of teachers in public and secondary schools identify as African American, 8.8% as Hispanic, and 4.3% as another racial group (Snyder, De Brey, & Dillow, 2018). The differences between educator and student experiences with diversity can result in many instructional challenges in the classroom. Individual and cultural experiences shape how students approach learning, how information is prioritized

http://dx.doi.org/10.1037/0000197-014

Healthy Development in Young Children: Evidence-Based Interventions for Early Education,
V. C. Alfonso and G. J. DuPaul (Editors)

and stored, and ultimately what decisions are made. When teachers and children have shared experiences, the use of language and context information is similar, and, as such, learning is easier (Espinosa, 2005). When there are differences in experiences and language, misperceptions and, at times, biases can form; the intentions driving behaviors can be easily misunderstood (Wang, Castro, & Cunningham, 2014). This chapter describes culturally sensitive practices, disparities that children from culturally and linguistically diverse backgrounds often face, and recommendations for early childhood professionals to implement culturally competent practices in their classrooms.

INTRODUCTION TO CULTURAL SENSITIVITY

To adapt teaching styles effectively to meet the needs of culturally and linguistically diverse children, one must understand what it means to be a culturally and/or linguistically diverse individual in the United States. One common misunderstanding educators face is the difference between racial and ethnic identity. Racial identity is based on an individual's appearance, whereas ethnic identity is based on an individual's culture, language, religion, and country of origin, among other variables (Worrell, 2007).

A strong racial identity may allow for an individual to have a strong sense of self as well as a sense of belonging when associated with a particular group or culture. Racial identity is associated with protective factors against racial discrimination and biases and is also correlated with lower levels of stress, increased affect, and other positive psychological outcomes (Jackson, Yoo, Guevarra, & Harrington, 2012). However, racial identity can become increasingly complex when individuals have a decreased understanding of their own identity, feel an increased pressure to feel or pass as Caucasian, and feel pressure to handle others' misunderstandings of their racial identity. For individuals of two or more racial backgrounds, the challenge can become especially complex (Lou, Lalonde, & Wilson, 2011). This complexity is often due to experiencing pressure to identify with one race and not feeling accepted by either racial group with which they identify. Furthermore, an educator in the school environment may unknowingly place children, on the basis of their appearance, into a racial category with which they do not identify.

An underdeveloped or rejected racial identity can lead to a lack of self-understanding and create an inner conflict for the child. This experience is often associated with a decrease in identity validation for the individual. Coupled with historical and systematic discrimination experienced over a lifetime, diverse children can experience a range of exclusion, rejection, and denial of advancement opportunities based solely on their racial and ethnic identities (Beatty Moody et al., 2019).

Academic Expectations

Understanding how diversity affects academic advancement is essential for educators and school practitioners to best support the unique needs of children.

In our educational system, there is disparity in academic performance between different groups of students, which is known as the achievement gap. Children and adolescents who experience the achievement gap often come from a racial/ethnic minority background, come from a low-income family, are English learners, have disabilities, and/or have a combination of these characteristics. In 2010–2011, children who were enrolled in kindergarten for the first time displayed observable patterns of academic score differences by race, ethnicity, and socioeconomic status (SES). For example, average mathematics scores were lower for children of low-SES, African American, Hispanic, and American Indian children than they were for their high-SES, Caucasian, and Asian counterparts (Snyder et al., 2018). However, the approach to addressing learning differences is often confounded by failing to disaggregate the impact of these characteristics. For a student of low SES, enrichment activities may be more applicable, whereas for a student from an ethnically diverse background, activities that are associated with the cultural expectations in pre-K–12 schooling may be more meaningful. Of course, children with a disability or who are English learners require tailored instruction to meet their needs. Because these groups overlap, a simplistic singular approach that ignores the unique challenges associated with diversity can leave children without appropriate support.

Consider the following example. Children's early literacy skills, including phonological awareness, print knowledge, and oral language, are measurable as early as the preschool years and are predictive of later reading abilities (Lonigan, Goodrich, & Farver, 2018). Preschool and kindergarten children are likely to engage in more voluntary literacy behaviors during free-play periods when literacy materials are introduced and teachers guide children to use those materials (Moon & Reifel, 2008). One way of encouraging literacy through play may be putting menus, pencils, and a notepad for food orders in a restaurant play area (Moon & Reifel, 2008). Although these play-based literacy learning activities are highlighted as particularly important for children who come to school with varying experiences in literacy and are praised as an opportunity to learn skills in a more relaxed and comfortable environment (Moon & Reifel, 2008), they also highlight how children from low-SES or culturally and linguistically diverse backgrounds may not have access to them and may not profit from them without guidance around this type of learning.

Adverse Childhood Experiences

Adverse childhood experiences (ACEs) include exposure to traditional traumatic events (e.g., abuse and neglect) as well as other types of household dysfunctions such as poor or compromised parental mental health and being a witness to domestic and community violence. ACEs present additional risk factors that can negatively impact children's health and well-being into adulthood (McLaughlin, 2017). ACE exposure can also reduce use of health and education services, which in turn impacts a child's development and educational outcomes (Woolfenden et al., 2015). Individuals of all races are susceptible to ACEs. However, 61% of African American children and 51% of Hispanic children have experienced at least one ACE, nationally, compared with 40%

of Caucasian and 23% of Asian peers (Sacks & Murphey, 2018). Recent data show that the majority of exposure occurs during early childhood (Substance Abuse and Mental Health Services Administration, 2011) and that rates are highest among children from families from a lower SES (American Academy of Pediatrics, 2017).

Inadequate Resources

Additional barriers that limit access to resources and services for children from low-SES homes include parents working long hours and/or multiple jobs and a lack of transportation to health services, mental health services, or learning resources such as a public library. One study found that Latinx and African American children have poverty rates 2.5 to 3 times as high as those of Caucasian children (Cartledge, Kea, Watson, & Oif, 2016). Undocumented immigrants and refugees may have no access to health insurance and proper medical or mental health care or early education experiences.

Low-SES households also tend to have less access to learning materials and experiences. In fact, families receiving public assistance may have fewer books at home, so the parents who know how to read are reading stories less often. This affects children's early literacy skills (Espinosa, 2005). Low-SES areas often have lower-achieving schools, greater numbers of minority students, and fewer resources. The lack of resources contributes to lower levels of academic performance, less classroom engagement, and a continuous cycle of low performance.

Ceballo, McLoyd, and Toyokawa (2004) found that African American students living in low-SES neighborhoods tend to deemphasize the importance of education and school, which results in decreased academic performance; however, low-SES African American students living in close proximity to middle-class neighborhoods where education was emphasized as important showed an increased academic performance. The authors suggested that the characteristics of the neighborhood, based on perceived crime, drug use, and upkeep of the community, have a significant impact on the educational values of low-SES children.

Stigma

Racial, ethnic, health, and metal health disparities result from pressures of poverty and racism, stigma associated with receiving mental health care, and lack of knowledge about mental health (Yasui, Pottick, & Chen, 2017). Of course, there is variation between groups. However, in general, ethnic minority children and families face additional sociocultural stressors such as discrimination, cultural isolation, and poverty that may increase their risk for psychopathology and reduce service use despite need (Yasui et al., 2017). Mainstream notions of mental health and appropriate treatment can counter specific cultural values and beliefs, thereby preventing ethnic and minority families from seeking help (Yasui et al., 2017). Parents may also feel denial, shame, fear, or guilt when it comes to their child's developmental delays, which keeps them from seeking problem identification (Woolfenden et al., 2015). Culture is something that is infused in one's individual and social understandings of health and well-being, thereby shaping what they might consider problematic as well as what treatment approaches families believe are acceptable, available, and preferable (Yasui et al., 2017). The barriers that young children face, coupled with the importance of having a cultural identity to increase protective factors, make it critical for educators and school practitioners to be aware of diversity as well as infuse culture into techniques and treatment when working with children and families who come from diverse backgrounds.

Disciplinary Disparities

Diversity comes into play in many other aspects of the education system, such as the use of disciplinary actions. As noted previously, the cultural mismatch between children and service providers can lead to bias. Implicit and explicit bias has often led to a misinterpretation of the motivations behind behaviors of young, diverse children. For example, teachers have been likely to view African American play fighting as aggression and cultural humor as disrespect (Cartledge, Singh, & Gibson, 2008). African American children tend to be viewed as older and more aggressive than they are and receive more disciplinary referrals in school than does any other ethnic group. This results in more severe disciplinary rates and decreases in positive educational outcomes (Counts, Katsiyannis, & Whitford, 2018).

African American preschool students are significantly more likely to be suspended than are students of other racial/ethnic groups. Specifically, 42% of students suspended once and 48% of students suspended multiple times are African American, even though they make up only 18% of the preschool population (Beatty, 2016; U.S. Department of Education, Office for Civil Rights, 2014). In addition, African American preschool students are 3.6 times more likely to receive out-of-school suspension than are their Caucasian counterparts (U.S. Department of Education, Office for Civil Rights, 2018). Disproportionate disciplinary actions in early childhood have been found to have significant long-term effects on children, including decreased kindergarten readiness, increased risk for school difficulties, and greater potential involvement in the juvenile justice system (Albritton, Mathews, & Anhalt, 2019). Specifically, African American males who are frequently suspended or expelled tend to become academically disengaged, increase their association with deviant peers, become resentful of school staff, and experience an increased sense of alienation. Increased disciplinary referrals, suspensions, and expulsions are linked to the school-to-prison pipeline (Darensbourg, Perez, & Blake, 2010). Critical consequences such as disciplinary actions or waiting years to receive special education services have thus resulted. This evidence proposes that exclusionary discipline techniques experienced by African American males alienate them from the learning process by steering them from the classroom toward the criminal justice system (Darensbourg et al., 2010). In light of the discrimination and stereotypes that exist between ethnic and racial groups, teachers and other school personnel need to recognize their own biases before working with diverse children.

ASSESSMENT AND INTERVENTION CONSIDERATIONS

It is important for educators and school practitioners to be aware that standardized testing does not always take into account nuances associated with diversity. Similarly, even interventions that have a documented evidence base require practitioners to consider how their application may require adjustments for diverse student populations. The use of assessment for intervention planning in diverse groups is presented next.

Inadequate Assessment Strategies

Many measures used in schools have a normative group that is referenced for comparing children's scores. Although some tests identify diverse groups, they often do not consider the multiplicity of factors that are shown in student groups. Children taking these measures may have different cultural backgrounds, levels of proficiency in English, access to educational materials, learning needs, and wide variation in their educational experiences. Standardized assessment results can also favor those who have socioeconomic advantages. As noted, a child who comes from a higher SES family may have more access to learning materials and experiences than does a child who grows up in a lower SES household. When test questions ask about information regarding experiences that children have never experienced, it is difficult for those students to answer them.

In regard to intelligence testing, not all cognitive abilities and skills are valued and practiced similarly across different cultures. In addition, societally defined measures of success in Western cultures may be important to some but are not universal to all. As conceptions of intelligence differ from one culture to another, parents also tend to emphasize different intellectual skills in raising their children. For example, Chinese people include interpersonal and intrapersonal skills as part of their conception of intelligence, whereas Kenyan conceptions of intelligence encompass ethical/moral skills. Thus, what might be considered as a comprehensive assessment of intelligence could differ from one culture to another (Sternberg, 2018).

Typical measures of cognitive and educational skills assess primarily memory, majority culture knowledge, and analytical reasoning skills but tend not to assess broader skills such as spatial relationships, musical skills, self-reflection, and social competence. The need to consider these additional attributes is based on the theory of multiple intelligence, which highlights that there are a variety of approaches to understanding and solving problems (Sternberg, 2018). The advantages of using broader measures are that it can capture knowledge and skills that are missed by assessments that focus on conventional academic abilities and that it also moves away from the concept of a static score as an indicator of the child's skills.

In contrast, dynamic testing approaches evaluate performance over time. For example, a child is given a pretest, then learns something, then is tested again. Thus, there is not just one indicator of overall learning but a consideration of a variety of learning experiences. Dynamic testing is based on the work of Vygotsky (1978), who proposed that an individual's learning is enhanced when appropriately supported in a manner in which they can readily learn new knowledge and skills (c.f., zone of proximal development). Dynamic testing is a useful technique to assess children who do not come from mainstream cultures because it enables them to learn in a testing situation that is not singularly situated in the school context (Sternberg, 2018). The addition of broader measures and dynamic assessment approaches may reduce the inequitable gap in cognitive and educational test scores between individuals of a dominant culture and individuals of other cultures. As such, professionals should use caution against overrelying on standardized, norm-referenced tests with culturally and linguistically diverse students and instead should seek to integrate alternative assessment approaches that consider the individual's background history, language, and culture (Counts et al., 2018; Ortiz, 2019).

A common challenge for educators and school assessment personnel is how to distinguish between language differences and learning disorders, especially in young, culturally diverse children. The challenge for professionals is distinguishing between children who are acquiring English as a second language and children who have a language-based disorder that would qualify for special education. For English learners, results of language assessments can underestimate the child's true language competency (Espinosa, 2005). Careful considerations must be made when interpreting results to differentiate developmental difficulties from differences in cultural and linguistic experience and exposure. Whenever possible, children should be assessed in their home language as well as in English to see how they are progressing. In addition, evaluators should remember that bilingual students may have a slower rate of learning vocabulary than that of students learning a single language (Méndez, Crais, Castro, & Kainz, 2015).

Professionals should also be familiar with the stages of acquiring a second language (e.g., silent or receptive phase, early language production, speech emergence, intermediate fluency, and ongoing language development or fluency) and how language learning develops differently in children exposed to two languages at the same time and in those exposed sequentially. In short, the automatic processes of language development occur easily in young children before the age of 3 and become the much more laborious process many of us are familiar with after that. However, although learning a second language adds challenges, it has also been linked to improved working memory, inhibitory control, cognitive flexibility, and executive functioning (Bialystok, 2015). There are also economic, personal, cultural, and communicative benefits associated with learning a second language such as enhancing higher thinking skills, marketability of bilingual skills for future employment, and psychological well-being and self-confidence (Bialystok, 2015). As with other areas, the challenge for teachers and school practitioners is to monitor how diversity adds to understanding the child and their language abilities. It is important that culturally and linguistically diverse children are frequently assessed and monitored for changes in language development (Espinosa, 2005).

When there is a language-based disorder, on average, children who are English learners tend to be identified for special education services 2 to 3 years after native English-speaking students (Weddle, Spencer, Kajian, & Petersen, 2016). As noted previously, the confusion in distinguishing between language acquisition barriers and a disability can result in these late referrals for special education services. Furthermore, the lack of resources available for addressing the specific needs of English-learning students can be discouraging and over-whelming to professionals (Naqvi, Thorne, Pfitscher, Nordstokke, & McKeough, 2012). The pressure to assist English-learning children, compounded by the lack of resources and understanding, can also often result in a push for special education services for a child who does not have a disability but rather a language acquisition problem (Hamayan, Marler, Sanchez Lopez, & Damico, 2007). Regardless of whether there is an overrepresentation or an underrepresentation of English learners receiving special education services, the misidentification results in poor educational opportunities and decreased academic success. It is apparent that a lack of resources and knowledge of how diversity affects culturally and linguistically diverse children is detrimental to their education (Hamayan et al., 2007). For this reason, it is imperative for professionals to be trained and educated on how to work with the rapidly growing population of children from linguistically diverse backgrounds in their schools to provide quality education for all children.

Evidence-Based Interventions for Diverse Learners

Selecting and implementing evidence-based interventions requires several considerations for children from diverse backgrounds. First, learning a second language in a school where few others speak a child's dominant language adds complexity to social, psychological, and cognitive development (Espinosa, 2005). Second, there is an underappreciation of the positive effects from long-term first language development.

A commonly accepted myth is believing that speaking and reading in a child's native language at home will not help them gain language skills in English. In actuality, having a more solid understanding of their primary language enhances their secondary language development (August & Shanahan, 2006). Kohnert, Yim, Nett, Kan, and Duran (2005) found that intense support of the first language during the preschool years improves second language attainment as well as a distinct advantage in reading and academic achievement in the second language. Despite this knowledge, many schools provide English immersion, which does not help with the development or maintenance of the child's first language nor does it foster support for the student's culture in school or at home. Instead, professionals should consider materials (e.g., print, songs, poems, dances, rhyming, counting) that are available in the child's home language at home and school in daily activities. It is important to avoid substituting English for children's native language and instead encourage an additive approach to discourage children from rejecting their first language (Espinosa, 2005).

A well-developed program would support the child's primary language while providing English learning alongside and in concert with the child's stage of language development. Naqvi and colleagues (2012) reported that the use of dual-language books (i.e., books that present the same story in the child's first and second languages) in the preschool years improves literacy in their first and second languages as well as fosters an understanding of their personal and cultural identity. Furthermore, small cooperative learning groups can be beneficial for children learning English to practice informal conversation in a collaborative, nonthreatening environment. This fosters an environment where English-speaking children can also act as a language resource.

SCHOOL PERSONNEL ETHNOCENTRISM

Often, teachers, school staff, and other mental health professionals have differing perceptions of their own experiences and the experiences of their students. This can lead to a lack of sensitivity to cultural differences and their effect on educational experiences because often the majority of educational professionals are Caucasian. In this way, a teacher's personal experiences with their own culture can make adapting the school environment to the needs of the culturally and linguistically diverse student difficult. As such, diverse children often experience culturally contradictory experiences at home and school (Li & Vazquez-Nuttall, 2009). Ethnocentrism, or how someone perceives another's culture based on their own cultural experiences, can be a huge barrier for teaching culturally and linguistically diverse children. For example, Douglas and Rosvold (2018) reported that students of Japanese culture were often perceived by American teachers to have poorer educational backgrounds because they were quiet, used fewer facial expressions, and were less likely to question authority. Although teachers in this study were found to perceive silence as a sign of poor educational background, silence was simply a cultural value exhibited by the students.

Teacher views about the educational preparation of children from diverse backgrounds strongly influence student educational opportunities. African American and Hispanic students are 50% less likely than Caucasian students to enter gifted programs, which may be due to a misunderstanding of the creativity and intellectual abilities in culturally and linguistically diverse students. Milner and Ford (2007) reported that culturally and linguistically diverse gifted students tend to be creative and complete assignments in ways that include more artistic and less formalized or linear patterns. Teachers without the appreciation of these students' approach to creativity can end up excluding gifted culturally diverse students from essential enrichment opportunities at school and successful academic engagement (Cartledge et al., 2008).

Ninety-five percent of preschool and early childhood centers do not have a formal gifted program, and many centers reported that they had little understanding of giftedness in early childhood (Kettler, Oveross, & Bishop, 2017). Kettler and colleagues (2017) reported several barriers to gifted programs in preschool, including a limited understanding of what being gifted means, difficulties in properly assessing for early childhood giftedness, and the inability to maintain gifted preschool programs due to lack of public funding and trained teachers. However, preschool gifted programs may assist young learners in the emergence and future development of their academic talents, especially those young learners who come from disadvantaged backgrounds.

High-achieving African American students often dissociate with their race and tend to adopt the attitudes, values, and behaviors of the majority population. A compromised racial identity can be detrimental to a child, often leaving them vulnerable to depression, anxiety, and feelings of cultural alienation (Worrell, 2007). This compromised racial identity often leaves culturally diverse students to feel as though they have to choose between being an authentic member of their racial or ethnic group or doing well in school (Erwin & Worrell, 2012).

RECOMMENDATIONS FOR EARLY CHILDHOOD PROFESSIONALS

Although culturally and linguistically diverse children face many barriers and challenges in the classroom, it is important to recognize that teachers also face barriers and challenges when addressing diverse student needs. First, there can be a language or communication barrier between the teacher and child, the teacher and the child's family, or both. Furthermore, teachers of English learners may confuse skills that are evident of a child's difficulties with the process of language acquisition with behaviors that are evident of possible learning disabilities. As previously mentioned, a lack of knowledge of the needs of English learners may result in special education referrals for a suspected learning disability when there is really a language acquisition problem or vice versa—which ultimately does not improve teacher knowledge but rather moves the challenge to a different set of individuals (e.g., speech and language pathologist, school psychologist, special education teacher, bilingual teacher) in the school building.

It may also be difficult for a teacher, or any member of school staff, to learn children's cultural norms, customs, and beliefs and adapt the classroom and learning environment to meet their needs. Learning the cultural needs of each diverse student on top of managing lesson plans, behavior referrals, and special education requirements can be a challenging task for teachers. It can be especially difficult when teachers do not know how the curriculum goals, social expectations, and cultural norms impact and are reflected in diverse students.

Chamberlain (2005) highlighted the challenge of professionals rating a child's social competence in use of language skills if they do not know the cultural and linguistic expectations of the child's ethnic group. Because of these complexities, adapting the classroom and teaching to each student's needs can be challenging. Consequently, cultural sensitivity should be a goal for all teachers and school personnel when planning for continuing their professional development that will support their everyday practice. School personnel need a realistic approach to be prepared to address diverse student needs.

Recognize and Celebrate Diversity

Culture deeply affects attitudes, beliefs, values, and approaches to teaching and learning. Racial color-blindness, the belief that race does not or should not matter, is often practiced by people with good intentions. However, practicing racial color-blindness ultimately ignores the privileges and obstacles that are associated with racial discrimination and results in a lack of cultural awareness (Wang et al., 2014). Furthermore, racial color-blindness approaches to teaching and classroom management are ineffective (Wang et al., 2014). In actuality, when students are taught with a racial color-blindness approach, they are being taught based on their teacher's cultural experiences and biases. Because 80% of teachers in the United States are Caucasian (Snyder et al., 2018), culturally and linguistically diverse children are often taught in ways that are not compatible with their own cultural experiences.

Implement Culturally Sensitive Practices

In order to be culturally sensitive, educators must be aware of and recognize their own biases, prejudices, and stereotypes before they can teach others (Bennett, Gunn, Gayle-Evans, Barrera, & Leung, 2018). Professionals need to recognize that their own privileges and experiences may not match the experiences of their students. It is also important to consider the range of risk factors (e.g., poverty; parental, marital, and mental health status; abuse; single-parent households; English learning; undocumented immigrant and refugee status), as well as the obstacles (e.g., limited access to learning materials, lower interest in traditional academic activities, cultural priorities that may not be viewed positively in mainstream classrooms) that they have had to overcome. Professional development programs should highlight these challenges and help to ensure that school teams understand how to be culturally aware and responsive.

Responsive practices can include participating in activities such as self-reflective writing, examining personal family histories, learning about the histories of diverse cultural groups, spending time in diverse communities, and reading about successful teaching in diverse settings (Richards, Brown, & Forde, 2007). School administrations can also assist with ongoing training, including demonstrations and coaching for culturally competent practices with persistent supervision and mentoring supports. These supports may enhance feelings of self-efficacy, attitudes, and beliefs that affect teachers' willingness to try new things and persist through difficulties (Klingner et al., 2005). Additional incentives should be provided for employees who complete trainings specific to the unique needs of the diverse population (Barksdale, Kenyon, Graves, & Jacobs, 2014). Above all, school professionals should demonstrate empathy, respect, patience, sensitivity, flexibility, acceptance, and openness (Douglas & Rosvold, 2018). In short, teachers need to be able to (a) allow children to preserve their own cultural identity, (b) facilitate positive identity formulation during the critical periods when young children are building their sense of self, (c) create an environment that facilitates respect for cultural and linguistic diversity, and (d) ensure children have access to a warm and supportive environment that fosters growth and development (Douglas & Rosvold, 2018).

Create a Culturally Competent Environment

A culturally competent environment can be established in several ways. Professionals can take the time to learn about each child's family, history, cultural experiences, and background. Gaining knowledge of an individual's home culture, family values, and parental expectations can provide valuable insight into the individual's strengths and needs in order to tailor instruction to the unique demands of the child and choose appropriate interventions. Additionally, taking the time to learn more about the child as a whole relays the message that one cares about the student's culture, experiences, and family and builds a positive, trusting relationship necessary for success (Kirmani, 2007).

Teachers can structure small-group interactions that foster positive peer relationships. These groups should allow for opportunities to share individual and cultural experiences that help to establish relationships and build understanding and acceptance of individual differences and unique experiences. Introducing materials such as books, videos, musical instruments, toys, games, and songs that reflect the racial, cultural, and linguistic backgrounds of children is important for the formation of a positive self-identity and provides opportunities for other children to learn more about their peers. As a result, this may build understanding, cultural competence, and acceptance among children from different backgrounds (Kirmani, 2007).

Also, professionals can provide appropriate and realistic skin colors for art projects, bulletin boards that portray diverse individuals, and dramatic play areas stocked with traditional articles of clothing. It is important for children to see people like themselves in a variety of roles. For example, seeing only male astronauts or older Caucasian scientists inadvertently sends the message that only those types of people can do those jobs (Bennett et al., 2018). Children need to see a variety of diverse men and women in a variety of roles.

Facilitate Meaningful Discussions

It is not sufficient for children to be surrounded by cultural clothes and diverse people. Children require systematic education about the differences in diverse cultures around the world. Teachers can provide learning opportunities for children by participating in activities that add different perspectives from many different cultures. Technology has created a world of many accessible opportunities for learning. Discussions can be enriched to promote mutual positivity and respect for each other. Teachers should provide culturally appropriate feedback, act as role models for equality and acceptance for all, and encourage children to think critically about their roles in society. Children need to be taught that they are a part of a diverse world in which they contribute ideas. It is their responsibility to create a fair and loving community and make the world a better place with their own actions. Children can be encouraged to continue gaining knowledge about current events and global issues and feel empowered to make changes in their community by participating in events such as local food drives or community cleanups (Richards et al., 2007).

Partner With Families

Professionals need to bridge communication and form relationships with families and communities to build a network of resources for children. As previously mentioned, children need to feel as though they are a part of the community in which they can elicit change and promote equality. Encourage families to participate in their child's education as much as possible. Building relationships with parents promotes trusting and positive relationships. These relationships help families develop a positive self-esteem and a sense of belonging in the school and community (Kirmani, 2007).

Teachers can build respect and trust in a number of ways. They should respect children's and families' names by not shortening or mispronouncing them. Shortening names could change the meaning of a name or deny cultural implications that may be important to the family (Kirmani, 2007). Some children may choose to display their name with its translated meaning and share it with their classmates to increase pride in their ethnic identity and open communication with peers about their culture. Activities such as morning meeting can open dialogue for children to share more about themselves and feel a sense of belonging.

Teachers can send invitations to school events in multiple languages to help parents feel more welcome. Technology has translation software that has made it easier than ever to accomplish this task. Some families do not speak English and have difficulties communicating with staff. Some may even rely on their child for communication with the school. Making an effort to communicate with families in their native language sends the message that they are welcome and the teacher is open to collaborating. Teachers may also invite parents to come into the classroom to label items around the classroom in their native language, create cultural bulletin boards within the school, or share special celebratory songs, articles of clothing, or dances (Vesely & Ginsberg, 2011). This encourages families to participate in school events, collaborate with professionals, find a sense of belonging in their child's education, and teach others their own personal customs and beliefs in an authentic way.

It is also the responsibility of school professionals to make sure families are aware of the resources in the community. Many communities have same-race and/or same-gender mentoring programs for those who would benefit from positive role models, mental health services, community events, and other after-school activities. Sending home a newsletter of resources in multiple languages can increase awareness and participation in community events (Vesely & Ginsberg, 2011). All of these actions build the families' network of resources, which helps them to feel less isolated and more supported.

Many parents want to be active participants in their child's education but do not know how. Sending home folder games, literacy bags, and books is very helpful for families (Klingner et al., 2005). Some parents may not know English. However, they can be provided with suggestions such as having children read to them or playing simple games even while speaking their native language, both of which can be beneficial for skill building in children.

SPECIAL CONSIDERATIONS FOR EARLY INTERVENTION

Special attention to implementing culturally responsive teaching for young children is particularly important to encourage school, community, and family collaboration for culturally and linguistically diverse children's success. Early intervention is especially important for the youngest of culturally and diverse learners. As previously mentioned, increased risk factors such as poverty as well as racial, ethnic, and health disparities are greatly associated with school failure (Duncan, Ludwig, & Magnuson, 2007). A longitudinal study found that disparities from factors such as low income and low maternal education were evident at ages as young as 9 months and increased with age (Halle et al., 2009). Specifically, Halle and colleagues (2009) found that infants and toddlers from low-income families scored lower on cognitive assessments, were less likely to be in excellent or very good health, and were less likely to receive positive teacher behavior ratings than were those from higher-income families. To address achievement gaps of culturally and linguistically diverse students, early intervention should occur during the first 3 years of life to ensure that these gaps do not persist and widen into adulthood.

Early childhood years are crucial, sensitive periods in which social, emotional, and cognitive development occurs. Brain development contributing to later skills such as executive functioning and self-regulation is very active during this time (Watts, Gandhi, Ibrahim, Masucci, & Raver, 2018). Researchers documenting the success of early intervention have shown the durable effects of cognitive and social behaviors in children into adolescence and even adulthood (Cartledge et al., 2008; Duncan et al., 2007; Watts et al., 2018). Specifically, early, intensive academic interventions have not only increased academic success but also decreased the likelihood of disruptive behaviors in the classroom (Cartledge et al., 2008). Early Head Start and preschool programs have been found to have positive effects on learning and development on children entering kindergarten, including increased performance on IQ, reading, and mathematics standardized tests (Barnett & Frede, 2010; Joo, 2010). Despite this information, studies indicate that children from immigrant families are less likely to attend preschool than are their nonimmigrant, Caucasian counterparts (Vesely & Ginsberg, 2011). Populations experiencing increased risk factors demonstrate a stronger need and should be exposed early to high-quality early interventions.

Universal Screenings

Universal screenings offer a pathway to subsequent services. Universal screenings can alert staff to all children, including culturally and linguistically diverse students, who have a need for early intervention. Screening processes allow for early interventions that target skills necessary for children's success (Miles, Fulbrook, & Mainwaring-Mägi, 2018). This is especially important around the time of the critical transition between preschool and early school age because test scores at this time can be predictive of academic achievement and school success (Miles et al., 2018). Quality programs identify children who might benefit from supports before they have a chance to fail, and progress monitoring helps establish if interventions are working and enables data-driven decisions (Klingner et al., 2005).

Choosing Evidence-Based Interventions

Although research is limited, positive results have been obtained for culturally and linguistically diverse preschool learners who receive culturally responsive pedagogy (Cartledge et al., 2016). A barrier to conducting research in preschool settings, particularly for culturally and linguistically diverse children, is ensuring access to a representative population. Not every child attends preschool. Often, those parents that can afford private day care do not send their children to income-based programs such as Head Start (Spencer, Petersen, & Adams, 2015). Therefore, preschool curricula and populations vary considerably across programs, which makes it difficult to simply apply research findings shown in elementary schools to preschools. Despite this challenge, some recommendations are the same across the age groups. For example, interventions should be chosen based on the unique needs of the child, keeping in mind the cultural and linguistic needs of the student (Spencer et al., 2015). A tiered system of support can help ensure that the appropriate level (i.e., intensity) of intervention is used. Progress monitoring is important to ensure that the intervention is resulting in the desired gains. All elements are required to determine if an intervention should be continued, changed, or discontinued. Table 13.1 provides several resources for professionals who work with learners who are culturally and linguistically diverse.

TABLE 13.1. Resources for Working With Culturally and Linguistically Diverse Learners

Resource	Description	Where to find it
National Education Association: Diversity ToolKit	An online toolkit providing an introduction to diversity. Basic information is provided, and diversity is considered from various viewpoints. A short list of suggested readings is included.	Web http://www.nea.org/tools/diversity-toolkit.html
National Education Association: English language learners	Information on English-learning students	Web http://www.nea.org/home/32346.htm
National Education Association: Culture Abilities Resilience Effort (CARE)	CARE describes approaches aimed at closing the achievement gap.	Book
Kids Matter: Diversity in Mental Health	Suggestions for schools and early childhood mental health services	Web https://www.kidsmatter.edu.au/mental-health-matters/cultural-diversity-and-childrens-wellbeing/suggestions-schools-and-early
The National Association for Multicultural Education: Biases in Teaching	Assessment for educators to evaluate their biases and how it impacts their teaching	Web https://www.nameorg.org/learn/how_do_i_know_if_my_biases_aff.php
National Association for the Education of Young Children: Promoting Young Children's Social and Emotional Health	Introduction to understanding young children's mental health	Web https://www.naeyc.org/resources/pubs/yc/mar2018/promoting-social-and-emotional-health
Teaching Tolerance	Provides resources to educators in K–12 to teach students to be active in the community	Web https://www.tolerance.org
International Center for Leadership in Education: English Language Learners Strategies Kit	Toolkit for teaching CLD students	Downloadable PDF through Brown University

Reading Rockets	Information and resources for reading instruction for English-learning students	Web	http://www.readingrockets.org/reading-topics/english-language-learners
Edutopia	Information and resources for teaching for English-learning students	Web	https://www.edutopia.org/article/resources-for-teaching-english-language-learners-ashley-cronin
Educating Everybody's Children: Diverse Teaching Strategies for Diverse Learners by Robert W. Cole	Strategies for teaching CLD students	Book	
Reading, Writing, and Talk: Inclusive Teaching Strategies for Diverse Learners, K–2 (Language and Literacy Series) by Mariana Souto-Manning, Jessica Martell (Author), Gloria Ladson-Billings (Foreword)	Strategies for teaching language and literacy to CLD students	Book	
PACER Center: Champions for Children With Disabilities: Engaging Culturally Diverse Families for Student Success	Research on parent involvement with diverse families; national research-based practice guides and tools for engaging families from diverse cultures; resources for parents from diverse cultures; resources for educators and parents; and information about educator perspectives and engagement organizations are available on this website.	Web	https://www.pacer.org/cultural-diversity
English Language Learners: Differentiating Between Language Acquisition and Learning Disabilities by J. Klingner and A. M. Eppolito (Authors)	This unique guide for special education teachers, teachers of English learners, and other practitioners provides the foundational information needed to determine whether the language difficulties experienced by English learners result from the processes and stages of learning a second language or from a learning disability.	Book	

Note. CLD = culturally and linguistically diverse.

CONCLUDING THOUGHTS

With the increasing diversity in today's society, it has never been more pertinent for early childhood education professionals to consider the needs of culturally and linguistically diverse children. Not only is there a need for awareness (e.g., why diversity matters in the educational process), but there is also a need for professionals who are competently equipped in providing quality education for all children. Because the vast majority of professionals are predominantly Caucasian females with limited cultural experiences, and a color-blind approach to teaching has clearly proven to be ineffective in ensuring success for diverse learners (Wang et al., 2014), it is critical for educational systems to prioritize continuous professional development in the areas of culturally and linguistically diverse populations. Early childhood professionals should strive to be active participants in cultural learning; this includes being self-reflective, being curious about the cultural backgrounds of children and families in one's class, and seeking supervision and support in providing the best ethical, professional educational opportunities for all children. In addition, educational professionals need to advocate for implementing best-practices assessments that are followed by tailored, relevant, evidence-based interventions.

REFERENCES

Albritton, K., Mathews, R. E., & Anhalt, K. (2019). Systematic review of early childhood mental health consultation: Implications for improving preschool discipline disproportionality. *Journal of Educational and Psychological Consultation, 29*, 444–472. http://dx.doi.org/10.1080/10474412.2018.1541413

American Academy of Pediatrics. (2017). *Adverse childhood experiences and the lifelong wconsequences of trauma.* Retrieved from https://www.aap.org/en-us/Documents/ttb_aces_consequences.pdf

August, D., & Shanahan, T. (Eds.). (2006). *Developing literacy in second language learners. Report of the national literacy panel on minority-language children and youth.* Mahwah, NJ: Erlbaum.

Barksdale, C. L., Kenyon, J., Graves, D. L., & Jacobs, C. G. (2014). Addressing disparities in mental health agencies: Strategies to implement the National CLAS Standards in Mental Health. *Psychological Services, 11*, 369–376. http://dx.doi.org/10.1037/a0035211

Barnett, W. S., & Frede, E. (2010). The promise of preschool: Why we need early education for all. *American Educator, 34*(1), 21–29. https://files.eric.ed.gov/fulltext/EJ889144.pdf

Beatty, L. A. (2016, September). *Disparities in preschool suspensions and expulsions.* Retrieved from https://www.apa.org/pi/about/newsletter/2016/09/preschool-suspensions

Beatty Moody, D. L., Taylor, A. D., Leibel, D. K., Al-Najjar, E., Katzel, L. I., Davatzikos, C., . . . Waldstein, S. R. (2019). Lifetime discrimination burden, racial discrimination, and subclinical cerebrovascular disease among African Americans. *Health Psychology, 38*, 63–74. http://dx.doi.org/10.1037/hea0000638

Bennett, S. V., Gunn, A. A., Gayle-Evans, G., Barrera, E. S., & Leung, C. B. (2018). Culturally responsive literacy practices in an early childhood community. *Early Childhood Education Journal, 46*, 241–248. http://dx.doi.org/10.1007/s10643-017-0839-9

Bialystok, E. (2015). Bilingualism and the development of executive function: The role of attention. *Child Development Perspectives, 9*, 117–121. http://dx.doi.org/10.1111/cdep.12116

Cartledge, G., Kea, C. D., Watson, M., & Oif, A. (2016). Special education dispropor-tionality: A review of Response to Intervention and culturally relevant pedagogy. *Multiple Voices for Ethnically Diverse Exceptional Learners, 16*(1), 29–49.

Cartledge, G., Singh, A., & Gibson, L. (2008). Practical behavior-management tech-niques to close the accessibility gap for students who are culturally and linguistically diverse. *Preventing School Failure, 52,* 29–38. http://dx.doi.org/10.3200/PSFL.52.3.29-38

Castro-Olivo, S., Preciado, J., Le, L., Marciante, M., & Garcia, M. (2018). The effects of culturally adapted version of First Steps to Success for Latino English Language Learners: Preliminary pilot study. *Psychology in the Schools, 55*(1), 36–49.

Ceballo, R., McLoyd, V. C., & Toyokawa, T. (2004). The influence of neighborhood quality on adolescent's educational values and school effort. *Journal of Adolescent Research, 19,* 716–739. http://dx.doi.org/10.1177/0743558403260021

Chamberlain, S. P. (2005). Recognizing and responding to cultural differences in the education of culturally and linguistically diverse learners. *Intervention in School and Clinic, 40,* 195–211. http://dx.doi.org/10.1177/10534512050400040101

Counts, J., Katsiyannis, A., & Whitford, D. K. (2018). Culturally and linguistically diverse learners in special education: English learners. *NASSP Bulletin, 102*(1), 5–21. http://dx.doi.org/10.1177/0192636518755945

Darensbourg, A., Perez, E., & Blake, J. (2010). Overrepresentation of African American males in exclusionary discipline: The role of school-based mental health professionals in dismantling the school to prison pipeline. *Journal of African American Males in Education, 1,* 196–211.

Douglas, S. R., & Rosvold, M. (2018). Intercultural communicative competence and English for academic purposes: A synthesis review of the scholarly literature. *Canadian Journal of Applied Linguistics, 21*(1), 23–42. http://dx.doi.org/10.7202/1050809ar

Duncan, G. J., Ludwig, J., & Magnuson, K. A. (2007). Reducing poverty through pre-school interventions. *The Future of Children, 17*(2), 143–160. http://dx.doi.org/10.1353/foc.2007.0015

Erwin, J. O., & Worrell, F. C. (2012). Assessment practices and the underrepresentation of minority students in gifted and talented education. *Journal of Psychoeducational Assessment, 30*(1), 74–87. http://dx.doi.org/10.1177/0734282911428197

Espinosa, L. M. (2005). Curriculum and assessment considerations for young children from culturally, linguistically, and economically diverse backgrounds. *Psychology in the Schools, 42,* 837–853. http://dx.doi.org/10.1002/pits.20115

Halle, T., Forry, N., Hair, E. C., Pepper, K., Wandner, L. D., & Whittaker, J. V. (2009). *Disparities in early learning and development: Lessons from the early childhood longitudinal study—Birth cohort (ECLS-B).* Washington, DC: Child Trends.

Hamayan, E., Marler, B., Sanchez Lopez, C., & Damico, J. (2007). *Special education con-siderations for English language learners: Delivering a continuum of services.* Philadelphia, PA: Caslon.

Jackson, K. F., Yoo, H. C., Guevarra, R., Jr., & Harrington, B. A. (2012). Role of identity integration on the relationship between perceived racial discrimination and psycho-logical adjustment of multiracial people. *Journal of Counseling Psychology, 59,* 240–250. http://dx.doi.org/10.1037/a0027639

Joo, M. (2010). Long-term effects of Head Start on academic and school outcomes of children in persistent poverty: Girls vs. boys. *Children and Youth Services Review, 32,* 807–814. http://dx.doi.org/10.1016/j.childyouth.2010.01.018

Kettler, T., Oveross, M. E., & Bishop, J. C. (2017). Gifted education in preschool: Per-ceived barriers and benefits of program development. *Journal of Research in Child-hood Education, 31,* 342–359. http://dx.doi.org/10.1080/02568543.2017.1319443

Kirmani, M. H. (2007). Empowering culturally and linguistically diverse children and families. *Young Children, 62*(6), 94–98.

Klingner, J. K., Artiles, A. J., Kozleski, E., Harry, B., Zion, S., Tate, W., . . . Riley, D. (2005). Addressing the disproportionate representation of culturally and linguistically diverse students in special education through culturally responsive educational systems. *Education Policy Analysis Archives, 13*(38), 1–45. http://dx.doi.org/10.14507/epaa.v13n38.2005

Kohnert, K., Yim, D., Nett, K., Kan, P. F., & Duran, L. (2005). Intervention with linguistically diverse preschool children: A focus on developing home language(s). *Language, Speech, & Hearing Services in Schools, 36,* 251–263. http://dx.doi.org/10.1044/0161-1461(2005/025)

Li, C., & Vazquez-Nuttall, E. (2009). School consultants as agents of social justice for multicultural children and families. *Journal of Educational & Psychological Consultation, 19*(1), 26–44. http://dx.doi.org/10.1080/10474410802462769

Lonigan, C. J., Goodrich, J. M., & Farver, J. M. (2018). Identifying differences in early literacy skills across subgroups of language-minority children: A latent profile analysis. *Developmental Psychology, 54,* 631–647. http://dx.doi.org/10.1037/dev0000477

Lou, E., Lalonde, R. N., & Wilson, C. (2011). Examining a multidimensional framework of racial identity across different biracial groups. *Asian American Journal of Psychology, 2*(2), 79–90. http://dx.doi.org/10.1037/a0023658

McLaughlin, K. (2017, April). The long shadow of adverse childhood experiences. *Psychological Science Agenda, 31*(4). Retrieved from https://www.apa.org/science/about/psa/2017/04/adverse-childhood

Méndez, L. I., Crais, E. R., Castro, D. C., & Kainz, K. (2015). A culturally and linguistically responsive vocabulary approach for young Latino dual language learners. *Journal of Speech, Language, and Hearing Research, 58*(1), 93–106. http://dx.doi.org/10.1044/2014_JSLHR-L-12-0221

Miles, S., Fulbrook, P., & Mainwaring-Mägi, D. (2018). Evaluation of standardized instruments for use in universal screening of very early school-age children: Suitability, technical adequacy, and usability. *Journal of Psychoeducational Assessment, 36*(2), 99–119. http://dx.doi.org/10.1177/0734282916669246

Milner, H. R., & Ford, D. Y. (2007). Cultural considerations in the underrepresentation of culturally diverse elementary students in gifted education. *Roeper Review, 29,* 166–173. http://dx.doi.org/10.1080/02783190709554405

Moon, K., & Reifel, S. (2008). Play and literacy learning in a diverse language prekindergarten classroom. *Contemporary Issues in Early Childhood, 9*(1), 49–65. http://dx.doi.org/10.2304/ciec.2008.9.1.49

Naqvi, R., Thorne, K. J., Pfitscher, C. M., Nordstokke, D. W., & McKeough, A. (2012). Reading dual language books: Improving early literacy skills in linguistically diverse classrooms. *Journal of Early Childhood Research, 11*(1), 3–15.

National Center for Education Statistics. (2018). Enrollment and percentage distribution of enrollment in public elementary and secondary schools, by race/ethnicity and level of education: Fall 1999 through fall 2027. *Institute of Education Sciences.* Retrieved from https://nces.ed.gov/programs/digest/d17/tables/dt17_203.60.asp

Ortiz, S. O. (2019). On the measurement of cognitive abilities in English Learners. *Contemporary School Psychology, 23*(1), 68–86. http://dx.doi.org/10.1007/s40688-018-0208-8

Richards, H. V., Brown, A. F., & Forde, T. B. (2007). Addressing diversity in the schools: Culturally responsive pedagogy. *Teaching Exceptional Children, 39*(3), 64–68. http://dx.doi.org/10.1177/004005990703900310

Sacks, V., & Murphey, D. (2018). The prevalence of adverse childhood experiences, nationally, by state, and by race or ethnicity. *Child Trends Research Brief* (No. 2018-3). Retrieved from https://www.childtrends.org/wp-content/uploads/2018/02/ACESBrief_ChildTrends_February2018.pdf

Snyder, T. D., De Brey, C., & Dillow, S. A. (2018). *Digest of Education Statistics 2016, 52nd Edition* (NCES 2017-094). Washington, DC: National Center for Education Statistics, Institute of Education Sciences, U.S. Department of Education.

Spencer, T. D., Petersen, D. B., & Adams, J. L. (2015). Tier 2 language intervention for diverse preschoolers: An early-stage randomized control group study following an analysis of response to intervention. *American Journal of Speech-Language Pathology, 24*, 619–636. http://dx.doi.org/10.1044/2015_AJSLP-14-0101

Sternberg, R. J. (2018). Context-sensitive cognitive and educational testing. *Educational Psychology Review, 30*, 857–884. http://dx.doi.org/10.1007/s10648-017-9428-0

Substance Abuse and Mental Health Services Administration. (2011). *Helping children and youth who have experienced traumatic events: National children's mental health awareness day.* Retrieved from https://files.eric.ed.gov/fulltext/ED525061.pdf

U.S. Department of Education, Office for Civil Rights. (2014). *Civil Rights Data Collection: Data Snapshot (School Discipline)* (Issue brief No. 1). Washington, DC: Author. Retrieved from https://ocrdata.ed.gov/Downloads/CRDC-School-Discipline-Snapshot.pdf

U.S. Department of Education, Office for Civil Rights. (2018). *2015-16 Civil Rights Data Collection: School Climate and Safety.* Washington, DC: Author. Retrieved from https://www2.ed.gov/about/offices/list/ocr/docs/school-climate-and-safety.pdf

Vesely, C. K., & Ginsberg, M. R. (2011). Strategies and practices for working with immigrant families in early education programs. *Young Children, 60*(1), 84–89.

Vespa, J., Armstrong, D. M., & Medina, L. (2018). Demographic turning points for the United States: Population projections for 2020 to 2060. *Current Population Reports* (No. P25-1144). Washington, DC: United States Census Bureau.

Vygotsky, L. (1978). *Mind in society.* Cambridge, MA: Harvard University Press.

Wang, K. T., Castro, A. J., & Cunningham, Y. L. (2014). Are perfectionism, individualism, and racial color-blindness associated with less cultural sensitivity? Exploring diversity awareness in white prospective teachers. *Journal of Diversity in Higher Education, 7*, 211–225. http://dx.doi.org/10.1037/a0037337

Watts, T. W., Gandhi, J., Ibrahim, D. A., Masucci, M. D., & Raver, C. C. (2018). The Chicago School Readiness Project: Examining the long-term impacts of an early childhood intervention. *PLoS ONE, 13*(7), e0200144. http://dx.doi.org/10.1371/journal.pone.0200144

Weddle, S. A., Spencer, T. D., Kajian, M., & Petersen, D. B. (2016). An examination of a multitiered system of language support for culturally and linguistically diverse preschoolers: Implications for early and accurate identification. *School Psychology Review, 45*(1), 109–133. http://dx.doi.org/10.17105/SPR45-1.109-132

Woolfenden, S., Posada, N., Krchnakova, R., Crawford, J., Gilbert, J., Jursik, B., . . . Kemp, L. (2015). Equitable access to developmental surveillance and early intervention—Understanding the barriers for children from culturally and linguistically diverse (CALD) backgrounds. *Health Expectations: An International Journal of Public Participation in Health Care & Health Policy, 18*, 3286–3301. http://dx.doi.org/10.1111/hex.12318

Worrell, F. C. (2007). Ethnic identity, academic achievement, and global self-concept in four groups of academically talented adolescents. *Gifted Child Quarterly, 51*(1), 23–38. http://dx.doi.org/10.1177/0016986206296655

Yasui, M., Pottick, K. J., & Chen, Y. (2017). Conceptualizing culturally infused engagement and its measurement for ethnic minority and immigrant children and families. *Clinical Child and Family Psychology Review, 20*, 250–332. http://dx.doi.org/10.1007/s10567-017-0229-2

14

Working With Young Children Living in Stressful Environments

Tammy L. Hughes and Cydney V. Quinn

Mental health and well-being are characterized by quality relationships, a satisfied sense of self, the ability to engage meaningfully in society, and the ability to cope with setbacks and daily challenges (Alegría, Green, McLaughlin, & Loder, 2015). Children develop these characteristics and skills through family relationships and social traditions. Later on, educators become primary partners with parents supporting children's social–emotional development with the purpose of developing resilient and academically able learners. For children living in stressful environments, development can be delayed or disrupted. Unmitigated distress can result in longstanding health and mental health problems. As such, it is important that skilled adults identify and respond to young children's needs during these early years. This chapter describes the impact of distress on child development as well as provides recommendations for parents, preschool educators, and early intervention providers.

MENTAL HEALTH

Children develop positive mental health and well-being as a response to their life experiences in combination with their ability to manage and benefit from these experiences. Variations in personal attributes, including temperament and emotional, social, and cognitive development, also influence mental health and well-being. Several factors are reported to promote positive mental health development regardless of cultural background (e.g., positive and nurturing

http://dx.doi.org/10.1037/0000197-015
Healthy Development in Young Children: Evidence-Based Interventions for Early Education,
V. C. Alfonso and G. J. DuPaul (Editors)

relationships, structure and expectations that are consistent and reliable, experiences that are developmentally appropriate, experiences tailored to the child's abilities, access to medical care and education) when delivered in a safe environment with access to adequate nourishment (Murray, 2003; Society for Research in Child Development, 2009).

Also, there are universal experiences that are known to have negative impact on children's health and mental health called *adverse childhood experiences* (ACEs). ACEs include abuse and neglect in addition to exposure to household dysfunctions (e.g., substance abuse, mental illness in household, parental separation or divorce, incarcerated family member, domestic violence; Felitti et al., 1998). Some experiences, such as maltreatment, family violence, and *toxic stress* (early prolonged exposure to trauma with the accompanying biological stress response of fight-or-flight), not only have immediate negative effects but can leave lasting devastating effects on child physiological development, health, and mental health (Alegría et al., 2015; Felitti et al., 1998). Ultimately, an individual's mental health status is a result of the competing elements of protection and threat (World Health Organization [WHO], 2014).

Risk and Resilience

Risks to mental health can occur at any time throughout the life span. A child's mental health can be influenced by events or circumstances occurring before birth or in very early infancy. For example, a mother's risky health behaviors during the pregnancy, low birthweight, exposure to malnutrition, inadequate attachments, and negative attitudes from caregivers regarding infant care can increase child stress and the risk for mental health difficulties (WHO, 2014). Exposure to negative experiences within the home (e.g., unstable resources and relationships, unsupportive parenting) or in day care/preschool (e.g., understaffed or chaotic learning environments) can have damaging effects on the development of children's cognitive and emotional skills. Additionally, sociocultural and geopolitical contexts can create threats to mental health. Sociodemographic characteristics (e.g., gender, race and ethnic grouping, place of residence, socioeconomic status) can increase the child's vulnerability when exposed to stigma and discrimination, violence and abuse, exclusion from societal groups, restricted access to health and social services, and impoverished education opportunities (Lopez & Gadsden, 2016).

The diathesis–stress model (Ingram & Luxton, 2005) is useful for considering how negative events, such as exposure to ACEs, toxic stress, and other early life stressors, can result in problematic emotions and behaviors in some children but not in others. We have since conceptualized the model as the diathesis–stress–coping model, recognizing the central role coping plays in mitigating expression of diatheses. In short, all humans—children and adults—carry biological predispositions. In day-to-day life we might refer to these as family traits that are carried in our genetics. In our medical history we might indicate a genetic weakness passed down through the family (i.e., a father with high blood pressure, uncle with diabetes, sister with breast cancer). Yet just because a weakness runs in the family does not mean that all will manifest the same illnesses; biology is not destiny. Rather, only when the body is under too much stress—maybe due to a poor diet, inadequate sleep, low levels of exercise, and employment at a high-stress job—do we see high blood pressure emerge, for example. In this scenario, it is also easy to imagine that under different conditions that same person would not have high blood pressure. In the future, with strong coping skills and networks, a person could be exposed to the same stressors and not manifest high blood pressure.

Problematic emotional, social, and cognitive behaviors—and ultimately mental health disorders—can occur in a similar way. Mental health problems often result from the child's liability and the amount of stress exposure. In general, children with more genetic risk can have problems even when they are in a lower stress condition. Likewise, children in highly stressful environments may show challenges even when they carry less genetic predisposition. Child psychopathology can be conceptualized as a combination of vulnerabilities that include biological predispositions and exposure to stressful environments (Ingram & Luxton, 2005). As such, when stress and vulnerability exceed the child's ability to cope and in the absence of coping mechanisms, underlying problems are more likely to become evident. For example, when toxic stress begins to surpass a developing child's limited coping skills, the child can become unable to regulate emotions and instead respond with problematic behaviors (Arvidson et al., 2011).

The diathesis–stress–coping model is greatly associated and interacts with an individual's level of resilience. *Resilience*, a personality trait correlated with positive affectivity, is the ability to adapt constructively when faced with stress and adversity. Thus, a highly resilient child may not experience the same level of distress to adverse situations and thus tend to require a less intense level of coping to adjust.

Protective factors that help children adjust are often parents, teachers, and other sources of support in the community (O'Connell, Boat, & Warner, 2009). These represent external coping mechanisms in the form of social support. As discussed above, the critical period when a child develops emotional control is an example of external support providing the coping *with* the child in stressful situations. Through these transactions the child begins to gain mastery over the intensity of her emotional responses. Later in the developmental period these positive influences can attenuate the effects of exposure to stress and vulnerability (Compas, Gruhn, & Bettis, 2017; Masten & Reed, 2002).

One of the most important roles for educators and early intervention providers is to identify the opportunities (Masten, 2014) that contribute to the child's ability to identify and apply coping mechanisms independently. A child's formation of coping ability is found within the interaction between situational risk and protective factors (Zolkoski & Bullock, 2012). In addition to establishing positive relationships, educators and early intervention providers can support the child's self-esteem, set clear expectations for behaviors that are reinforced, and ensure opportunities for engagement in play and other school and community activities. Such experiences move from novel to practiced and extrinsic to intrinsic. Coping becomes a metacognitive skill that over time becomes habit. Seeking and applying coping mechanisms when appropriate is a critical developmental achievement for children. The purpose or goal is for the child to feel proud of who she is and that she has some say in making life choices (internal locus of control), which promotes the feeling that she can accomplish goals she sets (self-efficacy) so as to be successful in managing feelings (effective coping) and behaviors (emotional regulation) at school (educational attainment and health status).

Educators and early intervention providers can also help to support (a) family protective factors such as family structure and cohesion, adequate housing, stable income, supportive parent–child interactions, and access to peer/social support, strong academic settings, and a stimulating environment as well as (b) community protective factors such as community connections and involvement, peer acceptance, supportive mentors, safe neighborhoods, access to quality schools, and access to quality health care (Child Welfare Information Gateway, 2014). Although this list is not exhaustive, any combination of these protective factors can help a child to cope more effectively when exposed to challenging or adverse situations (Masten, 2014; Murray, 2003). Educators and early intervention providers should expect that children require a variety of protective and supportive factors before typical and healthy patterns of developmental will be possible (Child Welfare Information Gateway, 2014; WHO, 2014).

Fortunately, even children with high levels of risk and exposure to stress can, and do, respond to prevention and early intervention (Center on the Developing Child, 2014). The challenge is to identify risks early, intervene strategically, and provide sustained multiyear efforts. For children with low resilience and a diathesis toward mental health problems, the loss of protective supports or the increase of stressors in the absence of adequate coping mechanisms likely increases the probability for onset or worsening of symptoms (Centers for Disease Control and Prevention [CDC], 2016; Perry & Conners-Burrow, 2016). Therefore, the effort to disrupt at-risk children from developing lifelong disabling conditions needs to include professionals prepared to select services that validly and comprehensively meet the family's needs.

Adverse Childhood Experiences

In the landmark CDC–Kaiser Permanente ACEs study, researchers identified environmental and interpersonal conditions that lead to problematic and lifelong health and mental health outcomes (Felitti et al., 1998). In this study, ACEs were defined as abuse (e.g., emotional, physical, sexual), household dysfunction (e.g., domestic violence, substance abuse, mental illness in the home, divorce, incarceration), and emotional and physical neglect (Felitti et al., 1998). ACEs were found to be common; almost two thirds of participants reported having had at least one ACE, and more than a fifth reported three or more ACEs during childhood. Recent data show that more than two thirds of children in the United States have reported having experienced a traumatic event by the age of 16 years (Substance Abuse and Mental Health Services Administration [SAMHSA], 2017) and that the majority of exposure occurs during early childhood (SAMHSA, 2011). Although ACEs occur in children ages 0 to 18 years, across all races, economic status, and geographical regions, the prevalence of ACEs is much higher for individuals with lower socioeconomic status (American Academy of Pediatrics, 2017). Children living in poverty tend to have the highest rates of exposure to ACEs and trauma (Bethell, Davis, Gombojav, Stumbo, & Powers, 2017).

Although trauma exposure is found among multiple ACEs, it is important to note that not all ACEs are considered to be traumatic (Jonson-Reid & Wideman, 2017). A traumatic event is defined as a frightening, dangerous, or violent event that poses a threat to a child's life or bodily integrity (National Child Traumatic Stress Network [NCTSN], 2018). Under the umbrella of trauma, witnessing a traumatic event that threatens the life or physical security of a loved one should also be considered, particularly for younger children who perceive the safety of their attachment figures as their own safety (NCTSN, 2018). Traumatic events can initiate strong emotions and physical reactions that can persist long after the event. Children may feel terror, fear, or physiological reactions after experiencing trauma. Less resilient children or children with less well-established coping mechanisms and who are exposed to trauma may experience distress and debilitating psychological outcomes (NCTSN, 2018).

A child's exposure to an adverse circumstance or traumatic stress may begin to have a detrimental effect on brain development, as would be predicted from the diathesis–stress model (Sameroff, Gutman, & Peck, 2003). Recent data show that exposure to two or three ACEs is a tipping point at which risk for unfavorable consequences increases (Mersky, Topitzes, & Reynolds, 2013). For some children, exposure to even one ACE can result in neurodevelopmental disruption (CDC, 2016). Children from birth to age 5 years are the most susceptible to the negative neurobiological consequences of distress that affect development and mental health status (Shonkoff, Garner, The Committee on Psychosocial Aspects of Child and Family Health, The Committee on Early Childhood, Adoption, and Dependent Care, & The Section on Developmental and Behavioral Pediatrics, 2012). In these young children, adverse experiences can result in permanent changes to the brain's neural functioning (Perry & Conners-Burrow, 2016).

Whereas having some exposure to stress is normal and is a needed element of proper psychological development when experienced in moderation and under supportive conditions, stress that is frequent and prolonged can become toxic. Toxic stress is known to wreak havoc on all systems of human functioning, ranging from emotional to physiological (Halfon, Wise, & Forrest, 2014), which lends a hand in explaining why impairment occurs across emotional, social, cognitive, behavioral, and physical domains. As noted, exposure to toxic stressors, in the absence of adequate protective factors, can lead to prolonged activation of the body's physiological stress-response system. The prolonged activation of the stress-response system has been found to lead to an overproduction of neural connections in the regions of the brain involved in fear, anxiety, and impulsive responses (CDC, 2016; De Bellis & Zisk, 2014; Franke, 2014). That is, under these conditions, the brain becomes overly responsive and can remain in a constant state of flight-or-fight. When the brain is stuck in survival mode, the overuse of these brain systems can result in flight-or-fight behaviors as the default/primary interaction style (Badenoch, 2008), with the result that children may be combative and ever-vigilant about potential future threats (Wolpow, Johnson, Hertel, & Kincaid, 2009).

Conversely, there is also research suggesting that in some children who experience toxic stress, the brain may develop in ways that lead to an under-active stress-response system, such as a numb, emotionally withdrawn behavior pattern (De Bellis & Zisk, 2014; National Institute of Child Health and Human Development, 2002). Furthermore, research on such children has also found fewer neural connections in brain regions responsible for planning, behavioral control, and reasoning (Bremner, 2006; Center on the Developing Child, 2014; Shonkoff et al., 2012). This deficit in neural connections may be observed when children withdraw and show low levels of engagement in creative play and social communication and interaction (American Academy of Pediatrics, 2017). Regardless of whether these toxic stress experiences lead to an overactive or underactive stress response, there is a significantly increased likelihood for debilitating physical and mental health outcomes (Ha & Granger, 2016).

Because of the significant impact that ACEs can have on the developing brain, coupled with the data showing children from low socioeconomic status and minority groups are likely to have higher rates of exposure to trauma and toxic stress, as well as the potential opportunity to mitigate risks via protective factors, it is important for educators and early intervention providers to take a close look at the children in their catchment area. To build early childhood learning environments that holistically promote child development, it is important to understand the needs of the broader child population, including the context where the child is living.

Disparities

In the early 1980s, Margaret M. Heckler convened the first group of experts to conduct a comprehensive study of the health status of minorities. Their research found significant health disparities between non-Hispanic Whites and racial and ethnic minorities in the United States (Heckler, 1984). In recent decades, the United States has made progress in improving access to health and mental health care and in recognizing how risk and protective factors relate to the development of psychopathology. However, ongoing economic, racial/ethnic, and other social and structural disparities in health and mental health access and outcomes are still evident. For example, economically disadvantaged populations experience differences in the overall burden of disease, injury, violence, or opportunities. These current health disparities have been attributed to the unequal distribution of social, political, economic, and environmental resources (CDC, 2018). Furthermore, health disparities have also been found to be related to the past and present imbalance of health care resources, especially for those with mental health disorders (CDC, 2018).

To better understand the context of disparities, it is important to understand the U.S. population and who is affected by these inequalities. Currently, the United States has a population of 328 million people (U.S. Census Bureau, 2019). On average, 60% of people received appropriate preventative services, 80% received appropriate acute care services, and 70% received management services for health-related concerns. Although all individuals should have equal access to high-quality care, or care at all, the data show that racial and ethnic minorities and people living in poverty face more barriers to receiving care (Agency for Healthcare Research and Quality [AHRQ], 2012). Because approximately 33% of the population identify as belonging to a racial or ethnic minority group (U.S. Census Bureau, 2018), this means a large portion of the U.S. population is experiencing barriers in obtaining appropriate health care. Those who are living in poverty are reported to have less access to and less provision of care than high-income individuals (AHRQ, 2012).

Overall, African Americans report the lowest rate of utilization of mental health services (Garland et al., 2005). Black, American Indian, Asian, and Hispanic people were found to have significantly lower quality of care than non-Hispanic Whites (AHRQ, 2012). In terms of mental health service use, non-Hispanic Whites had the highest rates, with Asian American/Pacific Islanders showing the lowest use (Garland et al., 2005).

Children's health and mental health service use show similar racial–ethnic disparities patterns. Children of Latin American descent and the uninsured have especially high rates of unmet need relative to other children (Kataoka, Zhang, & Wells, 2002). Compared with non-Hispanic White children, African American, Latino, and Pacific Islander children were found to have lower utilization of received individual, family, and group psychotherapy, medication management, assessment and evaluation, case management, residential treatment, and inpatient care (Popescu, Xu, Krivelyova, & Ettner, 2015). For children in contact with the child welfare system, compared with non-Hispanic Whites, African American children were less likely to receive mental health services (Gudiño, Martinez, & Lau, 2012). Though studies have drawn different conclusions regarding who is most disadvantaged, it is clear that minorities have disproportionately less access to services.

Often the disparities do not exist in isolation but are a part of a complex web of problems associated with inequality (Lopez & Gadsden, 2016). For example, for children living in poverty, their families also tend to experience inadequate and unhealthy housing, lower educational attainment, lack of equal opportunity in employment, and higher rates of mental health symptoms (Yoshikawa, Aber, & Beardslee, 2012). Children living in stressful environments require comprehensive and coordinated approaches that acknowledge the wide range of factors influencing child development. For those marginalized, these types of services tend to be delivered through the educational system rather than health care providers (Zeleke, Hughes, Tiberi, & Drozda, 2017). Efforts early in the life cycle offer the best opportunity to strengthen resilience, so the role of educators and early education experiences in combination with early intervention providers is critical for these young children (Center on the Developing Child, 2014).

EARLY CHILDHOOD SUPPORTS

There is a general consensus that early childhood has sensitive periods during which prevention efforts, early detection, and intervention most effectively promote child development, health, mental health, and wellness (Berger, 2011; Diamond, 2013). During the first few years of a child's life, access to prenatal and infant nutrition, education on how parenting practices are related to child development, and education or support for parents in coping with the challenges of infant and childhood care can help to reduce the prevalence of mental health problems in children and even adolescents (Mistry, Brown, White, Chow, & Gillen-O'Neel, 2015). Of primary importance is the interaction between caregivers and young children because this interaction serves as a source of reference for the child's subsequent development. A positive bond (e.g., patterns of healthy attachment and interaction) will be the foundation for developing feelings of safety and a source of comfort as the child learns. Parenting practices influence the child's conceptualization of the nature of relationships and belief in their abilities to accomplish goals (i.e., self-efficacy) as well as support the independence needed for subsequent cognitive development (Bronfenbrenner, 1974).

For children and families living in stressful situations, early identification and intervention in the home are associated with positive outcomes (Karoly, Kilburn, & Cannon, 2005). The recommended approach for service providers is to begin by forming a collaborative relationship with parents and caregivers. Of course, the goal of the alliance is to identify and determine how to address the child's needs, but the manner in which that is accomplished needs to be relationship focused; a supportive professional–parent consultative relationship serves as guide for supportive parent–child relationships (Kaufmann, Perry, Hepburn, & Duran, 2012). The focus on the relationship serves as a source of resilience for the parents and as a model for how to foster resilience in the child. As noted previously, for children exposed to adversity, having a predictable, child-centered daily routine/schedule is essential as it helps reduce anxiety and provides the groundwork for building trust and a sense of safety upon which other areas of development rely (Perry & Conners-Burrow, 2016). This is an early priority in the consultative relationship because parents may underappreciate how instability contributes to the risk for child mental health challenges.

Mental Health Care

Some families may need direct intervention to promote positive interactions. Parent–child interaction therapy is an evidence-based treatment that provides parents and/or caregivers with step-by-step, live coached sessions to change negative parent/caregiver and child interaction patterns (NCTSN, 2018). The Incredible Years, another evidence-based treatment, provides training to parents and/or caregivers on skills such as positive discipline, promoting academic success, and healthy interaction styles with their child (Webster-Stratton, Rinaldi, & Reid, 2011). Parent management training is an evidence-based treatment that was designed to help parents develop effective child behavior management skills such as effectively setting limits, enforcing consequences, reinforcing positive behaviors, and enhancing positive relationships at home (National Alliance on Mental Illness, 2007). Child–parent psychotherapy (Lieberman, Van Horn, & Ghosh Ippen, 2005; NCTSN, 2012) focuses on the way that trauma has affected the parent–child relationship and supports safety, child–caregiver relationship, and emotional regulation, all while having a goal of returning the child to a normal developmental trajectory. Families may also benefit from family-based therapy and/or individual therapy for parents addressing their mental health needs or specific challenges.

Early Childhood Education

Early childhood education is designed to support the development of the whole child. When early childhood programs provide safe environments, supportive relationships, an environment enriched with learning spaces, and the ability to build and grow positive social relationships, children are able to develop skills that will support them throughout childhood and into adulthood (American Psychological Association, Working Group for Addressing Racial and Ethnic Disparities in Youth Mental Health, 2017). Early childhood programs can also serve as a venue that coordinates the service needs of young children through early intervention services. If children are already connected to home or community services, educational services may supplement and/or coordinate with community providers. However, as with mental health care services, access and quality of early education programs vary.

The latest data from the National Center for Education Statistics (2019) show 86% of 5-year-olds, 68% of 4-year-olds, and 40% of 3-year-olds were enrolled in preschool programs in 2017, which is consistent with trends reported in 2000 (National Center for Education Statistics, 2019). These data also show that children from families that reported higher levels of education were accessing preschool more often than were those with low levels. Early Head Start and Head Start are well known federally funded programs that are available to children from low-income families and children with special needs. The vast majority of children qualifying for these programs live in families below the federal poverty level and are of minority status (Child Trends, 2015). It is estimated that 50% of children who qualify for Early Head Start and Head Start do not have services because of variations in state funding (Child Trends, 2015). In summary, not all children who could benefit from preschool are receiving it.

One perhaps obvious observation is that high-quality preschool programming has been shown to have better outcomes for children than low-quality programs (Cascio, 2017). However, once researchers consider who is attending preschool and who is not, a more mixed picture emerges. In general, children who attend preschool do much better (i.e., better prepared for school, less likely to be identified as having special needs or to be held back in elementary school) than do children who do not attend preschool (Meloy, Gardner, & Darling-Hammond, 2019). In general, programming that is tailored to meet the needs of specific populations is desirable for at-risk populations. Yet gains for specific groups of preschool children are more mixed especially when children are selected to attend preschool that is targeted to their at-risk status (Cascio, 2017). Although there are many potential reasons for this difference—lowered teacher expectations for at-risk students, less time to spend on universal content when targeted issues take priority—the variation in progress may simply reflect that students are receiving different experiences around universal content. It is well documented that preschool programming varies widely by state, teaching credentials, and funding support (Allen & Kelly, 2015). Therefore, before we turn to how trauma-informed teaching can improve the preschool experience for children in stressful environments, it is important to be clear that preschool programming should be of high quality and should consider the needs of at-risk groups in terms of how educational materials are delivered without needlessly narrowing the implementation of universal programming aimed at promoting development of the whole child.

The Trauma-Informed Lens

Preschool, preprimary school, early childhood education, and early intervention settings can offer experiences that promote healthy development by using a trauma-informed lens (Bartlett, Smith, & Bringewatt, 2017). Indeed, high-quality preschool education relies on many of the same approaches as trauma-informed teaching by prioritizing relationships, focusing on the needs of the whole child, and engaging family as part of the team of supports. Where trauma-informed practices differ from typical developmentally appropriate education is in the manner and approach to creating a safe environment. Trauma-informed teaching does not assume the child enters with feelings of safety but instead seeks to understand and identify what makes the child feel safe as well as the triggers that would make the child view that experience as unsafe, which may be observed in freeze, flight, or fight actions (Wright & Ryan, 2014). Once an approach onto safety is established, then there is (often simultaneously) an emphasis on relationship development so that the educators can better serve as a source of support (protective factor), which is followed by skill development. The combination of skills in trauma-informed teaching is what helps children exposed to ACEs, toxic stress, and other early risks to develop in a healthy manner (Perry & Conners-Burrow, 2016). For children with ACEs and trauma exposure, starting with skill development can be a recipe for failure. They are at high risk for problematic behaviors, which tend to result in punishment (Koomar, 2009) and a cycle of retraumatization that also impairs relationship development with the teacher (see Figure 14.1).

FIGURE 14.1. The Cycle of Retraumatization

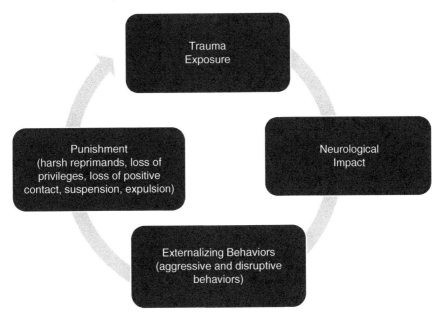

Adapted from *Unlocking the Door to Learning: Trauma-Informed Classrooms and Transformational Schools* (p. 5), by M. McInerney and A. McKlindon, 2015, Education Law Center. Retrieved from Education Law Center of Pennsylvania website: https://www.elc-pa.org/resource/unlocking-the-door-to-learning-trauma-informed-classrooms-and-transformational-schools.

Educators are in a unique position because they can serve as a protective influence for young children. Educators can increase resilience (Gorey, 2001), which will support child mental health and wellness. Yet, many educators indicate that they are unprepared to address the behaviors of children exposed to trauma (Maring & Koblinsky, 2013). The demands seem only to increase, and educators are overwhelmed. The ACEs experience itself can be unfamiliar, and it can be difficult to balance the demands of delivering universal preschool with the additional needs of a child who has experienced ACEs. Indeed, the conceptualization and implementation of intervention services is complicated because children's needs are unique. The younger the child, the less skilled she will be in communicating needs. However, there are some basic recommendations for engaging children living in stressful environments. This list is adapted in part from recommendations by the National Association for the Education of Young Children (NAEYC; Statman-Weil, 2015) for creating trauma-sensitive classrooms for young children:

- Focus on creating feelings of safety.
  - Identify what helps each child feel safe.
  - Identify and avoid triggers (if possible) that decrease feelings of safety.
  - Accept that threats may be real or perceived.

- Build relationships.
  - Respond with empathy and support when flight-or-fight behaviors take over.
  - Respond with understanding when children show fear and anxiety.
- Day-to-day interactions matter most.
  - Use consistent routines.
  - Give advance warning when there are going to be disruptions to a routine.
  - Give extra time to adjust to disruptions.
  - Prepare in advance for events that can be too stimulating.
  - Give developmentally appropriate choices.
  - Teach mindfulness and other self-calming strategies.
  - Model positive adjustment.

Trauma Practices in the Larger Educational Context

In light of the dissimilarity of professional training required for preschool directors and other educator leaders developing preschool programs, it is important to consider where trauma-informed approaches are related to other priorities in preschool education. Preschool program development should consider the following approaches for supporting children from stressful environments:

- Ensure educators have a working knowledge of the national standards (Statman-Weil, 2015) for high-quality universal preschool. NAEYC provides recommendations specifically for educators addressing trauma in the preschool classroom.

- Consider the use of universal social–emotional learning programs, such as The Second Step Curriculum. Not only do the lessons help build the foundational preskills for social, emotional, and behavioral competence, but randomized controlled studies have also shown the lessons to be effective for children exposed to high levels of neighborhood adversity, a common contributor to child stress (Committee for Children, 2011). Furthermore, the competencies learned in social–emotional learning programs have been linked with the development of subsequent protective factors (e.g., effective problem solving, optimism, impulse control, empathy) associated with childhood resiliency (Brooks & Goldstein, 2001; Masten & Reed, 2002).

- Stay attuned to the diversity in the classroom. Educational experiences should be inclusive and welcoming to the children and their families (Child Trends, 2015), including the multiply marginalized (e.g., more than one risk category as well as cultural and linguistical diversity, which can contribute to child stress and increased risk). All items used routinely in the classroom (e.g., toys, pictures, books, snacks) can and should reflect the diversity of the children coming to the preschool. Because many educators may be of a different ethnicity or socioeconomic status than the students (Oades-Sese, Kitzie, & Rubic, 2013), seeking input from parents is helpful. Simply inviting parents to label items in a variety of languages can begin the process of working together as a team.

- Consider how your program can help to address equity and social justice issues actively (e.g., access to health and mental health services). Identify opportunities to coordinate community services or to use community locations to reach parents and families together.

SUPPORT FOR SERVICE PROVIDERS

The extent to which educators and service providers can deliver trauma-informed practices depends in large part on the moment-to-moment, day-to-day interactions with children and families (Metz, Blase, & Bowie, 2007). Yet, working with children exposed to ACEs and other risks can also take a toll on adults. Just as we see in the responses of other helping professionals, educators and service providers experience compassion satisfaction (e.g., positive reactions to helping) as well as burnout (e.g., work-related stress and exhaustion) and compassion fatigue (e.g., preoccupation with the suffering of the children that results in your own distress). As such, it is important to watch for our own impatience, a shutting down of our empathy, blaming children for their emotional/social/cognitive/behavioral problems, using anger or sarcasm when trauma symptoms emerge, and using punishment, control, and compliance to address problem behaviors (Currier et al., 2013; Figley, 1995; Stamm, 1995). When you, or a coworker, notice professionals in distress, encourage them to take a break. Reframe (compassion) fatigue as simply the cost of caring, rather than as a sign of weakness or incompetence. Distressed adults only compound the challenges for distressed children, so make efforts to support each other and take seriously the need for self-care (Thomas & Otis, 2010). Consider seeking help from a mental health professional when burnout begins to interfere with your (personal or professional) functioning.

CONCLUSION

Trauma exposure and the experience of ACEs are so pervasive that they have been called a public health epidemic (Baker, Brown, Wilcox, Overstreet, & Arora, 2015). In response, there has been a call for initiatives aimed at helping institutions and individuals serving children with histories of adversity to adopt a trauma-informed practices approach. Yet education and training for educator and community service providers have not kept up with the need (Harris & Fallot, 2001). Furthermore, although the home, the community, and early intervention offer the opportunity to respond to the mental health needs of children (National Research Council and Institute of Medicine, 2009), access to evidence-based interventions (Alegría et al., 2015) and high-quality preschool programming (Cascio, 2017) remains a challenge, particularly in low-income communities and among children from diverse backgrounds.

It is clear that the health and mental health communities need to lead these efforts. When communities, families, and schools participate in evidence-based treatments to support the child comprehensively, the rate for resilience, healing, and positive psychological outcomes increases (Knapp, Ammen, Arstein-Kerslake, Poulsen, & Mastergeorge, 2007). As such, there needs to be a clear agenda that seeks to deliver mental health services where children live, play, and grow (Society for Research in Child Development, 2009; Tolan & Dodge, 2005). Implementation solutions for children and families require (a) shorter term consultative support (Albers, Mildon, Lyon, & Shlonsky, 2017) as well as (b) sustained multiyear multidisciplinary teams support to lessen the effects of adversity and reduce the prevalence of mental health disorders across the life span (Barnett, 1995; Campbell, Ramey, Pungello, Sparling, & Miller-Johnson, 2002; Center on the Developing Child, 2007; Parry, 1992).

REFERENCES

Agency for Healthcare Research and Quality. (2012). *National Healthcare Disparities Report*. Rockville, MD: U.S. Department of Health and Human Services.

Albers, B., Mildon, R., Lyon, A. R., & Shlonsky, A. (2017). Implementation frameworks in child, youth and family services—Results from a scoping review. *Children and Youth Services Review, 81*, 101–116. http://dx.doi.org/10.1016/j.childyouth.2017.07.003

Alegría, M., Green, J. G., McLaughlin, K. A., & Loder, S. (2015). *Disparities in child and adolescent mental health and mental health services*. New York, NY: William T. Grant Foundation.

Allen, L., & Kelly, B. B. (Eds.). (2015). *Transforming the workforce for children birth through age 8: A unifying foundation*. Washington, DC: The National Academies Press. http://dx.doi.org/10.17226/19401

American Academy of Pediatrics. (2017). *Adverse childhood experiences and the lifelong consequences of trauma*. Retrieved from https://www.aap.org/en-us/Documents/ttb_aces_consequences.pdf

American Psychological Association, Working Group for Addressing Racial and Ethnic Disparities in Youth Mental Health. (2017). *Addressing the mental health needs of racial and ethnic minority youth: A guide for practitioners*. Retrieved from http://www.apa.org/pi/families/resources/mental-health-needs.pdf

Arvidson, J., Kinniburgh, K., Howard, K., Spinazzola, J., Strothers, H., Evans, M., . . . Blaustein, M. E. (2011). Treatment of complex trauma in young children: Developmental and cultural considerations in application of the ARC intervention model. *Journal of Child & Adolescent Trauma, 4*, 34–51. http://dx.doi.org/10.1080/19361521.2011.545046

Badenoch, B. (2008). *Being a brain-wise therapist: A practical guide to interpersonal neurobiology*. New York, NY: Norton.

Baker, C. N., Brown, S. M., Wilcox, P. D., Overstreet, S., & Arora, P. (2015). Development and psychometric evaluation of the Attitudes Related to Trauma-Informed Care (ARTIC) Scale. *School Mental Health, 8*, 61–76. http://dx.doi.org/10.1007/s12310-015-9161-0

Barnett, W. S. (1995). Long-term effects of early childhood programs on cognitive and school outcomes. *The Future of Children, 5*, 25–50. http://dx.doi.org/10.2307/1602366

Bartlett, J. D., Smith, S., & Bringewatt, E. (2017). *Helping young children who have experienced trauma: Policies and strategies for early care and education.* Retrieved from https://www.childtrends.org/wp-content/uploads/2017/04/2017-19ECETrauma.pdf

Berger, A. (2011). *Self-regulation: Brain, cognition and development.* Washington, DC: American Psychological Association. http://dx.doi.org/10.1037/12327-000

Bethell, C. D., Davis, M. B., Gombojav, N., Stumbo, S., & Powers, K. (2017). *A national and across state profile on adverse childhood experiences among children and possibilities to heal and thrive.* Retrieved from https://www.cahmi.org/wp-content/uploads/2018/05/aces_brief_final.pdf

Bremner, J. D. (2006). Traumatic stress: Effects on the brain. *Dialogues in Clinical Neuroscience, 8*, 445–461.

Bronfenbrenner, U. (1974). Is early intervention effective? *Day Care and Early Education, 2*, 14–18. http://dx.doi.org/10.1007/BF02353057

Brooks, R., & Goldstein, S. (2001). *Raising resilient children: Fostering strength, hope, and optimism in your child.* New York, NY: Contemporary Books.

Campbell, F. A., Ramey, C. T., Pungello, E., Sparling, J., & Miller-Johnson, S. (2002). Early childhood education: Young adult outcomes from the Abecedarian project. *Applied Developmental Science, 6*, 42–57. http://dx.doi.org/10.1207/S1532480XADS0601_05

Cascio, E. U. (2017). *Does universal preschool hit the target? Program access and preschool impacts* (NBER Working Paper No. 23215). Cambridge, MA: National Bureau of Economic Research. http://dx.doi.org/10.3386/w23215

Center on the Developing Child. (2014). *Key concepts: Toxic stress.* Retrieved from http://developingchild.harvard.edu/key_concepts/toxic_stress_response

Center on the Developing Child. (2007). *Early childhood program effectiveness.* Retrieved from https://developingchild.harvard.edu/resources/inbrief-early-childhood-program-effectiveness

Centers for Disease Control and Prevention (CDC). (2016). *Adverse childhood experiences (ACEs).* Retrieved from https://www.cdc.gov/violenceprevention/acestudy/index.html

Centers for Disease Control and Prevention (CDC). (2018). *Adolescent and school health.* Retrieved from http://www.cdc.gov/healthyyouth/disparities/index.htm

Child Trends. (2015). *Head Start.* Retrieved from https://www.childtrends.org/?indicators=head-start

Child Welfare Information Gateway. (2014). *Protective factor approaches in child welfare.* Retrieved from https://www.childwelfare.gov/pubPDFs/protective_factors.pdf

Committee for Children. (2011). *Second Step: Skills for social and academic successes.* Seattle, WA: Author.

Compas, B. E., Gruhn, M., & Bettis, A. H. (2017). Risk and resilience in child and adolescent psychopathology. In T. P. Beauchaine & S. P. Hinshaw (Eds.), *Child and adolescent psychopathology* (3rd ed., pp. 113–143). New York, NY: Wiley.

Currier, J. M., Holland, J. M., Rozalski, V., Thompson, K. L., Rojas-Flores, L., & Herrera, S. (2013). Teaching in violent communities: The contribution of meaning made of stress on psychiatric distress and burnout. *International Journal of Stress Management, 20*, 254–277. http://dx.doi.org/10.1037/a0033985

De Bellis, M. D., & Zisk, A. (2014). The biological effects of childhood trauma. *Child and Adolescent Psychiatric Clinics of North America, 23*, 185–222. http://dx.doi.org/10.1016/j.chc.2014.01.002

Diamond, A. (2013). Executive functions. *Annual Review of Psychology, 64*, 135–168. http://dx.doi.org/10.1146/annurev-psych-113011-143750

Felitti, V. J., Anda, R. F., Nordenberg, D., Williamson, D. F., Spitz, A. M., Edwards, V., . . . Marks, J. S. (1998). Relationship of childhood abuse and household dysfunction to many of the leading causes of death in adults. The Adverse Childhood Experiences (ACE) Study. *American Journal of Preventive Medicine, 14,* 245–258. http://dx.doi.org/10.1016/S0749-3797(98)00017-8

Figley, C. R. (Ed.). (1995). *Compassion fatigue: Coping with secondary traumatic stress disorder in those who treat the traumatized.* New York, NY: Brunner/Mazel.

Franke, H. A. (2014). Toxic stress: Effects, prevention, and treatment. *Children, 1,* 390–402. http://dx.doi.org/10.3390/children1030390

Garland, A. F., Lau, A. S., Yeh, M., McCabe, K. M., Hough, R. L., & Landsverk, J. A. (2005). Racial and ethnic differences in utilization of mental health services among high-risk youths. *The American Journal of Psychiatry, 162,* 1336–1343. http://dx.doi.org/10.1176/appi.ajp.162.7.1336

Gorey, K. M. (2001). Early childhood education: A meta-analytic affirmation of the short and long-term benefits of educational opportunity. *School Psychology Quarterly, 16,* 9–30. http://dx.doi.org/10.1521/scpq.16.1.9.19163

Gudiño, O. G., Martinez, J. I., & Lau, A. S. (2012). Mental health service use by youths in contact with child welfare: Racial disparities by problem type. *Psychiatric Services, 63,* 1004–1010. http://dx.doi.org/10.1176/appi.ps.201100427

Ha, T., & Granger, D. A. (2016). Family relations, stress, and vulnerability: Biobehavioral implications for prevention and practice. *Family Relations: An Interdisciplinary Journal of Applied Family Science, 65,* 9–23. http://dx.doi.org/10.1111/fare.12173

Halfon, N., Wise, P. H., & Forrest, C. B. (2014). The changing nature of children's health development: New challenges require major policy solutions. *Health Affairs, 33,* 2116–2124. http://dx.doi.org/10.1377/hlthaff.2014.0944

Harris, M., & Fallot, R. D. (Eds.). (2001). *New directions for mental health services. Using trauma theory to design service systems.* San Francisco, CA: Jossey-Bass.

Heckler, M. M. (1984). *Report of the Secretary's Task Force Report on Black and Minority Health.* Washington, DC: U.S. Department of Health and Human Services.

Ingram, R. E., & Luxton, D. D. (2005). Vulnerability stress models. In B. L. Hankin & J. R. Z. Abela (Eds.), *Development of psychopathology: A vulnerability-stress perspective* (pp. 32–46). Thousand Oaks, CA: Sage. http://dx.doi.org/10.4135/9781452231655.n2

Jonson-Reid, M., & Wideman, E. (2017). Trauma and very young children. *Child and Adolescent Psychiatric Clinics of North America, 26,* 477–490. http://dx.doi.org/10.1016/j.chc.2017.02.004

Karoly, L. A., Kilburn, M. R., & Cannon, J. S. (2005). *Early childhood interventions: Proven results, future promises.* Santa Monica, CA: RAND Corporation. http://dx.doi.org/10.7249/MG341

Kataoka, S. H., Zhang, L., & Wells, K. B. (2002). Unmet need for mental health care among U.S. children: Variation by ethnicity and insurance status. *The American Journal of Psychiatry, 159,* 1548–1555. http://dx.doi.org/10.1176/appi.ajp.159.9.1548

Kaufmann, R. K., Perry, D. F., Hepburn, K., & Duran, F. (2012). Assessing fidelity for early childhood mental health consultation: Lessons from the field and next steps. *Infant Mental Health Journal, 33,* 274–282. http://dx.doi.org/10.1002/imhj.21337

Knapp, P. K., Ammen, S., Arstein-Kerslake, C., Poulsen, M. K., & Mastergeorge, A. (2007). Feasibility of expanding services for very young children in the public mental health setting. *Journal of the American Academy of Child & Adolescent Psychiatry, 46,* 152–161. http://dx.doi.org/10.1097/01.chi.0000246058.68544.35

Koomar, J. A. (2009). Trauma- and attachment-informed sensory integration assessment and intervention. *Sensory Integration Special Interest Section Quarterly, 32*(4), 1–4.

Lieberman, A. F., Van Horn, P., & Ghosh Ippen, C. (2005). Toward evidence-based treatment: Child-Parent Psychotherapy with preschoolers exposed to marital violence. *Journal of the American Academy of Child and Adolescent Psychiatry, 44,* 1241–1248.

Lopez, N., & Gadsden, V. L. (2016, December 5). *Health inequities, social determinants, and intersectionality* [Discussion paper]. Retrieved from National Academy of Medicine website: https://nam.edu/wp-content/uploads/2016/12/Health-Inequities-Social-Determinants-and-Intersectionality.pdf

Maring, E. F., & Koblinsky, S. A. (2013). Teachers' challenges, strategies, and support needs in schools affected by community violence: A qualitative study. *The Journal of School Health, 83*, 379–388. http://dx.doi.org/10.1111/josh.12041

Masten, A. S. (2014). *Ordinary magic: Resilience in development.* New York, NY: Guilford Press.

Masten, A. S., & Reed, M. G. J. (2002). Resilience in development. In C. R. Snyder & S. J. Lopez (Eds.), *Handbook of positive psychology* (pp. 74–88). New York, NY: Oxford University Press.

McInerney, M., & McKlindon, A. (2015). *Unlocking the door to learning: Trauma-informed classrooms and transformational schools.* Retrieved from Education Law Center of Pennsylvania website: https://www.elc-pa.org/resource/unlocking-the-door-to-learning-trauma-informed-classrooms-and-transformational-schools

Meloy, B., Gardner, M., & Darling-Hammond, L. (2019). *Untangling the evidence on preschool effectiveness: Insights for policymakers.* Palo Alto, CA: Learning Policy Institute.

Mersky, J. P., Topitzes, J., & Reynolds, A. J. (2013). Impacts of adverse childhood experiences on health, mental health, and substance use in early adulthood: A cohort study of an urban, minority sample in the U.S. *Child Abuse & Neglect, 37*, 917–925. http://dx.doi.org/10.1016/j.chiabu.2013.07.011

Metz, A. J., Blase, K., & Bowie, L. (2007). Implementing evidence-based practices: Six "drivers" of success. *Child trends: Research-to-results brief.* Washington, DC: The Atlantic Philanthropies.

Mistry, R. S., Brown, C. S., White, E. S., Chow, K. A., & Gillen-O'Neel, C. (2015). Elementary school children's reasoning about social class: A mixed-methods study. *Child Development, 86*, 1653–1671. http://dx.doi.org/10.1111/cdev.12407

Murray, C. (2003). Risk factors, protective factors, vulnerability, and resilience: A framework for understanding and supporting the adult transitions of youth with high-incidence disabilities. *Remedial and Special Education, 24*, 16–26. http://dx.doi.org/10.1177/074193250302400102

National Alliance on Mental Illness. (2007). *Choosing the right treatment: What families need to know about evidence-based practices.* Arlington, VA: Author.

National Center for Education Statistics. (2019). *The condition of education at a glance: Preschool and kindergarten enrollment.* Retrieved from https://nces.ed.gov/programs/coe/indicator_cfa.asp

National Child Traumatic Stress Network. (2012). *CPP: Child–Parent Psychotherapy.* Retrieved from https://www.nctsn.org/sites/default/files/interventions/cpp_fact_sheet.pdf

National Child Traumatic Stress Network. (2018). *Interventions.* Retrieved from https://www.nctsn.org/what-is-child-trauma/trauma-types/early-childhood-trauma/interventions

National Institute of Child Health and Human Development. (2002). *Stress system malfunction could lead to serious, life threatening disease.* Retrieved from https://www.nichd.nih.gov/newsroom/releases/stress

National Research Council and Institute of Medicine. (2009). *Preventing mental, emotional, and behavioral disorders among young people: Progress and possibilities.* Washington, DC: National Academies Press.

Oades-Sese, G., Kitzie, M., & Rubic, W.-L. (2013). Paving the way for cosmopolitan resilient schools: Promoting resilience and social justice in urban, suburban, and rural schools. In D. Shriberg, S. Y. Song, A. H. Miranda, & K. M. Radliff (Eds.), *School psychology and social justice: Conceptual foundations and tools for practice* (pp. 118–136). New York, NY: Routledge/Taylor & Francis Group.

O'Connell, M. E., Boat, T., & Warner, K. (2009). *Preventing mental, emotional, and behavioral disorders among young people: Progress and possibilities* (pp. 157–186). Washington, DC: National Academics Press.

Parry, T. S. (1992). The effectiveness of early intervention: A critical review. *Journal of Paediatrics and Child Health, 28*, 343–346. http://dx.doi.org/10.1111/j.1440-1754. 1992.tb02688.x

Perry, D. F., & Conners-Burrow, N. (2016). Addressing early adversity through mental health consultation in early childhood settings. *Family Relations: An Interdisciplinary Journal of Applied Family Science, 65*, 24–36. http://dx.doi.org/10.1111/fare.12172

Popescu, I., Xu, H., Krivelyova, A., & Ettner, S. L. (2015). Disparities in receipt of specialty services among children with mental health need enrolled in the CMHI. *Psychiatric Services, 66*, 242–248. http://dx.doi.org/10.1176/appi.ps.201300055

Sameroff, A., Gutman, L. M., & Peck, S. C. (2003). Adaptation among youth facing multiple risks: Prospective research findings. In S. S. Luthar (Ed.), *Resilience and vulnerability: Adaptation in the context of childhood adversities* (pp. 364–391). New York, NY: Cambridge University Press. http://dx.doi.org/10.1017/CBO9780511615788.017

Shonkoff, J. P., Garner, A. S., The Committee on Psychosocial Aspects of Child and Family Health, The Committee on Early Childhood, Adoption, and Dependent Care, & The Section on Developmental and Behavioral Pediatrics. (2012). The lifelong effects of early childhood adversity and toxic stress. *Pediatrics, 129*, e232–e246. http://dx.doi.org/10.1542/peds.2011-2663

Society for Research in Child Development. (2009). *Report of Healthy Development: A Summit on Young Children's Mental Health.* Washington, DC: Author. Retrieved from https://www.apa.org/pi/families/summit-report.pdf

Stamm, B. H. (Ed.). (1995). *Secondary traumatic stress: Self-care issues for clinicians, researchers, and educators.* Lutherville, MD: Sidran Press.

Statman-Weil, K. (2015). Creating trauma-sensitive classrooms. *Young Children, 70*, 72–79. Retrieved from https://www.naeyc.org/resources/pubs/yc/may2015/trauma-sensitive-classrooms

Substance Abuse and Mental Health Services Administration. (2011). *Helping children and youth who have experienced traumatic events: National children's mental health awareness day.* Retrieved from https://files.eric.ed.gov/fulltext/ED525061.pdf

Substance Abuse and Mental Health Services Administration. (2017). *Understanding child trauma.* Retrieved from https://www.samhsa.gov/child-trauma/understanding-child-trauma

Thomas, J. T., & Otis, M. D. (2010). Intrapsychic correlates of professional quality of life: Mindfulness, empathy, and emotional separation. *Journal of the Society for Social Work and Research, 1*, 83–98. http://dx.doi.org/10.5243/jsswr.2010.7

Tolan, P. H., & Dodge, K. A. (2005). Children's mental health as a primary care and concern: A system for comprehensive support and service. *American Psychologist, 60*, 601–614. http://dx.doi.org/10.1037/0003-066X.60.6.601

U.S. Census Bureau. (2018). *QuickFacts—United States.* Washington, DC: U.S. Government Printing Office. Retrieved from https://www.census.gov/quickfacts/fact/table/US/PST045218

U.S. Census Bureau. (2019). *U.S. and world population clock.* Washington, DC: U.S. Government Printing Office. Retrieved from https://www.census.gov/popclock

Webster-Stratton, C., Rinaldi, J., & Reid, J. M. (2011). Long-term outcomes of Incredible Years parenting program: Predictors of adolescent adjustment. *Child and Adolescent Mental Health, 16*, 38–46. http://dx.doi.org/10.1111/j.1475-3588.2010.00576.x

Wolpow, R., Johnson, M., Hertel, R., & Kincaid, S. (2009). *The heart of learning and teaching: compassion, resiliency, and academic success.* Olympia, WA: Washington State Office of Superintendent of Public Instruction Compassionate Schools.

World Health Organization. (2014). *Social determinants of mental health.* Retrieved from https://apps.who.int/iris/bitstream/handle/10665/112828/9789241506809_eng. pdf;jsessionid=1B75F737CB78000526D5A13F54A8F5AF?sequence=1

Wright, T., & Ryan, S. K. (2014). Too scared to learn: Teaching young children who have experienced trauma. *Young Children, 69*, 88–93.

Yoshikawa, H., Aber, J. L., & Beardslee, W. R. (2012). The effects of poverty on the mental, emotional, and behavioral health of children and youth: Implications for prevention. *American Psychologist, 67*, 272–284. http://dx.doi.org/10.1037/a0028015

Zeleke, W., Hughes, T. L., Tiberi, A. E., & Drozda, N. (2017). Healthcare and educational services used by children with autism spectrum disorders in poverty. *Perspectives on Early Childhood Psychology and Education, 2*, 31–60.

Zolkoski, S. M., & Bullock, L. M. (2012). Resilience in children and youth: A review. *Children and Youth Services Review, 34*, 2295–2303. http://dx.doi.org/10.1016/j.childyouth.2012.08.009

V

ADVOCACY FOR EARLY EDUCATION

15

National Policies and Laws Affecting Children's Health and Education

Tara C. Raines, Celeste M. Malone, L. Morgan Beidleman, and Noelita Bowman

Policy directly influences the experience of childhood and is often responsible for guiding perceptions of the role children play or should play in our society. For example, the formation of the National Child Labor Committee in 1904 was instrumental in the passage of the Keating-Owen Child Labor Act 12 years later (1916; U.S. Department of Health and Human Services [DHHS], 2020). This Act, although later ruled unconstitutional by the U.S. Supreme Court (see *Hammer v. Dagenhart*, 1918), set the standards for the treatment of children in the workforce and resulted in the inspection of hundreds of factories (U.S. DHHS, 2020). It also began the legal progression toward the first child labor and compulsory schooling laws. Thus, the stage was set to establish children as a vulnerable population warranting protection from abuse, neglect, and exploitation (U.S. DHHS, 2020).

Since these early attempts to provide protection to children, several policies and legislation have been passed that influence the daily well-being of children. However, it was only 30 years ago that the global community convened to resolve that children have certain inalienable rights (Human Rights Watch, 2014). This suggests that the practice of developing and defining policy to promote a positive childhood experience is ongoing work. This chapter reviews policies and legislative decisions (i.e., laws) that are tied to education and health services for children along the developmental spectrum, with an emphasis on early childhood. We also offer recommendations for advocacy to support children who are affected by the social and political climate generated by these

http://dx.doi.org/10.1037/0000197-016
Healthy Development in Young Children: Evidence-Based Interventions for Early Education,
V. C. Alfonso and G. J. DuPaul (Editors)

policies. Ultimately, it is through advocacy work that these policies can be enforced and/or challenged to promote best practice in supporting childhood well-being.

EDUCATION POLICIES AND LEGISLATION

Since the emergence of compulsory schooling laws in the 1850s, education has become central in the childhood experience (Katz, 1976). Schools are, for the most part, the common place through which all U.S. children pass. As such, the policies made regarding the content of public education, as well as who can access this education and how educational services are delivered, tend to have the most robust impact on the childhood experience.

Because the U.S. Constitution does not specifically refer to education as a duty of the federal government, pursuant to the Tenth Amendment, education has been deemed to be a function of the states. This Amendment states that, "the powers not delegated to the United States by the Constitution, nor prohibited by it to the States, are reserved to the States respectively, or to the people" (U.S. Const. amend. X). Therefore, state governments have assumed the duty to educate, the power to tax citizens to finance that education, and the power to compel school attendance. In addition to the Tenth Amendment, the Fourteenth Amendment, specifically the Equal Protection Clause and the Due Process Clause, have been applied to education (Yell, Rogers, & Rogers, 1998); states may not make a free public education available to some children and not to others.

Although, on the basis of the Equal Protection Clause of the Fourteenth Amendment, all students are entitled to an education, there have been incidents in which schools have attempted to restrict students' access to education on the basis of race (e.g., *Brown v. Board of Education of Topeka*; Brown, 1954) or ability status (e.g., *Pennsylvania Ass'n for Retarded Children v. Pennsylvania*; PARC, 1972). In each case, the courts have held that states must provide equal educational opportunity to all citizens within its jurisdiction and cannot restrict an individual's access to education. To further ensure equitable access to education, the federal government has enacted statutes (e.g., the *Elementary and Secondary Education Act* [ESEA]; the *Individuals With Disabilities Education Improvement Act* [IDEIA]; see Ralabate & Foley, 2003); however, these statutes have their roots in right to education case law.

Right to Education Case Law

The decision of the U.S. Supreme Court in *Brown* is arguably the most significant and influential case regarding children's access to education. It provided the legal precedent for subsequent cases to challenge schools that attempted to deny children's access to education. In the *Brown* case (1954), the Court held that state laws establishing racial segregation in public schools were unconstitutional, even if the segregated schools were otherwise equal in quality, and that these laws violated the Equal Protection Clause of the Four-teenth Amendment.

The ruling in *Brown* provided the groundwork for subsequent lawsuits regarding the right to education for all students under the Equal Protection Clause, including support for the education of students with disabilities. For example, in the *PARC* case (1972), the District Court struck down a Penn-sylvania law that allowed schools to deny education to students with intel-lectual disabilities, holding that Pennsylvania was responsible for providing free public education to all students, regardless of their ability status and perceived potential to learn, and that the quality of this public education must be compa-rable to the education of students without disabilities. Specifically, the Court required Pennsylvania to locate and identify all school-age individuals excluded from public school, to provide all children with a free and appropriate educa-tion, and to provide tuition grants for children in need of alternate school placements. Additionally, the ruling in *Mills v. Board of Education of District of Columbia* (1972) stated that students with disabilities must be provided with a free public education and be given an educational program suitable to their learning needs. Taken together, the outcomes of these cases and the follow-up state actions mandated by the courts are the basis of special education law.

IDEIA

The Education for All Handicapped Children Act (1975) provided funds to state and local educational agencies that deliver a free and appropriate educa-tion to children with disabilities in conformance with the requirements of the law (U.S. Department of Education, 2020). This Act has undergone several amendments and reauthorizations since its inception, and was renamed the Individuals With Disabilities Education Act (IDEA) in its 1997 reauthorization. Under its most recent reauthorization in 2004, it was renamed the IDEIA, which is composed of four parts. Part A states the general provisions of the law and definitions of terms used throughout the statute. Part B, entitled Assistance for Education of All Children With Disabilities, provides funds to states for the education of children with disabilities ages 3 through 21. Part C, entitled Infants and Toddlers With Disabilities, provides funds to states that offer early intervention programs for infants and toddlers under age 3 with known or suspected disabilities. Part D, entitled National Activities to Improve Education of Children With Disabilities, provides discretionary grants to sup-port state personnel development, technical assistance and dissemination, technology, and parent training and information centers. We focus on Part C here, because that is the mechanism by which young children with disabilities or suspected of disabilities receive early intervention services.

Most of the IDEIA is focused on the education of children ages 3 years or older; however, to mitigate future problems, it is important for children with disabilities to be identified early and receive preventative/early inter-vention (EI) services. To increase access to early intervention services, Part C of IDEIA was originally included in the 1986 reauthorization of the law. The purpose of Part C is to

> enhance the development of infants and toddlers with disabilities; reduce educational costs by minimizing the need for special education through early intervention; minimize the likelihood of institutionalization, and maximize independent living; and enhance the capacity of families to meet their child's needs. (20 U.S.C. §1435[a])

In recognition of the unique needs of infants and toddlers, Part C places emphasis on providing care in the home and in community settings and mandates family involvement in the evaluation and intervention process.

Although Part C is funded through the federal government, states develop their own EI systems consistent with federal guidelines. States are required to have (a) a rigorous definition of the term *developmental delay*; (b) offer appropriate, evidence-based EI services to all infants and toddlers with disabilities; (c) provide timely and comprehensive multidisciplinary evaluations of children's needs; (d) provide an individualized family service plan (IFSP) and service coordination; and (e) have public awareness programs focused on early identification of infants and toddlers with disabilities and provide information to parents. Additionally, states must designate a state lead agency (e.g., health/human services or education agencies) and establish a state Interagency Coordinating Council (Bradley et al., 2011).

Infants and toddlers suspected of a disability are typically connected to EI through primary referral sources (e.g., physicians, hospitals) or their parents, who contact EI programs directly to request an evaluation (Lipkin et al., 2015). Pending parental consent, children are evaluated in five major developmental areas to determine if they meet the state's definition of developmental delay or disability and, therefore, are eligible for EI services. The five developmental areas evaluated are cognitive development, physical development (including vision and hearing), communication development, social and emotional development, and adaptive development. Once eligibility is determined, an IFSP team meets to identify the appropriate needed services.

The IFSP team includes: parents, advocates, or other family members requested by the parents; the agency service coordinator assigned to the family; individuals involved in the evaluation; and individuals who will provide the EI services. The IFSP must include the child's current levels of developmental functioning; family's resources, priorities, and concerns about the child's development; the measurable results or outcomes to be achieved; the EI services appropriate for the child's needs; the settings where those services will be provided; and other services the child will receive. The IFSP is reviewed and revised as needed every 6 months. To the greatest extent possible, EI services should be provided in children's natural environments or settings that are typical for a same-aged child without a disability, such as the home, day care, or other community settings (Lipkin et al., 2015).

Part C services end at age 3 years; the lead agency must hold a conference with parents to develop a transition plan at least 90 days before the child's third birthday. Available program options are reviewed and may include pre-school services under Part B of IDEIA; elementary school or preschool services for children participating in a state's extended Part C option; early education, Head Start, or child care programs; or other appropriate services (Bradley et al., 2011). Although IDEIA focuses on children with disabilities, the federal government supports the education of all children through the ESEA.

ESEA

Another significant education law is the ESEA, which was first passed in 1965 as part of President Lyndon Johnson's War on Poverty. Its purpose was to pro-mote educational equity by providing federal funds for school districts serving low-income students. At the present time, ESEA is the largest source of federal spending on elementary and secondary education (Gamson, McDermott, & Reed, 2015). In exchange for these federal funds, states and school districts must collect student outcome data to show they are providing quality educa-tion services and moving towards attainment of specific educational goals. In addition to supporting education for disadvantaged students, the original authorization of the law also allotted federal funds to improve school libraries and purchase instructional materials, to support education research and devel-opment, and to improve the capacity of state education agencies (Gamson et al., 2015). Subsequent reauthorizations have included the Bilingual Edu-cation Act (1967) to support the learning needs of students who are English learners, mandates for states to develop education standards with aligned assessments, and accountability plans for schools not making adequate yearly progress (Thomas & Brady, 2005).

ESEA has been reauthorized eight times with the most recent reauthoriza-tion, the Every Student Succeeds Act (ESSA), signed into law in 2015. Several provisions in ESSA are germane to early childhood education. The Preschool Development Grant helps states and communities plan, coordinate, and expand early childhood programs for low-income children; and the Literacy Education for All, Results for the Nation grant program requires that states use a portion of these funds to support programs serving children from birth through kinder-garten entry (First Five Years Fund, 2016). The expansion of early childhood interventions and programs to include Head Start have resulted in positive outcomes for many children (U.S. DHHS, Administration for Children and Families, Office of Planning Research and Evaluation, 2010).

Head Start

Early learning programs, such as Head Start and Universal Pre-K, have had a major impact on children, especially those from low-income households (Bitler, Hoynes, & Domina, 2014; Bloom & Weiland, 2015). These programs provide high-quality early-childhood care that positively impact children's cognitive, language, and social development. For children, especially those from low-income households, these programs significantly enhance the foundational skills needed to succeed in kindergarten. Studies show children who attend high-quality early-childhood learning programs are more likely to perform higher academically, attain higher levels of education, and secure employment post-high school. Findings from the Abecedarian Pre-School Project found that children who attended preschool (i.e., an intervention group) had higher scores on intellectual and academic measures at age 21, attained more years of total education, were more likely to attend a 4-year college/university, and were less likely to have had a child as a teenager compared with the control. Findings support the need for high-quality early-learning programs, such as Head Start, Ready Set Leap, and the Early Literacy and Learning Model, as lack of access to these resources often result in underachievement and the maintenance of the achievement gap (Chambers, Cheung, Slavin, Smith, & Laurenzano, 2010; Karoly, Kilburn, & Cannon, 2005).

POLICIES AND LEGISLATION IMPACTING CHILDREN'S HEALTH SERVICES

In addition to improving access to education, legislation has also been instrumental in ensuring that children have access to health care through the establishment of health insurance entitlement programs. Approximately 95% of children in the United States have health insurance (Murphey, 2017). Although many children are insured through private insurers, the proportion receiving public health insurance is steadily increasing (Murphey, 2017; Perrin, Boat, & Kelleher, 2016). In 2017, over 46 million children received health insurance through Medicaid and the State Children's Health Insurance Program (CHIP) who likely would not have been insured otherwise (Centers for Medicare and Medicaid Services [CMMS], 2018). These programs are critical sources of health coverage for many vulnerable children, including those in or near poverty, those with special health needs, children who are members of historically marginalized racial/ethnic groups, and those living in rural communities. Young children have also benefited greatly from these programs; 45% of children under the age of six are insured through receiving Medicaid and CHIP benefits compared with 36% of children between the ages of six and 18 (Chester & Burak, 2017).

Without question, access to health care has a significant positive impact on child outcomes. Children with health insurance are more likely to have a usual source of care, receive medical care when sick, be immunized, and receive preventive care (e.g., regular checkups, dental care; Institute of Medicine, 2009). These regular visits with a pediatrician are important for making sure that children are developing normally and for finding and treating any problems as early as possible. Relatedly, insured children tend to stay healthier, receive more timely diagnosis of serious health conditions, and experience fewer hospitalizations than children without health insurance (Institute of Medicine, 2009). Public health insurance programs, such as Medicaid and CHIP, remove the financial barriers to health care, reduce parents' stress about addressing their children's health care needs, and reduce racial/ethnic health disparities. Across all racial/ethnic groups, CHIP enrollees noted greater access to care, were more likely to have a usual source for medical care and receive preventive dental care, and less likely to have emergency room visits and unmet health needs (Kenney, 2007). Moreover, CHIP has been found to eliminate preexisting racial/ethnic disparities in health care access, continuity of health care access, and unmet health care needs (Shone, Dick, Klein, Zwanziger, & Szilagyi, 2005).

Children's health directly affects their ability to learn (Murphey, 2017), and child health disparities are closely linked with disparities in educational outcomes (Friedman-Krauss & Barnett, 2013). Therefore, it is important to have coordination between child health policy and educational policy to mitigate health-related factors that affect children's functioning which, in turn, likely affect school performance (Fiscella & Kitzman, 2009). Access to health insurance through Medicaid or CHIP may help to reduce education disparities for vulnerable child populations (Paradise, 2014). There is consistent evidence that Medicaid access when young is associated with later educational attainment, including better grades, fewer missed days of school, and higher graduation rates (Cohodes, Grossman, Kleiner, & Lovenheim, 2016; Perrin et al., 2016). The details of Medicaid, CHIP, and other federal health care legislation and their impact on young children are described below.

Medicaid

Medicaid was authorized by Title XIX of the Social Security Act in 1965 to assist states in providing medical assistance to low-income individuals at or below the federal poverty line (FPL). Children comprise approximately 40% of Medicaid recipients (Murphey, 2017), but millions of other Americans, including eligible low-income adults, pregnant women, elderly adults, and people with disabilities receive health coverage through Medicaid. It is the largest source of funding for medical and health-related services in the United States (Klees, Wolfe, & Curtis, 2015). Medicaid programs are administered by states, according to federal requirements, and are funded jointly by states and the federal government. Although state participation in the program is voluntary, all the states, the District of Columbia, and the U.S. territories have Medicaid programs. As part of administering Medicaid programs, states determine their own eligibility standards, as well as the type, amount, and duration of services that are covered. Although this leads to variability among state Medicaid plans, there are basic health services that states are mandated to cover. These include physician visits and vaccines for children; prenatal and postnatal care for pregnant women; and early periodic screening, diagnostic, and treatment (EPSDT) services for children under the age of 21. States may also provide optional services, such as diagnostic services, clinic services, optometrist services and eyeglasses, rehabilitation and physical therapy services, and targeted case management services (Klees et al., 2015).

One important and unique feature of Medicaid is the EPSDT services benefit. The provision for EPSDT services for children guarantees children access to comprehensive and preventive health services, including regular well-child exams; hearing, vision, and dental screenings; and other services to treat physical, mental, and developmental illnesses and diseases. EPSDT services are intended to provide preventive screenings to children to identify those at-risk for health problems, provide diagnostic services and assessment if found to be at-risk, and treatment services if a child does have a health problem. States are required to provide a schedule of recommended screenings and preventive services at regular intervals that meet reasonable medical or dental practice standards, follow up with relevant diagnoses, and provide those services (Burak & Odeh, 2018). The EPSDT services benefit ensures that vulnerable children receive all pediatrician-recommended health services that they need. It also provides for case coordination and case management to ensure medical services are linked and that service providers and agencies are in coordination with each other to help children obtain needed services (Schor, Abrams, & Shea, 2007). These services are particularly important for children with special health care needs who may be treated by multiple health providers.

Children insured through Medicaid are not limited to physician offices and hospitals to receive care, as Medicaid pays for health and related services provided in schools (CMMS, 2003). Provided that the school meets federal and state requirements for Medicaid providers, schools can receive Medicaid payments when covered services are provided to Medicaid-enrolled children and adolescents, or when services are provided to children with disabilities receiving special education services under the IDEIA (CMMS, 2003). Additionally, schools and early intervention centers can receive Medicaid funds for Medicaid outreach and enrollment activities (CMMS, 2003). For students with disabilities, Medicaid helps to ensure that they receive the health and related services needed to access school curricula.

CHIP

CHIP was established in 1997, under Title XXI of the Social Security Act, to provide additional insurance coverage for children in households with incomes too high to qualify for Medicaid but unable to afford private insurance (Perrin et al., 2016). States are provided with federal matching funds to expand their Medicaid coverage or to create programs separate from Medicaid. All states have expanded children's coverage significantly through their CHIP programs with almost every state providing coverage for children whose family income is up to at least 200% of the FPL. This expansion of coverage helps to protect low-income families who are above the FPL from financial insecurity by reducing their medical expenses and having more to spend on food and housing (Murphey, 2017).

With regard to preventive services, CHIP programs that are Medicaid expansions include EPSDT services coverage; many states with separate CHIP programs provide benefits similar to those found in EPSDT services. Even in the absence of specific early-prevention screening programs, children enrolled in

CHIP have access to benefits most other types of insurance do not cover, including speech and language therapies, hearing tests and hearing aids, and pediatric dental services.

Patient Protection and Affordable Care Act

The Patient Protection and Affordable Care Act (ACA) was signed into law in 2010 and went into effect in 2014. It is the most significant regulatory over-haul and expansion of health care coverage since the passage of Medicare and Medicaid (Bauchner, 2015). The ACA has had a significant impact on private and public health insurance. In the private insurance market, insurers are required to cover all applicants and charge the same rates regardless of pre-existing health conditions, cannot have annual or lifetime benefit caps, and must cover preventive services without cost sharing. With regard to public health insurance, the ACA provides states with the authority to expand Medic-aid eligibility to individuals under age 65 with incomes below 133% of the FPL (CMMS, 2020). Additionally, the ACA standardized rules for determining eligibility and providing benefits through Medicaid, CHIP, and the health insurance marketplace. States are also required to ensure the availability of insurance for individual children who do not have coverage via their families. The ACA also expands access to mental health services, as any insurer in the marketplace that offers mental health and substance use treatment benefits must provide coverage comparable to that for general medical and surgical care (Beronio, Po, Skopec, & Glied, 2013) In addition to individual services to children and families, the ACA authorized over $200 million in funding for the expansion of school health clinics and the purchase and modernization of equipment for school clinics (Perrin et al., 2016).

The Basic Health Program is part of the ACA and provides states with the option to establish health-benefits cover programs for low-income individuals who would otherwise be eligible to purchase coverage through the health insurance marketplace. This provides affordable coverage and better conti-nuity of care for people whose incomes fluctuate above and below Medicaid and CHIP levels (CMMS, 2020). The aforementioned policies were designed with the well-being of young children in mind. However, there are policies that are not directed toward young children but do have an impact on their well-being. A few examples of this are discussed in the next section of this chapter.

POLICIES AND LEGISLATION THAT INDIRECTLY IMPACT CHILDREN

Taking an ecological or systems perspective, the climate and culture of society as a whole has an impact on the well-being of children (Bronfenbrenner, 1977). Similarly, although the policies that emerge from the larger social con-text may not be directly aimed at children, those policies often have an impact on their well-being. Similar to the enactment of Jim Crow and segregation laws and their marginalization of students of color, other laws and policies enacted for the general public can inadvertently, disproportionally negatively affect the well-being of certain groups of children. Some of these include discipline and immigration policies designed to promote public safety but in actuality are detrimental to the well-being of young children (Skiba & Knesting, 2001).

Zero Tolerance

Zero tolerance emerged as a criminal justice reform platform in the 1980s and was seen as a way for political candidates to both demonstrate that they were tough on crime and declare the war on drugs (Skiba & Knesting, 2001). This approach was solidified as an educational policy with the Gun Free Schools Act, part of the Improving America's Schools Act (1994). States that received Title I funding are required, under this Act, to expel or remove students from schools for no less than 1 year if they bring a gun or firearm on school grounds (Curtis, 2014; Improving America's Schools Act, 1994; Pigott, Stearns, & Khey, 2018). Zero tolerance policies are embedded in mandated consequences for specific offenses committed in school. These policies can also be extended to behaviors that occur outside of the school day and off school grounds (e.g., cyberbullying or fighting; Bell, 2015; Curtis, 2014; Mallett, 2017; Pigott, Stearns, & Khey, 2018). These draconian policies are defined by mandated, predetermined, punitive consequences for specific offenses with the intention of deterring students from engaging in these behaviors (Curtis, 2014; Mallett, 2017). Zero tolerance has had a ripple effect resulting in the adoption of these policies for more than weapons. Other behaviors included in zero tolerance policies include bullying, substance use, fighting, and cyberbullying (Curtis, 2014). Data from the U.S. Department of Education's Office for Civil Rights Data Collection (2020) showed an increase from 1.7 million to over 3 million students suspended or expelled from 1974 to 2010. This is believed to be largely due to the emergence of these policies.

Due to the definitive nature of zero tolerance policies, young children have not been exempt from the consequences, suspension, and expulsion if found to engage in behaviors falling under the policies. Preschool settings suspend and expel children almost three times more frequently than K–12 settings (Gilliam, 2005). Zero tolerance policies, in general, have been found to impact students of color disproportionately. African American and Latinx youth are more likely than their White peers to be suspended or expelled under this disciplinarily approach. Moreover, African American and Latinx boys in early childhood are overwhelmingly subjected to the consequences of these policies (Bryan, 2017). Although African American preschoolers make up 19% of preschool enrollment, they constitute 47% of suspensions in early childhood settings. Despite the lack of data or research demonstrating the effectiveness of suspension and expulsion, these approaches persist. Fortunately, some large school districts are moving away from applying these policies to youth from preschool to second grade (e.g., Chicago Public Schools, Denver Public Schools). However, this is not sufficient for the millions of other young children who are negatively impacted by this approach.

Immigration

The current zeitgeist in the United States has placed substantial attention on immigration and reform of existing immigration policies (Doucet & Adair, 2018; Matthews, Ullrich, & Cervantes, 2018). The United States has historically been perceived as a place where people from all nations are welcome to come and build their dreams. Many of the greatest accomplishments in our nation's history were contributed by individuals who were born in other countries (McCorkle, 2018). Currently there are 19.6 million immigrant children—one quarter of all children in the United States (Child Trends, 2018). With the rise in nationalism in the 2016 presidential election, a major shift in the ideology that welcomes immigrants into this country was brought to light. This rhetoric was consistent with an anti-immigrant sentiment that began to have an impact on the well-being of children in the schools who identify as immigrants. We know that strengths-based approaches are more advantageous in early childhood. These anti-immigrant sentiments have resulted in a reduction of strengths-based approaches to providing services for young children from immigrant families (Doucet & Adair, 2018).

Since the 2016 election, schools have reported a rise in bullying incidents experienced by students from immigrant and Muslim backgrounds (Mthethwa-Sommers & Kisiara, 2019). This is believed to be directly linked to policy being enacted at the federal level to dissuade immigration from Latin American and Islamic countries. Although these policies, colloquially termed the *Trump Border Policy*, continue to have their legality challenged, their ripple effect on the well-being of children in schools is apparent. These policies have compromised access to education and health care. In response to this changing climate, students who identify as immigrants are experiencing strains on their mental and physical health as well as compromised economic security (Cervantes, Ullrich, & Matthews, 2018; Page & Polk, 2017; Vargas & Ybarra, 2017). As these policies have expanded, the reach of immigration services is making it increasingly hazardous for undocumented families to engage in typical daily behaviors, such as transporting children to schools and medical appointments (Cervantes & Walker, 2017). Therefore, these policies that have been presented as safety measures are, in essence, compromising the safety of millions of U.S. children (Cervantes, Ullrich, & Matthews, 2018; Finno-Velasquez, Cahill, Ullrich, & Matthews, 2018; Lovato, Lopez, Karimli, & Abrams, 2018).

RECOMMENDATIONS FOR ADVOCACY

The key to supporting historically marginalized children and families is through advocacy. General tips for advocating for policies and laws are provided below. Table 15.1 lists organizations providing early childhood resources.

- Get to know your community—every community is unique. The education and health needs of the children in your community are likely influenced by your unique context. Getting to know what these needs are can inform

TABLE 15.1. Organizations Focused on Early Childhood Advocacy

Resource	Description
Child Care and Early Education Research Connections	Promotes high-quality research in child care and early education and the use of that research in policymaking. https://www.researchconnections.org/childcare/welcome
Child Care Aware of America	Works with state and local child care agencies nationwide to ensure that every family in the United States has access to a high-quality, affordable child care system. https://usa.childcareaware.org/
Early Care and Education Consortium	Nonprofit alliance of multistate/multisite providers, key state child care associations, and premier educational-services providers. Advocates for strong federal and state policies that bring quality to scale. http://www.ececonsortium.org/
First Five Years Fund	Works to sustain and expand support for early learning at the federal level and advances innovative ways to increase access to high-quality early-childhood education for children from low-income families. https://www.ffyf.org/
Frank Porter Graham Child Development Institute	Conducts research to influence children's lives, support families, and inform public policy. https://fpg.unc.edu/
National Association for the Education of Young Children	Professional membership organization that works to promote high-quality early learning for all young children by connecting early-childhood practice, policy, and research. https://www.naeyc.org/
National Association on Family Child Care	Represents child care providers to promote high-quality early-childhood experiences in the unique environment of family child care programs. https://www.nafcc.org/Public.Policy
National Collaborative for Infants and Toddlers	Committed to advancing the most promising policies and programs that ensure families have the supports they may need. https://www.thencit.org/make-the-case
The Ounce of Prevention Fund	Gives children in poverty the best chance for success in school and in life by advocating for and providing the highest quality care and education from birth to age five. Their Early Childhood Advocacy Toolkit is available here: https://www.theounce.org/wp-content/uploads/2017/03/EarlyChildhoodAdvocacyToolkit.pdf
Zero to Three Advocacy Action Center	Works to ensure that babies and toddlers benefit from the early connections that are critical to their well-being and development. https://www.zerotothree.org/advocate

areas in which you seek professional development, so you can better serve this community as an education or mental health service provider.

- Offer support to decision makers—state and local legislative bodies often have committees dedicated to education and health services. Take the time to learn more about the individuals on those committees. As an educator or mental health service provider, you may consider reaching out to these individuals and sharing your knowledge on emerging policy. Often, policymakers welcome white papers, infographics, and brief research reviews that will help guide their decisions.

- Understand impact versus intent—historically, policymakers have designed policies with good intent but without fully considering the impact of the policy on all populations. Slowly, policymakers are moving in the direction of using empirical evidence to guide their decisions and evaluating the outcomes of policy on special populations, including young children. Jurisdictions using these models are few and far between; as a result, measuring their effectiveness has been a challenge (Head, 2016). As advocates, we can support the use of evidence-based policy and ongoing evaluation of the impact of that policy.

CONCLUSION

Since the recognition of children as a special population, legislation and policy have played an indelible role in shaping their experiences. Without these laws, many young children, particularly those in poverty or from marginalized groups, would have limited access to health care and education. An investment in youth is an investment in the future. The creation of education laws and programs, such as IDEIA, ESEA, and Head Start, and social entitlement programs, such as Medicaid and the ACA, reflects the country's commitment to promoting education and health outcomes. But, as beneficial as these programs have been in increasing access, it is important to note that legislation and policy can also limit access to education and health services by indirectly setting a tone and culture that deter access to available resources. Although much has been accomplished over the past 120 years to protect children, many young children still remain unserved or underserved.

Over time, policy has been used to support the education and health care of young children. However, most recently, the policy has also resulted in fear and reduction of access to the programs designed to support young children and their families. Parents and educators must continue to advocate for the expansion of existing federal education and health care laws and the development of state and local policies to promote children's well-being.

REFERENCES

Bauchner, H. (2015). Medicare and Medicaid, the Affordable Care Act, and US health policy. *JAMA, 314*, 353–354. http://dx.doi.org/10.1001/jama.2015.8587

Bell, C. (2015). The hidden side of zero tolerance policies: The African American perspective. *Sociology Compass, 9*, 14–22. http://dx.doi.org/10.1111/soc4.12230

Beronio, K., Po, R., Skopec, L., & Glied, S. (2013). *Affordable Care Act expands mental health and substance use disorder benefits and federal parity protections for 62 million Americans.* Retrieved from U.S. Department of Health and Human Services website: https://aspe.hhs.gov/report/affordable-care-act-expands-mental-health-and-substance-use-disorder-benefits-and-federal-parity-protections-62-million-americans

Bilingual Education Act, Pub. L. 90-247 (1967).

Bitler, M. P., Hoynes, H. W., & Domina, T. (2014, August). *Experimental evidence on distributional effects of Head Start.* (NBER Working Paper No. 20434). Cambridge, MA: National Bureau of Economic Research. http://dx.doi.org/10.3386/w20434

Bloom, H. S., & Weiland, C. (2015). *Quantifying variation in Head Start effects on young children's cognitive and socio-emotional skills using data from the National Head Start Impact Study.* Retrieved from SSRN website: http://dx.doi.org/10.2139/ssrn.2594430

Bradley, M. C., Daley, T., Levin, M., O'Reilly, F., Parsad, A., Robertson, A., & Werner, A. (2011). IDEA National Assessment Implementation Study. Final Report (NCEE 2011-4027). Retrieved from the National Center for Education Evaluation and Regional Assistance website: https://ies.ed.gov/ncee/pubs/20114026/pdf/20114027.pdf

Bronfenbrenner, U. (1977). Toward an experimental ecology of human development. *American Psychologist, 32*, 513–531. http://dx.doi.org/10.1037/0003-066X.32.7.513

Brown v. Board of Education of Topeka, 347 U.S. 483 (1954).

Bryan, N. (2017). White teachers' role in sustaining the school-to-prison pipeline: Recommendations for teacher education. *The Urban Review, 49*, 326–345. http://dx.doi.org/10.1007/s11256-017-0403-3

Burak, E. W., & Odeh, M. (2018). *Developmental screenings for young children in Medicaid and the Children's Health Insurance Program.* Retrieved from the Georgetown University Health Policy Institute Center for Children and Families website: https://ccf.georgetown.edu/wp-content/uploads/2018/03/Developmental-Screenings-Report.pdf

Centers for Medicare and Medicaid Services. (2003). *Medicaid school-based administrative claiming guide.* Retrieved from https://www.cms.gov/Research-Statistics-Data-and-Systems/Computer-Data-and-Systems/MedicaidBudgetExpendSystem/Downloads/Schoolhealthsvcs.pdf

Centers for Medicare and Medicaid Services. (2018). *Unduplicated number of children ever enrolled in CHIP and Medicaid.* Retrieved from https://www.medicaid.gov/chip/downloads/fy-2017-childrens-enrollment-report.pdf

Centers for Medicare and Medicaid Services. (2020). *Program history.* Retrieved from https://www.medicaid.gov/about-us/program-history/index.html

Cervantes, W., Ullrich, R., & Matthews, H. (2018). *Our children's fear: Immigration policy's effects on young children.* Retrieved from Center for Law and Social Policy website: https://www.clasp.org/publications/report/brief/our-childrens-fear-immigration-policys-effects-young-children

Cervantes, W., & Walker, C. (2017). *Five reasons Trump's immigration orders harm children.* Retrieved from Center for Law and Social Policy (CLASP) website: https://www.clasp.org/sites/default/files/public/resources-and-publications/publication-1/Five-Reasons-Immigration-Enforcement-Orders-Harm-Children.pdf

Chambers, B., Cheung, A., Slavin, R. E., Smith, D., & Laurenzano, M. (2010). *Effective early childhood education programs: A systematic review.* Baltimore, MD: Center for Data-Driven Reform in Education. Retrieved from http://repositorio.minedu.gob.pe/bitstream/handle/123456789/5030/Effective%20Early%20Childhood%20Education%20Programmes%20A%20Systematic%20Review.pdf?sequence=1&isAllowed=y

Chester, A., & Burak, E. W. (2017). *Medicaid's role for children.* Retrieved from Georgetown University Health Policy Institute, Center for Children and Families website:

https://ccf.georgetown.edu/wp-content/uploads/2016/06/Medicaid-and-Children-update-Jan-2017-rev.pdf

Child Trends. (2018, December 28). *Immigrant children.* Retrieved from https://www.childtrends.org/?indicators=immigrant-children

Cohodes, S. R., Grossman, D. S., Kleiner, S. A., & Lovenheim, M. F. (2016). The effect of child health insurance access on schooling: Evidence from public insurance expansions. *Journal of Human Resources, 51,* 727–759. http://dx.doi.org/10.3368/jhr.51.3.1014-6688R1

Curtis, A. J. (2014). Tracing the school-to-prison pipeline from zero-tolerance policies to juvenile justice dispositions. *Georgetown Law Journal, 102,* 1251–1277.

Doucet, F., & Adair, J. (2018). Introduction: A vision for transforming early childhood research and practice for young children of immigrants and their families. *Bank Street Occasional Paper Series, 39.* Retrieved from https://educate.bankstreet.edu/cgi/viewcontent.cgi?article=1268&context=occasional-paper-series

Education for All Handicapped Children Act, Pub. L. 94-142 (1975).

Elementary and Secondary Education Act, 20 U.S.C. §§ 6301–8961 (1965).

Every Student Succeeds Act, Pub. L. 114-95 (2015).

Finno-Velasquez, M., Cahill, B., Ullrich, R., & Matthews, H. (2018). Heightened immigration enforcement and the well-being of young children in immigrant families: Early childhood program responses. *Zero to Three, 39,* 27–32.

First Five Years Fund. (2016). *Summary and analysis of the early learning provisions of the Every Student Succeeds Act.* Washington, DC: Author. Retrieved from https://ffyf.org/wp-content/uploads/2016/02/ESSA_ECE_ProvisionsNarrativeSummaryAnalysis_020316.pdf

Fiscella, K., & Kitzman, H. (2009). Disparities in academic achievement and health: The intersection of child education and health policy. *Pediatrics, 123,* 1073–1080. http://dx.doi.org/10.1542/peds.2008-0533

Friedman-Krauss, A., & Barnett, W. S. (2013). *Early childhood education: Pathways to better health* (NIEER Policy Brief Issue 25). Retrieved from Rutgers University, National Institute for Early Education Research website: http://nieer.org/wp-content/uploads/2016/08/health20brief.pdf

Gamson, D. A., McDermott, K. A., & Reed, D. S. (2015). The Elementary and Secondary Education Act at fifty: Aspirations, effects, and limitations. *RSF: The Russell Sage Foundation Journal of the Social Sciences, 1*(3), 1–29. http://dx.doi.org/10.7758/rsf.2015.1.3.01

Gilliam, W. S. (2005, May). *Prekindergarteners left behind: Expulsion rates in state prekindergarten programs* (Policy Brief Series 3). New York, NY: Foundation for Child Development. Retrieved from https://medicine.yale.edu/childstudy/zigler/publications/National%20Prek%20Study_expulsion%20brief_34775_5379_v1.pdf

Hammer v. Dagenhart, 247 U.S. 251 (1918).

Head, B. W. (2016). Toward more "evidence-informed" policy making? *Public Administration Review, 76,* 472–484. http://dx.doi.org/10.1111/puar.12475

Human Rights Watch. (2014). *25th Anniversary of the convention on the rights of the child.* Retrieved from https://www.hrw.org/news/2014/11/17/25th-anniversary-convention-rights-child

Improving America's Schools Act, Pub. L. 103-382, 108 Stat. 3518 (1994).

Individuals With Disabilities in Education Act, Pub. L. 101-476, 104 Stat. 1142 (1997).

Individuals With Disabilities Education Improvement Act, Pub. L. 108-446, 118 Stat. 2647 (2004).

Institute of Medicine, Committee on Health Insurance Status and its Consequences. (2009). *America's uninsured crisis: Consequences for health and health care.* Retrieved from http://www.nationalacademies.org/hmd/Reports/2009/Americas-Uninsured-Crisis-Consequences-for-Health-and-Health-Care.aspx

Karoly, L. A., Kilburn, M. R., & Cannon, J. S. (2005). *Early childhood interventions: Proven results, future promise.* Santa Monica, CA: RAND. http://dx.doi.org/10.7249/MG341

Katz, M. S. (1976). *A history of compulsory education laws.* Phi Delta Kappa Educational Foundation (Fastback Series No. 75). Retrieved from https://files.eric.ed.gov/fulltext/ED119389.pdf

Keating-Owen Child Labor Act, 39 Stat. 675 (1916).

Kenney, G. (2007). The impacts of the State Children's Health Insurance Program on children who enroll: Findings from ten states. *Health Services Research, 42,* 1520–1543. http://dx.doi.org/10.1111/j.1475-6773.2007.00707.x

Klees, B. S., Wolfe, C. J., & Curtis, C. A. (2015, November 16). *Brief summaries of Medicare & Medicaid Title XVIII and Title XIX of The Social Security Act.* Baltimore, MD: Centers for Medicare and Medicaid Services. Retrieved from https://www.cms.gov/Research-Statistics-Data-and-Systems/Statistics-Trends-and-Reports/MedicareProgramRatesStats/downloads/MedicareMedicaidSummaries2015.pdf

Lipkin, P. H., Okamoto, J., the Council on Children with Disabilities, & the Council on School Health. (2015). The Individuals With Disabilities Education Act (IDEA) for children with special educational needs. *Pediatrics, 136,* e1650–e1662. http://dx.doi.org/10.1542/peds.2015-3409

Lovato, K., Lopez, C., Karimli, L., & Abrams, L. S. (2018). The impact of deportation-related family separations on the well-being of Latinx children and youth: A review of the literature. *Children and Youth Services Review, 95,* 109–116. http://dx.doi.org/10.1016/j.childyouth.2018.10.011

Mallett, C. A. (2017). The school-to-prison pipeline: Disproportionate impact on vulnerable children and adolescents. *Education and Urban Society, 49,* 1–30. http://dx.doi.org/10.1177/0013124516644053

Matthews, H., Ullrich, R., & Cervantes, W. (2018). *Immigration policy's harmful impacts on early care and education.* Retrieved from Center for Law and Social Policy website: https://www.clasp.org/sites/default/files/publications/2018/03/2018_harmfulimpactsece.pdf

McCorkle, W. D. (2018). Using history to inform the modern immigration debate in the United States. *Journal of International Social Studies, 8,* 149–167.

Mills v. Board of Education of District of Columbia, 348 F. Supp. 866 (D.D.C. 1972).

Mthethwa-Sommers, S., & Kisiara, O. (2019). Refugee parents' perceptions of bullying practices of their children in urban schools. In G. Onchwari & J. Keengwe (Eds.), *Handbook of research on engaging immigrant families and promoting academic success for English language learners* (pp. 378–392). Hershey, PA: IGI Global. http://dx.doi.org/10.4018/978-1-5225-8283-0.ch019

Murphey, D. (2017, May 12). *Health insurance coverage improves child well-being.* Retrieved from the Child Trends website: https://www.childtrends.org/publications/health-insurance-coverage-improves-child-well

Page, K. R., & Polk, S. (2017). Chilling effect? Post-election health care use by undocumented and mixed-status families. *The New England Journal of Medicine, 376,* e20. http://dx.doi.org/10.1056/NEJMp1700829

Paradise, J. (2014). *The impact of the Children's Health Insurance Program (CHIP): What does the research tell us?* Retrieved from the Kaiser Family Foundation website: http://kff.org/medicaid/issue-brief/the-impact-of-the-childrens-health-insurance-program-chip-what-does-the-research-tell-us

Pennsylvania Ass'n for Retarded Children v. Pennsylvania, 343 F. Supp. 279 (E.D. Pa. 1972).

Perrin, J. M., Boat, T. F., & Kelleher, K. J. (2016). The influence of health care policies on children's health and development. *Social Policy Report, 29,* 3–17. http://dx.doi.org/10.1002/j.2379-3988.2016.tb00085.x

Pigott, C., Stearns, A. E., & Khey, D. N. (2018). School resource officers and the school to prison pipeline: Discovering trends of expulsions in public schools. *American Journal of Criminal Justice, 43*, 120–138. http://dx.doi.org/10.1007/s12103-017-9412-8

Ralabate, P., & Foley, B. (2003). *IDEA AND NCLB: Intersection of access and outcomes.* Alexandria, VA: National Education Association.

Schor, E. L., Abrams, M., & Shea, K. (2007). Medicaid: Health promotion and disease prevention for school readiness. *Health Affairs, 26*, 420–429. http://dx.doi.org/10.1377/hlthaff.26.2.420

Shone, L. P., Dick, A. W., Klein, J. D., Zwanziger, J., & Szilagyi, P. G. (2005). Reduction in racial and ethnic disparities after enrollment in the State Children's Health Insurance Program. *Pediatrics, 115*, e697–e705. http://dx.doi.org/10.1542/peds.2004-1726

Skiba, R. J., & Knesting, K. (2001). Zero tolerance, zero evidence: An analysis of school disciplinary practice. *New Directions for Student Leadership, 2001*, 17–43. http://dx.doi.org/10.1002/yd.23320019204

Social Security Act, Pub. L. 89-97, 79 Stat. 286 (1965).

Thomas, J. Y., & Brady, K. P. (2005). Chapter 3: The Elementary and Secondary Education Act at 40: Equity, accountability, and the evolving federal role in public education. *Review of Research in Education, 29*, 51–67. http://dx.doi.org/10.3102/0091732X029001051

U.S. Department of Education. (2020). *About IDEA.* Retrieved from https://sites.ed.gov/idea/about-idea/#IDEA-History

U.S. Department of Education, Office for Civil Rights Data Collection. (2020). *Civil Rights Data Collection.* Retrieved from https://www2.ed.gov/about/offices/list/ocr/data.html

U.S. Department of Health and Human Services. (2020). *Children's Bureau timeline.* Retrieved from https://cb100.acf.hhs.gov/childrens-bureau-timeline

U.S. Department of Health and Human Services, Administration for Children and Families, Office of Planning Research and Evaluation. (2010). *Head Start impact study: Final report.* Retrieved from https://www.acf.hhs.gov/sites/default/files/opre/hs_impact_study_final.pdf

Vargas, E. D., & Ybarra, V. D. (2017). U.S. citizen children of undocumented parents: The link between state immigration policy and the health of Latino children. *Journal of Immigrant and Minority Health, 19*, 913–920. http://dx.doi.org/10.1007/s10903-016-0463-6

Yell, M. L., Rogers, D., & Rogers, E. L. (1998). The legal history of special education: What a long, strange trip it's been! *Remedial and Special Education, 19*, 219–228. http://dx.doi.org/10.1177/074193259801900405

INDEX

ABOUT THE EDITORS

Vincent C. Alfonso, PhD, is interim dean of the Ferkauf Graduate School of Psychology at Yeshiva University and former dean of the School of Education at Gonzaga University. He is past president of Division 16 (School Psychology) of the American Psychological Association (APA); Fellow of Divisions 5, 16, and 43 of the APA; and a certified school psychologist and licensed psychologist. Most recently, Dr. Alfonso received the Jack Bardon Distinguished Service Award from Division 16. He has been providing psychoeducational services to individuals across the life span for more than 25 years and is the coeditor of *Essentials of Specific Learning Disability Identification* (2nd ed.) and coauthor of *Essentials of Cross-Battery Assessment* (3rd ed.). He is a member of the APA Coalition for Psychology in Schools and Education.

George J. DuPaul, PhD, is a professor of school psychology at Lehigh University. He has extensive experience providing clinical services to children with attention-deficit/hyperactivity disorder (ADHD) and their families, as well as consulting with a variety of school districts regarding the management of students with ADHD. He has been an author or coauthor of more than 225 journal articles and book chapters, as well as nine books and two videos related to ADHD and pediatric school psychology. He is codeveloper of the *ADHD Rating Scale–5,* which is widely used for screening, diagnosis, and treatment evaluation for children and adolescents with ADHD. Dr. DuPaul was School Psychologist of the Year in Pennsylvania in 1999, was the recipient of the 2008 Senior Scientist Award from APA Division 16 (School Psychology), and was named to the Children and Adults With ADHD Hall of Fame in 2008. He is a member of the APA Coalition for Psychology in Schools and Education.